INSIGHT GUIDE

CRETE

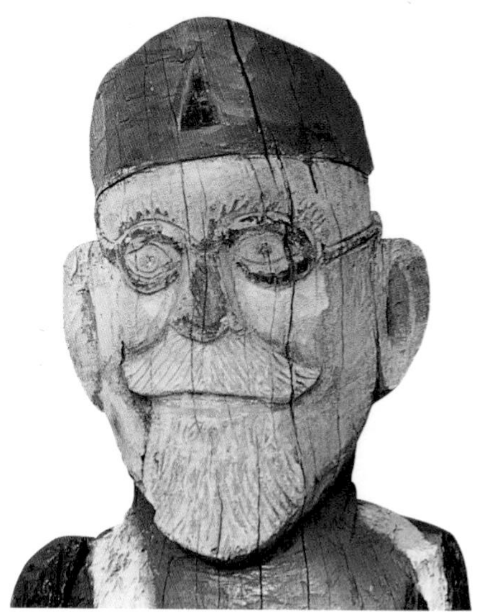

About This Book

Editorial
Project Editor
Jeffery Pike
Editorial Director
Brian Bell

Distribution

UK & Ireland
GeoCenter International Ltd
The Viables Centre, Harrow Way
Basingstoke, Hants RG22 4BJ
Fax: (44) 1256-817988

United States
Langenscheidt Publishers, Inc.
46–35 54th Road, Maspeth, NY 11378
Fax: (1) 718 784-0640

Canada
Thomas Allen & Son Ltd
390 Steelcase Road East
Markham, Ontario L3R 1G2
Fax: (1) 905 475 6747

Australia
Universal Press
1 Waterloo Road
Macquarie Park, NSW 2113
Fax: (61) 2 9888 9074

New Zealand
Hema Maps New Zealand Ltd (HNZ)
Unit D, 24 Ra ORA Drive
East Tamaki, Auckland
Fax: (64) 9 273 6479

Worldwide
Apa Publications GmbH & Co. Verlag KG (Singapore branch)
38 Joo Koon Road, Singapore 628990
Tel: (65) 865-1600. Fax: (65) 861-6438

Printing

Insight Print Services (Pte) Ltd
38 Joo Koon Road, Singapore 628990
Tel: (65) 865-1600. Fax: (65) 861-6438

First Edition 1989
Fifth Edition 2001

CONTACTING THE EDITORS
We would appreciate it if readers would alert us to errors or outdated information by writing to:
Insight Guides, P.O. Box 7910, London SE1 1WE, England. Fax: (44) 20 7403-0290. insight@apaguide.demon.co.uk

www.insightguides.com

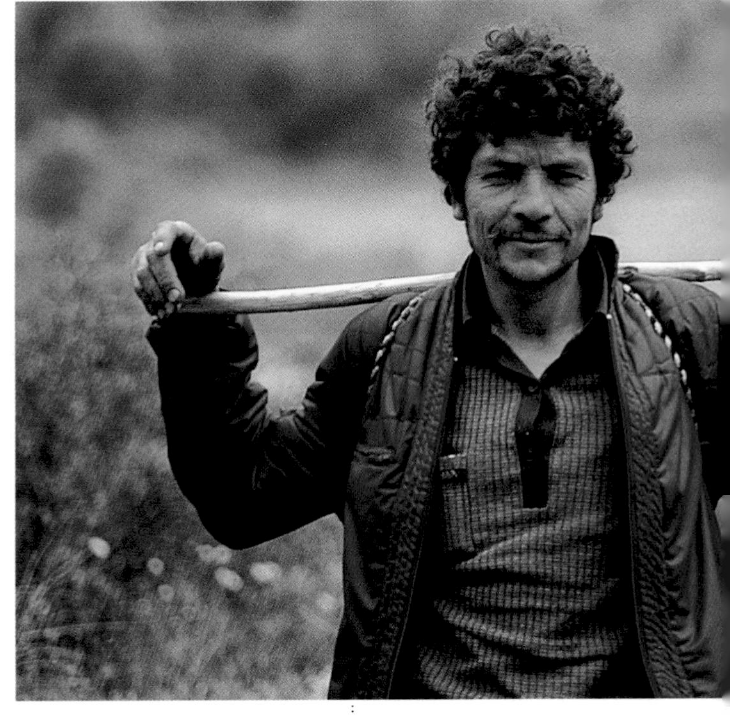

This guidebook combines the interests and enthusiasms of two of the world's best known information providers: Insight Guides, whose titles have set the standard for visual travel guides since 1970, and Discovery Channel, the world's premier source of nonfiction television programming.

The editors of Insight Guides provide both practical advice and general understanding of a destination's history, culture, institutions and people. Discovery Channel and its website, www.discovery.com, help millions of viewers explore their world from the comfort of their home and also encourage them to explore it at first hand.

This fully updated edition of *Insight Guide: Crete* is structured to convey an understanding of the island and its culture, as well as guiding readers through its sights and activities:

◆ The **Features** section, with a yellow bar at the top of each page, covers Crete's unique history, and the culture and character of its people.

◆ The main **Places** section, with a blue bar, is a complete guide to all the sights and areas that are worth visiting. Places of special interest are coordinated by number with the maps.

◆ The **Travel Tips** listings section, with an orange bar, provides a point of reference for information on travel, hotels, restaurants, shops and more.

The contributors

This new edition of *Insight Guide: Crete* was edited by **Jeffery Pike**, a London-based Hellenophile, who has also masterminded the current edition of *Insight Guide: Greek Islands.* This book contains a wealth of new material contributed by three Cretan experts.

Tony Fennymore is a freelance writer, historian and archaeologist who lives for much of the year in Haniá, returning regularly to the UK to lecture on Crete. He has researched and written new chapters on Knossós, Around Iráklion, From Iráklion to the Libyan Sea, Haniá and Surroundings, and Western Crete, as well as supplying a comprehensive all-new Travel Tips section. Fennymore was aided in his research, writing and translation by the Haniá-based team of **Tim Powell**, **Mike Stevens**, **Eva Maragoudáki** and **Michael Mylne**.

Lance Chilton first visited Crete in 1982 and has returned regularly since. He lived in Iráklion for four years, working for a UK travel company, and now leads botanical walks on the island every spring. He is the author of several major botanical works on Cretan flora, and also publishes walking guides on Greece and Cyprus. His favourite parts of Crete are the high mountains and the "remote, unbotanised bits". For this book, Chilton wrote a new chapter on Flora and Fauna, the picture spreads on Birds and Spring Flowers, and the chapters on Iráklion, Réthymnon and Surroundings, and South of Réthymnon.

The chapters on Food and Drink, Ághios Nikólaos and eastern Crete were written by **Marcus Brooke**, a Scot and regular Insight contributor who has returned to Crete many times since his first visit nearly half a century ago. "Then," he recalls, "the only flights were from Athens, hotels rented a bed rather than a room, and an order for *rakí* was invariably accompanied by a complimentary *méze.* Still, the wonderful warmth that is Crete persists."

This edition has drawn on an earlier Insight Guide, written and edited by **Gerhard Sasse**, with contributions by his wife **Nadja Sasse** and historical essays by **Hans-Gerd Schulte**, and translated from the original German by **Marianne Rankin**.

Thanks are due to **Penny Phenix** for proofreading and indexing this edition of the guide, and also to **Cynthia Howell**, who meticulously checked the maps.

Map Legend

—— - -	International Boundary
- - - -	Province Boundary
— • —	National Park/Reserve
- - - -	Ferry Route
✈ ✈	Airport: International/ Regional
🚌	Bus Station
ⓘ	Tourist Information
✉	Post Office
✝ ✝ ✝	Church/Ruins
✝	Monastery
☪	Mosque
✡	Synagogue
♜ ♜	Castle/Ruins
∴	Archaeological Site
∩	Cave
♙	Statue/Monument
★	Place of Interest

The main places of interest in the Places section are coordinated by number with a full-colour map (eg ❶), and a symbol at the top of every right-hand page tells you where to find the map.

INSIGHT GUIDE
Crete

CONTENTS

Maps

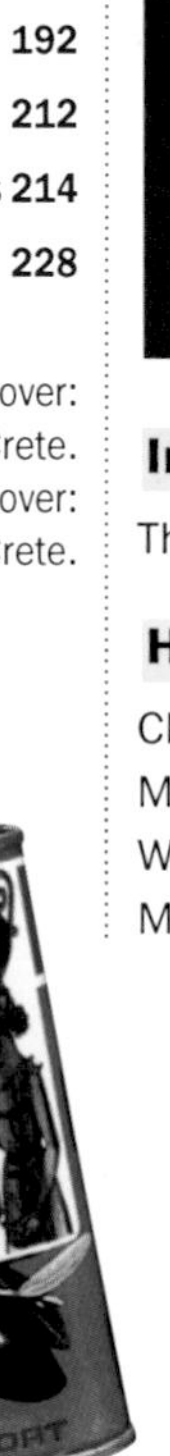

Introduction

History

Features

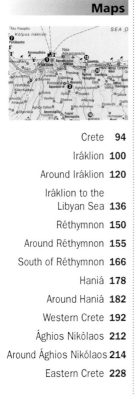

Caves at Mátala

Insight on ...

Information panels

Places

Travel Tips

◆ **Full Travel Tips index is on page 243**

THE CRADLE OF EUROPE

Megalónissos, the "Great Island", has a climate, a landscape and a culture that are uniquely Cretan

The shape of Crete is reminiscent of a gnarled branch, or perhaps a snail. A wise old Cretan likened the island to the crown of King Minos – tempered and battered by numerous battles and wars but, above all, ravaged by time.

With an area of about 8,350 sq. km (3,225 sq. miles), it is the largest of Greece's islands and the fifth largest island in the Mediterranean Sea. From west to east, the island is over 256 km (160 miles) long, and between 15 and 60 km (9–38 miles) wide.

Crete lies between the 34th and 35th degrees of latitude, on a plane with Tunisia and Syria and, with more than 300 days of sunshine a year, it's the most pleasant of all the Mediterranean islands. It is also the most significant historically for here, more than 4,000 years ago, European culture first blossomed with the Minoan civilisation.

There are so many different sides to modern Crete that there is something here for everyone. The northern coast is the tourist area, with wonderful beaches and bustling resorts, while the southern coast is still relatively deserted and undeveloped. Those looking for solitude can take refuge in the peninsulas of Gramvoúsa, Rodhopoú and Akrotíri, or just go up into the mountains.

There's beautiful scenery wherever you look, but it's not of the soft and gentle kind. It is a rugged place – in stark contrast to the friendly openness of the inhabitants. Plant lovers can find many different species unique to the island. If you are interested in caves, there's no lack of choice: there are more than 3,000 of them. Then there's the Samariá Gorge, 18 km (11 miles) long, which makes it the second longest in Europe (after the Gorge du Verdon in Provence), and many shorter gorges, no less spectacular.

Crete is exceptionally rich in places to see. Most of these can be easily reached on the 2,000 km (1,240 miles) of asphalt road. Apart from excavation sites of the Minoan period – especially Knossós, Phaestos, Aghía Triádha, Mália and Káto Zákros – there are many interesting Greek-Dorian and Roman sites; then a wealth of Byzantine monuments – over 1,000 churches, chapels and paintings; in the towns there are old buildings dating from the Venetian and Turkish occupations. Between Chryssoskalítissas in the far west and Toploú in the east, there are more than 30 impressive monasteries. ❑

PRECEDING PAGES: a Sfakiot man from Western Crete; an old woman in traditional black; young people relax in Haniá's Municipal Gardens; bringing in the olive harvest. **LEFT:** Zeus, diguised as a bull, wins the heart of Europa.

Decisive Dates

6500–2600 BC New Stone Age. Earliest settlers, from Asia Minor or North Africa, live first in caves, later in primitive dwellings of stone and brick.
2600–2000 BC Pre-Palace Period. More immigrants bring the potter's wheel and copper.
2000–1700 BC Old Palace Period. Discovery of bronze. Language written down. The first palaces.
circa 1700 BC Palaces destroyed, possibly by earthquake. Rebuilt on an even grander scale.
1700–1450 BC New Palace Period. The golden age of Minoan culture.

circa 1450 BC Minoan palaces destroyed by fire.
circa 1400 BC Knossós palace rebuilt.
1375 BC Knossós destroyed again, and with it the whole of Minoan civilisation.
1375–1100 BC Post-Palace Period. Mycenaeans rule; Kydonia (now Haniá) the island's chief city.
circa 1100 BC Dorians from northern Greece conquer most of Crete, bringing iron weapons.
1000–600 BC Hundreds of small city-states established, often fighting between themselves.
6th–4th centuries BC Greece's Classical Age largely bypasses Crete, which plays no part in the war against the Persians or the Peloponnesian War.
circa 480 BC The Code of Górtyn is inscribed on stone in Dorian Cretan dialect.

ROME AND BYZANTIUM

168–146 BC Rome defeats the Achaean League, annexes most of Greece and Macedonia.
67 BC Crete becomes a Roman province under Quintus Metellus. Górtyn becomes the capital.
1st–2nd centuries AD Romans build roads, aqueducts, irrigation systems, and create major cities at Górtyn, Knossós, Áptera, Lýttos and elsewhere.
AD 59 St Paul visits Crete, begins conversion to Christianity. Titus becomes first Bishop of Crete.
circa 250 The Holy Ten (Águii Dhéka) are martyred at Górtyn for refusing to worship the Roman gods.
395 The Romen Empire splits into two: Crete is part of the Eastern Empire, ruled from Byzantium.
5th–6th centuries About 70 basilica-style Byzantine churches built on Crete.

ARABS AND VENETIANS

7th century Crete suffers attacks from Arab raiders based in North Africa.
824 Arabs capture Crete, proceed to plunder the Aegean for over 100 years.
828 Arabs make their headquarters at fortress el-Khandak (Iráklion), destroy the old capital, Górtyn.
961 Byzantine army under Nikefóras Fókas retakes Crete after the siege of el-Khandak.
circa 1090 Cretan attempt to gain independence is quelled by Byzantine fleet.
1204 The Fourth Crusade sacks Constantinople. Crete is sold to the Venetians by crusade leader Boniface of Montferrat.
13th century Venetians put down a series of rebellions led by Byzantine Cretans.
1363 Short-lived "Republic of St Titus" is quashed and punished by Venice.
1453 Ottoman Turks capture Constantinople, rename it Istanbul and make it their capital.
15th–16th centuries Refugees from Constantinople settle in Crete, which becomes the centre of Byzantine art and scholarship.
1560s Turkish attacks on Crete; Venice strengthens fortifications in coastal cities.
1645 Turks attack in force: capture Haniá after a bloody siege, then Réthymnon.
1648 Turks control all Crete except Iráklion.
1669 Iráklion falls to Turks after 22-year siege.

THE STRUGGLE FOR INDEPENDENCE

1770 Rebellion against the Ottomans in Sfakiá, led by Dhaskaloghiánnis ("Teacher John"), who is captured and executed by the Turks.
1821–27 Greece revolts against Turkish rule: the War of Independence.

1825 Egyptian Pasha Mehmet Ali helps to crush rebellious Cretans; is given control of Crete by the Turks as a reward.
1827 The Great Powers (Britain, France, Italy, Russia) arrange armistice which gives Greece autonomy, though still under Turkish sovereignty.
1832 Greece becomes an independent kingdom, but Crete is still under Egyptian control.
1840 The Great Powers take Crete away from Egypt, return the island to Turkey.
1866 The Monastery of Arkádhi is the Cretan stronghold in another rebellion. As the besieging Turks attack, the ammunition stores are detonated, killing hundreds of Cretans and Turks.
1878 Amateur archaeologist Mínos Kalokerinós begins excavation of what he believes is the "Palace of King Minos" at Knossós.
1894 Arthur Evans visits Crete for the first time.
1897 After more violent clashes between Cretans and Turks, the Great Powers occupy the island with an international force.
1898 Crete becomes an independent principality under Prince George, within the Ottoman Empire.
1899 Evans buys the land on which the Palace stood and begins excavations at Knossós.

REVOLUTION AND UNIFICATION

1905 Cretan lawyer Elefthérios Venizélos summons illegal Revolutionary Assembly at Thériso. Prince George abdicates.
1909 Army officers revolt against political establishment in Athens, invite Venizélos to form new government.
1910 Venizélos becomes Prime Minister. His Liberal Party dominates Greek politics for 25 years.
1911 Arthur Evans is knighted for his archaeological discoveries at Knossós.
1912–13 First Balkan War: Greece takes Crete from Turkey (as well as Macedonia and northern and eastern Aegean islands).
1913 Crete becomes part of the Greek nation.
1917 Greece enters World War I, fights alongside the Allies against Germany and Turkey.
1919 Venizélos sends Greek troops to try to annex parts of Asian Minor from Turkey.
1921 Greek expeditionary force crushed by Turks.
1923 Exchange of populations takes place: 30,000 Muslims are forced to leave Crete in exchange for a similar number of Christian refugees from Turkey.
1924 Greece becomes a republic.
1941 Battle of Crete: German forces drive Allies off the island. Heavy casualities on both sides.
1941–44 Crete occupied by Germany. Resistance punished by brutal reprisals.
1944–45 Allied forces liberate Crete.
1945 The site of Knossós is handed over to the Greek nation. Níkos Kazantzákis publishes *Zorba the Greek*.
1947–67 Constitutional monarchy in Greece.
1953 US establishes military bases on Crete.
1955 English linguists Ventris and Chadwick decipher Linear-B script, the earliest written Greek.

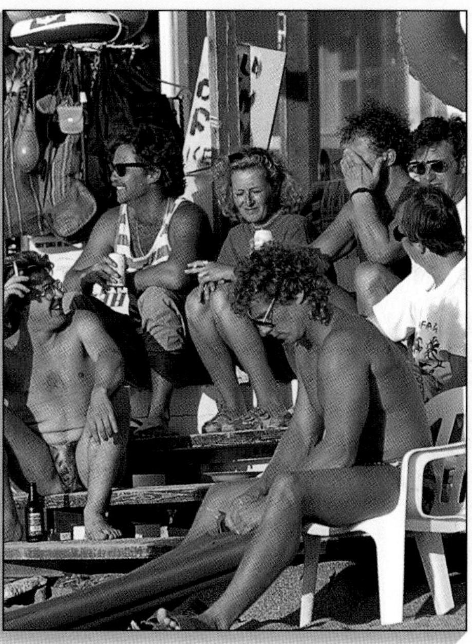

1960s Tourist boom begins.
1967–74 Greece ruled by junta of right-wing colonels; King Constantine in exile.
1972 Iráklion becomes the capital of Crete.
1974 Colonels overthrown; republic established.
1981 Greece joins the European Community. Papandréou's PASOK party, with strong support in Crete, forms first Greek Socialist government.
1989 PASOK government is brought down by corruption scandals; out of office for three years.
1996 Papandréou dies. His successor as leader of PASOK, Kóstas Simítis, steers the party to an election victory.
2000 Simítis is re-elected Prime Minister for another four-year term. ❑

PRECEDING PAGES: the "Ladies in Blue" fresco from the Minoan palace at Knossós.
LEFT: seated figure from Górtyn, 4th century BC.
RIGHT: seated figures in Mátala, 20th century AD.

MINOAN MAJESTY

Its beginnings are swathed in myth, its sudden end remains a mystery, but Crete's Bronze-Age civilisation was Europe's first great flowering of culture

Until the second half of the 19th century the early history of Crete lay buried in the myths of late Greek civilisation, hidden for over 4,000 years since the first of the splendid palaces were built. But even the earliest legends attest to the high level of cultural development on the island. We hear of the god-like Minoan dynasty and its great sense of justice and beauty. The Minoans loved dancing and sport and their settlements reflect their ability to combine the practical and the aesthetic. It was this social complexity which made Crete the first great historical centre in Europe, now so richly documented in Crete's museums and excavated sites.

The sensational discoveries made by the archaeologist Arthur Evans after 1900, as well as numerous other finds and continuing excavations, while not providing evidence of the godliness of the Cretan kings, certainly point to the existence of an independent culture far in advance of the later Mycenaean civilisation.

Today the evidence revealed by excavation and research completes a picture of the art, architecture, religion and everyday life of Europe's first sophisticated civilisation.

The New Stone Age

No evidence has been found of Palaeolithic or Mesolithic habitation on Crete. It is assumed that in Neolithic (New Stone Age) times, perhaps as early as the 7th millennium BC, a hunter-gatherer culture arrived on the island. At first these early islanders lived in caves, such as the Eileithyía Cave near Amnissós or the Yeráni Cave near Réthymnon. Later they built primitive dwellings of stones and bricks. This development took place before the "Neolithic Revolution" – the advent of agriculture.

With the introduction of cultivated crops, the domestication of cows, sheep and goats, and the use of fire for the production of pottery, a unique island civilisation developed. Through fishing and sea voyages, the early Cretans made contact with the neighbouring islands of Gávdhos and Dhía, and with the Cyclades. They made tools such as hammers, cudgels and axes from stone, occasionally from bone.

They made pottery vessels without the aid of a wheel. The pots had a rustic appearance with a simple shape, and were decorated with polished patterns and slits. Some discoveries of marble and baked idols (Neolithic pieces in cabinets 1 and 2 of the Archaeological Museum in Iráklion – abbreviated as AMI) point to the worship of the Mediterranean Goddess of Fertility, the Great Mother, Mother Earth. But there was still little indication of the unique way in which early civilisation on Crete was to develop in the future.

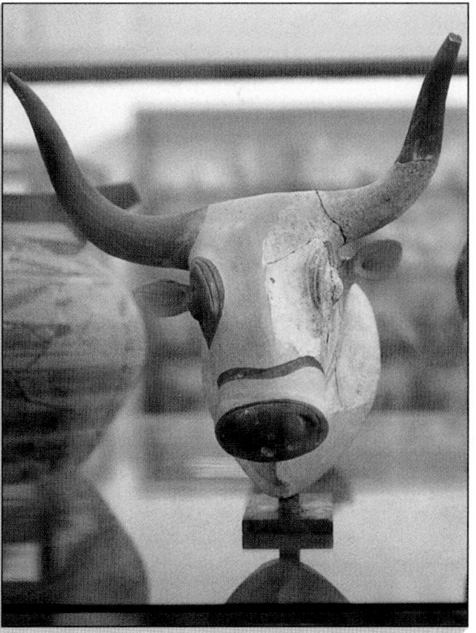

LEFT: storage jars *(píthi)* in the palace of Knossós.
RIGHT: a Minoan bull's head in clay.

The Pre-Palace Period

At the beginning of the Cretan Bronze Age, around 2600 BC, there was a further wave of immigration to the island from the Aegean and

Asia Minor. These newcomers were relatively more advanced. They had the potter's wheel and also had experience in obtaining and working copper, which soon became a valued commodity for the far-reaching sea trade. Furthermore, glassy, volcanic obsidian was imported from the islands of Mélos and Yiáli. New trading routes and cultural links were established with Anatolia and Syria, Cyprus, the Cyclades, Libya and Egypt.

These contacts with neighbouring civilisations, some of which were highly developed, combined with Cretan receptivity and inventiveness, led to the rapid evolution of an original and unique Mediterranean culture – the Minoan palatial civilisation.

It was probably during this era, referred to as the Pre-Palace Period, that Knossós and Phaestos got their names, both reflecting the influence of Asia Minor. The first mansions such as Mýrtos and Vassilikí were occupied and larger buildings were erected, some with a second storey.

The ceramics of the Pre-Palace Period still show signs of the New Stone Age, as the wheel was seldom used and the pieces were not baked in an oven but over an open fire. The Pýrgos style, which was influenced by the rich Cycladic culture (AMI, cabinet 3), demonstrates the distinct further development of late Neolithic ceramics. A vivid example of the polished lattice pattern is the often reproduced dark chalice-like cup (AMI, No. 74855).

Dating from the same period is an example (AMI, No. 2719) of a *pyx*, a shallow, round soapstone box with a lid, decorated with slit patterns and with a handle in the shape of a dog lying down. Other variations in the style of creative works in clay are the Ághios Onoúfrios style with its profusion of line decorations; the early Vassilikí style, characterised by uneven baking; and the Barbotine style with three-dimensional decoration (examples in AMI, Room 1, cabinets 3, 4, 6, 9, 12).

Just as remarkable as the ceramic art was the technique of stoneworking which developed. The stone pitchers found on the island of Mólchos in Mirabéllo Bay (AMI, cabinet 7) are notable for their attractive shape and the natural texture of the material. The harmony of shape and decoration of the vessels is particularly impressive.

There were also innovations in the art of seal

Beehive Burials

The practice of burying the dead in beehive tombs originated in the Pre-Palace Period, as shown by archaeological finds in Krási and in Foúrni, near Archánes.

moulding. Small *objets d'art* used for decoration or protection were made in a variety of designs. Precious stones, rock crystal and ivory were used, and shaped into geometrical and figurative forms, pyramids or cylinders. The rich variety of ideas is astonishing. The seal-makers produced graceful representations of animals and even, more rarely, human figures.

DEFINING AGES

The periods of Bronze-Age Crete now known as Pre-Palace, Old Palace and New Palace were classified by Arthur Evans as Early, Middle and Late Minoan.

In metallurgy too, there were new trends being developed. Goldsmiths had reached a high level of skill as early as the Pre-Palace era

(AMI I, cabinets 5, 14, 16, 17, 18a). The Cyclades were still the leaders in the artistic field (compare AMI I, cabinet 18a, found on Crete) but by the end of the Pre-Palace Period they had been superseded by Cretan craftsmen.

The Old Palace Period

Around 2000 BC, Cretan society took another major step forward. As the population increased, the first palaces were built. Most of them were sited in prominent positions, such as on the heights of Knossós and Phaestos. In order to prepare the ground for building, the hilltops were flattened. Then the unique and unprecedented residences were built with hundreds of rooms interconnecting in labyrinthine form. The palace of Mália was built on somewhat more modest lines.

Newer palaces erected later on the same sites make excavations under the foundations difficult. However, parts of early courtyards have been discovered, as in the old palace theatre arrangement in the West Courtyard at Phaestos and at the Louloures in Knossós, where round, well-like sacrificial shafts were built on Pre-Palace foundations. (In general, the new palaces differed little from the old, except in one major respect: the new palaces were far larger, and eventually almost took on the dimensions of small towns.)

Archaeological finds seem to indicate that there was a monarchical central power in Knossós. The growing influence of the Cretan rulers paved the way for the development of an island kingdom, giving Crete economic and political pre-eminence in the whole of the Aegean. This in turn led to the *"Pax Minoica"*, an

LEFT: Europa takes the bull by the horn, unaware of its divinity – *see page 26.*
ABOVE: griffin in a field of lilies on the walls of the Throne Room, Knossós.

extended period of peace, during which extensive fortifications were unnecessary and all the arts reflected the people's peaceful way of life.

Thanks to its favourable situation at the intersection of east Mediterranean trade, Crete's fleet was able to make wide-ranging contacts. Cretan ships sailed as far as Italy and Ugarit in Syria, and to Troy, Mélos and Lerna in the Peloponnese. At these Mediterranean trading posts, many Kamáres style pots have been found. The name was derived from a grotto in the Ida Mountains below the snowcapped peak of Psiloritis, where many such pots were found. In ceramic terms, the Kamáres style denotes the New Palace period, but it still retains decorative elements from an earlier era. Its main features are its wide variety, range of colours and, above all, its beauty.

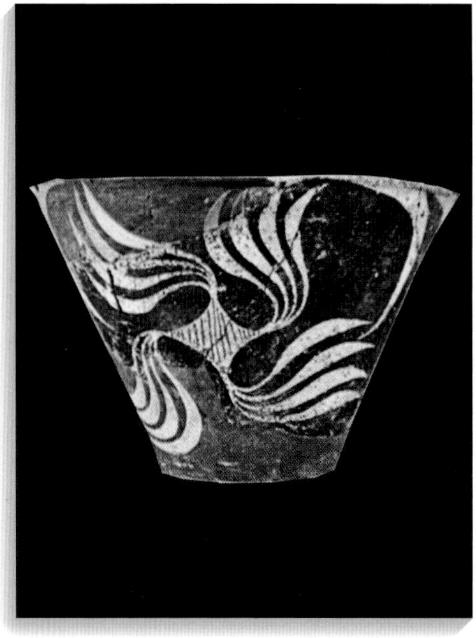

Grottos such as the Kamáres Cave and other mountain shrines were the destinations of pilgrims. People laid down offerings to placate the goddesses of fertility and maturity, and those of birth and death. Finds from this period also reveal the way the pilgrims were dressed. The women had wide skirts and elaborately coiled hair. The men wore loincloths and carried daggers in their belts. Some offerings – depictions of sick parts of the body, hands or chest – indicate the extent of the power ascribed to the goddess of nature. This tradition of votive offerings to the deity has continued unbroken on Crete since Minoan times.

The palaces were not merely the dwelling places of the rulers, but were also centres of production and administration. It has been discovered that even at the beginning of the Old Palace period, a script composed of symbols was in use. This was only preserved on a few objects and tablets (AMI II, cabinet 25); all documents in ink – if any existed – have been lost. This first European picture writing, still undeciphered, possibly had its origins in Egyptian hieroglyphics. In this script each sign represented a word, whereas in the Linear-A script which developed from it after about 1700 BC, each sign stood for a syllable.

Despite many years of study, this script has still not been deciphered either. It probably corresponded with the far-reaching bureaucratic necessities of the palatial trade organisation. It is assumed that the few clay tablets which have been preserved contain references to stocks and trade. However, it is the invaluable and singular Phaestos Disc which symbolises the transition to the New Palace period. This is a clay disc embossed on both sides with characters, the text of which, reading from the outside to the centre in spirals, would perhaps give more cultural information. The text is composed from 45 symbols but, unfortunately, it has never been deciphered. It has been dated at about 1600 BC.

The end of the old palaces came suddenly. In fact, in about 1700 BC they were all destroyed almost simultaneously. Their destruction is generally attributed to a massive earthquake, although it has been conjectured that a hostile invasion from North Africa could have been responsible. But the fact that the palaces were speedily rebuilt, and Minoan civilisation continued to develop with barely a pause, suggests that a natural calamity was probably responsible for the destruction.

The New Palace Period

The extensive sea trade which provided the basis for the flowering of Minoan culture also served to supply the island with any materials it lacked. Lead, silver, steatite (soapstone), jasper, rock crystal, manganese and ochre, all essential for the paintings, were extracted from the island itself. There was local timber too; cypress trees abounded. But copper was imported from Cyprus, gold from Nubia, ivory from Syria, obsidian from the island of Melos and possibly papyrus from Egypt. Tin, imported from Asia Minor, was of great importance as it was increasingly used in bronze alloys.

In fact, the development of Minoan civilisation in the middle of the 2nd millennium BC can only be understood against the background of this economic exchange. In the civilised lands of the Near East, particularly in Egypt, Cretan products were greatly sought after. Not only was wine in high demand, but also olive oil, timber, ceramic pots, bronze weapons and many other commodities. Foreign trade from Crete was extensive, reaching as far as Ugarit and Phoenicia, and Cretan wares have been found in Syria and former Yugoslavia as well as Egypt and Asia Minor.

REMAINS TO BE SEEN

Some archaeological sites not yet fully excavated may contain the remains of yet more Minoan palaces – at Tourkoginotiá/ Archánes, Monastiráki, Profítis Iliás, Hamálevri and Haniá.

After the destruction of the old palaces, new ones were constructed, including Knossós, Phaestos and Mália – which have been the destination of numerous visitors for years. In 1900, the English archaeologist Arthur Evans and his team, led to the site by Greeks, created a sensation when they unearthed the palace of Knossós. At around the same time, the archaeologists Federico Halbherr and Luigi Pernier were at work in Phaestos. These excavations were continued after 1950 by Doro Levi.

Mália was revealed by the Cretan archaeologist Joseph Hadzidhákis from 1915 until 1920 when French teams took over. A fourth palace was discovered in 1960–61 in Zákros in eastern Crete, although its existence had been suspected for some time. Since 1962, it has been researched by Nikolas Pláton. These excavations are of particular interest as large parts, some preserved beneath the sea, have been found untouched.

The four Minoan palaces already excavated are similar in some respects. They are not imitations of the residences of Mari or Ugarit, nor are they comparable to the palaces of Anatolia, Egypt or Mesopotamia. Most notable are the north/northeast-facing quadrangles, the asymmetrical layout of the buildings and the irregular shape of the outer walls. There are no facades to provide outside shelter while extend-

LEFT: a decorated cup in the Kamáres style.
ABOVE: the inscription on the Phaestos Disc, from *circa* 1600 BC, remains undeciphered

The Myth of Minos

Homer, Herodotus, Horace and Ovid all tell of the part supposedly played by Zeus in the foundation of the first great Cretan dynasty. As king of the gods, Zeus was able to take on any form he chose – a skill he often practised in his amorous pursuits. One day he fell in love with Europa, a beautiful Phoenician princess. Disguised as a bull, he approached the Phoenician coast, Europa leapt onto his back and Zeus immediately jumped into the sea and swam to Crete.

There, under an evergreen plane tree, he either

revealed himself as a god and seduced the princess, or turned himself into an eagle and raped her. Three sons were born: Minos, Rhadamanthys and Sarpedon. Soon Zeus deserted Europa for other loves. She married the Cretan king Astarios who adopted her sons.

Minos was the only son who kept up his relationship with his father. He spent nine years in the Dhíkti Cave, learning the art of leadership from Zeus. Then, armed with tablets of law, he returned to humankind, banished his brothers, and became the sole ruler of Crete. Wishing to discourage other aspirants to the throne by a show of power, he asked Poseidon for a miracle: a white bull was to emerge from the waves to be sacrficied. Poseidon granted him his wish but the bull was so beautiful that Minos could bring himself to kill it, and offered a different one to Poseidon. But the god was not deceived and punished him by making Pasiphae, Minos' wife, fall in love with the bull.

In her anguish, Pasiphae confided in the court engineer Daedalus, who constructed an ingenious model of a cow. Pasiphae hid herself inside the beast, and was immediately mounted by the bull. The result of their coupling was the Minotaur – half-man, half-beast. Minos was beside himself with fury, and wanted to kill the monster. But Ariadne, his daughter, begged for mercy for her half-brother.

The white bull, saved from sacrificial offering, gained fame as an exceptionally strong and dangerous creature. Later, Herakles (Hercules) was ordered by the Delphic Oracle to perform 12 heroic deeds, one of which was to capture the Cretan bull. He succeeded, and took the beast to the Peloponnese, where it did much damage.

At this time, Androgeus, the son of King Minos, had just won the pentathlon in the Panathenian Games. While out hunting for the bull, Androgeus was ambushed and murdered by a jealous rival. As soon as he heard of this, Minos sent his fleet against Athens. After a long struggle, the Athenians surrendered.

As recompense for his son's murder, Minos demanded the sacrifice of six youths and six maidens each year. He then ordered Daedalus to construct a labyrinth below the Palace of Knossos where the Minotaur must live. Whoever entered it was faced with two challenges: the confusing labyrinth and the monster itself.

One day Theseus, the son of the King of Athens, was chosen as a sacrifice – or perhaps he took it upon himself to go to Crete to fight the Minotaur. Once on the island, he fell in love with Ariadne. She reciprocated his feelings, and promised to help him overcome the monster. She turned for advice to Daedalus, who suggested that she should give Theseus a ball of thread. Theseus fastened one end at the beginning of the labyrinth, felt his way into the maze, killed the Minotaur and, with the aid of the thread, returned to daylight and fled to Athens with Ariadne.

When Minos discovered that it was his engineer who had helped the lovers to escape, he locked Daedalus and his son Icarus in the labyrinth, from which they later escaped with the aid of home-made wings. But that's another story. ❑

Left: another bull from a Knossós fresco.

ing the living space. These features give a clear impression of how the Minoans lived.

Other unique features are the palace halls, which were open at the sides, and the enormous staircases. There are "bathrooms" too, lying lower than the adjoining rooms, and light shafts and gardens in terrace formation with porticos. The upper rooms were used as offices, sanctuaries and staterooms.

EXPORTED DESIGN

Cretan architectural styles of the New Palace Period were copied as far away as Santoríni, where houses of this design have been found preserved in lava.

The whole ensemble is quite spectacular. The labyrinthine arrangement of the building is evi-

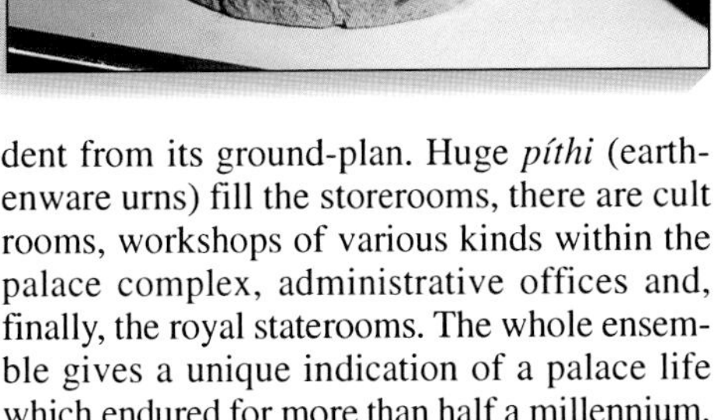

dent from its ground-plan. Huge *píthi* (earthenware urns) fill the storerooms, there are cult rooms, workshops of various kinds within the palace complex, administrative offices and, finally, the royal staterooms. The whole ensemble gives a unique indication of a palace life which endured for more than half a millennium.

Outside the palace buildings, both at Phaestos and Knossós, there were theatre-like courtyards and stairways, with "processional paths" leading at an angle (Phaestos) or at right angles (Knossós) linking the steps to the "small" palace, which at Knossós was at a distance from the main building.

ABOVE AND RIGHT: well-preserved Minoan vases have been found in a wide variety of shapes and designs.

Around the palaces and also in other parts of the island, townships with several thousand inhabitants grew up as regional centres and market places. The freedom-loving nature of the Cretans was reflected in the towns. Of course, the architecture of a town was greatly influenced by its location; for example whether it was built on a slope (Phaestos, Psíra, Arkalochóri) or on a level plain (Mália). The geographical position of Zákros, Gourniá and Palékastro called for narrow streets, while at Mália and Knossós there were blocks of houses divided by courtyards and gardens.

In this completely original and varied style of building even the mostly flat-roofed stone town houses showed a highly developed sense of creativity. Excavations have revealed more details, as in the simple two-storey brick house in Gourniá with a store-room on the ground floor, and living rooms above. Its counterpart is House E at Mália. This "villa" has about 50 rooms on the ground floor, with bathrooms and a room decorated with murals. It is respectfully, if inaccurately, called the "Small Palace".

The wide variety of housing at Knossós can be seen from about 50 faïence plaques, part of a complete picture, giving an indication of the facades of the houses at the beginning of the New Palace period (AMI II, cabinet 25). The two- and three-storey houses are of varied design; the ochre-coloured windows indicate that there was a covering of transparent material. A clay model of a typical, fairly large house complete with light shaft and balcony was discovered at Archánes in 1970.

SAFE AS HOUSES

Minoan society must have been secure and untroubled by threats of attack from within or without: there are virtually no defences, internal or external, at any excavated site.

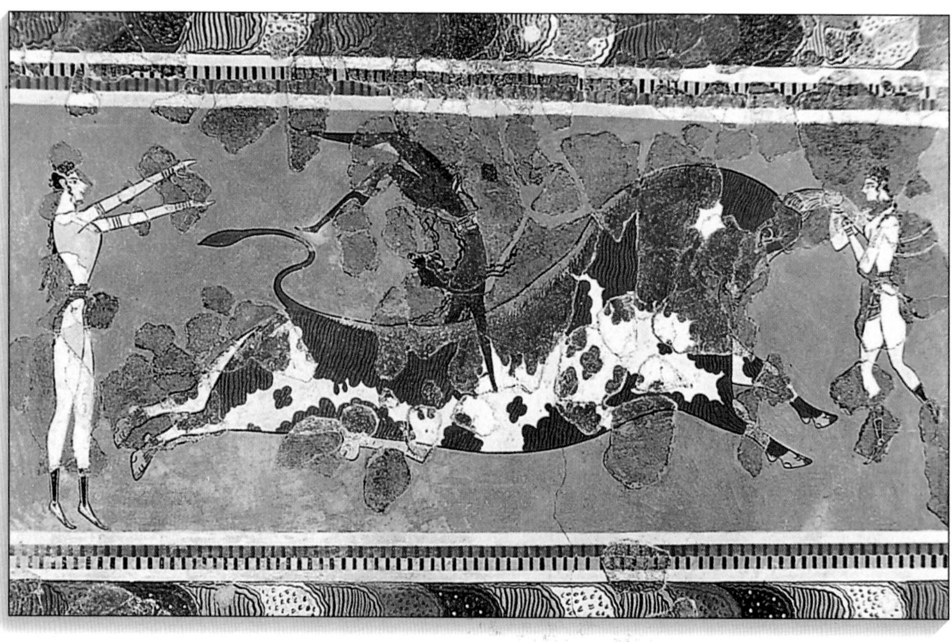

In the countryside, life was less varied and free. Olives and grapes grew abundantly on the island, but the eternally repeating demands of viticulture and the olive harvest, and the drudgery of agriculture and cattle raising left little scope for the development of the individual. Various forms of collective ownership, as well as clan associations, had been a feature of Cretan life for centuries. But now clear social divisions became evident and the old order was broken up. This is shown in various excavated country houses, which clearly reflect the difference between rich and poor. Houses from the area around Síva were poor, without kitchen, lavatory or even a stable. Then there was the typical country house, such as the one unearthed in Achládhia, with servants' rooms and a reception room next to the entrance. Finally, at the top of the accommodation scale, there were the splendid and plush Minoan villas. Each of the "manor houses" of Týlissos comprised many apartments with a two-roomed porter's lodge (Villa B); they also had running water.

Life in the New Palace society unfolded in many directions. There were athletic competitions featuring bulls and processions, dances and plays, which can clearly be seen as early forms of the different categories of sport, religion and theatre. Religious life was primarily influenced by the cycles of nature and the seasons of the year which determined growth. Despite the fact that Crete was an important trading and sea power, the fundamental growth of plants and ripening of crops was still a mystery. The autumnal withering and dying was observed with awe and hope was always renewed with the advent of rebirth in spring. The wonder at nature's regeneration had found expression in the concept of a great Mother Nature. She was the mother, and also the wife of the younger, lesser god who died each year, yet always came back to life. As Díktynna, Briómartis or Eileithyía, with regional variations, this goddess was also recognised in neighbouring regions and she appeared impressed on seals and golden rings, which are among some of the most valuable finds dating from the New Palace period.

EPONYMOUS KING

Minoan civilisation was so-called by the archaeologist Arthur Evans, after the (probably legendary) King Minos. It is possible that "Minos" was a royal title applied to all Cretan rulers.

Some of the scenes captured on such rings – and again the difference between country and Palace life is evident – indicate that many events took place out of doors, as shown on the golden ring of Isópata (AMI VI, cabinet 87, No. 424). Other cult events, however, are depicted as taking place in stone areas (the golden ring from Mycenae, National Museum Athens No. 3179), or staircases, which lead one to visualise a theatre-like central courtyard (ring from Archánes, AMI VI, cabinet 88, No. 989). There is still much to learn about the origins and early history of European theatre.

Ceremonies and sports

Religious ceremonies and processions grew in importance within palace life. With the development and transformation of New Palace customs, the significance of the holy caves, the importance of which dated back hundreds of years, began to diminish. Some were still revered, but new centres of worship had sprung up as well. In the caves, for example, the power of the great goddess was manifest. The goddess of women in labour, the birth helper, was sought in the Grotto of Eileithyía. The Cave of Psychró was thought to have been the birthplace of the young god who later became known to the Greeks as Zeus.

Numerous votive objects, sacrifice tables, small statues, tools and double axes give an insight into this religion of nature, which endured for a considerable period of time.

The sports involving bulls, where the worldly and religious ceremonials were inextricably bound, were held in the theatre area. The bull was worshipped in Eastern cultures as a godlike creature. Stylised bull horns were found dating from the 6th millennium BC in Catal Hüyük in southern Anatolia. On Crete the bull was probably the embodiment of virility. The mythological union of the beautiful bull and Pasiphae, wife of Minos *(see page 26)*, may have its origins in Minoan theories concerning fertility. Minoans believed that the holy marriage between the god of heaven and the Great Mother resulted in the fertility of plants on earth. The ubiquity of bull worship is indicated by sculptures and horns and their proximity to the double axes. This cult aspect mustn't be overlooked when one admires the agile athletes.

The acrobatic bull games probably caused injury or death to athletes from time to time, and occasionally there may have been a sacrificial offering of one of the bulls. But on the whole the games were nowhere near as gory as bullfights are now. The venue for these tests of courage seems to have been the so-called "royal road", a narrow street leading to the wider theatre area, which in itself was probably less suitable. The discovery of a long stone foundation edging the street, which could well have offered seating for spectators along the way, would certainly seem to indicate this arrangement.

LEFT: daring athletic displays featuring bulls seem to have been a pastime at Knossós.
RIGHT: the beautiful partridge fresco from the Knossós Caravanserai (Guest House).

Details of the games are shown in various representations: one of Crete's most beautiful murals has the games as its subject (AMI XIV). The unique representation of movement, one of the most important characteristics of Minoan art, is nowhere more evident than in the fine ivory sculpture of the suspended somersaulting bull leaper (AMI IV, cabinet 56) which is prized as one of the first examples of such movement in art. In addition, the cult container from the Small Palace in Knossós, the stone bull's head with lifelike rock crystal eyes, the golden horns and the wonderful slit and relief decoration covering the head, clearly demonstrate the special place held by this revered animal (AMI IV, cabinet 51 No. 1368).

Music and dance

A totally different aspect of Minoan art is seen in a ceramic model, dating from a somewhat later period, from Palékastro (AMI X, cabinet 132, No. 3903). Three women are dancing a round, with a lyre player in the centre. They are holding hands, and make a circle around the musician. Their long, bell-like robes accentuate their light swaying movements. This alluring scene is described by Homer with the words: "...circling round, just like the rounded wheel the seated potter wields..."

In the ancient world, Crete was the cradle of dance, and several signet rings show ecstatic dancers. Some dances have even been handed down to the present day. Scenes of dancing are documented in the miniature frescoes at Knossós. Almost a thousand years later, the Greek poetess Sappho wrote:

The Greek women,
Harmony in their light feet,
Danced around the altar of Eros,
Stepping on softly swelling flowers.

The dance performed for the protection of the newborn offspring of Zeus has its origin on the island of Crete. So do the choral songs in

A WRITER'S WONDER

Níkos Kazantzákis, the author of *Zorba the Greek*, was spellbound by the Knossós murals. He described: "noble, dignified women with lush, sensual lips, and birds, pheasants, partridges, blue apes, kings' sons with peacock feathers on their heads, wild holy bulls, maiden-like priestesses with snakes winding around their arms, blue boys in wonderful gardens: joy, strength, wealth, a secret world, Atlantis arisen from the depths of Cretan soil looked at us with huge black eyes, but with sealed lips. What world is this, I wondered, when will she open her mouth and speak? What great deeds had been performed by these ancestors from the soil of Crete?"

praise of Dionysos from which Attic drama was to develop.

Special mention must be made of some treasures of the purely Minoan New Palace works of art. In ceramics, where the forms become more slender, two new styles emerged with the building of new palaces. The flora style came a little earlier with its dark colours on a light background. Very naturalistic, particularly in the depiction of grasses (AMI IV, VIII), this was used to portray the world of plants. The marine style eloquently expressed the other dominant side of island life: octopuses, corals, shells and starfish. Here, particular attention should be paid to the works from eastern Crete (AMI IX, cabinets 120, 125; AM Ághios Nikólaos, room 3).

EQUAL OPPORTUNITIES

Minoan frescoes show women participating in games, hunting and religious festivals on apparently equal terms with men.

However, some of the most remarkable pieces of art in the world must be the famous snake goddesses from the central sanctuary of Knossós (AMI IV, cabinet 50) whose interpretation as depicting mother and daughter is still controversial. Even though the third figure, like some of the others, is not complete, the clothing of these sacred figures clearly indicates the various fashions of the New Palace era. The arms and upper parts of the older goddess are covered with snakes, cult-like attributes of the female godheads. They may be seen as chthonian animal companions of the Earth Goddess, although in Minoan times they were looked upon as protective house demons.

Some of the most glorious works of Minoan art are to be found in the unique frescoes of the palaces. It is here, above all, that the love of life and the glorious creativity of Cretan artists is expressed. Here the combination of the grace and originality in the depiction of the themes and the rich colour composition are shown at their height.

As frescoes, but also applied dry, the paintings adorned the walls and filled the surfaces of the rooms. Simple but durable mineral and metallic oxide colours glowed red, blue and green. They conjured up ornamental spirals and lines, painted over stucco relief work with bull scenes and pictures of cult festivals in the miniature frescoes. Here in the Mycenaean versions as well, and particularly in the Minoan paintings which were uncovered on Santoríni, the attractive youthfulness of this art has been well preserved and can still be appreciated today.

Minoan mystery

In about 1450 BC, this colourful splendour came to a sudden end. The cities of the Minoan civilisation collapsed in ruins. All the major palaces were flattened, and all except Knossós were consumed by fire. The suddenness of the event and the widespread destruction have presented historians with a puzzle.

What actually happened? At least three conflicting theories have been advanced to explain the devastation: natural disaster, internal revolt and invasion.

Was it the eruption of the volcano of Santoríni (more devastating than the 1883 eruption of Krakatoa, which killed 36,000) – and the ensuing earthquake and tidal wave that caused the destruction of Minoan culture? Today, the catastrophe of Santoríni is dated at about 1500 BC, about 50 years before the widespread destruction on Crete. It is quite possible that there were

LEFT: a reconstruction of daily life at Knossós in the Archaeological Museum of Iráklion.
RIGHT: one of the famous snake goddesses from the central sanctuary.

many indirect repercussions of the disaster, as the Cretan trading fleet must have suffered great losses, and clouds of volcanic ash may have ruined many a harvest. But the complete destruction of all the palaces and the cities? And why should Phaestos have been burnt, situated as it was on the south of the island and presumably protected from waves and fire in the north? The theory of an island-wide fire following the Santoríni eruption can no longer be upheld today.

The second theory is that Crete was swept by an internal revolt by the population against its rulers, possibly triggered by the eruption. Some evidence can be seen to fit this explanation: at Mýrtos on the south coast, for instance, a villa dominating the site was burnt but the surrounding settlement remained untouched. A "peasants' revolt" against the aristocracy? The evidence from elsewhere is not convincing. Great social inequality may have led to disputes, but there is nothing to suggest a violent uprising across the island.

The third theory is equally difficult to uphold: that Mycenaean invaders from the Greek mainland overwhelmed the Minoan culture by force of arms and systematically destroyed its finest creations. It is true that Mycenaeans took the place of Minoans in Crete within a generation or so of the calamity. But were they the cause of it?

If the Mycenaeans came to conquer the island, it was surely not in their interest to destroy the society and its infrastructure. And if they did, why did they leave the major centres of population deserted for a generation? Moreover, there is evidence that Mycenaeans were well established in Crete before the destruction of the palaces, and possibly even before the Santoríni eruption.

It is at Knossós in particular that the slow process of change can be seen. Certainly some time after the disaster, Mycenaean regents ruled

The First Written Greek

The Mycenaean script known as Linear-B was brilliantly deciphered by a young Cambridge scholar, Michael Ventris, in 1952. It turned out to be an early form of Greek (the same dialect was also spoken in Pylos in the Peloponnese, where similar clay tablets have been discovered). The Knossós tablets turned out to be mainly administrative documents – such as stock lists, records of transactions and taxes – although mention was also made of some of the Greek gods. It is not clear exactly when Linear-B supplanted Linear-A, an earlier script used to record the original language of the Minoans, which has yet to be deciphered.

in the rebuilt palace, which they altered and developed in a completely different way.

The previously unknown and all-conquering Mycenaean war chariot was in use – although the Cretans used it mainly for outings. The throne room in the palace of Knossós was erected during this period.

Another change was that Linear-A, the script used for the palace book-keeping, was replaced by Linear-B. This script, which was preserved on baked clay tablets, records an early form of the Greek language and was almost certainly introduced by the Mycenaeans.

Linear-B tablets have been found at Haniá too, and further discoveries in Tourkogitonía/ Archánes and Aghía Triádha from this period (1600–1450 BC) point to a Mycenaean presence in numerous other places in Crete before the sudden destruction of the palaces.

Warlike and masculine

The royal grave of Isópata, situated to the north of Knossós, is definitely Mycenaean, as can be seen from its unfamiliar construction and arrangement of rooms. The warlike, masculine character of the new rulers is also evident in the knights' graves discovered near Phaestos, which contained swords, daggers and spears – all extremely unusual grave furnishings on peaceful Crete.

Also attributable to this warring spirit are the mercenary figures in the fresco scene *Leader of the Blackamoors* from Knossós (AMI XIV, No. 3); and in general the subjects of the murals became harsher during that time (for example the *Procession* fresco, AMI XIV, No. 21).

Even in Egypt, which continued to be an important trading partner of the island, the change in Cretan clothing to a loincloth tapered at the front was observed. In areas under foreign domination, ceramics too evolved a new style known as the "Palace Style". Although the Minoan creative skill is still in evidence, for example in stoneworking, there are some signs of decay. Now, instead of the octopus motif, reflecting the graceful Minoan style of movement, on a palace style amphora we see a swarm of battle helmets.

The questions When? How? and Why? remain unanswered. All that we know for certain is that, in a relatively short space of time, Greek-speaking Mycenaeans became dominant in Crete, usurping and replacing Europe's first great civilisation. ❏

LEFT: Minoan tablets in Linear-A script.

ABOVE: an ornate sarcophagus found at the palace of Aghía Triádha, showing tributes imported from Africa.

WAVES OF INVADERS

The sudden collapse of Minoan culture marked the beginning of centuries of invasion, as one race after another occupied Crete

Around the year 1375 BC, the Palace of Knossós was destroyed – this time completely – and with it disappeared several other Minoan settlements and Mycenaean centres on the island. As with the mass destruction of 1450, the cause of this widespread devastation hasn't been firmly established. Some theories suggest that there was an unsuccessful uprising on the island against the foreign overlords. Perhaps the governor was evicted by Mycenaean mainland forces. However, it is clear that, from around the start of the Post-Palace Period (1375–1000 BC), the Mycenaeans held areas in central Crete and were steadily extending their influence.

Other Greek tribes forced their way on to the island and Crete's influence abroad began to decline. It became essentially a Mycenaean province of the Greek "community" (*koiné*), which included other islands such as Sámos, Rhodes and Híos as well as parts of Thessaly and Asia Minor. Now Mycenae and Tyrins, Thebes and Pylos, Sparta and Athens were far more important as fortified centres of Mediterranean power, as the Greek world continued to suffer from internal disputes.

Emigrating art

Although Crete was in decline, politically, culturally and artistically, Cretan artists who had emigrated to the new centres of power continued to produce art and artefacts in the island's characteristic style. One outstanding example of Cretan metalworking from this period is the dramatic depiction of the conquest of a walled city on a silver *rhyton* (drinking cup) found in Mycenae (National Museum of Athens, Mycenaean Room, cabinet 27, No. 481). This is in fact the oldest example of historical representation in the Occident.

During this period of decline, the palaces and buildings which had been destroyed were resettled. Unfortunately, there is very little historical evidence of this era. It is not known, for instance, to what extent the palace at Knossós was rebuilt, but the small shrine of the double axes does date from this time. Life went on as usual in Phaestos, Knossós, Górtyn and Aghía Triádha, and new cities sprang up, such as Tegea, Pergamos and Láppa.

LEFT: a Roman statue unearthed at Ierápetra shows Emperor Hadrian exulting over a defeated enemy. **RIGHT:** the "poppy goddess" found at Gázi is believed to be a goddess of fertility and healing.

A typical example of Mycenaean art is the "poppy goddess" found at Gázi. But the typical Mycenaean stylisation in ceramic decoration and the degeneration in thematic representation marked an artistic decline, particularly in stonework. The collapse of Minoan culture, which had so long stimulated and enriched that of the Mycenaeans, caused a paralysis in Mycenaean artistic development, which was apparent further afield than Crete. In room X of the Archaeological Museum in Iráklion, where the works of art and craft from this period are on view, their Mycenaean uniformity is there for all to see, despite traces of Minoan influence.

The greater political picture is known in broad outline: the deadly feuds between Greek tribes may have led to the brutalisation and weakening of the Minoan kingdom. The vagabonds, pirates and plunderers to whom the destruction of the cities and palaces of Hattuscha and Ugarit, Mycenae and Tyrins, Pylos and Thebes is attributed, may also have included Cretan and Mycenaean adventurers.

But the Trojan War is dated at this period of Mycenaean decline too (see panel below). The legends of the journeys of the Argonauts and the return of the Heraclidae indicate mass movements of peoples. Thucydides writes: “After this war [against Troy] the Hellenes moved and went to live elsewhere, and so there was no peace in the land and no power was gained. The late return of the warriors from Troy brought much strife. The conquered felt the need to leave and to found new cities.”

Arrival of the Dorians

Around 1100 BC members of another Greek tribe, the Dorians from the north, migrated from mainland Greece to Crete, bringing with them iron weapons and tools. They became the dominant group in a multilingual mix of peoples that included Eteo-Cretans (the “real” Cretans), Pelasgers and Kydonians (West Cretans). The original inhabitants fled to remote and inaccessible parts of the island, there to guard their own cultural identity. They preserved their own ancient customs and forms of expression, although showing some Mycenaean influence (AMI XI, cabinets 148, 154). Above all they kept their own original language.

By the end of this Post-Palace Period, the Minoan dream of peaceful coexistence in a flourishing culture was lost. But the efforts of archaeologists, who have painstakingly unearthed traces of this civilisation, have revealed that Minoan culture was not completely over-

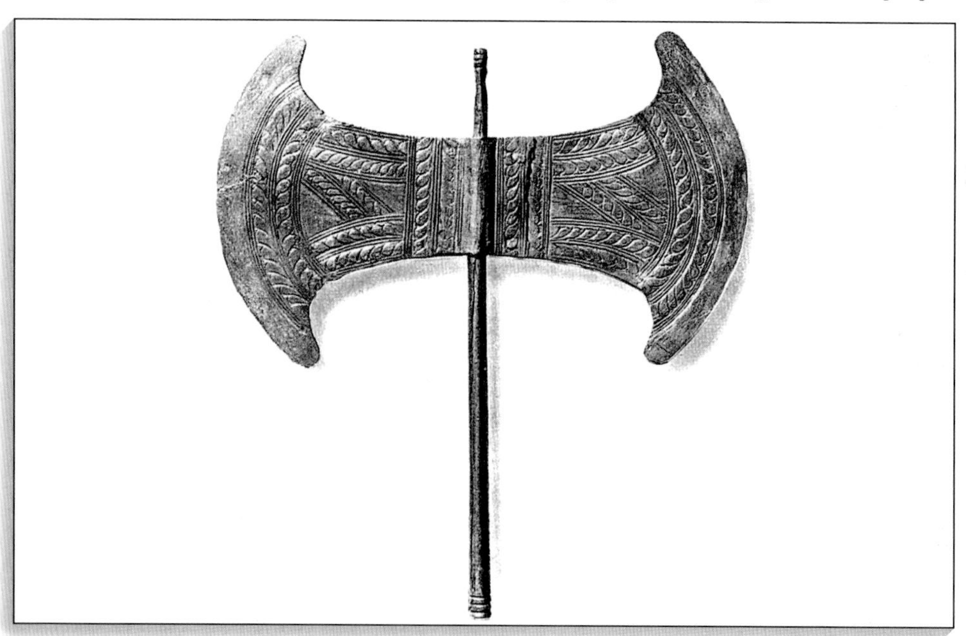

Cretans go to War

According to Homer, Cretans participated in the Trojan war (traditionally dated around 1184 BC), contributing a fleet only just smaller than that of Agamemnon:

But the renowned spear thrower Idomemeus led the Cretans,
Who came from Knossos and the fortress of Gortyn,
Lyktos, Milet and Lycastos on chalk shimmering cliffs,
Phaestos, Rhytion too, those populous towns
Others too, from Crete of a hundred cities,
These Idomeneus led, he of the skill with the lance,
And Meriones, like the murderous Ares,
They were followed by a squadron of eighty dark ships.

whelmed. There are traces of Minoan customs in the regional development of the new Dorian "three-class system" (see Homer, *Odyssey*, XIX, 171).

The newcomers and their warriors became the new ruling class; the burghers were guaranteed specific rights by a binding legislation. Then there was a third group of non-Dorians which seems to have constituted an oppressed servants' class.

FINAL SOLUTION

The Dorians introduced a new way of dealing with their dead: urn cremation replaced burial in tombs as practised by the Minoans and Mycenaeans.

Slowly, a political system of "Spartan" strength was formed on Crete. The towns were heavily fortified and youths eligible for military service were trained.

Between 900 and 725 BC a new style of pottery evolved. The somewhat clumsy ceramic works from the earliest years of this genre (Proto-Geometric) are displayed in the Archaeological Museum in Iráklion, Room XI. With the development of the early Geometric Style that followed, starkly stylised figures, quite unlike those from the mainland, were created (AMI, cabinets 146, 155). In the later, mature Geometric phase there was a resurgence of original creativity, although the works cannot compare with the Attic amphoras or the Olympic bronze sculptures dating from the same period. The impression of a provincial, reactionary place poor in ideas slowly receded, and a period of isolation drew to a close for Crete. As a Dorian port of transshipment and centre of maritime trade, it was no longer cut off from the neighbouring Mediterranean cultures.

LEFT: a miniature gold double-headed axe found in the cave of Arkalochóri, near Iráklion.
ABOVE: little horses adorn this ceramic *pyxis* (decorated pot) from the Geometric period.

The Archaic Epoch

In the century and a half following 650 BC, Crete was drawn into the upheaval and radical change that characterised this period of strife, poverty and over-population in the Greek world. A colonisation movement led to the formation of almost 1,500 city-states, some of which were tiny. This movement of peoples stimulated the region, both politically and economically. The high turnover of goods through the new trading centres of Ionian Asia Minor, and throughout the Levant, brought about an economic upsurge.

In the realm of art, the years of relative isolation were over and the stereotyped repetition of circular and rectangular ornamentation and uniform geometric figures was at an end. In the visual arts, Homeric myths were presented in a more varied and lively way, breathing new life into long-buried creative ability.

Perhaps Crete had already been stimulated artistically by the completely different cultures of Syria or Assyria, for there was much trade with those regions, or perhaps its location had attracted foreign artists to settle, enriching the artistic creativity on the island. Whatever the reason, for the last time in its long history, Crete developed its own form of artistic expression: the Daedalic Style. Among the numerous workshops on the islands in the Aegean and on the mainland, the school of Daedalus and his pupils was considered of decisive importance in the renewal of Greek sculpture.

BABY ALARM

According to legend, the cymbals found in the Ida Cave were crashed together to drown the cries of the infant Zeus hidden in the grotto, to save him from being swallowed by his father Kronos.

In the Ida Cave, the grotto long associated with the childhood of Zeus, unique bronze shields and cymbals were discovered first by Cretan shepherds and later in 1885 by Fabricius, Halbherr and Aerakis as a result of systematic excavation. Because of their oriental relief work, these cymbals were ascribed to functions in the cult of Zeus. The bronze work demonstrates a transformation of oriental form and content. From the oriental hero Gilgamesh, the hand of either a Cretan or an immigrant North Syrian master has fashioned a wonderful drawing of the Cretan Zeus (AMI XIX, cabinet 209).

The importance of early Cretan sculpture is apparent from the stone sculptures of the goddesses of Górtyn, a town in the region of Phaestos, which was growing more powerful (AMI XIX). This may be a representation of Artemis and Leto. The statuette with a helmet (AMI XVII, cabinet 193) which was found at Górtyn in a holy place on the Acropolis, is generally taken to represent the goddess Athena.

The oldest of the temples built in the archaic period with Minoan architectural elements have been excavated near Priniás on the eastern foothills of the Ida Mountains. The unique late Daedalic portal sculptures of two goddesses seated opposite one another clearly reflect traces of Egyptian and Syrian/Phoenician iconography.

The picture of the Archaic epoch may be completed by a visit to the Dorian city of Lató, which was founded at this time. With its streets lined with houses and its ground plans of the stores, particularly the *agora*, or meeting place, and the show staircase area, it gives a significant insight into the early history of Greek city life and theatre.

Looking at the old steps, reminiscent of the arenas of Phaestos, Gourniá or Aghía Triádha, one can sense the *joie de vivre* of the Minoans across the ages which Homer so vividly describes:

Glowing youths there and much acclaimed
young women danced around, hand in hand.
Soft clothes covered the youths, light as oil's
soft glow, and the maidens were veiled in
linen.
Every dancing girl was adorned with a lovely
garland, and the youths had golden daggers
at their sides in silver belts...
Many were those crowded around the lovely
dancers, rejoicing with all their hearts...

–Homer, *Iliad*, XVIII, 5593/5604

As the Archaic epoch finally drew to a conclusion, Crete sank back into the obscurity of an island province.

The Classical Period

From around 500 BC, the political and cultural focus of the Greek world was finally established on the mainland. Athens, which rivalled Sparta, had been waging war for centuries – not only against the threatening enemy of Persia – and Attica had grown to become the new centre of Greece. Crete was relegated to the cultural and political sidelines. Although tradition and poetry helped preserve the island's artistic reputation, there was no new notable creativity in the field of art during this period.

There is, however, one extraordinary document that must be mentioned: a stone inscription which affords the visitor a glimpse into the ancient Cretan legal system. "King Minos" was renowned for his wisdom, although he was also known as a stern lawmaker and judge. It is said that the legendary Spartan lawmaker Lykurgos studied on Crete. Even Solon enriched early Athenian legislation from Cretan law. So, for the ancients, Crete was also an island with a high reputation in legal matters.

In 1884, Federico Halbherr, soon to be assisted by Ernst Fabricius, found the great inscription of Górtyn. Standing in the mill canal of Dhéka, they deciphered a total of 17,000 signs carved in broadstone: it was the legal code of the up-and-coming town of Górtyn.

This settlement on the Messará plain had long lain in the shadow of the older royal residence of Phaestos, but now the city was on its way to becoming the centre of this fertile region. With its trading ports of Kommos and Mátala in the south, it was able to outstrip Phaestos, and possibly the other cities of the island too. There are 12 columns each with 52 lines expertly carved in the stone in an old Dorian dialect. The lines follow a so-called "ox turn", that is, the lines turn like the ox when ploughing *(Bustrophedón)*. They do not simply follow each other but alternate and reverse with the letters set in the mirror image. In the early Greek alphabet, the letters Phi, Chi, Psi, Zeta, Eta and Omega are missing. The 20 tablets of law, each about 70 cm (27 ins) wide and about 170 cm (67 ins) high, make up the longest Greek inscription ever found and reflect a previously unknown set of laws. The inscription is generally dated to 480–460 BC.

There is no clear separation of the different branches of the law. The work deals with civil and criminal law, substantive and procedural

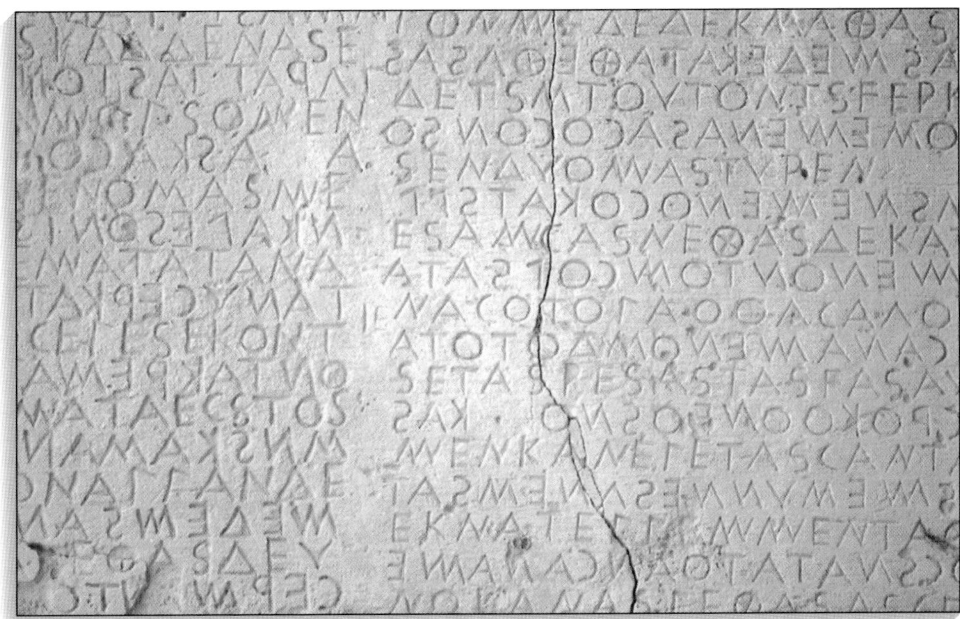

LEFT: a steatite (soapstone) vase in Iráklion Archaeological Museum depicts olive gathering.
ABOVE: the famous Górtyn Code, 20 tablets of laws in a Dorian dialect, dates from 480–460 BC.

law, and deals with the punishment for adultery and claims following a death. Different sanctions were imposed for both free and unfree burghers (the latter presumably refers to the descendants of the old suppressed Minoan peoples). Here is an example: "Whoever assaults a free male or female, must pay one hundred *strate*... If a slave assaults a free male or female, he must pay double... Whoever assaults his own slave, must pay two *strate*..."

UNEQUAL RIGHTS

The Gortyn Code reveals how, since the arrival of the Dorians, the status of women had declined. Their legal rights were now hardly better than those of slaves.

Even the rights of possession of the slaves' children had been dealt with: the child of an unmarried slave woman was allocated to her father's master; the child of a married slave woman, to her husband's master.

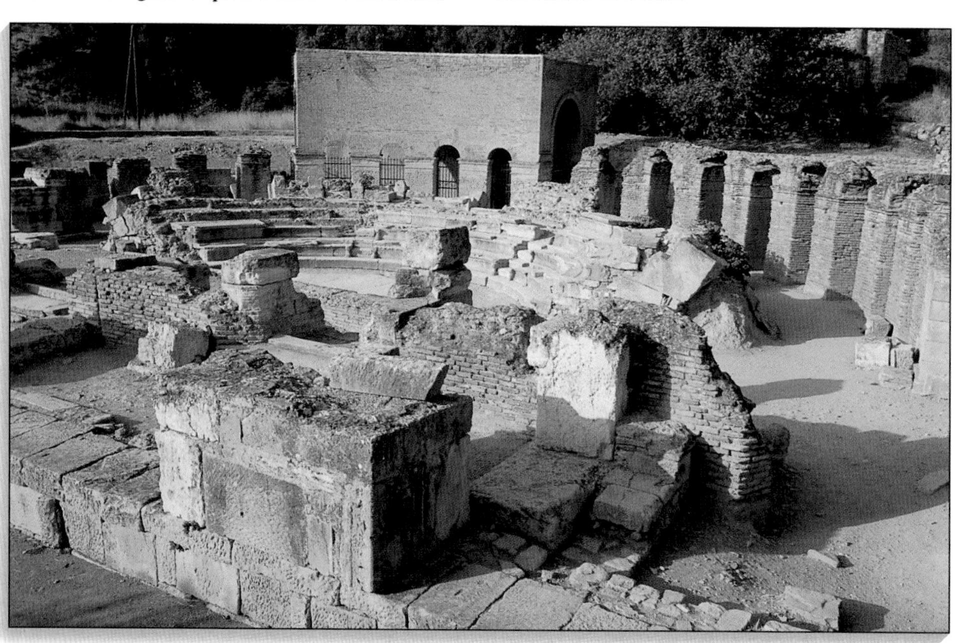

Interesting information is also provided on the methods of giving evidence: "If the case concerns a slave (or any other possession) and each party maintains that he is the owner then, if a witness testifies, the judge will rule in accordance with that evidence; but if witnesses support the claims of both parties, or of neither, then the judge must rule in accordance with his conscience under oath." (Tablet I, lines 16–24).

Not much took place on or around Crete at this time. Górtyn had almost attained its goal of becoming the main city, and in the changeable Cretan city-state history there were many short-lived agreements and contracts. Sometimes the Cretans backed the wrong horse, as when they supported the Persian fleet in the sea battle against Alexander the Great at Issos (333 BC). He remained unvanquished. The Hellenic events which influenced world history, from the death of Alexander (323 BC) to the death of Julius Caesar (44 BC) were only followed from a distance on the island of Crete.

Roman occupation

For nearly 1500 years, since the first arrival of the Mycenaeans, various groups of Greek-speakers had held sway in Crete, gradually eroding the influence of the Minoans and driving the pre-Greek Cretans into isolated inland communities. For the next two millennia, Crete was occupied by a succession of non-Greek powers, unbidden intruders and their hostile armies, who saw the island as a breadbasket or as an important strategic naval base. However, throughout the period, the Cretans always put up a strong resistance.

By the 1st century BC, the Romans had become the unchallenged power in the Mediterranean.

So it is not surprising that Rome was the dominating factor in Cretan life for around 400 years. In 69 BC the Praetor Quintus Caecilius Metellus and his troops landed near Haniá and, after several years of resistance, conquered the island which then became another Roman province (Crete-Cyrere). As Górtyn had been friendly to the Romans, helping them in their conquest, the town was made the island's capital as a reward.

One of the first things the Romans did was to eradicate the hordes of pirates who had been terrorising the Mediterranean from bases on Crete, often with the support of the islanders. The Roman general Gnaeus Pompeius (Pompey the Great) swept them off the sea with 500 ships and 120,000 soldiers.

Ruins and archaeological finds give evidence of a Roman way of life, but also reflect the restraints imposed on the foreign rulers by the Cretans, and the compromises they were eventually obliged to make after many years of suppression and rebellion. That the island experienced a modest flowering is indicated by the theatres and temples, villas and water systems, especially in Górtyn and the new garrison city of Knossós.

Crete also played a part in the early history of Christianity: St Paul, whose companion Titus became the first Bishop of Crete, stopped at Kalí Liménes on his way into captivity in Rome in AD 59. As the new religion spread, the island had its martyrs, such as the "Holy Ten" (Aghii Dhéka) who were beheaded in around 250 for refusing to worship the Roman gods. With the decline of Roman imperial power, *Pax Romana* – the long reign of Roman stability – and the suppression of piracy came to an end.

The rule of Byzantium

Crete maintained its non-central role during the rule of the Byzantines, who dominated this Mediterranean region during the 4th century after the split-up of the Roman Empire. On 11 May 330 the old city of Byzantium was renamed Constantinople, after Rome's first Christian emperor, Constantine, and it became the capital of the new Eastern Empire with a state system which was to last for a thousand years. Crete was administered from there and was left to its shadowy existence.

Christianity was promoted on the island. Many churches were built, of which the most important architecturally and from the point of view of ecclesiastical history is perhaps the domed basilica of Ághios Títos in Górtyn. This dates from the 6th century and was probably built on the site of a more ancient building near the Roman odeon and theatre. Dedicated to St Titus, who was appointed the first Bishop of Crete by St Paul, it remained the seat of the Archbishops of the Church of Crete until the invasion of the Arabs during the 9th century.

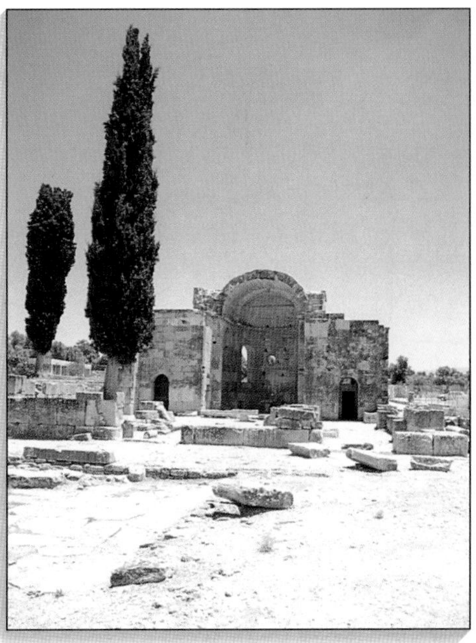

Between the 4th and 6th centuries Crete can be assumed to be politically stable. Like the rest of the Aegean, the island remained unaffected by assaults by Germanic tribes which were the first convulsions to shake the Byzantine Empire. But, in AD 623, the island was disturbed by the Slav migrations and from the mid-7th century, Crete was the scene of Arab attempts to move northwards to conquer Constantinople, the cultural and political centre of the known world at that time. After decades of fighting for supremacy, the Byzantines lost Crete along with Sicily in 824. Both islands were ceded to the Arabs.

LEFT: the Romans built this odeon (small theatre) in Górtyn in the 1st century AD.
RIGHT: the most important church on Crete – the 6th-century basilica of Ághios Títos at Górtyn.

Arab occupation

The ports of Crete soon became used by the Saracen pirates, who made life dangerous throughout the whole Aegean up to the Dardanelles. This was a permanent feature of life under the Arabs, whose rigid exercise of power was to last for more than a century. However, worse was to come with the complete destruction of all Christian monuments on the island and the gruesome pursuit and persecution of Cretan Christians. Once again many islanders

ATTACKING HEAD-FIRST

The Byzantines' battle to regain Crete was extremely bloody, even by the standards of those days: Saracen heads were used as catapult ammunition against the fortress of el-Khandak.

retreated to their hide-outs in the mountains. In AD 828, the Arabs set up their headquarters in the fortress el-Khandak, near the present-day city of Iráklion, and the old city of Górtyn was irrevocably destroyed.

Return of the Byzantines

Finally in 961, after several unsuccessful attempts, the Byzantine army, led by Nikefóras Fokás retook Crete. The siege of el-Khandak lasted for months, and was not helped by a great famine, but nevertheless it culminated in the eventual storming of the city. As the Byzantines began to display their power once again, Crete's rule was returned to Constantinople. Thanks to the retaking of Crete, and of Aleppo in 926, Fokás was made emperor two years later. By then Crete had become a relatively independent military and administrative region.

Its location led to a certain isolation and agriculture soon went back to the feudal system. Merchants from Constantinople and allied neighbouring lands came to Crete, reinvigorating the sea trade, which was mainly controlled by Genoese families. The capital was the new town of Chandax, close to the Arabs' fort of el-Khandak on the site where Iráklion stands today.

As life became more stable, both politically and culturally – architecture and fresco painting experienced a revival – so the power of Constantinople declined. This was demonstrated by the big landowners being exempted from paying tax and the emergence of a bureaucracy. According to tradition, an attempt to gain autonomy took place at the time of the Byzantine defensive action against the Seljuks (1090–92), but it ended with the arrival of the imperial sailing fleet, commanded by Johannes Dukas.

The reconquest of Crete led to a flowering of Byzantine art on the island, of which sadly little now remains. The Byzantine church buildings of Myriokéfala (Panaghía Church, 11th–12th century) with its many frescoes was constructed shortly after the recapture of Crete from the Arabs. Byzantine art treasures from the following Venetian epoch are more numerous, but equally admirable, in Assómatos (Archánes, Church of the Archangel Michael, 14th century) or in Kritsá (Panaghía Kerá, 13th–14th centuries).

Sold to the Venetians

In 1204 Byzantium was finally forced to surrender its hold on Crete – but not to the Arabs. The catalyst that heralded the decline of the Byzantine Empire was the sacking of Constantinople by the Fourth Crusade, at the instigation of Venice. In an attempt to regain control of the empire, the deposed emperor Alexios III made a gift of Crete and other Byzantine possessions to the leader of the crusade, Prince Boniface of Montferrat. His donation was to no avail. Constantinople was sacked by the crusaders, who installed their own emperor, and in return for their assistance Boniface sold Crete to the Venetians for a nominal sum.

Their first task was to expel their arch-rivals, the Genoese, who had established a powerful commercial base on the island, with strong local support. By 1210 Venice had made Crete their own – although for more than a century, the Genoese gave active assistance to any local rebels, in the hope of regaining a foothold.

The Venetians were able to make good use of the island to widen their maritime interests. By means of only a few representatives stationed on Crete, these new strong and dictatorial rulers managed to put down 14 major uprisings and a rebellion during the ensuing four and a half centuries, while at the same time expanding the economy. The island of Crete was completely transformed and brought in line with Venetian ideals. The church of Rome was made the "official" religion, supplanting Eastern orthodoxy. Place names were changed – the capital, Chandax, took the name of Candia, which was soon applied to the whole island. Building began to change the face of the island – not entirely to its detriment.

LEFT: a Byzantine icon of the Madonna and Jesus. **ABOVE:** retelling the story of Arkádhi Monastery, one of many abortive rebellions against the Turks.

In some parts of the island, the Cretans were able to escape Venetian political influence. Elsewhere, the islanders rose up against the ruling nobles and proclaimed a "Republic of Saint Titus". Finally, a concession for religious tolerance of the Eastern Christians ensured the solidarity of the people, but the gruesome end of the uprising in 1363–64 was inevitable.

Only after the final fall of Constantinople in 1453 to the Ottoman Turks did Byzantine artists and learned men come to Crete. They were to enrich this Greek- and Byzantine-influenced island considerably. Some ships and volunteers had, in fact, taken part in the defence of Constantinople against the Turks. Now this coming together of the Latin early Renaissance spirit and the Greek Orthodox antique heritage was to bring forth its own results. This was most clearly demonstrated in the new capital Candia (Iráklion) where features still visible today, such as the Morosini Fountain, the Loggia and the Ághios Márkos Basilica, reflect this new culture.

During this time, too, the threat of attack from the increasingly powerful Ottoman Empire encouraged the Venetians to build their most ambitious public works – the solid fortresses that can still be seen today in cities such as Iráklion, Haniá and Réthymnon.

Turkish occupation

An attack on an Ottoman convoy in 1645 provided the excuse for a Turkish assault on Crete. The Ottoman Turks took Haniá after a bloody battle, then Réthymnon, and soon had control over the whole island except the capital, Candia. It was not until 1669, after a gruelling 22-year siege, that the Turks took the city and now ruled all of Crete.

"Freedom or Death"

Crete celebrates its National Day on 8 November, the anniversary of the explosion in 1866 at Arkádhi Monastery, where hundreds of Cretan rebels died rather than surrender to the Turks.

By this time, the Ottoman Empire had grown from a band of clans who made their first conquest of the town Bursa (Brusa) in 1326, to the most important power in the Eastern Mediterranean. For the Turks, Crete was not only a source of tax revenue but, more crucially, also a base of great military importance, so that even when the islanders refused their economic cooperation and the towns grew desolate, the retention of this island, so dearly paid for, still seemed justified.

In Cretan lore the famous attempted uprising of 1770 has never been forgotten. Before the Cretan Dhaskaloghiánnis ("Teacher John") could organise a coalition with Russia during the Russo-Turkish War of 1768–74, he was tricked and executed by the Sultan. But Crete remained an inspiration to revolt for the other Aegean islands, and the constant battles that were necessary to safeguard conquered territory slowly eroded the strength of the Ottoman Empire. Gradually a Greek national consciousness was born. In 1821 the Greek mainland and some of the islands rebelled. The Peloponnese was free.

In the winter of 1824–5, Mehmet Ali, viceroy of Egypt and the new commander in chief of the occupational fleet, landed on Crete, which had been given to him by the Turks as a reward for his punitive expedition against the Greeks. Once again the island was conquered. Meanwhile, other great European powers had decided to try to intervene and deal with this centre of conflict. The result was that on 6 July 1827, an armistice was arranged between the Great Powers (Britain, France, Italy and Russia) in which Greece – but not Crete – was guaranteed autonomy, but still under Turkish sovereignty.

It was not until 1830, after continued acts of war, that a peace settlement came into force. In 1832, Greece became a kingdom, now chafing under the rule of a Bavarian king's son (Prince Otto). But there was still no peace on Crete, and in 1841, after another bloody uprising, the Great Powers took it away from Egypt and returned it to Turkey.

In 1869 the Paris Conference extended autonomy to Crete but it was too late for the hundreds of Cretans who, three years earlier, had blown themselves to bits by exploding a cache of arms in the monastery of Arkádhi, rather than be captured by the Turks.

In 1897, an attempt by the mainland to win back the island failed. Then in the following year Crete acquired "autonomous status" under Ottoman supremacy, with the full support of the great powers. The high commission of Prince George became the party responsible for the island's administration. An almost incidental event, when some British soldiers were killed, finally led to the end of the Turkish presence on Crete and in 1899 the first Cretan government was sworn in. ❑

LEFT: Turkish Cretans in the late 19th century.
RIGHT: Haniá lighthouse was rebuilt in the form of a minaret in the 1820s, when Egypt held sway in Crete.

MODERN TIMES

Free from foreign domination at last, and eventually part of Greece, Crete has nevertheless remained on the fringe of mainstream Greek affairs

Crete entered the 20th century with many issues of nationality unresolved. True, there was now a Cretan Assembly presided over by Prince George, the son of King George of Greece, but in reality he was governing the island on behalf of the Great Powers, Britain, France, Italy and Russia. The Turkish army had been driven out, yet Turkey still had a voice in the assembly, which was jointly Christian and Muslim. Most frustrating of all to most Cretans, Crete was still not part of Greece.

The *Énosis* (Unity) that Cretans had awaited for so long still had to be fought for. The struggle was led by the charismatic Elefthérios Venizélos. He had fought in earlier uprisings against the Turks, and now became a member of the Cretan Assembly and minister of justice under Prince George. But, when George refused even to consider unification, Venizélos took matters into his own hands.

In 1905 he summoned an illegal Revolutionary Assembly at Thériso, which raised the Greek flag and declared unity with Greece. Although the Great Powers quickly stamped on this latest rebellion, they had to concede that Prince George had lost all support in Crete. He was forced to resign and a new governor appointed, the veteran Alexander Zaïmis.

But this was not enough for Venizélos and the unification movement. In 1908, the Cretan Assembly issued a unilateral declaration of *Énosis* with Greece – to the embarrassment of the Greek government which, like the Great Powers, was fearful of antagonising Turkey. In an extraordinary move, the government invited Venizélos to Athens to become Prime Minister of Greece, yet still refused Cretan deputies seats in the Greek Parliament.

In 1912 Greece, Serbia and Bulgaria declared war on the Ottoman Empire over Macedonia. Previous fears of antagonising the Turks were now irrelevant, and Cretans were finally allowed into the Athens Parliament. This First Balkan War was ended in 1913 by the Treaty of Bucharest, which also formally recognised Crete as part of the Greek state.

LEFT: a naïve painting of Elefthérios Venizélos.
RIGHT: memorial to Cretans killed in the Balkan Wars.

Perhaps because of its remoteness from Athens, Crete was spared the worst repercussions of the political strife that plagued Greece in the early decades of the century. World War I, for instance, brought dissension between King Constantine, who favoured neutrality, and Prime Minister Venizélos, who wanted to join the Allies against Germany and Turkey.

Eventually, after Venizélos had set up a rebel government, pressure from the Allies persuaded Constantine to step down in 1917. Greece entered the war and Greek troops served with distinction on the Allied side. But Crete was largely unaffected by the conflict.

The island suffered far more serious consequences from Venizélos' next enterprise – an attempt to seize territory in Asia Minor from a war-weakened Turkey. A Greek expedition was crushed and humiliated by Turkish forces under

Mustafa Kemal (later Ataturk), and the Treaty of Lausanne which followed this debacle in 1923 forced an exchange of populations between Turkey and Greece. Nearly 400,000 Muslims were expelled from Greece; nearly 1.5 million Orthodox Christians left Turkey. For Crete, this meant the expulsion of 30,000 "Turks" – many of them Cretan Muslims whose ancestors had lived on the island for centuries – in exchange for the same number of Greek-speaking refugees from Turkey.

The political upheavals of the 1920s and '30s also made little impression on Crete. While Athens witnessed coups and counter-coups, the establishment of a republic and the restoration of the monarchy, the exile of Venizélos and the rise to power of dictator Yioánnis Metáxas, the islanders in the eastern Mediterranean were scarcely affected. But their peaceful existence was soon to be brutally shattered.

The Battle of Crete

Greece entered World War II in 1941 and was rapidly overrun by German troops. The Prime Minister, Emmanuel Tsoúderos, set up a government in exile in his native Crete, which was defended by British and Commonwealth forces.

On 20 May 1941, German parachutists and mountain infantrymen landed near Haniá, followed by further airborne contingents. Fired on by Allied troops and Cretan civilians, the Germans suffered appalling losses. But after 10 days of fierce fighting, Haniá, Réthymnon and Iráklion were under German control.

The Allied troops were forced to retreat. About 12,000 men trudged down the Ímbros Gorge to the south coast, to be evacuated to Egypt from Hóra Sfakíon. The few that remained were sheltered and aided by Cretans, who also organised resistance activities against the German troops – but at great cost. If Cretans were suspected of guerrilla actions against the occupying forces, the Germans retaliated by destroying whole villages and arbitrarily shooting civilians. Their orders were "10 Cretans for every German shot". In some mountain villages, the entire male population was killed.

The long occupation and terror did not succeed in breaking the Cretans' resistance. On the contrary, the islanders continued a guerrilla campaign against the occupiers, culminating in the surprise attack on the German headquarters in 1944. The reprisals were harsh: the mountain village of Anóghia was completely destroyed.

When the Germans finally surrendered and withdrew in 1945, they left behind them bombed-out cities, burnt villages and destroyed roads. The island was in economic ruins.

Post-War chaos

In most of Greece, resistance against the Germans had been organised by Communist groups, who now expected to play a part in Greek politics. The post-war struggle between Communists and the British-backed monarchy led to a bloody civil war which lasted until 1949. But in Crete pro-British sentiment and British post-war reconstruction aid made Communism an unpopular option: thus the island was spared the bloodshed and bitterness that wracked the rest of the country.

In 1947, the monarchy of George II was replaced by a republic, with Crete as one of Greece's 10 administrative provinces. Because of Greece's strategic importance on the eastern flank of NATO, and what the Pentagon continued to see as a communist threat, the US supported a series of right-wing governments until 1964, when George Papandréou's centrist coalition came to power – but not for long. On 21 April 1967, a group of right-wing colonels staged a *coup d'état* against the elected government and established a military dictatorship. Any opposition was rigorously suppressed, detention camps were set up, and the regime supported the foreign policy of the American protecting power. Student unrest in 1973 and the Junta's involvement in Cyprus in 1974 resulted in the final downfall of the dictatorship. In 1981 PASOK, the socialist party led by George Papandréou's son Andréas, came to power on the promise of freeing the country from US influence.

REPRESSIVE COLONELS

The military regime of 1967–74 censored the press, suppressed intellectual debate, and closed the frontiers to long-haired or mini-skirted foreigners – at least, until they realised the implications for Greece's tourist trade.

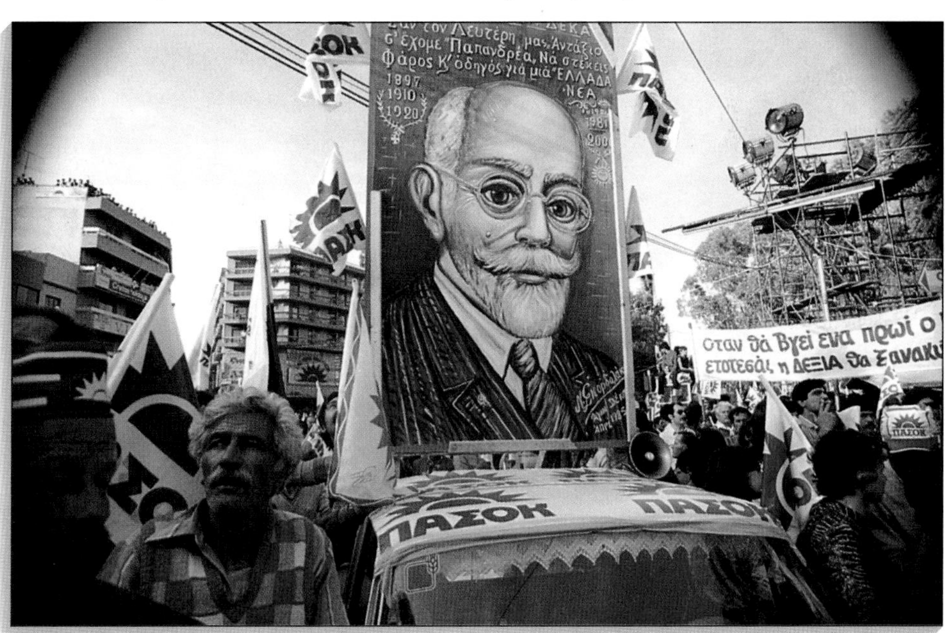

The American military presence was reduced, but the US still has military bases on the island. However, relations with the Americans have become increasingly strained since the NATO bombing of Kosovo in 1999, which was strongly opposed in Greece. The US naval base in Soúdha Bay has been a frequent target for protests.

Meanwhile, Papandréou's successor, Kóstas Simítis, has taken the PASOK party towards the right, while striving to knock Greece's economy into shape to qualify for entry into European Monetary Union in 2001. ❑

LEFT: Andréas Papandréou, leader of Greece's first socialist government, came to power in 1981.
ABOVE: the socialist PASOK party still uses images of Venizélos to attract popular support in Crete.

ΑΝΕΚ
22
1-3 ΙΟΥΛΙΟΥ 1984
Φ/Γ «ΕΛΛΗ»

ΟΛΥΜΠΙΑΚΗ
ΒΕΡΓΑΝΕΛΑΚΗ
ΧΡΟΝΙΑ
διαλεξε και αποφασισ

A Rugged Beauty

With its unique geology, geography, flora and fauna, the island is a precious gem that even expanding tourism can do little to damage

Homer was full of admiration for the island, as the *Odyssey* shows. But even for Homer, around 800 BC, the Minoan epoch was ancient history and shrouded in that same mystery which captures and fascinates visitors to Knossós to this day.

In middle of the sable sea there lies
An isle call'd Crete, a ravisher of eyes,
Fruitful, and mann'd with many an infinite store;
Where ninety cities crown the famous shore

Historians believe that the 90 cities he refers to had about 1.2 million inhabitants. Today just over half a million people live on the island, but the mixture is still as colourful. The appearance of Crete has, however, changed dramatically. Ancient authors tell of huge cypress forests, but centuries of plunder have denuded the island, leaving bare limestone scenery. Only further inland, mainly in the west, are there wooded areas.

The physical island

The Aegean Sea was formed by the sinking of a block of land and the islands that remain are the peaks of former mountains. Subsequent earth-folding created the chain of uplands that curve south from the Balkans through the islands of Kýthira, Crete, Kárpathos and Rhodes, to the Taurus mountains in Turkey. Crete itself has been an island and unconnected to the mainland for about 5½ million years.

The fifth largest island in the Mediterranean, it is 256 km (160 miles) long by 56 km (35 miles) at its widest, and consists largely of porous limestone overlaying an impermeable crystalline base. The landscape has many features of karst scenery – high plateaux surrounded by higher mountains, limestone pavements, caves, sinkholes, subterranean rivers and, in particular, deep gorges leading to the south coast. Four high mountain ranges, and their connective hills, form the island's backbone: the Lefká Óri (White Mountains) in the west with Páchnes at 2,454 metres (8,051 ft); the central Ida (Ídhi) or Psiloritis Mountains with Tímeos Stavrós at 2,456 metres (8,056 ft); the eastern Dhíkti Mountains with its highest summit at 2,148 metres (7,045 ft); and in the east the Sitía Mountains with the highest peak, Aféndhis Stavroménos, reaching 1,476 metres (4,841 ft). Overall, half of Crete is mountainous and another quarter is hilly.

The remaining quarter, flat land, is mostly devoted to agriculture which is, after tourism, the island's main industry. Vegetables, olives, grape-vines, citrus fruit, bananas and avocados are cultivated. On the Messará Plain, with its vast expanse of about 140 sq km (55 sq miles), and in other smaller areas, production has been increased by the introduction of polythene-covered greenhouses enabling the farmers to provide mainland Greece with the first spring

PRECEDING PAGES: contemplation in a *kafeníon*; a shepherd and his flock on Psilorítis.
LEFT: a weatherbeaten face under the Cretan sun.
RIGHT: ploughing the fields in western Crete.

crops of tomatoes, peppers, cucumbers, aubergines and strawberries. The fertile, mountain-ringed plateaux of Omalós, Askýfou, Nídha, Lassíthi and Katharó provide a sharp contrast to the limestone summits around, and are the only places where cool climate crops such as apples can be grown on any scale, although most of these still have to be imported.

Offshore Depths

To the southwest of Crete, the Mediterranean sinks to its deepest point of 4,926 metres (16,157 ft).

Population and organisation

Crete is divided into four administrative provinces, with the four governing cities and their

infrastructure based on the north coast. It is quite impossible to say which is the most typical city, as with Knossós, Phaestos or Kydonia in ancient times, for the four are completely different from one another in character.

This northern bias is mirrored by tourism, due to ease of access and the presence of many of the best beaches. Almost 50 percent of all holidaymakers stay on the 70-km (44-mile) stretch between Iráklion and Ághios Nikólaos, with the busiest secondary areas east of Réthymnon and west of Haniá.

Iráklion, with its eponymous capital city, is the colossus of the provinces, covering almost one third of Crete. Some 264,000 people live in the province, nearly half the total population of the island. Here too are found more ancient sites than in the rest of the island put together, indicating that even in the earliest days this was the most populous region. The other provinces have their own attractions: Haniá, with around 133,000 inhabitants, is full of scenic contrast, of lush valleys and huge mountains; Lassíthi, with 71,000 people in a large area, is the least densely populated; and Réthymnon, with 69,000 people, is the smallest but with the largest percentage of upland areas.

A variety of weather

Blue skies, and glorious views over mountain, sea and beach: most brochures picture Crete as having eternal summer weather. In fact, there are several climatic zones on the island. The east and southwest have a dry Mediterranean climate, the northwest has a wetter, summer-humid Mediterranean climate, while parts of the high interior have mountain desert weather with very cold winters.

There are only two seasons: dry, from April to October, with July and August as the hottest, windiest months and temperatures often reaching 40°C (104°F); cool and damp from November to March, with 70 percent of the rainfall between November and February. Inland and upland there are snowfalls every winter. Rainfall varies widely from year to year, and can in places be below the annual total of 30 cm (12 inches) that technically defines a desert. There is no real autumn, but the short spring brings beautiful, clear weather without intense heat.

There are powerful winds, which can change suddenly. The hot, dry, south winds, which often carry sand from the Sahara, are felt even in the north of the island. The northwesterly winds, however, can cool the air in the baking summer heat. In the waters around the island, sailors have to beware the strength and extremely changeable nature of the winds.

These climatic changes do, of course, have an effect on the choice of holiday period. The summer months are better for beach holidays, as the sometimes almost unbearable heat precludes much walking and sightseeing. The cooler, sunny weather in April and early May is a good time to explore the south coast, when the profusion of glorious flowers is a sight to behold. By the early summer harvest, the colours have faded. Fields are empty and brown, though the sea is warm from midsummer right through until the end of October.

WHITE MOUNTAINS

The snow that falls on Psiloritis and the Lefká Óri lasts from October through to May, with small patches lingering into July.

The tourist trade

About 110 years ago, according to the *Illustrated Manual of Geography and Ethnology*, for the traveller arriving by sea, "In the distance the jagged mountains of the isle of Crete appeared, with the highest peak the Ida, where Cretan Zeus was born. From these people... Lykurg took his strict laws for the Spartans, and today the island is a sad reflection of unlawfulness. No one knows to whom the island belongs, least of all the Cretans, who in the past, and in recent times have shed so much blood trying to free themselves from the yoke of Islam, but in vain. The valiant sons of this classic isle fight this national battle bravely, and at the head of the warriors... are enthusiastic priests for whom the fight for freedom of the land is consecrated to God. The capital city, Candia, and the important port of Canea have little attraction for us today as things stand, we'll leave them behind, and sail to the island of Milo [Mílos], where there is peace."

This impression seems to have lasted for a long time. In the 1920s the Imperial flying boat

LEFT: viticulture plays a role in the rural economy.
ABOVE: tourism is now one of the major employers.

services called at Águios Nikólaos en route to East Africa, but up until the 1950s, most travellers would pass Crete by. In 1953, for example, only 450 visitors were counted. Since then the numbers have steadily increased and today more than 1.5 million visit the island each year.

In accordance with Arthur Koestler's remark that "tourists are more easily milked than cows" (sheep and goats on Crete, of course) the revenue from tourism has exceeded that of agriculture, previously the most important sector of the economy. This change has brought with it a range of problems, some direct, others less obvious. It's easier to earn money as a waiter

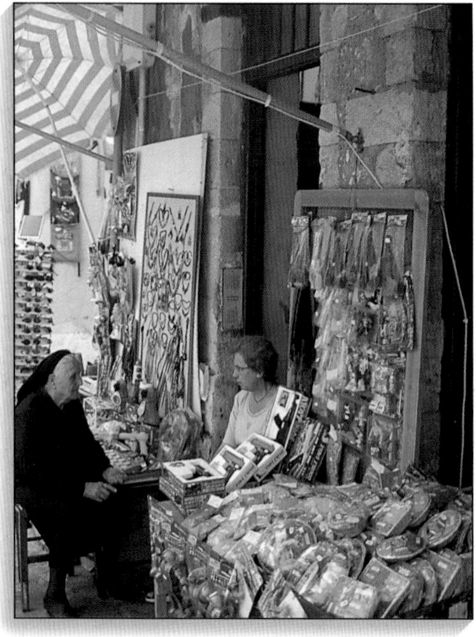

than as a farmer, so many young people are leaving the villages, which are left with just the middle-aged and old. This is causing a decline in the rural economy, but already the environment has benefited from the decreased grazing.

There has definitely been a decline in local traditions – most notably, from the tourists' point of view, with regard to hospitality. In practice, the legendary iron law of Cretan hospitality in olden days was only applied to certain foreigners, who were then a very small minority. Nowadays, if one arrives alone, speaks a little Greek, or visits older folk, particularly in the interior or south, everything is still as it used to be and the *rakí* still flows.

Food, however, has had to match international tastes in tourist areas, often to the detriment of the local cuisine. Nowadays, much of the best food is to be had in the cities, where there are substantial and affluent discerning local populations.

Conflict of interests

Prosperity alters much that it touches and brings modern Western criteria into conflict with traditional local values. The difference in living standards, between those people directly benefiting from the tourist trade and those who are not involved, has in some cases led to social divisions. This happens today, not just around the coastal resorts, but inland – even in isolated mountain settlements – particularly as the newly-enriched return to build opulent mansions in dilapidated ancestral villages.

There are other, unanticipated difficulties. Most tourists don't just come for the Minoans or the climate, but want to experience something of the "real" Crete. On arrival, they find that tourist money has changed both the country and the local lifestyle in a way which does not match their expectations. Tiny ancient Cretan houses may be photogenic, but uninhabitable by modern standards. The people who have to live in them would usually prefer an airy, three-storey concrete building, with running water, power, an inside flush toilet, and space to park the boat and pick-up truck underneath.

It would be a mistake to see only the negative side of tourism on Crete. There are no natural resources on the island and, apart from a few food and textile factories, no non-agricultural industry either. Jobs would be very scarce here, if it were not for the tourist. The majority of people live more comfortable lives than their parents did. The environmental loss around the coastline is probably balanced by the gains inland with the reduction of agricultural pressure. Overall, tourism is probably as much a blessing to the island as Crete is a boon to the tourists. One must hope that development is kept within reasonable limits, thus preserving the intrinsic charm and loveliness of the island, so that tourism will remain a blessing for visitors and islanders alike. ❑

LEFT: tourist tat for sale in Haniá.
RIGHT: a musician in traditional Sfakiot dress playing Crete's most characteristic instrument, the *lýra*.

A People under the Sun

Brave, proud, passionate, critical, self-sacrificing, hospitable and often deceitful, the people of Crete are unlike any other Europeans

When studying the Cretan character, one could be forgiven for supposing that the words "Cretan" and "critical" were perhaps related, or even had exactly the same meaning. Etymologically, however, there is no connection: critical comes from the verb *krínein*, to decide, via *kritís*, a judge. But Cretans are definitely highly critical.

As they are interested in any kind of politics, their own or other people's, the main target of their criticism is usually clear. But not far behind is their propensity for criticising each other. Cretans are proud to be Cretan, and this is evident in their criticism of other groups and nationalities. But within the island, this critical attitude can sometimes lead to a kind of hierarchy of superiority. The educated feel superior to the uneducated, the city-dwellers to the farmers, those who live in the mountains to the fishermen, the rich to the poor, the modern to the old-fashioned – which makes Crete rather like the rest of the world.

The lie of the land

Over two thousand years ago, the philosopher Epimenides remarked that all Cretans were liars. When you know that Epimenides himself was a Cretan, born in Phaestos, the saying takes on paradoxical dimension. What might have been an objective truth becomes something more. He would not have made such a remark casually. At the time, Crete was ruled by the Dorians, and one can suspect that his remark was meant to sow seeds of doubt in the minds of the rulers, making them feel that there was nothing in either the character or action of the Cretans which they could take at face value.

It was only after St Paul had quoted Epimenides' remark (Epistle of Paul to Titus, 1:12-13) adding "This witness is true" that the remark took on the gravity of a judgement. So how do the Cretans stand today as regards their attitude to the truth?

LEFT: lace is still made in many parts of the island.
RIGHT: most shops are privately owned and run.

All things considered, the following picture emerges: Cretans are given to showing off and making up stories. They talk a lot, promise a lot, and the next day they've forgotten it all, or it doesn't matter any more. And whether from necessity or for fun, they do undoubtedly tell lies – sometimes for no obvious motive. Wait at

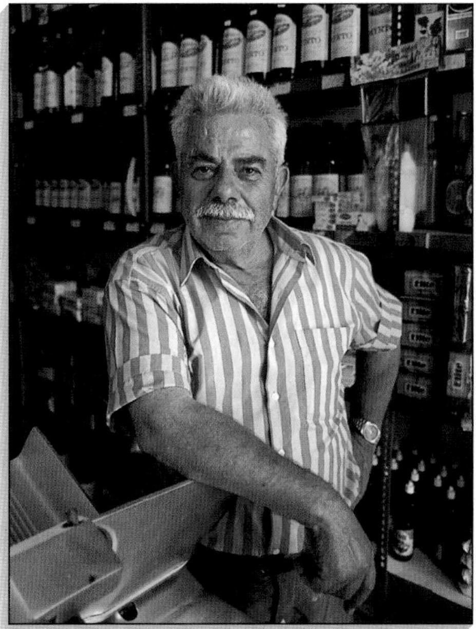

a bus stop, and a passing stranger may come over to inform you, incorrectly and apparently gratuitously, that the last bus has gone. Ask for information, and even if they don't know the answer they will come up with one that combines what they think you want to hear with what would be, in their opinion, best for you. They will be quite unabashed when events prove them to have been blatantly wrong. Cretan truth is a seamless amalgam of what is, what could be and what should be.

Reliability is just not their strong point. They can seem undisciplined and seldom finish what they have started if it cannot be completed quickly. If you arrange something with a Cretan, you can be pretty sure it may not come off. They will arrive three hours late for an appointment, and be genuinely surprised that you are no longer waiting patiently.

Positive thinking

There is also a Cretan tendency to expect their actions always to have the anticipated result, without considering the possibility of a different outcome or of side-effects. When things go wrong there is very rarely an alternative plan ready to swing into place, and initial, apparently trivial, failure may cause complete depression and withdrawal.

One of many old sayings on the island goes: "He who doesn't cheat, stays poor." The author D. McNeil Doren, who lived in Crete for a long time, wrote of a Cretan woman friend who completely changed character when he entered her shop to buy something. Having just helped him as a friend, she immediately tried to swindle him as a customer. This strange phenomenon is apparently quite common, as Cretans try to find out in their own way just how clever someone is.

So, feeling disillusioned, you pass a garden and cast your longing eyes at a succulent fruit and the next minute it's yours. Or, in the evening, you ask the waiter at a hotel bar the name of a particular song that is being sung on television and the next morning there's the cassette at the reception desk, as a gift for you. The spontaneous generosity can be startling. Visit a small country *kafeníon* and you may well leave feeling that the few drachmas you paid for your coffee or lemonade – just half of the cost of these in your holiday resort – may, when compared with the gifts of *rakí*, biscuits, cake, fruit, nuts and pelargonium cuttings, mean that the kindly owner made a financial loss from your visit.

People you have never met before can be remarkably helpful – far beyond the call of any duty of hospitality. And yet a street café full of muscular local men can watch a 70-year-old woman struggle along the road with a large, heavy gas canister with no more assistance than the occasional word of encouragement.

A conspicuous and admirable feature of Cretan society is the lack of social segregation between the generations. Young people find no problem in being seen sharing a café table with pensioners, or conversing with them in the street.

Cretan Experiment

Arthur Miller wrote in 1940: "Greece is that which everyone knows, even if they have never been there…Crete is something else, a cradle, an instrument, a test tube in which a volcanic experiment is taking place."

As a result, elderly Cretan men are genuinely surprised that their attempts to chat up eligible foreign girls can cause offence, when overtures from their younger compatriots are welcomed.

Cretans and Greeks

As regards their fellow-countrymen, the local attitude is undeniably that one is first a Cretan, and only then a Greek. It is true that for centuries the Cretans aspired towards *énosis*, union with Greece, but ultimately this was for reasons of communal security, not because of any deep feeling of oneness. Greeks regard Cretans with a mixture of awe for their uncompromising resistance against invaders, curiosity as to their somewhat old-fashioned lifestyle and mores, and some amusement over their rural accents. Cretans regard Greeks as too easily influenced by modern ephemera, somewhat lacking in necessary integrity – and they probably wouldn't want their daughter to marry one. However, Cretans put aside their feelings of superiority and cheer loyally when football teams from Athens or Thessaloníki are beating clubs from other European countries, or their basketball teams are beating the world.

Fundamental to this feeling of superiority is the longing for freedom. Anything which appears to a Cretan as a curtailment of liberty is rejected, and there is always the underlying suspicion that Athens is not entirely to be trusted in this respect. The course of their history has forced the people to become experts at discerning enemy intentions. It's no wonder that at Greek election time, the results from the administrative provinces of Crete are always markedly different from those returned by the rest of the country.

Royalist Cretans are rare. When a referendum on the abolition of the monarchy was held in 1974, 69 percent of all Greeks voted for abolition – whereas 91 percent of the Cretan population voted against the monarchy.

And where else would ordinary people go into the streets armed, to protest against the removal of historical art treasures from their museums? That's what happened in 1979 in Iráklion when the then Prime Minister Karamanlís wanted to loan part of the Minoan collection abroad.

Generosity and indifference, spontaneity and calculation. How can these attributes be so intertwined? It's probably best simply to accept (and enjoy) the Cretans, rather than to attempt fully to understand them. ❑

LEFT: facing a bright future.
ABOVE: inside a local kitchen, near Réthymnon.

RELIGIOUS VALUES

The church may not be as influential in Crete as it once was, but there are still occasions for religious fervour and devout celebration

Almost all Cretans are, at least nominally, adherents of the Greek Orthodox Church, which has always played a special role on the island. During the centuries of foreign domination, the Church was far more than just a community of believers. As a social institution it funded and organised agricultural projects, hospitals and, more importantly in the long run, schools where Greek history and traditions were taught and kept alive. Most significantly, it was the focus of unity and resistance to oppression. The struggle of the people against various foreign rulers has always been closely associated with the Church.

The many attacks on the island's 34 monasteries are a clear indication of where the enemy suspected the centres of resistance to be. Monks, priests, bishops and archbishops died along with their compatriots. Just how seriously the Cretans took their maxim "freedom or death" was never more clearly demonstrated than at the monastery of Arkádhi in 1866. Although there have been similar struggles and battle cries elsewhere, nowhere has the fight against suppression equalled that which has taken place in Crete over the centuries.

In a novel by Pandelís Prevelákis, a Cretan worker and a monk are locked in an argument with each other.

Worker: "And to think I took you for a holy man."

Monk: "Here one is a man first, and only then holy."

This interpretation of Christianity is typically Cretan. Village priests in Crete are very much men of the people, married and with children, and often with a daytime job. The people accept them as subject to human foibles, frailties and indulgence, rather than as abstinent, self-righteous intermediaries between the people and God. Turning the other cheek has rarely been seen here as a desirable option, and 19th-century photographs show warrior-priests armed with swords and pistols rather than holy books.

Nowadays, in a unified and independent republican Greece, the influence of religion is waning. Younger generations are not prepared to grant the Church its traditional influence. Overt commercial greed over church land and politicking among the church hierarchy is much criticised, as is mainland Orthodox fundamentalism. However, devout belief still exists: even today you may see an elderly women making her penitent way on bleeding bare knees along the concrete road to a church or monastery.

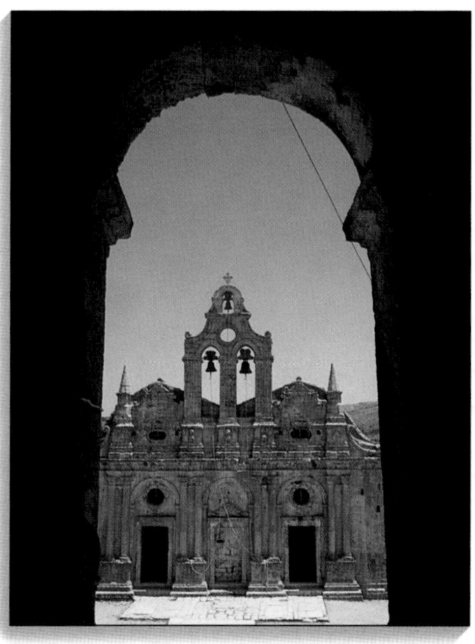

LEFT: celebrating St Nicholas' Day in Águios Nikólaos.
RIGHT: religion, politics and the fight for independence came together at Arkádhi Monastery in 1866.

Feasts and festivities

Of all the annual Church festivals, Easter *(Páscha)* is pre-eminent. The lead-up starts with *Apókrias*, the Greek equivalent of Mardi Gras, three weeks of pre-Lenten festivities including major carnivals in Kastélli, Soúdha, Réthymnon and Sitía. These are followed by *Katherá Dheftéra* (Clean Monday), theoretically the day when the overindulgence of Carnival ends and Lenten restraint begins. In practice, Crete becomes one big party, with everyone out in the countryside for lunch, and thousands of fathers and children flying elaborate kites.

Many remoter Cretan households still adhere to the strict dietary rules of Lent, which become increasingly rigorous as Easter approaches. Meat, fish and eggs are forbidden and during Holy Week even wine and cooking oil are not allowed. As a result, a particularly healthy and economical diet of vegetables, pasta, bread and legumes is followed. On *Megáli Paraskeví* (Good Friday), the blood of slaughtered lambs stains every roadside, and the *epitáfios*, the funeral bier of Christ, is carried through the streets. For the next two days local children throw fireworks at everyone, to the amusement of the Greeks, and the shock of tourists.

At Mass on Saturday night, churches are packed to bursting with the faithful – and the normally agnostic – all of whom have brought candles with which to carry home the light of the Resurrection. At midnight the priest announces *Christós anésti* (Christ is risen), candles are lit and firecrackers let off. In some of Crete's wilder villages, guns are fired in the air.

SUPPORT YOUR LOCAL SAINT

Panighýria are celebrations of saints' name-days, held in towns and villages where the local church is dedicated to that particular saint. In times gone by, the festivities could last for days and would be accompanied by street fairs and markets – an event that drew together all the people from the surrounding villages. Musicians would perform Cretan music on the *lýra* and *laoúto,* sing local songs and often accompany the recitation of *mandinádhes* (a poetic form, often improvised) by various villagers.

In many villages, *Panighýria* have ceased to exist, or are celebrated in a cursory way. The young people now have transport to the larger towns for entertainment, young girls no longer have to wait for village celebrations to dance, to be seen and to be chosen for marriage, and anyway everyone is far too busy working with tourism to be able to take time off. When *Panighýria* do occur today, they are often organised by the local tavernas for financial gain and involve the hiring of a professional band to play *laiká* (Greek pop music) at appalling volume.

But some villages have retained an authentic approach where the old customs are still observed and maintained. There is also a renewal of interest in village traditions, in which Cretans who are jaded with modern city life enjoy these festivals as an opportunity to reclaim their roots.

Outside in the churchyard, an effigy of Judas Iscariot is sometimes burnt on a funeral pyre.

During Easter Sunday, all make up for their recent deprivations, and family meals turn into festivals of music, song, dance and gunfire, with traditional Easter tripe soup, lamb roasted on the spit and dyed red hard-boiled eggs.

Other festivals

The most important date in the Orothodox calendar after Easter is 15 August, when Apokímisis tís Panaghías (the Assumption of the Virgin) is celebrated in towns and villages throughout Crete, particularly at the monasteries of Faneroméni, Chryssoskalítissa and Kolimbári. It is a time of family reunions, when people traditionally return to their home villages. Church services begin at dawn, but latecomers are welcome to the bread, lamb and wine served in the churchyard after the service, around lunchtime.

In typical Cretan style, religious and secular celebrations merge into one festival on 25 March, which is both Independence Day (marking the beginning of the 1821 revolt against the Turks) and Evangelismós (Annunciation Day, when Mary was given news of the Incarnation). It is a national holiday, when church services spill out into street parades, and there is music and dancing.

Ághios Yeórghios is the patron saint of shepherds, and his *panighýri* (name-day), 23 April, is cause for great festivities throughout Crete, especially in the rural areas. It is also a more important occasion than a birthday to every George on the island.

As befits an island where many work in agriculture, there are numerous harvest-related festivals, such as the Orange Festival in Skinés, the Cherry Festival at Kerásia, the Wine Festival in Réthymnon and the Sultana Festival in Sitía.

LEFT: bread is presented as an offering to St George.
ABOVE: a joyful wedding procession in Kritsá.

Family celebrations

The most important event in a family's year is a wedding. Before Crete had a proper road network, wedding celebrations often lasted a week. Travel was difficult, so the marriage would be a good opportunity for families to get together and to enjoy each other's company.

Civil weddings, conducted by local mayors, were introduced in 1983, and many younger Cretans now prefer this secular alternative. But for their mothers and grandmothers, particularly in more remote areas, the influence of the Church is as great as ever, and for them an unholy civil wedding is unthinkable.

Traditional weddings still take place, especially in rural Crete, and are conducted according to an unchanging set of rituals. First, an "inviter" chosen by the bride and groom's relatives goes to the couple's village(s), to announce the good news and to invite the guests.

BEST ADVICE

The best man (or sometimes, these days, best woman) is known as the *koumbáros* (or *koumbára*), and is more than just a wedding helper. He/she will act as a lifelong counsellor to the couple and a godparent to their children.

The wedding itself is always held on a Sunday. On the Saturday afternoon, some of the guests carry the trousseau, which has been on view for a few days, from the bride's house to that of the groom. Ballads are sung, often in the form of impromptu *mandinádhes* (improvised verse songs in rhyming couplets).

On the Saturday evening, the villagers from the place where the couple are to make their home bring symbolic gifts, the *kaniskiá,* mainly meat, cheese, oil and wine. Poorer people may bring bread, potatoes and onions.

On the Sunday morning, the bride, dressed in all her finery, holds a reception for the guests. This is an opportunity for many tears to be shed, as the marriage also means that the bride is leaving her parents' home for ever. Then the *pastiká* is sung (*mandinádhes* on the subject of the bride, especially composed for the occasion). The bridegroom is not allowed to hear these songs, and they have to be finished before he arrives to take the bride to the church.

After the wedding service, the dance for the bridal veil is usually held immediately outside the church. All the male relatives of the couple dance with the bride. The last to dance receives the veil, which means that he too will soon be married. Then the procession, led by a *lýra* player, goes to the bridegroom's house, and more *mandinádhes* are sung. This time the subject of the songs is broader, with plenty of good wishes and practical advice for the couple.

In the groom's house, the bride's mother-in-law presents the bride with honey and nuts, *melokário*, as a welcoming gift. Before the bride crosses the threshold, she must dip her finger into the honey, and make a cross on the door, to bring good luck to the household.

Before the guests sit down at tables laden with good things, everyone sings a prayer-like song in which the mothers-in-law are wished strength to accept their new son and daughter-in-law. Then, to the sound of gunshots, the festivities begin. A great deal of crockery may be broken during the proceedings.

Nowadays, this old-fashioned kind of wedding is only celebrated in the more isolated villages, but modern weddings may still feature the gunfire, along with remarkable traffic jams caused by hundreds of guests' cars.

Increasingly, Cretan men are marrying foreign women, a much easier process through civil marriage, but even today weddings between Cretan women and foreign men are very rare. Most Cretan families would still be very unhappy about a foreign suitor for their daughter; many would even disapprove of a Greek from outside Crete. Robust attempts will be made by the bride's father and brothers to discourage the relationship.

A christening is another very important occasion for a feast, although this event is usually less lavish than a wedding. The celebrations always take place in the evening, and often everything is over just after midnight. Here too, special songs have to be sung, and the health of the child is toasted. ❑

LEFT: processing the Bier of Christ on Good Friday.

Unorthodox Beliefs

In many Cretan churches and monasteries you will see small beaten-metal plaques hanging in rows, each depicting a person, or a part of the body. They have been hung there by people suffering from afflictions, or their relatives, to supplement a prayer and perhaps a donation, in the hope of bringing about a divine cure for their ailment – which can be anything from madness to tennis elbow.

Although these modern votive offerings are directed towards the saints of the Orthodox Church, their origins pre-date Christianity by thousands of years. In Minoan peak sanctuaries and caves including Kamáres, Skotinó and Dhíkti, archaeologists have unearthed clay figurines depicting parts of the body in exactly the same way. It is safe to assume that these were offered to whatever gods resided in these holy places, for just the same reasons as today's metal plaques – as votive offerings for the deliverance from infirmity or suffering.

Many other heathen customs have been so completely integrated into Orthodox belief that people are now quite unaware of their origins. Cretans still observe countless practices that could be summarily dismissed as superstition, but which derive from ancient pagan religions, or early Christian observance, or actual historical events, or communal folk memory, all blurred into an unquestioning belief in what will bring good fortune, or the opposite.

Here are more examples of Cretan superstitions. In some cases their origins are obvious, or can be guessed at; others are as obscure and perplexing as superstitions the world over.

● After Mass early on Easter Day, believers take home candles lit from the holy flame and use their smoke to mark a cross on the door lintel. This protects the house from bad luck and evil spirits for the rest of the year.

● Hard-boiled eggs are painted red on Holy Thursday, to symbolise the blood of Christ. On Easter Day, people strike their eggs against other people's: the owner of the last egg to remain unbroken is considered lucky.

● A knife that was made during Holy Week offers protection against evil spirits.

● In eastern Crete, it is bad luck to give a knife as a present; but in western Crete, giving a knife to the best man at a wedding brings good luck.

● The eyes of saints are often missing from frescoes in old churches: it was once believed that if you fed the plaster from a saint's eye to the object of your affection, your love would be reciprocated.

● If an unexpected and unwanted guest arrives, someone creeps outside the door and spills salt on the ground. This is supposed to ensure the speedy departure of the visitor.

● On the first day of the quarter, it is important to note who first crosses your path. If that person is bad, it will bring bad luck. So on those days, a reliable family member is sent out on to the road to pave the way. Without this precaution, no superstitious person would set foot outside the door.

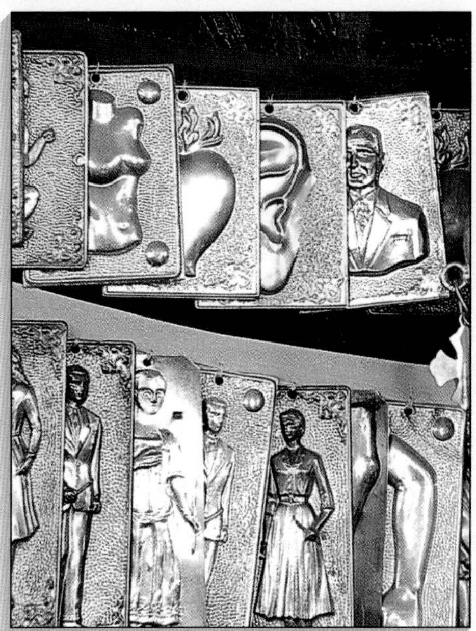

RIGHT: votive offerings for all manner of afflictions are hung in churches as a supplement to prayers.

● Constantinople fell to the Turks on 29 May 1453 – a Tuesday. Many Cretans still believe in Unlucky Tuesday and are reluctant to do important business on that day.

● The hated Turks, it was believed, were reincarnated as dogs, which may explain why dogs are treated so poorly in Crete, often with contempt. A Cretan may name his dog after an enemy, so as to have the pleasure of yelling at it.

● Black cats and broken mirrors have no significance in Crete, but it is considered very lucky to own a black hen. ❏

TWO LITERARY GIANTS

Kazantzákis is best known for Hollywood adaptations of his novels; Prevelákis is hardly known at all. But both authors shed startling light on their native Crete

Modern Cretan literature is stamped by the influence of the writers Níkos Kazantzákis and Pandelís Prevelákis. Kazantzákis was born on 18 February 1883 in Iráklion. He qualified as a lawyer, and saw his first play performed in Athens in 1906. He spent the next few years in Paris studying political science and philosophy. In 1915 he was a volunteer in the Balkan War and, four years later, Elefthérios Venizélos appointed him Minister of Welfare in the Greek government.

On leaving politics, Kazantzákis travelled to England, Spain, Russia, Japan and China. These journeys inspired him to write a series of critical travel books. In addition, he wrote lyric poetry, stories, novels and tragic plays with predominantly historical or religious themes, as well as philosophical essays and epic poems such as the *Odyssey*, which appeared in 1938. In 1945 he returned to politics and took a ministerial position in Soufoulís' cabinet, but soon resigned because of inter-party quarrels.

International fame came to Kazantzákis with his later works, particularly through his 1946 novel *Zorba the Greek*, a book that has often been misunderstood. Many believe that Zorba is a superhuman creation, heavily influenced by Nietzsche and incorporating a side of Kazantzákis' character, much embellished and with delusions of grandeur. In fact, although the novel cannot be regarded as a factual account, Zorba is supposedly modelled on a man with whom Kazantzákis lived and worked on a Cretan beach for six months in 1917.

A further misunderstanding arises from the fact that Alexis Zorba is more widely known through the rather shallow film of the book than through the original. He is often considered to be the archetypal noble Cretan. But Zorba is not a Cretan at all, but a Macedonian. As a Greek from the mainland, he brings a breath of freedom to the Cretans caught up in their ghostly traditions. In the novel, Zorba, the man of action, comes face to face with the intellectual ditherer, Kazantzákis. Zorba stands at the centre of life, accepting things as they are. He has no inclination to improve the world.

Taken in isolation, this is a conservative standpoint. But Zorba does in fact alter the world around him – even if unintentionally. He is a kind of "mystical realist", who views things in daily life always as new and wonderful. He does not separate this sense of wonder from reality as a believer or an intellectual would; for him it is the substance of reality itself. This infatuation is infectious. In contrast, there is the "boss" full of questions, doubts and problems. He makes grandiose plans, none of which ever comes near to being put into practice. He fails to "come alive".

Here we come to another misunderstanding: the book is no mere adventure story, but a philosophical novel dealing with existential questions, questions of life and death. As in all

LEFT: the grave of Níkos Kazantzákis.
RIGHT: the real-life Yeórghi Zórba, the inspiration for Kazantzákis' memorable character.

Kazantzákis' works, the central theme is the relationship of man with God.

There is no doubt, however, that in his indisputable love for his homeland, Níkos Kazantzákis himself is the archetypal Cretan. He is always aware of the special nature of the island, and of its past. "Being a Cretan is a duty," he says. It is certainly in no small measure due to this wholehearted patriotism that Kazantzákis, despite the criticism, embodied in his works that he became and has remained so popular on Crete.

GOETHE IN GREEK

Kazantzákis' works include translations into modern Greek of such classics as Dante's *Divine Comedy* and Goethe's *Faust.*

However, in the depiction of his contemporaries – and particularly of former friends – Kazantzákis is sometimes very severe. If someone has surrendered to fate, become complacent and stopped fighting, Kazantzákis' contempt and despair is plain. In his autobiography, *Report to El Greco*, he describes a small rural scene: a bluebird has just flown past and Kazantzákis wishes to know what kind of bird it is. The peasant he asks replies, "Why do you want to know? You can't eat it." To mollify the reader, Kazantzákis adds, "I was no misanthrope; I always loved people, but from a distance..."

Almost as well-known as *Zorba the Greek* is *Freedom or Death* (1950), an exceedingly pessimistic depiction of the uprising of 1889 against the Turks. Here a different characterisation of God is given: "If you are a wolf, eat; if you are a lamb, let yourself be eaten! And who is God? He is the Great Wolf – who eats both lambs and wolves and all their bones!" Certain passages in this book, and much of the later novel *The Last Temptation of Christ*, have offended the Church. However when the Vatican announced that it intended to excommunicate Kazantzákis, there was such an uproar in the literary world that it was decided simply to put both works on the Index – the Vatican's list of forbidden books.

What is amazing is not so much the fact of the Church's initiative, but the timing. As early as 1928, in his book *Askitikí*, Kazantzákis had expressed what he saw as insurmountable contradictions in the so-called message of salvation: it is not God who saves man, but man who must save God. In his 1948 novel *Christ Recrucified,* the author takes up Dostoyevsky's dark vision that the Crucifixion is extremely necessary to the Church, and that it may need to be repeated throughout eternity.

When Martin Scorsese filmed the novel *The Last Temptation of Christ* more than 30 years after it had been put on the Index, the Church's inability to come to terms with Kazantzákis was remarkable. The objections raised sounded like a parody of the earlier criticism, which was perhaps predictable, since Scorsese interpreted the novel entirely as the author intended. Kazantzákis brought out the human side of this exceptional being, Jesus Christ, and portrayed him as "the animal that questions", a man who thinks but who also has natural desires.

A Cretan's Epitaph

Kazantzákis' own words are inscribed on his tombstone in the Martinengo Bastion: "I hope for nothing. I fear nothing. I am free."

Kazantzákis was nominated for the Nobel Prize for Literature in 1955 – by Albert Schweitzer, among other eminent persons – but the Church managed to prevent this honour being bestowed upon him.

From 1950 onwards, Nikós Kazantzákis and his wife lived in Antibes on the French Riviera. He died on 26 October 1957 in Freiburg im Breisgau, Germany. His coffin was brought to Iráklion where it was received by enormous crowds and he was buried in the Martinengo Bastion of the old city wall, with the striking profile of Mount Yioúchtas as a backdrop.

It is often maintained that Kazantzákis was posthumously "banished" to the Martinengo Bastion, having been denied burial in consecrated ground. This is certainly not true, as it is a Cretan custom to allocate special burial places to prominent citizens. Not only did he receive a proper funeral service in 1957, but later, in 1977, a special memorial Mass was celebrated for him.

Pandelís Prevelákis

Crete's second major literary figure was born in Réthymnon on 18 February 1909 – 26 years to the day after Níkos Kazantzákis. Prevelákis studied philology in Paris and Thessaloníki and, from 1939 to 1975, was professor of Art History at the Academy of Arts in Athens. From around 1930 he was closely associated with Kazantzákis, as disciple, literary agent, confidant and, eventually, biographer.

All his life Prevelákis remained in close contact with his birthplace. Perhaps more than in any other Cretan city, the "geological layering" of time is clearly in evidence in Réthymnon. So perhaps it is no wonder that Prevelákis became known as an author of "historical dimensions". For the interpretation of the changes wrought by time, he invented a new genre, that of "Mythistory", a mixture of historical interpretation and subjective mythological impressions.

In 1938 his first effort in this direction, *Chronicle of a City,* appeared to great acclaim. Later novels received a varied reception by critics and readers. There was, however, widespread agreement that the historical and the subjective mythical did not complement one another and in the end should be treated as separate entities. Perhaps his most successful novel, on all counts, was *The Sun of Death*, published in 1959, which depicts a boy coming to terms with mortality.

While Kazantzákis' international fame lives on, Prevelákis reputation was soon eclipsed after his death in March 1986. Bookshops and librarians no longer remember his name. But while not enjoying the same level of recognition, Prevelákis is nevertheless an interesting and revealing writer. ❑

LEFT: huge crowds paid their last respects to Kazantzákis at his funeral in Iráklion in 1957.
RIGHT: Pandelís Prevelákis (left) pictured in Dimitsaná, in the Peloponnese.

ΣΚΟΡΠΙΟΙ
ΔΡΑΚΑΙΝΕΣ
3.000
ΜΟΥΡΜΟΥ
32

2800

FOOD AND DRINK

In tourist areas, you can find any food you want. Elsewhere in Crete, take the trouble to try local specialities

Thanks to the ubiquitous use of greens, grains and olive oil, Cretan cuisine is, according to many authorities, the healthiest in the world. Exemplifying this cuisine is *dhákos*, the Cretan national dish, which is barley rusks soaked in olive-oil and smothered with tomato pulp, eaten as a starter: the equal of the best *bruschetta.*

However, in the main, the dishes you encounter in tavernas in Crete are the same as those served throughout Greece. As elsewhere the country, the diner in Crete is often invited to enter the kitchen and inspect what is on offer. Undoubtedly the dishes will be served luke-warm and often "swimming in grease". Complain about these matters and be told that tepid food is better for the digestion than hot. And this might well be true. Food without olive oil is unimaginable to the Greeks who believe that it aids digestion and that it is a laxative. If you want food without olive oil, ask for dishes *horís láthi* (without oil). You may or may not get it.

Carnivores can enjoy mutton, lamb, goat, kid or rabbit. These are usually prepared as a *stifádho* (a stew) cooked with fennel, artichokes and wild mountain greens and served with tomato or egg and lemon sauce. It is said that 50 percent of the rabbits in Greece are found in Crete, a figure difficult to accept when one considers the Cretans' appetite for rabbit. It's even more strange considering there are no wild rabbits on the island; however, many individuals breed rabbits in hutches or sheds, or even in a back room of the house. Traditionally, in the mountains, a bride to be was chosen not only for her dowry but for her ability to cook a rabbit *stifádho.*

Kid is often stewed in fruit juice and served with rice pilaf. But it is with lamb that Cretans really go to town. A gastronomic delight is *Sfakía* pasty, which is lamb and creamy white cheese in a pastry dough baked in the oven.

The waters that bathe Crete are those of the Mediterranean which, at times, would appear to be "fished out", so fish is much rarer than one might expect. When available, some of the most popular fish are *barboúnia* (mullet), *xifías* (swordfish), *tónnos* (tuna), *sargós* (white bream) and *fagrí* (common sea bream). It is said that cats would never eat the heads of *fagrí*: the fish is so expensive that people eat the heads.

But best of all is *skáros* (parrot fish), known as the "cow of the sea", a tasty white meaty fish. In Crete the best fish is never fried but boiled or grilled (broiled) and the scales are not removed.

Don't be alarmed by the prices of fish on the menu: they are by kilo. You choose the fish you want, it is weighed and priced accordingly.

Octopus is invariably available. Grilled octopus (*chtapódhi*) is served as a starter or a main dish while octopus stew, made of equal weights of onions and octopus cooked with capers, oil and vinegar, is a popular dish. An expensive and unusual starter is *achinosaláta* (sea-urchin salad) which is made from the ovaries of these spiny creatures.

PRECEDING PAGES: fresh fish for sale in Réthymnon.
LEFT: octopus hanging out to dry.
RIGHT: typical Cretan hors-d'oeuvre – *dhákos.*

Even when fish is not on the menu one may find *psarósoupa*, a fish soup with vegetables, and spicy *kakaviá*, an authentic bouillabaisse rich in seafood. Both can be extremely rich and satisfying. Other thoroughly enjoyable, although possibly less filling soups are *fasoládha* (haricot bean soup) and *soúpa avgolémono* (egg and lemon soup, usually prepared from a chicken stock). None of these is unique to Crete.

Snails from Crete are much prized throughout Greece and are even exported to France.

Although eaten throughout the year snails are a Lenten speciality. They are prepared in a variety of ways: scalded in salted water, cooked with rice, tomatoes and garlic, cooked in *rakí* or, best of all, fried with ground tomatoes, potatoes and thyme, a dish called *eghíni*. *Salingária stifádho* is snail stew.

Vegetarians will delight in *hórta*. These are wild greens which are collected in the mountains especially in spring and autumn. They are boiled and served lukewarm or cold after being lavishly dressed with oil and vinegar.

The fields are also rich with herbs: dittany, which is indigenous to Crete, and more familiar herbs such as dill, oregano, thyme and sage. These are used not only in cooking but, especially in mountain villages, for making herbal infusions. Of these, *dhíktamos,* tea that is prepared with dittany, is the most popular. Other herbal teas are *tsái méndai* (peppermint tea), *tsái kamoumílo* (camomile tea) and *tsái tou vounoú*, made with an infusion of mountain herbs.

When it comes to fruit and vegetables, Crete is a cornucopia. Many of these are available throughout the year as a result of the greenhouse revolution that began in the early 1960s. Visitors to the fruit and vegetable market in any of the larger towns can well believe that Crete was the granary of Rome and might well recall Pliny's statement that whatever is produced in Crete is incomparably better than that produced in other parts.

EATING HABITS

Cretans regularly eat out, often in large parties of family and friends. Meals are taken late – lunch between 2 and 3pm, followed by a siesta, and dinner at 9–11pm.

Sweets and cheese

Desserts other than fruit or yoghurt are rarely served in tavernas: rather, as is the case throughout Greece, one adjourns to the *zacharoplastíon* (patisserie) which specialises in all kinds of sweets. Here you might order such Cretan specialities as *xerotígana*, a delicious traditional sweet pancake filled with honey and nuts, or *amygdalópitta*, an equally delicious almond pie; or savour sugary tarts called *kalzoúni*.

Honey and cheese have long adorned the Greek table: both are frequently served at breakfast. Indeed, the Greek consumption of cheese per capita is one of the highest in the European Union. The cheeses are made from ewe's or goat's milk. Apart from *féta*, cheese preserved in brine, semi-hard yellow *graviéra*, the equivalent of a gruyère, and *ladhótyro*, cheese that has been cured in olive oil, Cretan cheeses are soft and white. Most creamy of all Cretan cheeses is *stáka*. Then there is *mýzithra* (in western Crete it answers to the name of *anthótyro*), an unsalted skim-milk cheese sold in bags similar to fresh ricotta.

Saganáki (deep fried cheese) is a popular starter. A much enjoyed snack is *kalitsoúia*, small hand-made pasties filled with cheese and eggs with or without aniseed and sesame seeds but with a little cinnamon and cooked in oil. They may also be filled with spinach or wild herbs. Or try *macaronía*, thin pasta cooked in potent goat broth and garnished with *anthótyro*.

Wine, oúzo and rakí

Crete boasts a long tradition of wine making as evidenced by the discovery of wine-making equipment in the ruins of a Minoan villa at Vathípetro. Today, 20 percent of all Greek wine is produced in Crete yet only about one-third of the one million hectares (2.25 million acres) on the island that are devoted to grapes go to the making of *krasí* (wine). The remainder are made into sultanas for which Crete, especially the Sitía region, is renowned.

HOME BREW

Until recently, the only beers available in Crete were imported, at least from the Greek mainland, but now there is Mýthos, a locally brewed Continental-type lager.

The principal wine producing areas are Archánes, Pezá and Dhafnés in the hills south of Iráklion, the region around Sitía in the eastern part of the island and, to a lesser extent, Haniá in the west. The Iráklion region is noted for its red (*mávro*, literally black) wines; Sitía for its whites (*áspro*) and Haniá for an old-fashioned heavy red. The grapes from which these wines are made – Kotsifali, Mandilaria, Vilana and Liatiko – are all old varieties that are seldom grown outside of Greece.

Every village, every farm, produces its own wine called *híma*. This is the house wine served in tavernas. It is sold by weight rather than volume, is invariably served in a battered pink tin container and is a dark rosé. It is especially good around Kastélli in the west and Sitía in the east. If you want resinated wine (retsina is not nearly as popular as on the mainland), ask for a *retsínato*. The best bottled wines are *Kritikós Topikós Ínos*, the Greek equivalent of *vin de pays*. Kourtakis and Boutari have the reputation for being the best merchants.

Although *oúzo*, the national aperitif of Greece, is drunk in the towns of Crete, in the countryside it is considered a drink for wimps and is replaced by *rakí*, which in western Crete is called *tsikoudhiá*. This firewater drink is made by distillation of the must (the remains of grapes whose juice has been made into wine) to which aromatic herbs have been added.

Rakí is drunk from tiny glasses and, unlike the aniseed flavoured *oúzo*, is not diluted with water. It is often offered in tavernas as a complimentary drink at the end of a meal. No need to look for excuses when drinking *rakí*. It aids digestion, enables you to relax, wards off the evil eye, is an aphrodisiac and makes a good rub for chest colds. If perchance you get hungover then try the Cretan cure of *zigoúri vrastó*, a long-simmered garlic goat brew.

Gone are the days when the simplest Cretan taverna would never dream of serving an *oúzo* or a *rakí* unaccompanied by *mezédhes* ("nibbles"). This may have consisted of a couple of olives, a slice or two of tomato, a piece of *féta* cheese, but the mere thought of drinking without eating was inconceivable. Now, the *rakí* will come alone and you will have to order and pay for your *mezédhes*.

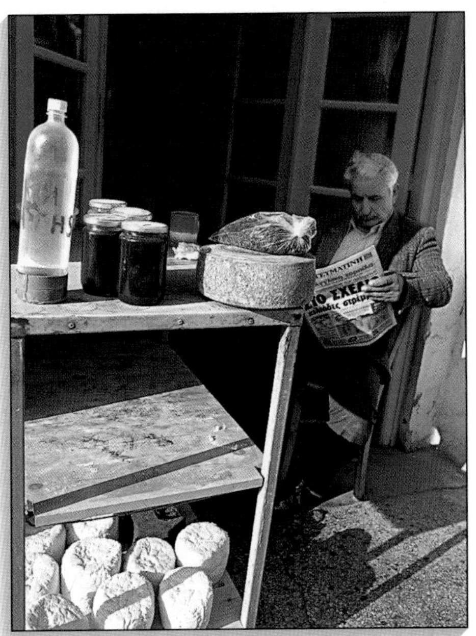

On rare occasions you may be offered *mástika*, which is a liqueur made from the bark of the mastic tree. Then there is brandy or, as the Greeks almost invariably call it, Metaxas (the brand name), available in three degrees of smoothness 3-, 5- or 7-star. Round it all off with a *kafé ellinikó* (Greek coffee) which is served *skéto* (without sugar), *métrio* (with some sugar) or *glykó* (very sweet). If Greek coffee is too pungent for your taste, "regular" coffee is invariably instant and known as *Nes* (for Nescafé). *Nes me gála* is with milk. ❑

LEFT: at work in a taverna kitchen, Haniá.
RIGHT: local produce – cheeses, honey, sultanas, *tsikoudhiá* – for sale in western Crete.

FLORA AND FAUNA

Its diverse landscape and geographical location have endowed Crete with a stunning range of plants – many of them unique to the island

Travel through Crete in the blazing heat of high summer and it can seem like an outlying district of the Sahara or of Arizona. Dead tumbleweeds roll across sere landscapes, each movement of the hair-dryer wind raises clouds of dust, and the only flowers visible are in carefully nurtured village window-boxes.

But arrive in spring – which starts in early February in the far east and lasts until late May in the west – and the contrast is amazing. The dominant colour is green, overlaid by swathes of white, yellow, red and purple flowers. Every roadside strip, patch of waste ground and rock crevice is a garden, bursting with life in the urgent rush to produce fruit before the summer drought. Where the plants flourish, so does other wildlife. Insects repopulate; insect-eaters fatten up; food-chains expand.

Seeds remain dormant during the baking summer, then the first seedlings and new leaves sprout in response to the first rains of autumn, which may be in September, but sometimes not until November. Winter light levels are high, and average temperatures sufficient for active growth during this period, until flowering resumes a few weeks into the new year.

Because the climatic extremes of the Ice Ages affected southern Greece very little, a number of Crete's plant species are ancient, pre-glacial relics. The Cretan flora – approximately 1,710 species – includes a larger percentage of Asian and North African plants than mainland Greece's, and most of the alpines of the high mountains have their origin in Asia Minor rather than in Europe. Nearly 9 percent of the species are endemic – plants found wild and native nowhere else but Crete. They are particularly common in very specialised habitats such as gorge cliffs.

As the site of the first major European civilisation, Crete has been subject to human disturbance for more than 8,500 years. Before man, the island had a mixture of some woodland, some tall, dense, impenetrably shrubby maquis vegetation, and much garrigue of low spiny bushes. Little of the original woodland cover remains, except as fragments in the higher mountains and inland valleys in the west. Tree felling for fuel, charcoal and timber for houses and boats started the process of deforestation. It is said that the saw was invented in Crete, in Minoan times. Massive forest fires lasted for years at a time, and regeneration was prevented by stock-grazing and clearance for cultivation. As early as AD 1414, the Venetians banned the export of cypress wood from Crete in order to protect stocks.

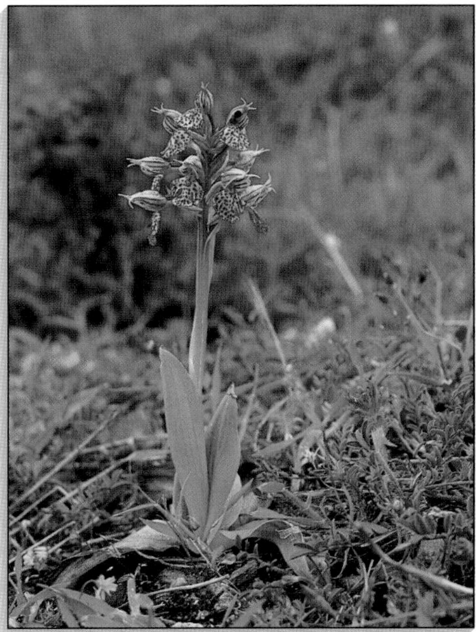

However, it is a myth that man and his flocks destroyed a verdant Greek Eden of continuous forest. Before man's arrival on the island, large areas were intensively grazed by a number of deer species and a pygmy hippopotamus, all now extinct, but then essentially without preda-

PRECEDING PAGES: a large pod of common dolphins play off the coast of Crete.
LEFT: sea holly and marram grass on a coastal dune.
RIGHT: a milky orchid flowers on garrigue (scrubland).

tors. The plant population combated this grazing by developing foul tastes, bristles, spines, and other features to discourage edibility. They were then well prepared for the comparatively recent arrival of early humans bringing sheep and goats, and for the modern-day bare-legged walker. Intermingled with the shrubs are aromatic herbs, colourful annuals and, gaining protection from those spines, fragile orchids.

The recent growth of tourism has affected the landscape considerably, particularly around the coast. However, by providing alternative and more profitable employment for local farming populations, it has eased the pressure of some agricultural practices on the natural environment. There is less cultivation and grazing in many areas, which means that, not only is much of the wild flora making a comeback, but land fertility and stability are being slowly restored. In particular, bare inland areas, heavily grazed by huge flocks of goats until the early 1980s, are reverting to lush green shrubland. Relic areas of ancient woodland are expanding. There are probably more trees in Crete today than there have been for the past millennium.

Most visitors will see the coastal flora first – or remnants of it. Sadly, humans prefer bare sand for their enjoyment of the seaside, and early season beach-cleaning operations remove all traces of plant life from many popular beaches. The coastal strip is probably the most damaged of Crete's native habitats. Where it survives, particularly on dunes, it includes the gorgeous white sea daffodil, which can be recognised from Mycenaean frescoes. Confirming Crete's subtropical connections, *Phoenix theophrasti*, the Cretan date palm, lives in eight coastal localities around the island, with the biggest colony at Vái.

HOME-GROWN PALMS

Contrary to popular myth, the palm trees that grow at Vái and elsewhere are a native species, and do not derive from Roman legionnaries dropping date stones on their way home from Egypt.

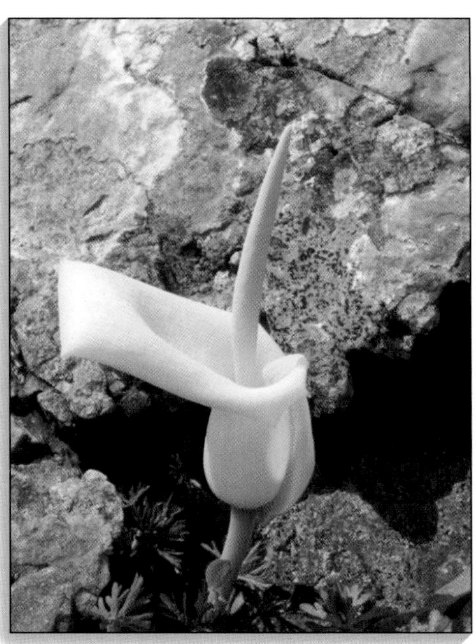

The woodland is a mixture of trees, mainly evergreen oaks and cypresses, with deciduous oaks on more fertile soils, sweet chestnuts in the west, and pines in the drier uplands. The increasing number of pines brings its own hazards for other wildlife, since these resinous trees are dangerously flammable and seriously exacerbate any forest fire. Pale-leaved oriental planes line watercourses and make huge shade trees in many Cretan village squares. The richer woodlands often have an understorey of tree heather and strawberry tree, and perennials such as cyclamen and peonies

Garrigue (uncultivated scrubland) is characteristic and widespread on drier limestone, and one of Crete's most species-rich habitats. There are no trees, except for small, continuously nibbled-down hummocks of evergreen oak or maple. Large shrubs are scarce, but there are many subshrubs, often with open ground between, where bulbs and orchids may be common. Phrygana, from a Greek word for dry firewood, is an extreme form of garrigue, with hedgehog-like dwarf shrubs. Away from the limestone, it is dominated by spiny burnet with protective twigs resembling wire-netting.

Many botanists visit Crete in April specifically to see orchids. These terrestrial species are not as spectacular as their bigger, tropical hothouse cousins, but just as variable, beautiful and complex when seen close to. Taxonomic boundaries between species are often blurred, but, on our current understanding, 67 species are confirmed to occur on Crete. Of these, the 30 species of Ophrys, the bee and spider orchids, are the most interesting and frequently most controversial.

They use subtleties of colour and false female hormonal scents to lure small male wasps. The insects' deluded attempts at courtship of the flowers result in pollination of the plant. All species are officially protected, but many Cretans still gather them for decoration of the home and of graves.

Some of the most specialised habitats are the cliffs of gorges – near-vertical surfaces that grazing animals have difficulty in reaching and which are refuges for vulnerable plant species. Three of the richest gorges are Samariá, Ímbros and the Kotsifoú. Many of Crete's endemic plants are more or less restricted to this habitat – and to man-made walls, where conditions are often similar.

A few lowland plants, such as the shrubby thyme, continue to flower during the summer and are often mobbed by butterflies during this nectar-lean time. Increasing altitude delays the flowering period, and above 1,200 metres (3,940 ft), there is more to see between June and August. Above 1,800 metres (5,900 ft), the landscape may appear to be bare rock and scree, but careful inspection shows a unique community of cushion-shaped dwarf shrubs and tiny herbs.

FAR LEFT: kermes oak, also known as holly oak because of its prickly leaves. **LEFT:** the beautiful Cretan arum, found only on the island.
RIGHT: the elusive *agrími* or *krí-krí*.

Mammals

There are wild mammals on Crete, but most are shy and reclusive. The ibex-like wild goat or *agrími (krí-krí)*, is a rarely seen inhabitant of the White Mountains. Because of fears of its extinction through excessive hunting, some animals were relocated to Dhía island, off Iráklion, where they multiplied like rabbits, decimating the rare native plants.

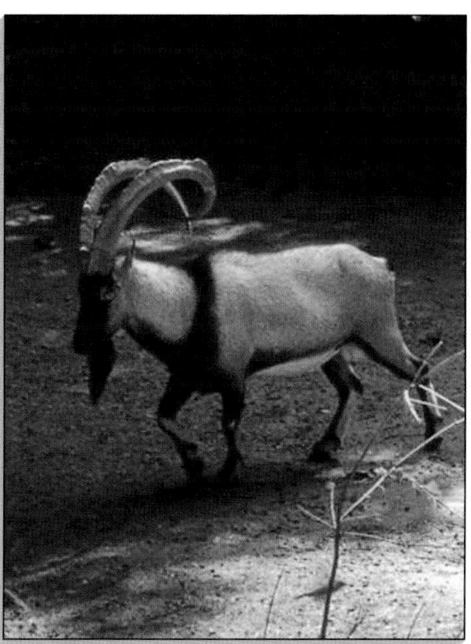

Otherwise, the largest mammal is the badger, but far more often seen is the ferret-like stone-marten (beech-marten), named from its territorial marking of stones with droppings. Agile and fast-moving, but with no road sense, they become frequent victims of the taxidermist's art, and many specimens feature on the walls or shelves of country tavernas. There are no foxes or wild rabbits, but hares occur and are hunted, along with partridges, in the higher mountains.

Most other mammals are small: weasels, rats, mice and shrews, and a variety of bats that can move from island to mainland and vice-versa. In the seas around Crete, look out for dolphins speeding alongside ferries.

On the wing

While the mammal-watcher may find himself underemployed, the bird-watcher should not be. Spring brings a huge variety of migrating species up from Africa, usually heading for a final destination further north. After the long sea crossing, Crete will be their first landfall, in sheltered bays and in quiet areas of coastal marsh and scrub.

Many of the warblers tend to be small and inconspicuous, and are often best distinguished by ear rather than by eye. In startlingly colourful contrast are the bigger hoopoes, golden orioles, kingfishers, rollers, and the multicoloured bee-eater – the latter usually high-flying and the chatter of the flocks generally heard before they are seen.

For many ornithologists, the greatest excitement comes from the raptors: hawks, falcons, eagles and vultures, although the most frequent species – and most frequently misidentified as something more unusual – is the common buzzard. The larger species inhabit mountain areas, where gorges and cliffs provide secure nesting and the necessary isolation. Golden eagles may be the most romantic, but vultures are undoubtedly the most spectacular. Griffon vultures, sometimes in flocks of up to 20, patrol the skies, soaring effortlessly on broad wings spanning a door and a half. The very much scarcer lammergeier, which has narrow wings, is the ultimate flying machine in its search for bones to drop on to rocks and smash open. The nine or 10 pairs in Crete are now the only viable breeding population left in Greece and the entire Balkans, and a conservation project is being co-ordinated by Iráklion's Natural History Museum. *(For further information about Crete's birds, see pages 222–3.)*

Cooler-blooded

The most abundant reptiles are several species of lizard, of which the Balkan green is the most

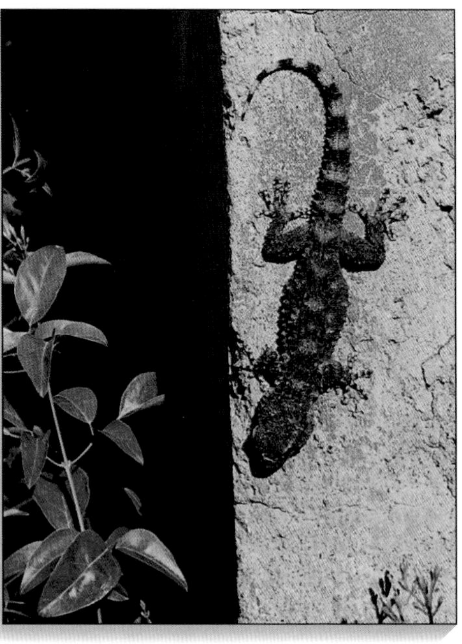

conspicuous. Their relatives, the geckoes, are to be found at night, clinging to walls and ceilings in houses, attracted by the insects around lights, appreciated by tourists but regarded as a pest by locals.

Perhaps surprisingly, tortoises do not occur on Crete; their relatives, the terrapins, like streams with bare muddy banks for sunbathing, but they are vigilant and quick to dive out of sight. Until recently, marine loggerhead turtles used to breed on Crete, but most of their nesting beaches have been lost to tourist activities.

Frogs, toads and tree frogs are most likely to be heard near wet places during the spring breeding season. Seeing them can be more difficult. Small, brilliant green tree frogs are noisy by night, but hard to spot in the day, as they rest among the leaves of shrubs and trees.

Creepy-crawlies

Crete is always busy with insect life, mostly harmless although frequently irritating. At night, the whine and attack of mosquitoes makes them the most obvious insects but, in the sunshine, butterflies in quantity and variety add their colours to the flowers, joined by the hummingbird hawk-moth, whose blurred wingbeats make it infinitely manoeuvrable as it feeds in flight. Rare, but found near strawberry trees, the two-tailed pasha is the largest butterfly of all.

The slow-flying glossy black carpenter bees may cause alarm by their size and noise as they search for suitable nesting sites, usually a hollow cane, but they are rarely a problem; domestic honey-bees should be treated with more caution. The loudest summer noise comes from the cicada, really an overgrown aphid, which perches – usually on a pine tree – and keeps up a deafening whir. Despite their size and volume, they are surprisingly hard to see. Indoors in older buildings, the unstoppable, high-pitched chirping of house crickets can become equally irritating

The praying mantis keeps its barbed forearms in a position of supplication until an unwary insect moves nearby – whereupon the mantis becomes a hungry atheist. Even the male of the species is devoured, from the head down, as he romances the female, his protein helping to nourish the next generation.

Mosquito bites can be uncomfortable, but more serious (though far less common) are the bites of the large Scolipendra centipede or the trapdoor spider, and the sting of the scorpion.

When they are seen scuttling across dry hillsides, far from water, land-crabs are likely to cause surprise. They spend most of their life away from water, only going to streams to breed, and are very common in some areas. The village of Arkalochóri in central Crete was even named after them. ❑

HANDS OFF

There are no dangerous snakes on Crete. The cat snake does have venom in its rear fangs, but its mouth is far too small to bite a human – unless you push your little finger in its mouth.

FAR LEFT: a griffon vulture soars through a gorge.
LEFT: geckoes are usually seen only at night.
ABOVE: tree frogs chorus at night in wet places.
RIGHT: the voracious praying mantis awaits food.

PLACES

A detailed guide to the entire island, with principal sites clearly cross-referenced by number to the maps

For thousands of years this sunny island, the fifth largest in the Mediterranean and just 320 km (200 miles) from the shore of Africa, has been casting its spell over foreign invaders. In recent times, the invasion has been largely benign. In the 1960s, the island's ancient culture and the simple Cretan way of life beckoned to the disillusioned youth of industrialised northern Europe. Attracted by the world of Zorba, they saw Crete as a place where dreams could come true, and settled in small communities where they enjoyed a carefree lifestyle in idyllic surroundings.

More recent tourism has left its mark on Crete in many ways. There are now hundreds of charter flights to Iráklion and Haniá airports from all over Europe. Thousands more modern invaders arrive each year on ferries from Piraeus or from other Greek islands. Concrete and asphalt have undeniably altered some of the unspoilt charm of Crete. But if you take the time and make the effort, a fascinating and unique island is waiting to be explored, off the tourist track.

To help you on your journey of discovery, the following chapters have been compiled to offer inspiration as well as practical advice, starting with Iráklion. To avoid the capital's heat, dust and tourist rabble, you should attempt a cool, quiet visit to the city's two excellent museums of archaeology and history, for

PRECEDING PAGES: an ancient church looks over the White Mountains; windmills look over the Lassíthi Plain; a modern hotel looks over the Sea of Crete.

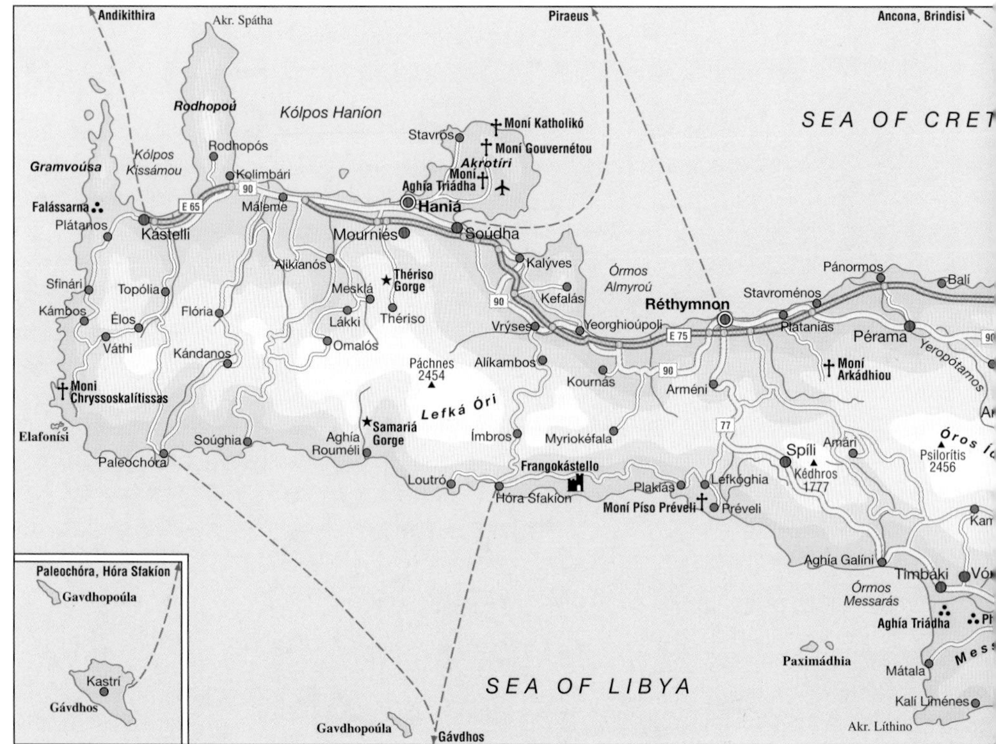

some insight into the island's turbulent past. From Iráklion, move on to Knossós, the most important archaeological site on Crete.

More Minoan palaces can be found in Archánes, Mália, Aghía Triádha and Phaestos, as you follow the road south. From Réthymnon you can follow a trail of discovery to numerous old monasteries before continuing westwards the island's second city, Haniá. For wild countryside and a proud, unchanging lifestyle, explore the rocky expanses of western Crete.

Then it's eastward, back to the tourist centres, the bustle of the beach resort of "Ag Nik", and on to Sitía in the east and Ierápetra in the far south. For good measure, there is another fascinating Minoan palace in Káto Zákros.

A note about our spelling of place names: the Greeks themselves have never settled on a uniform system for transliterating their language into Roman characters, so you will encounter many variant spellings as you travel round Crete. On road signs you may see the town we are calling Haniá also spelt as Chaniá, Khaniá or even, curiously and erroneously, Xaniá. We have tried to be consistent in the way we spell names in the text and on the maps, and where there are variations, we have indicated the options.

The transliteration scheme used in this book is an attempt to portray the pronunciation of words in modern Greek. For instance, the common word Ághios (Saint, masculine) should be pronounced with a guttural "y" sound. But you will also see it spelt Agios and Ayios. *For further explanation, see Travel Tips Language section, page 271.*

But don't let erratic spellings spoil your enjoyment of this magical island. If the name on the sign you are reading looks approximately the same as the spelling in this book, you're probably on the right road. ❑

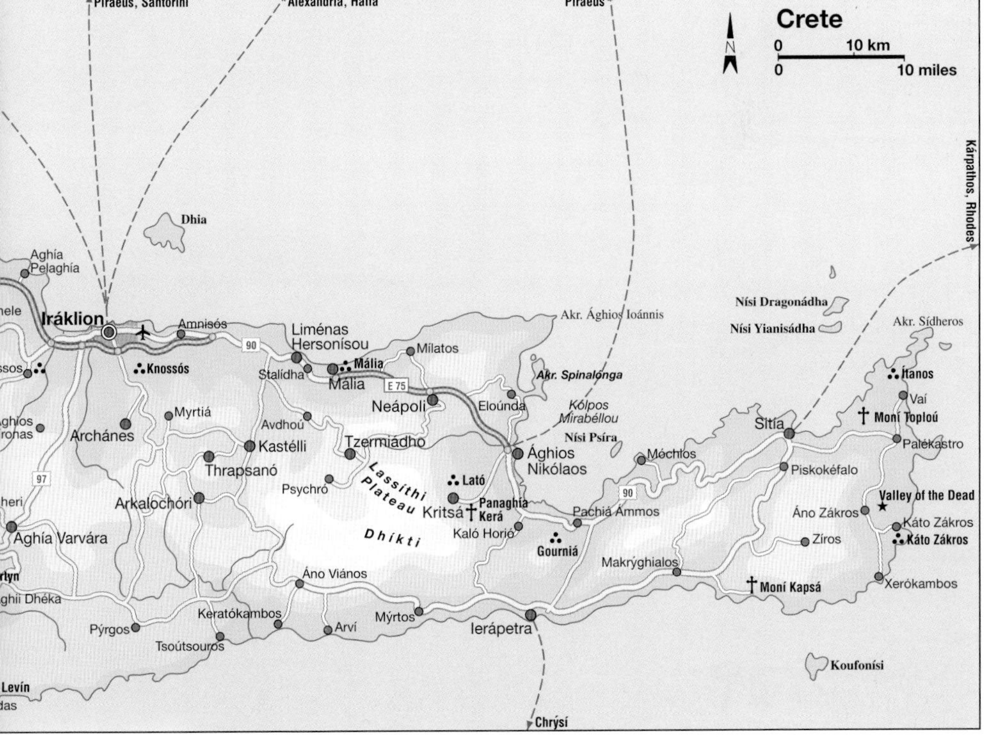

Ἑνετική
Λότζια
Venetian
Loggia
KNOSSOS HOTEL
HONDA
KREIDLER

IRÁKLION

Dusty, noisy and not altogether beautiful, Crete's capital city does not immediately appeal to the senses. But it has much to offer – not least its generous and charming populace

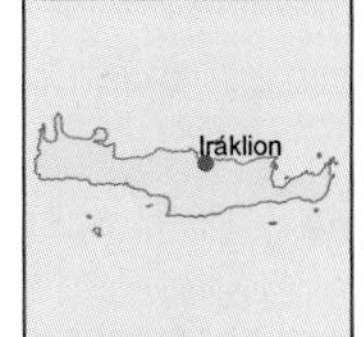

There was a city named Iráklion on Crete as early as the Minoan epoch, probably as the harbour of Knossós. Greek mythology tells that it was here that Hercules (Herakles or, in modern Greek, Iraklís) performed the seventh of his 12 labours: slaying the fire-breathing Cretan bull. The Greeks probably called the city Herakleion or Herakleia, in honour of their hero. Later, under the Romans and Byzantines, this region was only sparsely populated. It was not until after the conquest of Crete by the Saracens in AD 824 that Iráklion once again gained importance. It was expanded and fortified, and given the name Rabdh el-Khandak, "castle of the moat". The Saracens made the town the piracy and slavery centre of the eastern Mediterranean.

In 961 Nikefóros Fokás reconquered Crete for the Byzantine Empire. In doing so, he destroyed el-Khandak, which was later rebuilt and named Chandax. With the destruction of Byzantium by the crusaders, the Venetians took ownership of Crete in 1204. Chandax became Candia, and not long afterwards the whole island was given that name. During the 465 years of Venetian rule, Candia became a centre of culture. In practice this meant that the new rulers lived in luxury in Candia, Haniá and Réthymnon, while the native inhabitants were stripped of their land and possessions and reduced to slavery. Once they had subdued them, the Venetians had little to fear from the Cretans, who referred to Candia by its old Greek name of Megalo Kastro, "great fort".

PRECEDING PAGES: the Sea of Crete pounds against Iráklion's harbour.
LEFT: the rebuilt Venetian Loggia.
BELOW: the Lion of St Mark on the Koulés fortress.

The Turkish threat

Turkey now threatened the island, and in 1462 work began on a huge perimeter wall to encompass all the suburbs of the city. Work continued for over a century, incorporating after 1536 the designs of the great Venetian fortifications engineer Michele Sanmicheli. When the Turks captured Haniá in two months and attacked Candia in 1647 (with what was then the world's strongest army), few thought the siege would be maintained for 22 years. Eventually, after 30,000 casualties on the Cretan side and an estimated 117,000 Turkish deaths, the Venetians could hold out no longer, and in 1669 the Turks took Crete. Once again the city of Candia changed its name, this time to Megalo Kastro, but its influence waned. The Turks preferred Haniá as their centre, and in 1850 the western city was elevated to the island's new capital.

When Crete acquired "autonomous status" under Ottoman supremacy in 1898, Megalo Kastro once again became Herakleion – or Iráklion in modern Greek. After the island became part of the Greek nation in 1913, Iráklion took on the aspect of a metropolis. During World War II the city suffered heavy bombing by German and British forces. It was not until 1972 that it once again became the capital city of Crete.

Most post offices (tachydhromía) *will change foreign money as well as handle mail.*

Museums and monuments

Many travellers have the same problem with the city of Iráklion as they do with Greek cuisine. They are disappointed before ever really giving it a chance. However, there's no denying that Iráklion is difficult to fall in love with at first sight. Particularly in the city centre, it seems to be exactly what the tourist is trying to escape – dirt, noise and nothing but traffic and ugliness – but if you explore behind the scenes, you'll discover the true nature of the city. It has, in fact, much to offer; not least its people, who manage to combine metropolitan open-mindedness with unspoilt warmth.

Most tourists to the city head straight for Knossós, but you should definitely combine this with a visit to the **Archaeological Museum of Iráklion** ❶ (Tues–Sun 8am–6pm, Mon 12.30–6pm), itself almost as controversial as the archaeological site. Some say it is the most beautiful museum in the world; others maintain it is quite the opposite. Here in one single museum is the ultimate documentation of the Minoan civilisation – although the vast quantity of material on display can be overwhelming and insufficiently supported by the labelling. Visitors sink down on benches outside completely exhausted after their visit. Nevertheless, this is the place to see the surviving traces of a culture that led to Crete being labelled the "Cradle of European civilisation".

The tourist office is almost next door, and the **Municipal Museum of the Battle of Crete and the National Resistance** is just around the corner on Bofor. Both are a few moments' stroll from the expensive cafés and restaurants of **Platía Eleftherías** ❷ (Freedom Square). Recent radical reorganisation of the square has narrowed the traffic routes away from the cafés, but has increased the concrete coverage. Many will prefer instead to head down Idhomenéos to the

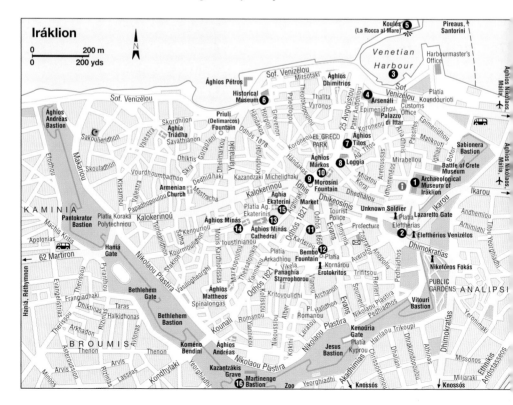

Iráklion

0 200 m
0 200 yds

Venetian Harbour ❸ · Arsenáli ❹ · Koulés (La Rocca al Mare) ❺ · Historical Museum ❻ · Ághios Títos ❼ · Loggia ❽ · Morosíni Fountain ❾ · Ághios Márkos ❿ · Odhós 1866 ⓫ · Bembo Fountain ⓬ · Ághios Minás Cathedral ⓭ · Ághios Minás ⓮ · Aghia Ekateríni ⓯ · Martinengo Bastion ⓰

Pireaus, Santoríni · Harbourmaster's Office · Platía Koundourioti · Customs Office · Sabionera Bastion · Battle of Crete Museum · Unknown Soldier · Platía Eleftherías · Lazaretto Gate · Eleftherios Venizélos · Nikefóros Fokás · Public Gardens · Analipsi · Vitouri Bastion · Kenoúria Gate · Platía Kyprou · Jesus Bastion · Zoo · Kazantzákis Grave · Koméno Bendíni · Ághios Andréas · Bethlehem Bastion · Bethlehem Gate · Haniá Gate · Pantokrator Bastion · Platía Koraka Polytechniou · Kaminia · Broumis · Ághios Andréas Bastion · Armenian Church · Aghia Triádha · Priuli (Delimarcos) Fountain · Ághios Pétros · Ághios Dhimitrios · Palazzo di Ittar · El Greco Park · Market · Tourist Police · Prefecture · Platía Kornárou · Erotokritos · Panaghia Starrophorou · Ághios Mattheos Spinalongas · Platía Arkadhiou · Pl. Romanou · Knossós · Haniá, Réthymnon · Aghios Nikolaos, Mália

cafés on the southeast side of the old **Venetian harbour** ❸, overlooking a mixture of private yachts and local fishing boats. Other monumental Venetian memorials are the huge barrel-roofed boat-building yards, **Arsenáli** ❹, which before the building of the road opened directly into the water.

At the end of a causeway on the far side of the harbour is the **fortress of Koulés** ❺ (Mon–Sat, 8am–6pm, Sun 10am–3pm). Constructed by the Venetians in the 13th century to protect this most important military and commercial port, and known as La Rocca al Mare, it frequently had to be rebuilt after earthquake or storm damage. The present building dates from 1523–40 and still bears marble high-reliefs of the Lion of St Mark, but it has lost its smaller twin which once stood on the opposite side of the harbour entrance. During the Turkish occupation it was used as a prison for Cretan rebels.

With a population of 110,000, Iráklion is the fifth largest town in all Greece.

Slightly out of the way, west along the seafront road Sofoklís Venizélou, but well worth a visit, is the **Historical Museum** ❻ (Mon–Sat, 9am–5pm, except Sat afternoons), which chronicles the Post Minoan epoch up to the present day. Exhibits include Byzantine-Medieval, Historical and Folk Art collections, plus eclectic memorabilia of the author Níkos Kazantzákis and the World War II prime minister in exile Manólis Tsoudéros. It also has Crete's only El Greco painting. Nearby, the medieval Dominican monastery church of **Águios Pétros**, badly damaged by bombing in 1941, is currently being restored.

From the Koulés causeway, head inland on 25 Avgoústou (25 August) Street, the scene of the massacre in 1898 which led to the Great Powers finally invading Crete and ending the Ottoman occupation. The Turks killed the British consul, 17 British soldiers and an unknown number of Cretans, and torched many of the buildings. The elegant houses on the corner of 25 Avgoústou and Epi-

BELOW: fishermen at work in Iráklion harbour.

menídhou are preserved examples of the early 20th-century neoclassical style employed in the post-occupation reconstruction.

Further up the street, in its own little square, is the church of **Ághios Títos** ❼, dedicated to Titus, St Paul's apostle to Crete, its first bishop and now the patron saint of the island. Following the expulsion of the Saracens from Crete, the Christian bishopric was moved from distant Górtyn to Chandax and a basilica was built here. Earthquakes and fire took their toll, and the church was rebuilt several times, but for many years remained the seat (and burial place) of the Archbishops of Crete. As the metropolitan church, it was spared by the Turks for a long time, but eventually it was turned into the Vizir Köprülu Mosque. The earthquake of 1856 damaged the building so much that the renovation project of 1872 almost amounted to a rebuilding job, and during these changes elements of Ottoman style were incorporated. Among its treasures of particular note, are the iconostasis and the golden vessel containing the skull of St Titus, exiled at St Mark's Basilica in Venice from 1669 to 1966.

Next on 25 Avgoústou, you reach the **Venetian Loggia** ❽. A two-storey building was built here by the Venetian governor Francesco Morosini (1626–28) and served as a club for the Venetian aristocracy. It fell into disrepair during the Turkish period, and the second storey collapsed soon after independence. During World War II the little that remained was so badly damaged that the post-war authorities decided to pull it down and rebuild it in the original style. Behind is the present **Town Hall**, on the site of the Venetian Armeria or armoury.

Platía Venizélou (Venizélou Square), locally known as Leondária (Lions) Square, takes its popular name from the **Morosíni Fountain** ❾ which was built by Francesco Morosini in 1628, at the end of a 15-km (9-mile) water pipe.

The Morosini Fountain originally had a giant statue of Poseidon on top, matching the sea gods around the basin, but it went missing during the Turkish occupation.

BELOW: the church of Crete's patron saint, Ághios Títos.

This aqueduct brought water to the city from Mt Yioúchtas. The four water-spouting lions are probably three centuries older, and are the emblems of the city, but few notice that the fountain is also decorated with ancient mythological scenes. The pedestrianised square and the cafés around it are the meeting point of the city – the place to see and to be seen for the youth of Iráklion.

Leading off to the west is **Hándakos Street**, with more cafés and late-night bars, while to the east is **Dhedhálou Street**, another pedestrian precinct, with shops to suit every taste. Also on the eastern side of Platía Venizélou is the **Ághios Márkos Basilica** ⑩. This church with three aisles is the oldest Venetian basilica on Crete and impressively illustrates the eventful history of the island. It was built in 1239 in honour of the patron saint of Venice and restored several times after earthquakes in 1303 and 1508. From 1669 to 1915, it served as a mosque; later it was used as a warehouse, then as the branch of a bank and finally as a cinema. After renovation to its original Venetian style in 1961, it is now an exhibition centre.

Parts of the ancient aqueduct that brought water to Iráklion can be seen behind Knossós, above the motorway.

Oriental flavour

At the end of 25 Avgoústou, cross over the main road, **Kalokerinoú-Ídhis-Dhikeosínis**, and diagonally into **1866 Street** ⑪, popularly known as "Market Street". Lined with stalls and incredibly crowded during mornings and evenings with both locals and tourists, its noisy oriental atmosphere makes a visit an interesting experience. You can buy fruit, sweets, bread, fish and drinks as well as clothes, reproductions of antique works of art and souvenirs, although prices are lower elsewhere in the city. The true local markets take place in Iráklion's suburban streets.

BELOW: the dome of Ághios Minás cathedral.

When the Greek War of Independence spread to Crete in 1821, the archbishop and four bishops were killed by the Turks inside Ághios Minás church.

Halfway down the market street, **Fotíou Street** leads off to the left. This used to be the place to enjoy the relaxed atmosphere of little tavernas, but these days everything is brisk and profit-orientated. The food is usually good, but far too expensive. The market street leads to **Kornárou Square** with its lovely Turkish well house and the Venetian **Bembo Fountain** ⓬, dating from 1588. The headless Roman statue was brought from Ierápetra by governor Zuanne Bembo.

If you turn to the right just before the end of the market street, you find yourself at the city's handicraft centre. Here the quaint shops are huddled together as they were 100 years ago in the time of the guilds. Continue further, across 1821 Street, to reach a square with three churches. The largest of these is **Ághios Minás Cathedral** ⓭ (1862–6 and 1883–95). However, apart from its huge dimensions (it is one of the largest churches in Greece) it has nothing special to offer, except perhaps surprise at the Turks having permitted the building of so large a place of Christian worship. Near the cathedral is the little church of **Ághios Minás** ⓮, noted for its remarkable iconostasis.

In the northeast corner of the square is the church of **Aghía Ekateríni** ⓯ (Mon–Sat, 9am–1pm), with a distinctive circular oculus window over the door, which was built in 1555 as part of the "Convent School of Mount Sinai". This unusual school, connected with the monastery in Sinai, produced, among others, the writers Vitzéntzos Kornáros and Yeórghios Hortátzis, and the painters Michaílis Dhamaskinós and Domeniko Theotokopoulou, later known as El Greco. During Turkish rule it was also turned into a mosque. Today the church is used as an exhibition hall for Christian art. The greatest treasures are the six icons painted by Dhamaskinós in 1580 for the Vrondísi Monastery near Zarós.

BELOW: local produce for sale in 1866 Street.
RIGHT: waves break over the Venetian Koulés fortress.

From the cathedral you can head in a southerly direction to the **Martinengo Bastion** ⓰, the most southwesterly point of the city walls and the burial place of the Irákliot writer and iconoclast Níkos Kazantzákis. It is not easy to find the way there, but it leads through fascinating little lanes and alleyways; you may need to ask for directions now and then. Alternatively, walk part of the great 15th-century city walls which stretch for nearly 4 km (2½ miles), are 29 metres (95 ft) thick in places, and were in their day the most formidable in the Mediterranean.

In the moat, between the **Kenoúrghio Pórta** (Kenoúria Gate) and the Martinengo Bastion, are the open-air theatre where the summer festival of music and song is held, the little zoo, and the home ground of Iráklion's OFI football team. But pause at Martinengo, by the monument, to enjoy the views, to visualise a siege lasting an incredible 22 years, and perhaps to ponder on the tomb's brief inscription from the works of Kazantzákis regarding the relationship between hope, fear and freedom.

Beyond the walls, in the southern suburbs on the road to Knossós and Archánes, is the excellent, modern, but insufficiently publicised, **Natural History Museum of the University of Crete** (daily, 9am–5pm). Exhibits on the island's flora and fauna are imaginatively displayed, as is a section on the geomorphology of Crete. Outside is a small new botanic garden inhabited by a family of tortoises. ❑

CENTRE OF EUROPE'S FIRST CIVILISATION

Until a century ago, the Minoan civilisation was little more than a myth. Now its capital is one of the largest and best restored sites in all Greece

Knossós is a place of questions, many of them unanswered. Some visitors to the site find the concrete reconstructions and repainted frescoes (often from very small existing fragments) aid comprehension. But for many, used to other, more recent, ruins that are clearly defensive or overtly religious, the site is mysterious. Can we hope to look back at fragments of a culture from 3,500 years ago and understand its imperatives and subtleties?

In legend, Knossós was the labyrinth of King Minos, where he imprisoned the minotaur, the human-bovine child of his wife Pasiphae. In reality, the role of the Minoan palace was probably not in the modern sense of a palace, but perhaps as an administrative and economic centre, unified by spiritual leaders.

Among the 1,300 rooms of the main palace were both the sacred and the commercial: lustral baths for holy ceremonies; store rooms for agricultural produce; workshops for metallurgy and stone-cutting. Nearby are the Royal Villa and the Little Palace.

Try to visit early or late in the day, to avoid the worst of the crowds, and to avoid being swept along by the flow. Look for the subtle architectural delights – light wells to illuminate the larger rooms; hydraulic controls providing water for drinking, bathing and flushing away sewage; drains with parabolic curves at the bends to prevent overflow.

Combine that with a midday visit to the archaeological museum on the site – to take full advantage of the air-conditioning inside.

△ OVERVIEW
The scale of the site is most apparent from the air – nearly 2 ha (4 acres) of palaces ruled a population of perhaps 100,000.

▽ EMPTY VESSELS
Huge earthenware jars, *píthi*, were used to store grain, olive oil, wine or water. Similar jars are still made in a few Cretan villages today.

△ CHAIR OF STATE
The throne room, possibly a court or council room, has a gypsum throne flanked by benches, and frescoes of griffins. These may have symbolised the heavenly, earthly and underworldly aspects of the rulers.

△ **THE PLAY'S THE THING**
The theatre was used for plays and processions. An engineered road, one of the oldest in Europe, leads from here to the Little Palace.

▽ **ALL AT SEA**
The fresco in the Queen's apartments (which included an *en suite* bathroom) features dolphins, fishes and sea urchins.

◁ **BULL AND GATE**
A (replica) fresco depicting the capture of a wild bull decorates the ramparts of the north entrance, leading to the road to Knossós' harbour at Amnissos.

▽ **DILEMMA OF HORNS**
The famous double horns now sitting on the south façade were once regarded as sacred symbols, though perhaps this is an overworking of the bull motif of the site.

◁ **COLOUR CODING**
The South Propylon (pillared gateway) has near life-size frescoes of processionary youths, including the famous slender-waisted cup-bearer. In Minoan art, male figures were coloured red, female white.

CONTROVERSIAL EXCAVATIONS

In 1878 a local merchant, Mínos Kalokairinós, uncovered a fragment of the remains at Knossós, but the Turkish owners of the land prevented further excavation and even the wealthy German Heinrich Schliemann couldn't afford their asking price when he attempted to buy the site.

However, once Crete gained autonomy from the Turks at the turn of the 20th century, the way was open for the English archaeologist Arthur Evans to purchase the area and begin excavating. He soon realised that this was a major discovery. He worked at Knossós over a period of 35 years, though by 1903 most of the site had been uncovered.

Evans' methods of using concrete to reconstruct the long-gone timber columns, and to support excavated sections of wall have received much criticism. While these preserved some of the structure *in situ*, it also involved much interpretative conjecture on the part of Evans (pictured above with a 1600 BC steatite bull's head from the Little Palace).

Excavation continues to this day, under subtler management.

Knossós

The largest of Crete's Minoan palaces, extensively excavated and controversially restored, Knossós is the island's major tourist attraction

Maps: Site 110 Area 120

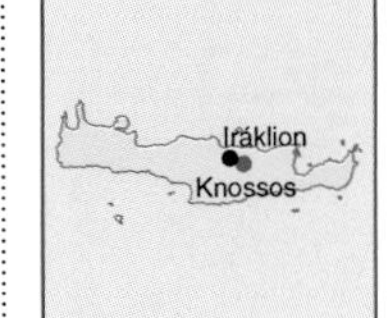

Just to the south of **Iráklion** ❶, amid the vineyards of the hill of Kefála and near the banks of the Kératos River, stands Crete's most famous ancient site and one of the archaeological wonders of the world – the Minoan palace of **Knossós** ❷ (daily 8am–6pm). The very name immediately conjures up memories of the Labyrinth and the Minotaur, King Minos, Daedalus and Icarus, Theseus and Ariadne, and all those other fabled figures. Yet it was only 100 years ago that this fundamentally important period of Greek history was revealed to us for the first time – by an Englishman, Arthur Evans.

Forgotten under the earth for 3,500 years, this Bronze-Age civilisation was the forerunner of the Classical Greek world. Not even the ancients of later periods had any knowledge of the Minoan world, apart from a few words of reference in Homer. Evans may not have been the discoverer of Knossós, but his systematic excavations over a long period uncovered the vast riches of the Bronze Age of Greece, and what he called "the first civilisation of Europe".

Many people decry Evans's reconstruction works, but, apart from preserving the fragile fabric of the structures, he has given the layman some idea of the size of a Minoan palace and what it could well have looked like. (If you desire to see sites as dug by the archaeologist's spade then there are Phaestos, Mália, Gourniá and Káto Zákros to visit.) Evans's ultimate gesture in giving the site he had bought to the British School of Archaeology in Athens and the subsequent gift to the Greek Nation not only secured for the Greeks part of their heritage, but provided them with one of the most visited archaeological sites in the world.

LEFT: the Prince of the Lilies fresco in the South Porch. **BELOW:** visiting Crete's leading tourist attraction.

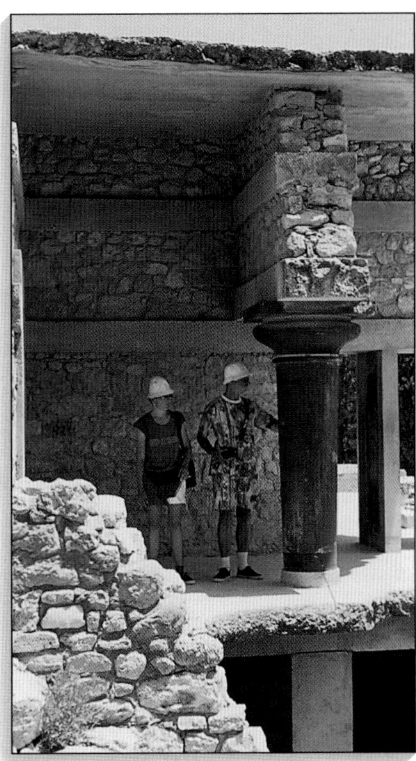

A great centre

The word "palace" is not the most accurate title for this and the other similar, highly complex structures. These areas constitute not only the seat of political power, but also a place of religious worship, a focus of cultural activities, and a centre for the distribution of goods and other aspects of the island's economy.

Of the 90 towns mentioned in Homer's *Odyssey,* Knossós is described as a "great city" in the sense of "the most famous". That Knossós was great in size as well was established in Roman times by the geographer Strabo, who calculated the diameter of the city as almost 6 km (3½ miles). The site of the palace is roughly square, about 150 metres (165 yards) across, and covers an area of approximately 2.25 hectares (5½ acres) The building comprised some 300 chambers on the ground floor and with the upper floors may well have had 1,300 rooms on up to four storeys. Some estimates consider that 80,000–100,000 people once lived there, but this would seem to be a dramatic overstatement. However the general settlement area at

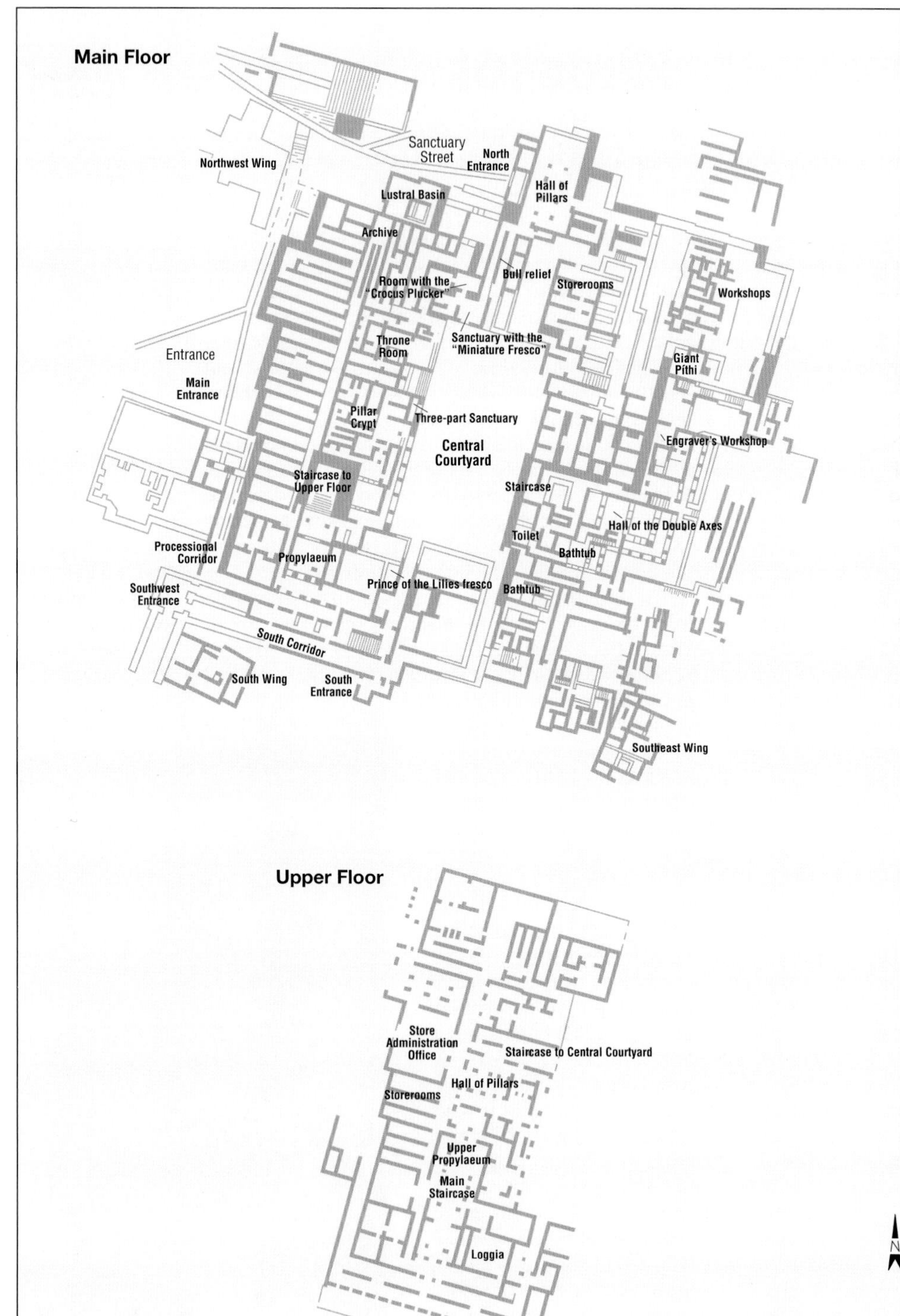
Main Floor
Sanctuary Street
North Entrance
Northwest Wing
Lustral Basin
Hall of Pillars
Archive
Bull relief
Room with the "Crocus Plucker"
Storerooms
Workshops
Throne Room
Sanctuary with the "Miniature Fresco"
Entrance
Giant Píthi
Main Entrance
Pillar Crypt
Three-part Sanctuary
Engraver's Workshop
Central Courtyard
Staircase to Upper Floor
Staircase
Hall of the Double Axes
Toilet
Processional Corridor
Bathtub
Propylaeum
Prince of the Lilies fresco
Bathtub
Southwest Entrance
South Corridor
South Wing
South Entrance
Southeast Wing
Upper Floor
Store Administration Office
Staircase to Central Courtyard
Hall of Pillars
Storerooms
Upper Propylaeum
Main Staircase
Loggia
N
Knossós
0
20 m
0
20 yds

Maps:
Site 110
Area 120

the height of the Minoan period (1600 BC) is now considered as being some 750,000 sq metres (2.5 million sq feet) and more conservative modern estimates put the population of the Minoan town at between 12,000 and 20,000.

Due to a lack of funds and many of the original building materials not being readily available, Evans was forced to use concrete for much of his preservation, repair and reconstruction. The science of reinforced concrete was still in its infancy and much of Evans's work has unfortunately not stood the test of time thanks to the use of incorrect aggregates and sands, and inadequate cover to the untreated metal reinforcement. Yet it is certain that, without Evans's works, the palace of Knossós would have been destroyed in the earthquake of 1926.

Arthur Evans spent 35 years in all – and some £250,000 of his own money – on the excavation and partial reconstruction of the palace.

His efforts have not escaped criticism from purists, for various reasons. He felt obliged to paint the concrete to distinguish between the stone and timber elements. The sacred horns of consecration and *píthi* (large storage jars) are set out together in artistic arrangements. Also some of the rebuilt sections were deliberately left incomplete: mouldings can end abruptly to create a dramatic impression. Evans devised some misguided names for the rooms and artefacts, such as the "Hall of Double Axes" and the "Bath of the Queen" (a vessel without a drainage hole and found far from the bathroom) and these were used in his monumental work, *The Palace of Minos at Knossós*. The bulk of Evans's excavation works were completed between 1900 and 1906. The frescoes on site today are all copies of the originals which are in the Archaeological Museum in Iráklion.

A tour of the palace

In recent years access to certain parts of the palace has become more and more restricted. The site is always subject to the considerable restoration works that are now necessary. So this tour is not a specific route, but more a comprehensive indication of the rooms and other spaces that have been excavated.

The main entrance to the site is on the west side, set off by a line of jacaranda trees and a festive arcade of magenta bougainvillaea. The palace has a complicated layout with lots of narrow zig-zagging corridors and stairways with L-shaped, T-shaped and X-shaped landings; all of which could be interpreted as a way to foil invading enemies or evil spirits; or be a part of the sacred rituals – perhaps even just a playful maze.

A bronze bust of Evans stands to the right of the paved entrance courtyard with its slightly raised walkways, one of which leads up a grand flight of steps to the **Small Palace** (on the other side of the main road and not accessible). To the left are three deep circular walled pits which may have served as granaries or as a store for devotional offerings which had been removed from the palace shrines. During the rebuilding at the end of the Old Palace period, they were filled with rubbish, including fine pottery fragments, and then paved over. Looking down into the central pit, a staircase from an earlier house (circa 2000 BC) is visible. The courtyard is overlooked by the remains of the **West Facade**, whose huge masonry blocks were once faced with gypsum derived from a quarry south of the palace. These blocks are blackened by fire from its destruction by an earthquake around 1450 BC.

BELOW: re-creation of the procession fresco in the South Propylaeum.

Only the reconstructed foundations of the **West Porch** and the polythyron complex remain. This led through heavy wooden doors (the sockets for the door posts survive) into the **Processional Corridor** which is paved with gypsum flagstones and eventually leads out into the **Central Court**.

The **South Propylaeum** is an example of the "idealised" ruins created by Evans. It was an imposing roofed gateway supported on four impressive columns and has been partially restored. A version of the large procession fresco adorns the wall. The large Mycenaean *píthi* nearby were left there by Evans to show that by circa 1400 BC, in the New Palace Period, the Mycenaeans were already well established in Knossós. The pair of stone **Horns of Consecration** to the right once decorated the eaves of the south facade of the palace.

A rhyton, *often in human or animal form, was a vessel for pouring libations.*

The monumental **Staircase** leads north up to the reconstructed upper storey, or *piano nobile* as Evans called it, borrowing the term from the Italian Renaissance for the loftier state reception rooms of an upper storey. The lobby, Evans's porticoed vestibule, leads into a large hall with a small room to one side which held a considerable number of stone *rhytons* (drinking cups) including the Lioness Head Rhyton now to be found in the Archaeological Museum of Irák-lion. A long upper corridor on a north–south axis had rooms opening off both sides, but a gap was left in the reconstruction works to allow a fine view over the ground floor into the **Corridor of the West Magazines** immediately below and the long narrow **Storerooms** opening off it. Separated from each other by strong walls, there are 18 of these rectangular storerooms and, below ground, 93 box-shaped cists or depressions (stone chests) known as *kassélles*, some of which were lined with lead and were probably created for the storage of precious items. The huge *píthi* in these magazines held a variety of goods and provided

BELOW: Evans's excavations before the start of the controversial reconstruction.

cool underground storage for tributes and bartered goods such as oil, wine, grain and cloth. One estimate reckons there was room for at least 400 pots with a total capacity of more than 75,000 litres (16,500 gallons) of wine or oil.

To the left of the Upper Corridor are two large interconnecting rooms which Evans partially restored. Across the corridor are smaller rooms, one of which contains copies of several frescoes now in the Archaeological Museum of Iráklion. Among them are the Bull-leapers, the Captain of the Blacks and two panels of miniature frescoes; one depicts a tripartite shrine of the kind found in the palace. Five columns surround a light well, the main source of light and ventilation for the inner rooms of the palace. To the left, a small staircase leads down to the Central Court near to the famous **Throne Room**. A rounded corner at the bottom of the stairs is part of the remains of the Old Palace.

The Throne Room, which is no longer accessible, can be viewed through a wooden grille. The alabaster throne is made of gypsum and has a tall wavy back. It dates from the Early Palace Period and stone benches line either side of the room. The fresco of heraldic griffins in a field of lilies are copies of originals dating from Knossós' Mycenaean era, after 1450 BC. Evans found overturned jars on the floor, which he interpreted as part of a last-minute ritual to avert the disaster that led to the palace's destruction. A replica of the throne can be seen in the outer chamber. Another replica is on view in the International Court of Justice in The Hague, as in Greek mythology King Mínos was believed to be a wise judge. Adjacent is the Light Well and steps lead down to the **Lustral Basin** or *Ádyton*, one of the small gypsum-panelled spaces that still baffle archaeologists today. They are generally thought to have been used for religious rituals. Off the Throne Room was a small shrine.

Maps:
Site 110
Area 120

To reach Knossós by bus from Iráklion, go to the Harbour Terminus (near the main Bus Station), from where bus No. 2 leaves every 15 minutes.

BELOW: the Throne Room, with copies of frescoes dating from the Mycenaean era.

This palace does not offer the symmetry and geometrical architecture of Greece. Here fantasy reigns, and the free expression of man's creativity. This palace grew like a living organism, like a tree...

– NÍKOS KAZANTZÁKIS

Just south of the Throne Room, past a staircase leading to the *piano nobile*, is a **Tripartite Shrine** similar to the one pictured in the miniature frescoes, where the sanctuary lies behind a facade of twin columns standing on either side of a central section supported by a single column. Beside the shrine is the **Lobby of the Stone Seat**, from which you can peer into one of two dark pillar crypts, possibly used for religious rituals – perhaps involving sacrifice. Troughs sunk into the floor at the base of the pillar may have been receptacles for liquid offerings. The Lobby leads into the **Room of the Tall Píthi** and the **Temple Repositories**. These two large chest-shaped pits in the floor originally had lids. A smaller one between them was inserted at a later date. The outer chest contained the faïence (glazed earthenware) figures of the snake goddesses and the other shrine equipment now displayed in the Archaeological Museum of Iráklion. The other large chest had been robbed: in it Evans found only a few fragments of gold leaf.

The heart of the palace

The **Central Court** is 53 metres (175 ft) long and 26 metres (85 ft) wide. It was once paved and is aligned northeast–southwest like those at Phaestos and Mália. Scholars are divided over whether it was used for bull games. (Evans believed these were more likely to have been held outside the east wing of the palace beside the Kératos stream.) The **South Porch** to the inner courtyard is decorated with (a copy of) the Prince of the Lilies fresco.

Approaching the **North Entrance Passage** from the Central Court, to the left is a series of rooms where the Saffron Gatherer and other miniature frescoes were found. Beneath these rooms were deep stone-lined pits from the Old Palace

BELOW: Evans's reconstruction of the pillars of the North Entrance.

period which may have been granaries or, as Evans suggested, dungeons. The entrance is guarded by a reconstruction of a splendid relief fresco of a charging bull in an olive grove, perhaps a scene from a bull-catch. Evans believed that this fresco may have remained above the level of the ruins for a considerable time after the destruction of the palace, so embedding the legend of the minotaur in popular memory.

The entrance was narrowed when the later palace was built and the North Pillar Hall/Customs House was added, with a double row of gypsum pillars. According to one theory, the palace banqueting hall was located above the Pillar Hall. Domestic utensils were found in the neighbouring magazines. To the left and past the **North Portico** is the **North Lustral Basin**, the biggest of the lustral basins at Knossós. Evans thought that visitors to the palace underwent a ritual cleansing and anointing before being admitted. **Storerooms** and **Workshops** lie, somewhat surprisingly, directly adjacent to the living quarters.

On the east side of the Central Court the elegant **Grand Staircase** leads down into the **Royal Chambers** – what Evans considered to be the living quarters of the king and queen of Knossós. Originally built into the side of the hill, four flights of gypsum steps survive and there may have been a fifth. They are lit by a deep light well. This part of the palace shows off Minoan architecture at its best, with rooms divided by pier-and-door partitions to ensure warmth and privacy when closed, or an airy coolness in summer. Three smaller staircases linking the different storeys and corridors contribute to the labyrinthine atmosphere. The brightly painted reproduction of the Shield Fresco shows animal hides stretched on a frame into a figure of eight shape, which may have decorated the **Hall of the Double Axes** or King's Hall located below and just along the cor-

Maps: Site 110 Area 120

Evans's reconstructed columns all have a characteristic downward taper. He believed the originals were made from cedar or similar tree trunks, erected in this way, ie upside-down, to allow the sap to run out of the capillary tubes, thus avoiding wet rot.

BELOW: a modern bank near Knossós designed in "Minoan" style.

Minoan ablutions: the clay tub in the Queen's Bathroom.

ridor from the **Hall of the Colonnades**. The Hall of the Double Axes is so called because of the *lábrys* or double-headed axe symbols (masons' marks) which have been incised into the blocks of the adjoining light well.

Nearby lies the **King's Megaron** – a reception area divided by double doors with a sheltered L-shaped portico at one end. A passage leads southwest into the **Queen's Mégaron** which is decorated with copies of the lively Dolphin Fresco with colourful rosette borders and furnished with stone benches. An Old Palace floor with irregular paving is visible below the later floor level. Beside the Queen's Mégaron is a bathroom complete with a clay tub behind a screen, and frescoes of Minoan ladies and a dancer on the walls. Beyond, a narrow corridor leads to the **Queen's Toilet** with a drainage system. When Evans discovered this room, he is said to have exclaimed: "Now I am the only person on Crete to possess a toilet that flushes!" Grooves in the wall and floor suggest that a wooden seat was fixed above the outlet to an elaborate drainage system which channelled waste water down to the Kératos River.

The **Court of the Distaffs**, also named after the mason's marks found on its wall, provides light for this area. Leaving the living quarters from the Queen's verandah and then turning left, you pass by the terrace flanking the Hall of the Double Axes to the **East Portico**. This is the area of the Palace Workshops. A parallel corridor leads past a narrow storeroom containing pieces of lapis lacedemonios, a speckled green stone found only in the southern Peloponnese region of mainland Greece and used for making stone vases and seals. This would indicate a mason's or lapidary's workshop and some stone pieces show traces of work in progress. To the north is a room with a stone bench which could have been a potter's workshop.

BELOW: Sandy MacGillivray, former Knossós Curator of the British School at Athens, studies Arthur Evans's *Knossós Fresco Atlas.*

Continuing north is the **Court of the Stone Spout**, located high up on the west wall, which channelled rainwater to a cistern outside the court. Ahead are the **Magazines of the Giant Píthi**, part of a storeroom complex of the Old Palace with the huge vases dating from circa 1800 BC. North again are the **Royal Pottery Stores**, also a remnant from the earlier palace, where some fine pottery from Kamáres was found. A staircase leads down to the **East Bastion** marking the east entrance to the palace. Beside the steps is a series of carefully cut stone water channels with settlement basins.

Above this area you pass more giant *píthi* and arrive in the **Corridor of the Chess Board** where the intricate and richly decorated gaming board dating from the New Palace Period was found (now in the Archaeological Museum of Iráklion). The line of a drainage system of tapering clay pipes can be seen beneath the corridor before you reach the **Magazine of the Medallion Píthi**. From here the **Corridor of the Beys** leads to the **Grand Staircase** (there is an alternative way back to the Central Court via a staircase to the right).

The Theatre

Outside the main palace area to the northwest, is the paved palace **Theatre Area**, which could hold 500 spectators for rituals, dances and also perhaps boxing and wrestling. It overlooked a flight of stairs overlooking the end of the **Royal Road** at the west side, which may have formed a reception area. The road continued west into the Minoan town and branched north down to the Little Palace (where the Bull's Head Rhyton was found). Access is no longer available to this area, or to the Royal Villa, the Arena, the Guest House (Caravanserai), the House of the High Priest or the Royal Temple Tomb. ❑

Maps:
Site 110
Area 120

TIP

The best time to visit Knossós in summer is two hours or so before closing time: it is cooler and most of the tour groups have left.

BELOW: the Horns of Consecration provide a platform for a tour guide.

AROUND IRÁKLION

In the verdant countryside to the south and east of the capital there are more relics of Crete's ancient past, as well as memorials to recent artists

Map on page 120

About 7 km (4½ miles) from **Iráklion ❶**, south of **Knossós ❷**, there is a superb two-tiered aqueduct spanning a gorge. It was built between 1830 and 1840, during the interval of Egyptian rule, on the site of a previous Roman construction. A further 8 km (5 miles) down the road is the thriving town of **Archánes ❸**. With a population of over 3,500 inhabitants, it is at the heart of a major agricultural and vine-growing region, the centre of Cretan wine production. The dessert grape Rosakiá is also grown here. Apart from the churches of Aghía Panaghía (the Virgin Mary), with its icon collection, and Aghía Triádha (the Holy Trinity), with a few remains of Byzantine frescoes, the town is best known for being constructed on the site of an important Minoan palace, and for the extraordinary treasures made in other Minoan excavations nearby.

Thanks to its abundant water supplies, this area has been inhabited since Neolithic times (6000 BC), and in 1900 BC the **Palace of Archánes** was built, coinciding with the great Minoan palaces of Knossós, Phaestos and Mália. Although it was Sir Arthur Evans who first recognised signs of Minoan occupation in the centre of Archánes, it was not until 1964 that evidence of a major building was revealed by the archaeologists Éfi and Ioánnis Sakellarákis. Floral frescoes (now in the Archaeological Museum of Iráklion) were found on some of the sizeable walls, some of which reached a height of 3 metres (10 ft); their thickness suggested a building rising to three storeys. Unfortunately only a small portion of this potentially large site has been excavated, because it is located in the town centre and lies beneath existing houses. Various ceramics and copies of artefacts from the site are currently well displayed in the delightful **Archaeological Museum** (Wed–Mon 8.30am–3pm), established in 1993, though the more valuable pieces are in the Archaeological Museum of Iráklion.

LEFT: a church bell in the morning sun. **BELOW:** baking loaves for Easter.

Grave goods

The second most important site is the Minoan cemetery at **Foúrni**, named after the hill upon which it sits, 1 km (½ mile) to the northwest of the town. This is a unique site: the burial ground was in constant use from 2400–1200 BC and, with more than 20 structures and tombs, is the most extensive in the entire prehistoric Aegean. Discoveries here include not only the sole intact royal burial chamber in Crete, but also many imported objects showing contact with the Cyclades, Egypt and the Middle East. As you enter the site, the circular tomb of Thólos E is on the left. Dating from the Pre-Palace Period (2500–2000 BC), it housed 31 stone sarcophagi and 21 burial urns (*píthi*) as well as six early Minoan sealstones. A smaller tomb, Thólos D, dating from the Mycenaean period

Crete's buses, run by a group known as KTEL, are modern, reliable and cheap. There are frequent buses connecting major towns, and services to the main archaeological sites, the Samariá Gorge and many of the island's villages.

(1300 BC) is at a lower level to the south and was probably a burial chamber for women, to judge from the quantity of jewellery found there.

Thólos C and Thólos B to the north (and to the right-hand side of the site entrance) form a larger complex. Cycladic idols were found buried below the sarcophági and *píthi*, which were the resting places for 47 bodies, so this tomb must date from the Pre-Palace Period, when there was an identification with Cycladic culture. Just to the north is Thólos B, a two-storeyed mortuary temple, and on the ground behind was the site of the ossuary where 200 human skulls, bronze objects, ceramics and sealstones were found.

Thólos A, further to the north, was discovered in 1965. This vaulted, bee-hive tomb, resembling in shape a baker's oven (*foúrnos*, hence the name of the hill), had been used by the farmers as a storeroom for many years. However Ioánnis Sakellarákis recognised it as a Mycenaean tomb (circa 1400 BC) and started to excavate. First he found the systematically dismembered skeleton of a horse, followed by the skull of a sacrificial bull, and then, on the removal of a side wall, he found the last resting place of a princess. Although the outer chamber had been plundered by grave-robbers, this chamber contained more than 140 pieces of gold jewellery, glass paste necklaces, bronze vessels, ceramics and 87 ivory fragments which had adorned the front panel of a footstool. Although the wood of the furniture had rotted away, this was a unique find in Crete (all these pieces are now in the Archaeological Museum of Iráklion).

Cave of the Wind

At the third site, on the northern slope of Mt Yioúchtas, the most extraordinary and controversial discovery of all was made in the shrine of **Anemospília** (Cave

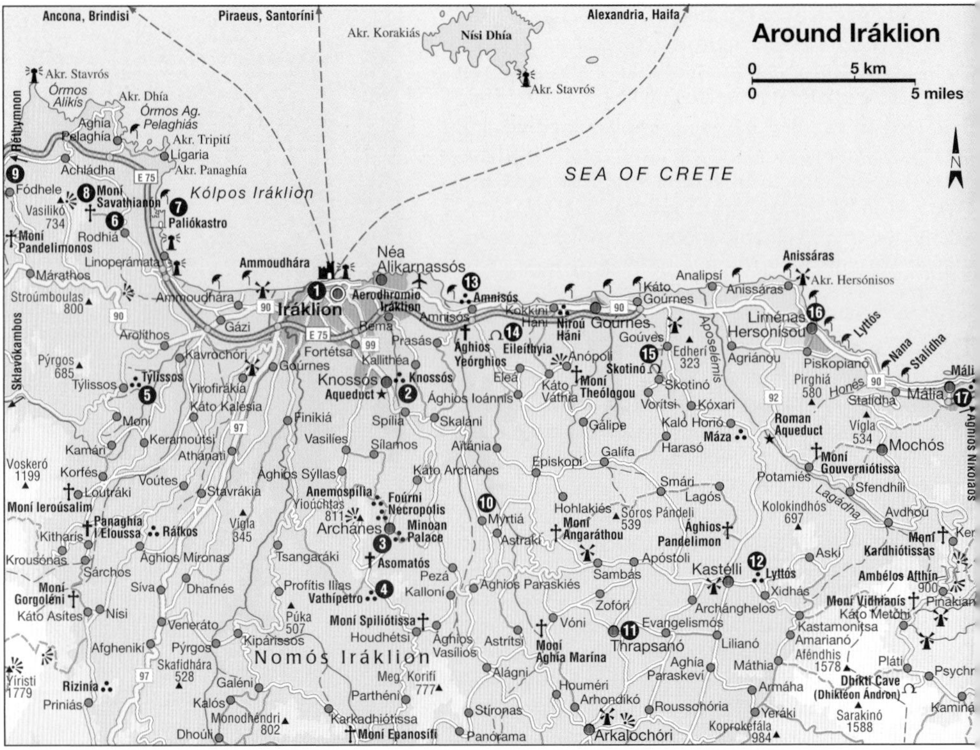

Around Iráklion

0 5 km
0 5 miles

SEA OF CRETE

of the Wind). A central portico leads into a corridor or ante-chamber which gives access to three separate rooms – a simplicity unusual in the often labyrinthine Minoan architecture. In the corridor, apart from the bones of cattle and goats, was the skeleton of a man who had obviously been killed by falling masonry caused by the earthquake of 1700 BC, with the shattered remains of the ceremonial vessel he was carrying beside him. In the east room, many more of these ritual vessels were found on top of the stepped altar. In the central room, along with ceramic pots and *píthi* (storage urns), was a pair of clay feet which would have supported the cult statue of the Xóanon (wooden idol).

But it was the three skeletons found in the west room that were to make this excavation one of the most famous in Crete. In the southwest corner were the remains of a woman, about 28 years of age, who had fallen face down. The skeleton of a man, about 38 years old and 1.78 metres (5 ft 9 ins) tall, was found on his back with his arms in a position implying he was trying to protect his head. Thus it has been assumed that these were deaths caused by the earthquake and ensuing fire, which reached temperatures that even melted the enamel on some of the teeth. Two items, found on the remains of the tall male, show that he was a person of some standing, probably a priest. On his left wrist was an ornate agate sealstone and on his left hand he wore a silver ring covered with iron – an extremely valuable adornment as iron was a more precious metal than silver in the 18th century BC. It is probably the earliest iron object to be found in Crete, as it is generally accepted that iron did not appear on the island until the Dorian occupation of 1100 BC.

However, the third skeleton found in this room was the most sensational. Instead of being on the floor, this one was lying on the altar in a foetal position,

Map on page 120

Ioánnis Sakellerákis found himself unpopular in Greek archaeological circles after reporting evidence of a human sacrifice at Anemospília. His explanation is still disputed by some.

BELOW: Ioánnis Sakellarákis at the Minoan cemetery of Foúrnes.

with its feet bound together and a bronze dagger or lance placed against its belly. More importantly, the colour differentiation between the left and right side of the skeleton indicates that the deceased, a male youth of about 18 years of age and 1.65 metres (5 ft 5 ins) tall, had lost his blood while still alive. Here, then, we have the remains of a human sacrifice. It is conjectured that this was an attempt to appease the gods during the pre-seismic tremors of the major earthquake of 1700 BC.

You can drive to the top of Mt Yioúchtas on the track (signposted) that leaves the road 2 km (1 mile) west of Archánes. It takes about an hour to climb on foot.

Mt Yioúchtas (811 metres/2,660 ft) lies to the west of Archánes and dominates the region in the proximity of Knossós. In the Minoan era this would have been the most prominent landmark for those travelling by sea to the palace. There are two large caves in the area, **Hostó Neró** and **Stravomíti**, both candidates for being the burial site of Zeus. Seen from the northwest, the skyline of the mountain does resemble the profile of a reclining male head ("the sleeping giant"). The Minoan peak sanctuary of **Psilí Korfí**, set at the highest altitude of its kind, includes a *témenos* (sacred precinct) and rooms that may have been priests' cells. A large number of votive offerings were discovered, including figurines, and in prehistoric times this was a place where Poseidon, the god of the sea, was worshipped. Unfortunately this site is not open to the public.

Vathípetro ❹, 5 km (3½ miles) south of Archánes, is a Minoan villa and agricultural estate from the 16th century BC, with spectacular views to the west and south (open daily 8.30am–3pm). Still encircled by vineyards, the mansion originally had a courtyard, a shrine, spacious rooms and would have been two or three storeys high. The most interesting finds, however, were in basement workshops and included agricultural implements, an oil press, a loom and a wine press. Some of these objects are still on site, but you must ask the custodian to open up the rooms as they are kept locked.

BELOW: a wine-grower in the Archánes region.

West from Iráklion

Travelling west towards Týlissos, after 11 km (7 miles) you pass an impressive building, with two domes, which was used during the Turkish period as a travellers' rest-house because the gates of Megálo Kástro (Iráklion) were locked at night. It has recently been excellently restored with the aid of an EU grant. This location is an ideal spot from which to photograph the profile of the "Sleeping Giant" of Mt Yioúchtas.

Another 3 km (1¾ miles) further on is the village of **Týlissos** ❺ (Tílissos). Situated in the province of Malevísi, in a valley rich with vineyards and olive groves, this area has been renowned since Venetian times for the production of the sweet, dark, heavy wine known as Malmsey.

Being an independent and autonomous city in ancient times, Týlissos minted its own coins, including one depicting a huntsman with an arrow in one hand and the head of an *agrími* (Cretan ibex) in the other. The hunting of this wild goat was obviously a favourite pastime in Minoan times, as evidenced by the large number of bones that have been unearthed here. This practice has obviously been energetically pursued all over the island during the intervening years and would account for the near-extinction of what is now an officially endangered species.

Important Minoan finds were made here when three large houses (open daily 8.30am–3pm) were excavated by Iosíf Hadzidhákis from 1902 to 1913 (the rest of the site remains unexposed). Artefacts included *amphorae* (two-handled jars), ceramic wine-casks, kitchen utensils, tablets inscribed with Linear-A script, double-headed axes, a fine obsidian *rhyton* (libation vessel), a bronze figurine of a man in a typical stance of worship and three great bronze cauldrons. The exact purpose of these cauldrons, due to their sheer size (one of which weighs 50 kg/110 lb and has a diameter of 1.5 metres/5 ft), remains a mystery. They were probably used to cater for large gatherings, although whether ritualistic, festive or for military operations is unknown. Interestingly, these were the first items discovered on the site and initiated the excavation.

On the road to Anóghia, 6 km past Týlissos, are the remains of a Minoan villa (1500 BC) at **Sklavókambos**, which means "plain of slaves". The name probably derives from the fact that Slavic mercenaries (known as *skláves*, literally "slaves") were settled here after Crete was regained from the Saracen Arabs by Nikefóros Fokás in 961.

This large, late Minoan villa was excavated by the archaeologist S. Marinátos after it was discovered during the construction of the road to Anóghia in 1930. The house is not as sophisticated as those found in Týlissos, being built of rough stone from the local terrain, but fine examples of pottery and seal impressions were found. Several of the latter depict the same scenes of bull-leaping as those found in Káto Zákros, Gourniá and Aghía Triádha. Unfortunately, there is not a great deal to see and this site is fenced off – for enthusiasts only!

On the main E75 road, 8 km (5 miles) west of Iráklion, is a side-road on the right, which passes the Almyrós of Malevízi (salt pond), climbs up to a height

Map on page 120

If you are planning to hire a motorcycle or moped to get around Crete, check that your holiday insurance covers you for motorbike accidents – many policies don't.

BELOW: remains of Minoan mansions at Týlissos.

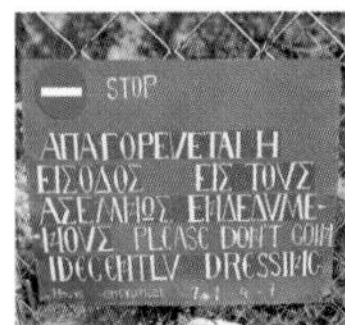

Out of respect for the nuns, "Please don't go in indecently dressing" at Savathianón.

of 300 metres (1,000 ft) above sea-level, and leads you to **Rodhiá ❻**. The village is notable for its Venetian Palazzo, part of the ruins of the Fiefdom of the Modino family which, from 1565, consisted of five churches, 48 houses, two windmills and the feudal mansion itself, which is located next to the church of Evángelos Theotókon.

The village, renowned for its citrus fruits and garden produce, has stunning views over the Kólpos Iráklion (Gulf of Iráklion) and overlooks the remains of **Paliókastro ❼**, the castle built by the Genoese pirate Enrico Pescatore in 1206. Having fought the Venetians and captured their commander-in-chief, Reniéris Dándalos (the doge of Venice's son, who starved himself to death while incarcerated), Pescatore eventually lost the fortress to them in the spring of 1209 and subsequently left the island. The castle was unoccupied until 1573 when, with a Turkish invasion looming, the Venetians rebuilt it at great expense, with its own chapel, arsenal, barracks and cisterns. It is said that the conditions for the surrender of Crete to the Turks were negotiated here.

To the west of Rodhiá, 5 km (3½ miles) up a steep road, is the **Monastery of Savathianón ❽** (Moní Savathianón). Often referred to as an "oasis", this Venetian monastery, encircled by cypress trees, is now used as a convent. The nuns tend to the lush vegetation with its abundant flowers and trees, including an orchard of quince from which they produce jam that they sell to visitors. Ághios Andónius (St Anthony), one of the two churches in the convent, has some interesting icons.

The village of **Fódhele ❾**, 25 km (15 miles) west of Iráklion, is best known for its claim of being the birthplace of the painter Doméniko Theotókopoulos, more commonly known as El Greco (1541–1614). Although this cannot be

BELOW: the convent of Savathianón. **RIGHT:** plaque at the Kazantzákis Museum, Myrtiá.

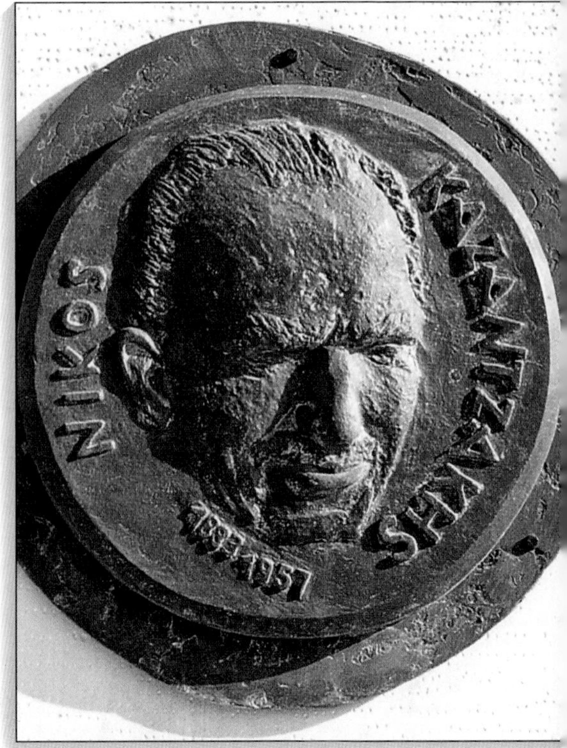

proved, and many counter-claims have been made, it is now generally accepted and has received a seal of approval in the form of a memorial plaque, presented by professors and students from the University of Valladolid, Spain, in 1934. El Greco had always claimed that his place of birth was "Candia", but, as this meant both the town of Iráklion and the island of Crete at that time, this only added to the subsequent confusion. However, documents from that period do record that a Theotókopoulos family did indeed live in Fódhele.

El Greco visited Rome in 1570 and it is believed that he then studied under Titian in Venice for several years before residing in Toledo, Spain, from the late 1570s until his death. He never saw Crete again. Unfortunately, there is only one original El Greco on the island (*View of Mount Sinai and the Monastery of Saint Catherine, circa* 1570, in the Historical Museum of Crete, Iráklion) but the village of Fódhele, of course, thrives on his reputation and has turned itself into a tourist attraction.

Locally made lace and embroidery is for sale at Fódhele.

Pedhiádha potteries

To the southeast of Iráklion is the largest province in Crete, which takes its name from the valley of Pedhiádha, a very fertile area, and one of the most extensive wine-producing regions in Crete. In the *platía* (square) of the village of **Myrtiá** ❿ (Mirtiá) is the **Kazantzákis Museum** (Fri–Wed 9am–1pm, also 4–8pm except Tues and Fri). Founded in 1983 in honour of the Cretan writer Níkos Kazantzákis (1883–1957), the museum is housed in a large mansion where his parents once lived. On display is a large quantity of his personal possessions and memorabilia, including manuscripts, first editions, film and theatre posters, photographs, diaries and sketches. Understandably, many items relate

BELOW: Byzantine church near Fódhele.

To make a píthos *by the traditional method, the process of preparing the clay, forming the jar, drying it, then firing it in the kiln takes about a week.*

to his most famous work, *Zorba the Greek*. The village is also known as "Várvari" (barbarians) because, as Kazantzákis wrote: "When the Byzantine Emperor Nikifóros Fókas reconquered Crete in the 10th century, he rounded up into certain villages those Arabs who survived the slaughter, and those villages were called Várvari."

Southeast of Myrtiá, 9 km (5½ miles) away, is the village of **Thrapsanó** ⓫, famous for its potteries. The large earthenware storage jars *(píthi)*, virtually unchanged since the Minoan era, are produced here. The potteries are open to the public and the potter's wares are for sale. There is also a church with a well, called Káto Panaghía, formerly Panaghía Pigadhiótissa in Venetian times (from *pigádhi*, Greek for well). This well was deemed to have miraculous powers, because if someone happened to fall in, the water level would rise up and return them to dry land. This was witnessed by Andréas Kornáros in whose family fiefdom the well was situated.

The village of **Kastélli** is 8 km (5 miles) to the northeast, in the heart of the Pedhiádha region. It takes its name from a Venetian castle that once stood on the site. From here, having passed through the village of **Xidhás** (also confusingly referred to as Lyttós) and about 3 km (1½ miles) in the direction of Askí is the ancient site of **Lyttós** ⓬. Described by the Cretan historian Sterghios Spanákis as "the Bethlehem of the ancient world", this is allegedly where Rhea came to give birth to Zeus far from her husband/brother Kronos who, having heard the prophecy that he would be deposed by one of his sons, had swallowed her two previous offspring.

However it is certainly the location of the oldest Dorian city state on Crete. Being autonomous, it minted its own coins (87 different kinds from various eras

BELOW: pottery is made today in Thrapsanó...
RIGHT: ...as it has been for centuries.

have been recorded) and it was referred to by Homer in *The Iliad* as having sent warriors commanded by Idomeneus in "eighty black ships" to fight with Agamémnon during the siege of Ilion (Troy). Lyttós was at war with Knossós over many years. In 220 BC Knossós formed an alliance with Górtyn and later, on learning that the Lyttians were away waging war on the Ierapytians on the south coast, invaded the city, abducted the women and children, and razed it to the ground. The Lyttians, on returning from their campaign, were so appalled and disheartened by the devastation that they abandoned the city and settled in Láppa, now known as Arghyroúpoli, in the *nomós* (county) of Réthymnon.

There is not a great deal visible on the site, but some recent excavations to the northwest reveal an impressive Corinthian-style capital and sections of fine quality stone columns, dressed-stone walls and other masonry. However, it is well worth a visit for its panoramic views and commanding position at the foot of the sacred mountain of Dhíkti.

Eastward along the North Coast

The area east of Iráklion, with its busy airport, defunct US air base and over-developed tourist spots, is not exactly attractive. However, almost buried under this onslaught are some rare and precious gems.

The ancient city of **Amnisós** ⓭ is 7 km (4 miles) along the coast road in the region of Karterós (named after the Byzantine General Karteros, who fought the Saracens here in AD 826). In Minoan times Amnisós was the seaport of Knossós, and Idomeneus sailed from here with his army for Troy. Theseus would also have passed through here when bringing the young Athenians to be sacrificed to the Minotaur.

Map on page 120

The municipal beach at Karterós is popular with tourists and locals alike. There is a bar and you can hire chairs and sunshades.

BELOW: white-washed simplicity in Kastélli.

Decorative glazed cakes are made for wedding parties.

Marinátos excavated the site in 1932–8 and discovered the harbour and the "Harbour-Master's House" at the northern foot of the hill. As the latter was buried under a layer of pumice stone, it reinforced the "volcanic catastrophe" theory. On the western side of the hill was a long wall, in front of which was found the Sanctuary of Zeus Thenatas, with an open-air temple and a large, circular altar with the remains of sacrificial animals. On the eastern flank Marinátos uncovered a house known as the Villa of the Lilies, so-called because of the fine, delicate frescoes of lilies found there. These are ancient and would have been the originals of designs subsequently found on vases from Knossós during the Middle Minoan period (*circa* 1600 BC). The frescoes of the lilies and the altar stone can be viewed in the Archaeological Museum of Iráklion.

In the 1920s Marinátos also excavated the sacred **Eileíthyia Cave** ⓮, otherwise known as Neriadhóspilios (the nymph's cave). Reach the cave by taking the turning for Episkopí south of Amnisós and after about 1 km (½ mile), the entrance is 25 metres (85 ft) below on the left-hand side, with a fig tree outside. It is said that here Zeus's wife Hera gave birth to Eileithyia, the goddess of fertility and childbirth. The cave, 60 metres (200 ft) long, up to 12 metres (40 ft) wide and 4 metres (15 ft) high, is mentioned by Homer in the *Odyssey* as being visited by Odysseus on his way to Troy, and has been a sacred site of cult worship since Neolithic times. There is also an extraordinary stalagmite, well described by Arthur Cotterell in his book *The Minoan World*: "Within the inner enclosure there rises a solitary stalagmite, the up-thrusting presence of universal fertility. The phallus. Here it is, in uncarved rock, unmistakably present in the 'holy of holies' of a feminine shrine. Here is pillar worship in its most primative and naturalistic form."

BELOW: a simple supper of lamb, *hórta* and oúzo.

Unfortunately the gate to the cave is locked and to obtain the key requires a detour to find the custodian (probably in the *kafeníon)* in **Niroú Háni**, 5 km (3 miles) east of Amnisós, where there is also an excavated Minoan villa containing a Mégaron (principal hall) – the same custodian holds the key to this. This is an impressive two-storey building covering 100 sq metres (1,075 sq ft) and built during the New Palace period (*circa* 1550 BC). Once considered to have been a palace, it is now generally accepted to have been a rather grand mansion, containing 40 rooms on the ground floor alone. Artefacts found on the site included many examples of objects pertaining to religious and cult activities which led to the site being referred to as the "House of the High Priest". Four impressive bronze double-headed axes were unearthed, along with jars, vases, amphorae, cups, incense burners and more than 40 circular, clay, sacred tables mounted on tripods and apparently unused, suggesting that this was a store for ritual paraphernalia. They were possibly distributed via the Minoan harbour of **Ághii Theódhori** (named after the ruined church nearby), remains of which can be seen under the water 1 km (½ mile) west of the villa.

The enormous bronze double-headed axes discovered at Niroú Háni are on display in Room VII at the Archaeological Museum in Iráklion.

"Dark Passage"

Further east a turning on the right leads to **Goúves** and then on up to **Skotinó** (5 km/3 miles from the main road). The **Skotinó Cave** ⓯ takes its name from either the church of Ághios Nikólaos Skotinós, built at its entrance in 1639, or from the Turkish census of 1671, where it is referred to as "*Skotinó Pérama*" (dark passage). This huge cave, situated northwest of the village at a height of 230 metres (765 ft), consists of four successive floors and is 126 metres (420ft) long, 36 metres (120ft) wide and 47 metres (155ft) high. A large number of

BELOW: the mobile fruit-seller calls.

Watersports of all kinds are on offer in modern Mália.

bronze and ceramic votive offerings, including three important bronze figurines from the Late Minoan period, were found there, which suggests that it was a cave-sanctuary shrine from Middle Minoan times up to the Roman period. Paul Fauvré, the French speleologist, believed that the moon deity and goddess of fertility, Vritómartis ("sweet virgin"), was worshipped there.

Roistering resorts

Liménas Hersonísou (Limín Chersonísou) ⓰, on the coast 26 km (16 miles) east of Iráklion, was once the port for the ancient city of Lyttós and later was an important Greco-Roman harbour. Now, however, it has been swamped by tourist hotels, "full monty" breakfasts, gift shops, "dancing bars" and Euro-louts. If this is not your cup of tea, the newly-constructed bypass means that you no longer have to drive through the town to get to **Mália** (34 km/ 21 miles from Iráklion), which has also been overdeveloped. However 3 km (1½ miles) to the east are the remains of the Minoan site of **Mália** ⓱ (Mállia), the third largest Minoan palace after Knossós and Phaestos. Situated between the Lassíthi mountains and the coast, on a flat agricultural plain, it probably took its name from the Greek word *omália* meaning "level ground". Tradition has it that this palace was the residence of King Sarpedon, the brother of Minos and Radamanthis.

But the ruins visible today are from a second palace, built after the earthquake of 1700 BC had destroyed the original edifice of 1900 BC, and the second palace was itself devastated in the catastrophe of 1450 BC.

Although the site was originally purchased and partially excavated by Iosíf Hadzidhákis in 1915, it was from 1922, when the French Archaeological School took over the site, that the palace was discovered. Like the other great Minoan

BELOW: taking it easy in one of Mália's many luxurious hotels.

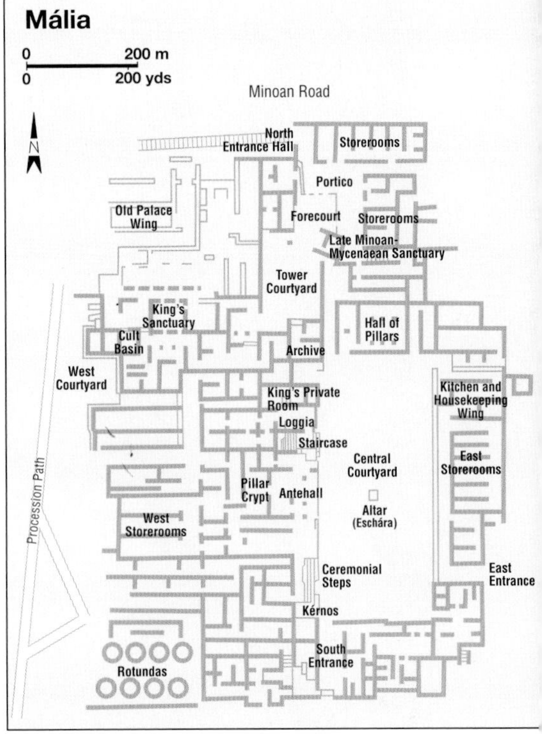

palaces, it is dominated by a large central courtyard surrounded by colonnades, royal quarters, sacred areas, rooms, corridors and storage areas (the storage silos to the west of the courtyard are particularly impressive). Next to the staircase and still in its original position is a *kérnos* made of hard limestone, 1 metre (3¼ ft) in diameter, with a central concave indentation and 34 other smaller indentations around its circumference. Its true usage is not known, but some scholars believe it is a kind of sacred altar on which seeds were placed around a central flame as an offering to the gods. Quite possible, when you consider how long the practice of blessing seeds to ensure a bountiful harvest has been retained in Orthodox churches.

Artefacts unearthed included a stone mace-head in the shape of an axe and a panther, bronze two-handled basins, stone lamps, jugs and two royal swords sheathed in gold. However, the most famous piece of all was actually found on an outlying site near the sea, 500 metres (1,665 ft) from the palace. A local story has it that long ago there was a black man living in the area who had a collection of gold objects which he would lay out to glitter in the sun. The area was known locally as Chryssólakos ("pit of gold") due to the number of pieces found there. When the area was fully excavated in 1931 by Pierre DeMargne, a large mausoleum with several burial chambers was discovered. Uniquely in Crete, the tombs lack "doorways", so the dead would have had to be lowered in from above and the aperture then covered with flagstones. The elegance of its construction and the quality of burial offerings found imply that it was the communal tomb of the royal family during the time of the Old Palace. Among these artefacts was the famous gold pendant with two honeybees, which is now on display in the Archaeological Museum of Iráklion and on a million postcards. ❏

Maps:
Area 120
Site 130

The main road from Iráklion divides Mália into two: to the north are the tourist hotels, restaurants, supermarkets and souvenir shops, to the south lies the (largely unspoilt) Old Town.

BELOW: Mália is Crete's third largest Minoan palace.

FROM IRÁKLION TO THE LIBYAN SEA

A journey south through the dramatic Ida Mountains brings you to more astonishing ancient sites, and finally to the bustling south coast resorts

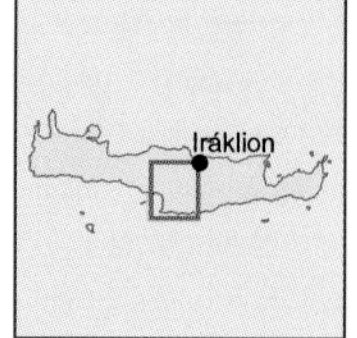

Leave Iráklion by the Haniá Gate and turn left at the first set of traffic lights. Once out of town, the road runs through a rich, fertile valley and then climbs up to the village of **Tsangaráki** (15 km/9 miles). From here it is 6 km (3½ miles) to **Profítis Ilías** in the province of Témenos. For many years the village was known as Kanli Kastélli (from the Turkish for "bloody" and the Venetian for "castle") after a fierce battle when the Venetians defeated the Turks in 1647. More recently it has taken its name from the Prophet Elijah, dedicatee of one of the village's two churches. Towering above the village is the site where Nikefóros Fokás built the castle he named Témenos after recapturing El Khandak (Iráklion) from the Saracens in March 961. On the summit of this impregnable location is the Rókka – literally "a stronghold built on a hill". His intention was to relocate the city of Iráklion there as protection from marauding pirates. However this was not a popular idea as most of the citizens did not want to move so far away from their harbour. By the time Nikefóros had been recalled to Konstantinópoli (Constantinople, now Istanbul) to become emperor in 968, only the castle had been completed.

PRECEDING PAGES: the mountain village of Zarós.
LEFT: peasant woman in the Ida Mountains.
BELOW: playing a bamboo flute.

This site, thought to have been the location of the Greco-Roman city-state of Lykastos, rewards a stiff climb with stunning, panoramic views. The area contains a double cistern, probably Roman, in a good state of preservation, as well as sections of the castle walls that had been repaired by the Venetians in the 16th century due to the threat of a possible Turkish invasion. There are also the ruins of five churches, some dating back to the time of Nikefóros Fokás. From the village you proceed 8 km (5 miles) to **Veneráto** where you can join the main Iráklion/Phaestos road.

The village of **Aghía Varvára** ❶, 9 km (5 miles) to the south, is situated on the peak separating the province of Malevísi to the north and the plain of Messará to the south. Its delightfully cool climate in the summer months and its abundance of fruits make for an idyllic stopover.

In 1866 the Turks destroyed five of its nine churches. However, there is still preserved in the remains of Aghía Pelaghía a Greek inscription that translates as "Jesus Christ gives light to all". On a rock at the northern end of the village is the church of Profítis Ilías (Prophet Elijah) which is regarded as the geographic centre of the island – from east to west and north to south. This explains why it also has the name Omfalós (navel).

The village of **Priniás** lies 5 km (3 miles) to the north. Its name means "the place of many evergreen

The small shrines (ikonostasía) *that you see by the roadsides are usually maintained by a family in memory of someone who was either killed or had a miraculous escape there.*

oaks". In 1906–8, the Italian archaeologist Luigi Pernier excavated a site northeast of the village and discovered the ruined acropolis of an ancient town known as **Rizinia** ❷. The plateau-like summit of this outcrop, sheer on every side, rises to a height of 686 metres (2,285 ft) and dominates the landscape. Remains of ceramic idols and vases show that it was occupied in the late Minoan, early Geometric and Hellenic periods. There are also the ruins of two important temples of the Archaic-Greek period (7th–6th centuries BC) from one of which the gateway to the temple, with two statues of seated goddesses and friezes of deer and lions, is now reconstructed in the Archaeological Museum of Iráklion as a fine example of the art of Daedalus.

Springs and strings

The village of **Zarós** ❸, 12 km (7 miles) west of Aghía Varvára, is renowned for its excellent spring water from the spring of Stérnia, for which the Romans even constructed an aqueduct to transport it the 15 km (9 miles) to the ancient city of Górtyn. These days the water is transported all over Crete by trucks leaving the bottling plant. The village is situated in the centre of a fertile valley, irrigated by the River Vótomos, and makes an ideal base for exploring the region. To the northwest of the village is the **Monastery of Ághios Nikólaos**, situated at the bottom of the beautiful **Róuvas Gorge**, where a small community of ageing monks (at the time of writing there were 15) reside. The church has two aisles but the northernmost, dedicated to St Nicholas, is the original church and has frescoes dating from the 14th century.

In the village of Zarós itself, it is worth visiting the workshop of Antónios Stefanákis, an instrument maker and one of the few craftsmen on the island still

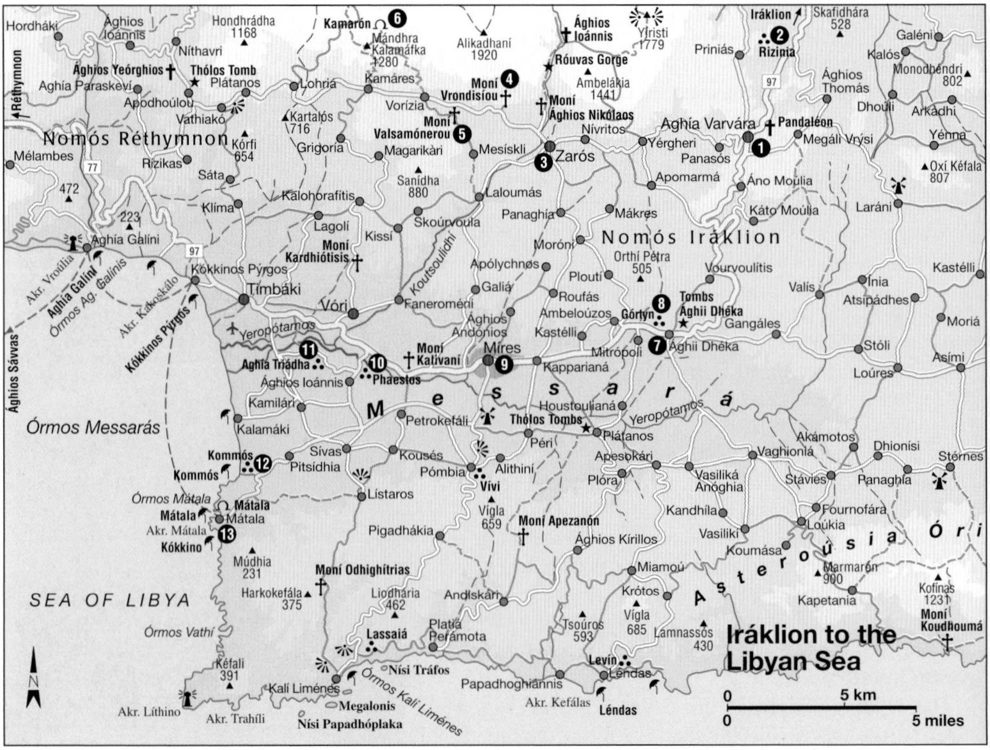

Iráklion to the Libyan Sea

making the Cretan *lýra*, an upright fiddle with three strings. Carved out of a single piece of mulberry wood and capped with a sheet of cedar, the instrument is bowed. Changes in pitch are achieved by pressing the fingernails of the left hand laterally against the strings, rather than conventional violin fingering. Stefanákis also makes Cretan *laoúta* (lutes), *bouzoúkis*, *baglamás*, mandolins, violins and guitars.

There are two adventurous excursions in the area – one to the Venetian church of Ághios Pandelímon, next to the deserted village of **Apólychnos**, and the other to the **Karékla tou Vasilliá** (King's seat), a large stone carved into a throne, where Minos's brother allegedly sat and surveyed the Libyan Sea for pirates. However, both these places are difficult to find and the best person to guide you is Michális, the owner of Kéramos studios – which happens to be an excellent place to stay *(see Travel Tips section: Where to stay)*.

Just 4 km (2½ miles) west of Zarós, on the right-hand side, is a road up into the mountains where, a little further on, you will find yourself in front of the **Monastery of Vrondísi** ❹ (Moní Vrondisíou). The forecourt alone makes the journey worthwhile, but it is merely a foretaste. On each side of the entrance to the monastery is an enormous plane tree. In the corner behind is a 15th-century fountain depicting Adam and Eve presiding over the four rivers of Eden, symbolised by four sculpted heads with water running from their mouths. This artistic fountain was so unusual in Crete that the Turks referred to the monastery as the "Santrivalli Manastir" because of its *sadrivan* (fountain). Unfortunately, the sculptures have been badly damaged and one can only guess at the former beauty of this extraordinary work.

It is not known when the Vrondísi monastery was built, because the dates

One of the huge plane trees at the entrance to the Vrondísi Monastery was once struck by lightning. Its trunk is now hollow and contains a tiny kitchen from which coffee is served.

BELOW: the lofty Nídha Plateau.

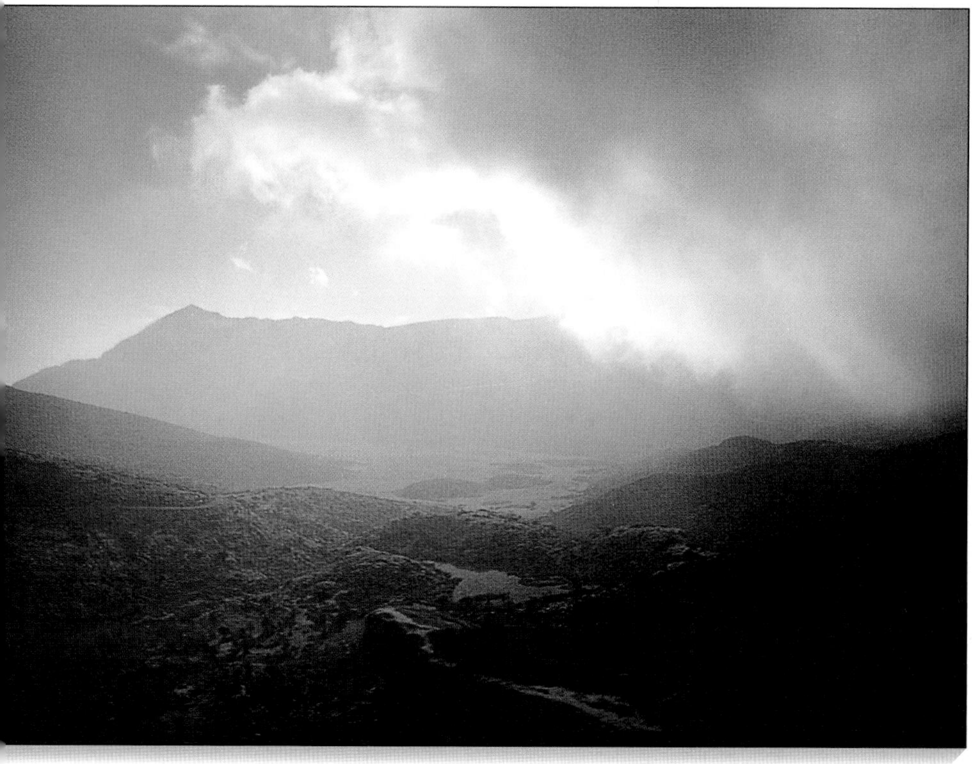

Hard-boiled eggs are painted red on Holy Thursday, to symbolise the blood of Christ, and eaten on Easter Sunday.

1630–39, which were inscribed in Byzantine script above the original main gateway (subsequently destroyed in 1913), may not be correct. According to experts, the building must date from at least 250 years earlier, and could have belonged to the monastery of Valsamónerou, which was much larger and more important before 1500.

The monastery has two naves, one of which is dedicated to St Anthony and the other to Thomas the Apostle. The inside, particularly the southern nave, is decorated with frescoes and icons. The fresco of the Last Supper is painted, uniquely for Cretan churches, in the vaulting of the apse. The icons are in fact from the church in Ághios Fanoúrios, which is all that is left of the enormous monastery complex of Valsamónerou. The works of art were brought here for safe-keeping, as there had been a considerable increase in church robberies during the Turkish period.

The six Cretan icons by the painter Dhamaskinós, for which Vrondísi was so famous, have been kept in the church of Aghía Ekateríni in Iráklion since 1800. They were taken there to be saved from the ravages of the Turks. That decision proved to be the right one for in 1866 the Turks destroyed everything they could find in the monastery, including the extensive library. In front of the church stands a belltower in the Venetian style and an impressive gateway leads to a beautifully paved inner courtyard.

Opposite the turn for Vrondísi, down in the valley to the south, are a group of unfinished houses. These were built by the villagers of **Vorízia**, whose homes had been bombed by the Germans in World War II. However, the land belonged to the village of Zarós and the Zarianí forced them back to rebuild their village on its original location, 3 km (1½ miles) further west. From there a 2-km (1-mile)

BELOW: thoughtful moment in a *kafeníon*.

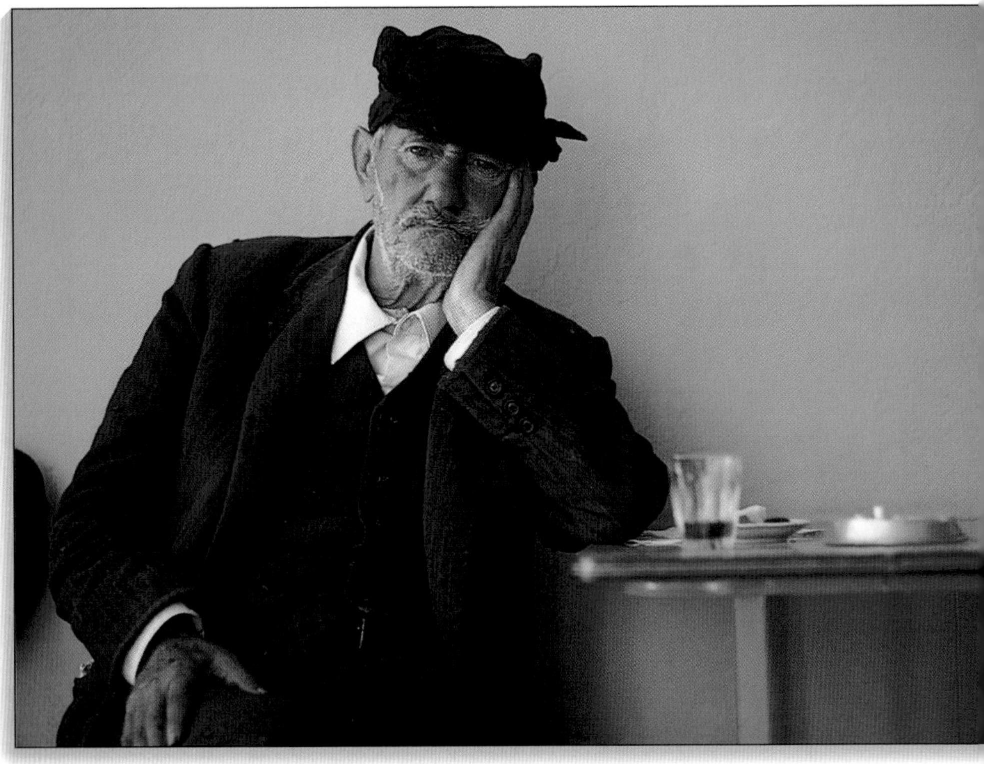

road leads to the **Monastery of Valsamónero** ❺ (Moní Valsamónerou; Tues–Sun 9am–3pm). The monastery has been devastated except for the church of Ághios Fanoúrios which, since work began in 1996, has been beautifully restored. The northern aisle is dedicated to the Virgin Mary, the southern one to Ághios Ioánnis (St John the Baptist) and the central one to Ághios Fanoúrios. The northern aisle is the oldest, with inscriptions on the walls dating back to 1332 and 1404. The walls and ceilings are covered with outstanding, well-preserved frescoes and icons by the Cretan painters Konstantínos Ríkos and Ángelos (the icon of Ámbelos, now in Vrondísi, is also by the latter).

St Fanoúrios, whose church is all that remains of Moní Valsamónerou, was martyred on Rhodes circa *1500. He is the patron saint of lost articles.*

To Kamáres Cave

Located in the foothills of the Ida (Ídhi) Mountains, 4 km (2½ miles) to the west, is the small village of **Kamáres**. This is a good starting point for mountain hikes or a stiff climb to the **Kamáres Cave** ❻ (Spílio Kamarón), situated 1,525 metres (5,083 ft) above sea level. Zacharías, the owner of the *kafeníon* opposite the track to the cave, has been walking these hills for many years and acts as a guide. But since he has marked the path with signs and dabs of red paint, it is quite possible to make this journey unaccompanied (there are also several places to drink water en route).

The cave is impressive, with a depth of about 80 metres (265 ft) and an entrance 40 metres (135 ft) wide and 20 metres (65 ft) high which can be seen from as far away as Phaestos. The cave was rediscovered in 1890 by a villager, then excavated by Italian archaeologists and, in 1913, by the English Archaeological School. Beautifully decorated vases, eggshell thin with polychrome spirals on a black background, were discovered. They had been produced in the

BELOW: the Kamáres Cave.

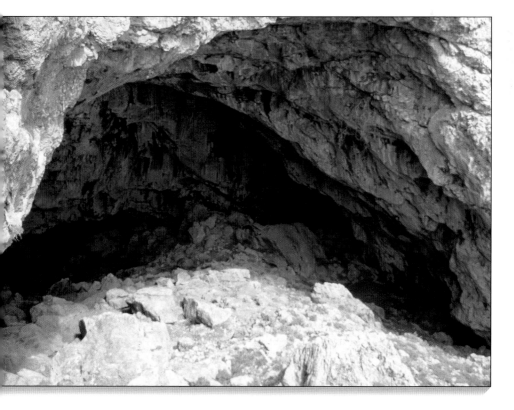

palace workshops of Phaestos and Aghía Triádha, but it was not until later, when examples of the Kamáres style were found in graves of the Middle Kingdom of Ancient Egypt, that the dates could be accurately assessed. Examples are displayed in the Archaeological Museum of Iráklion. The cave itself was inhabited during Neolithic times, and in the Minoan era it became a sacred place, with the earth goddess, Eileithyía, being the focus of worship.

The other important cave in the region is **Idhéon Ándron** or Ida Cave (see page 160), one of the two alleged birthplaces of Zeus, situated on the plateau of Nídha at a height of 1,495 metres (4,983 ft).

To the southwest of Ághii Dhéka is an ancient crypt (beside a modern chapel) where six tile tombs are venerated as the graves of some of the 10 martyrs.

South of Aghía Varvára

On the road south from Aghía Varvára is the **Vourvoulítis Pass**, from which you have your first view across the Messará Plain to the Asteroúsia mountains, inland from the Libyan Sea. It is a busy transport route for agricultural produce from the fertile areas of the south to Iráklion and thence to Europe. Depending on the differing atmospheric pressures between the north and south sides of the island, it often suffers from high winds.

About 5 km (3½ miles) south of the pass, and lying in a superb position among the olive groves, is the village of **Ághii Dhéka** ❼ (the Holy Ten) – the site of the martyrdom of 10 early Christians, who were decapitated during the persecution by the Roman emperor Decius in AD 250. In the nave of the 14th-century church is an icon depicting the martyrdom, and the stone which served as the execution block. The location of the village was recorded precisely by the Vatican Codex after their canonisation: "It lay at a little distance from the town [Górtyn] and was called by the natives *alóni* [threshing floor]."

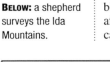

BELOW: a shepherd surveys the Ida Mountains.

Górtyn ❽ (Górtyna, Górtys; daily 8am–7pm), 1 km (½ mile) west of Ághii Dhéka, is a very important and extensive archaeological site built on either side of the River Lethéos, once known as Mitropolianós. This ancient city, originally settled in Minoan times, continued to grow during the Dorian period and by the 8th century BC commanded the valley of Messará. Plato wrote that it was the most powerful, well-governed and prosperous Cretan city, and that its inhabitants were respected above all other Cretans. This is borne out by the famous 6th-century Górtyn Code, the "Queen of Inscriptions" of Greek law. Originally carved into the walls of a public building, it is now found relocated in the back wall of the Odeon (small theatre), which was built by the Romans at the beginning of the 1st century AD. The laws relate to personal liberty and the regulations concerning human interaction, whether it be on a domestic or civic level, and is the basis for many clauses in the modern penal code. There were no barbaric penalties and the death sentence was unknown.

The most impressive building on the site is the 6th-century basilica-style church dedicated to Ághios Títos (St Titus), who was appointed the first Bishop of Crete by St Paul. The most important monument of Christianity on the island, it remained the seat of the Archbishops of the Church of Crete until the Arab invasion of 824. Although renovated in the 10th and 14th centuries, the remains of the triple-naved church as seen today are mainly the result of work undertaken in the early 1900's. There is only one service here a year – on 23 December, the feast day of St Titus.

To explore the southern part of the site, cross the main road and, after following the secondary road for about 250 metres (270 yards), turn left. Here are the Praetorium, built in the Roman period as the seat of the Governor of the

Map on page 136

The text of the Code of Górtyn is written in "ox-turn" fashion, reading from left to right along one line, then right to left on the next.

BELOW: steps of the Temple of Apollo Pythios, Górtyn.

A large number of earthenware píthi *were found at Phaestos, and most remain on the site.*

Province of Crete and Cyrenaica (North Africa); the Nymphaeum, a public bath originally decorated with statues of nymphs; the Temple of Apollo Pythios, the main sanctuary of pre-Roman Górtyn; and a small, well-preserved theatre. Further to the south are the Thérmai (thermal springs), the amphitheatre and the stadium, where chariot races could have been staged.

The city reached its height during the Roman period (67 BC–AD 330), when it had the largest population in Crete. In 1415 the Venetian traveller Boundezmont, wrote that he had counted over 2,000 fallen statues – some of which are now displayed adjacent to the tourist café.

The limestone used to construct the city was transported 5 km (3½ miles) from an area close to the village of Kastélli, where there was a quarry – which some people later believed was the "Labyrinth of the Minotaur".

Eight kilometres (5 miles) west is the market town of **Míres** ❾, the largest town of the Messará plain, with more than 3,500 inhabitants. Its name is thought to derive from the Greek word *moíres* (meaning allotments) due to the Venetians apportioning land to Nauplians and Monemvasians displaced after the capture of Moreas by the Turks in 1543. A similar area was allocated on the plateau of Lassíthi and the village now on that site also bears the same name.

Fortunate Phaestos

The **Palace of Phaestos** ❿ (Festós; daily 8am–5pm), the most significant archaeological site in Crete after Knossós, is 7 km (4 miles) west of Míres and 62 km (38 miles) southwest of Iráklion. The city receives a mention in Homer's *Iliad*: "Of Lictus, and Miletus' towers, of Lycastus' state, of Phaestos, and of Rhytius, the cities fortunate, and all the rest inhabiting the hundred towns of Crete."

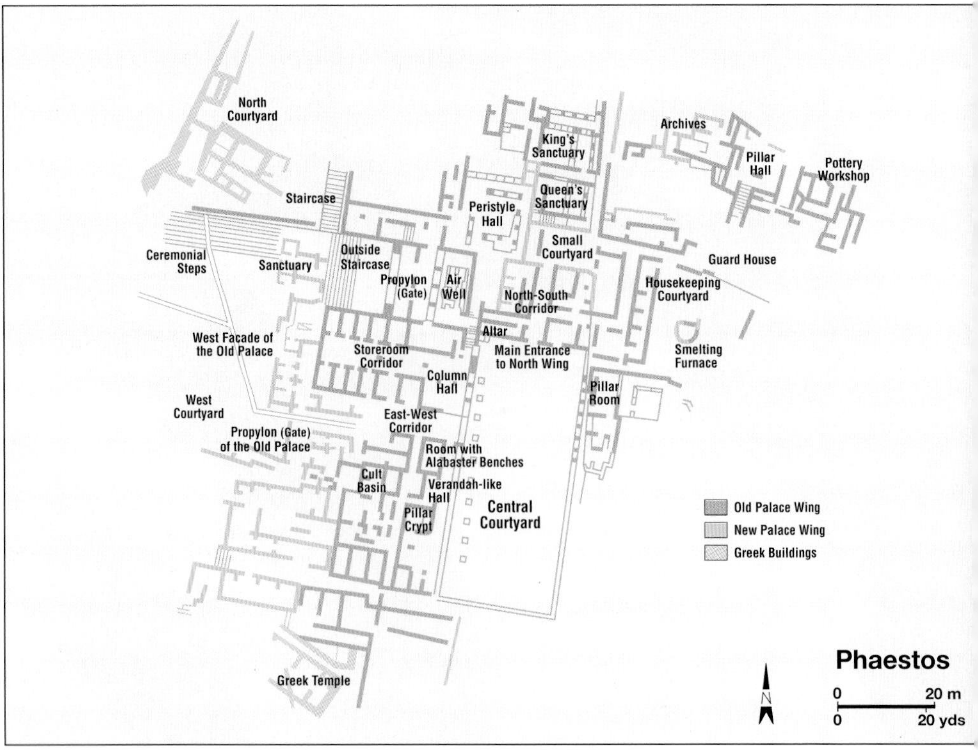

North Courtyard
King's Sanctuary
Archives
Pillar Hall
Pottery Workshop
Staircase
Queen's Sanctuary
Peristyle Hall
Small Courtyard
Ceremonial Steps
Sanctuary
Outside Staircase
Guard House
Propylon (Gate)
Air Well
North-South Corridor
Housekeeping Courtyard
Altar
West Facade of the Old Palace
Storeroom Corridor
Main Entrance to North Wing
Smelting Furnace
Column Hall
Pillar Room
West Courtyard
East-West Corridor
Propylon (Gate) of the Old Palace
Room with Alabaster Benches
Cult Basin
Verandah-like Hall
Pillar Crypt
Central Courtyard
Old Palace Wing
New Palace Wing
Greek Buildings
Greek Temple
N
Phaestos
0 20 m
0 20 yds

It is certainly a "fortunate" site with magnificent, panoramic views. Located on the summit of a hill formerly known as Kastrí, 60 metres (200 ft) above the centre of the valley, the palace dominates the rich, fertile plain of Messará. With the mountain ranges of Psiloritis to the north, Lassithiótika to the east, Asteroúsia to the south and a view to the Libyan Sea, the location is indeed strategic. Phaestos had the benefit of two ports, Mátala and Kommós, from which extensive trading relationships were established with other eastern Mediterranean and North African cities.

One story has it that Phaestos was founded by Rhadamanthes, the son of Zeus and brother of Minos, while another maintains that it was Phaestos, the son of Ropalos and grandson of Hercules. This latter story is supported by the fact that most of the coins minted there depicted Hercules.

Phaestos was the birthplace of Epimenides, the mystic, and one of the "seven wise men of Ancient Greece", who is renowned not only for sleeping continuously for 47 years, but also for his statement that "all Cretans are liars". This could have referred to their claim that their island was the birthplace of Zeus.

The site was first excavated by Federico Halbherr, the head of the Italian Archaeological School, at the beginning of the 20th century. It was established that the palace had been built in 1900 BC, on a site previously occupied from Neolithic times, but was apparently destroyed, along with Knossós, by a great earthquake circa 1700 BC. However, the Phaestians soon rebuilt an even grander palace, which survived until its destruction in 1450 BC, along with all the other palaces, after the volcanic eruption of the island of Santoríni.

Although Phaestos is smaller than Knossós (18,000 sq. metres/ 60,000 sq. ft), there is a similarity in its design and structure, with various buildings grouped

Maps: Area 136 Site 142

The north–south axis of the Palace of Phaestos points directly towards the huge entrance of the Kamáres Cave (see page 139)*, which is clearly visible 15 km (9 miles) away.*

MYSTERY DISC

On the northern borders of the Palace of Phaestos, in a strange department divided into seven small "coffers" where the archives were probably kept, the most extraordinary discovery of all was made: the so-called Phaestos Disc. This is a circular clay tablet with a pictographic script covering both sides in a spiral pattern *(see photograph on page 25).*

There are 241 signs, some repeating, separated into groups by vertical lines, with each grouping, supposedly, forming a "word". Amazingly, these symbols were not incised but were struck from a matrix and are therefore the earliest example of typography, 3,000 years before William Caxton.

The exact purpose of this disc, which dates from the end of the 2nd millennium BC, is a mystery – mainly because we have no idea what the signs signify. The meaning of this syllabic script has been lost, and its decipherment has remained one of the most intriguing riddles in archaeology. Despite a plethora of theories from scholars and amateurs alike – there are a number of books and pamphlets available on the island purporting to reveal its secrets – the Phaestos Disc, with the earliest known Minoan script, remains a complete enigma.

BELOW: visitors to Phaestos.

Detail from the highly decorated sarcophagus found at Aghía Triádha, now in the Archaeological Museum of Iráklion.

around a central courtyard. Stonemasons' marks found at both sites indicate that some of the same craftsmen worked on both palaces. However, the exact nature of the relation between the two and how closely they were linked is still not clear. Many interesting finds, including "the Jug of Reeds" and other examples of "Kamáres-ware", are now on display in the Archaeological Museum of Iráklion. The pottery kiln, exposed in the east courtyard, is one of the oldest to be found in the whole of Greece.

Summer residence

On leaving Phaestos, follow the signs for the 3 km (1½ mile) road which leads around the hill to **Aghía Triádha** ⓫ (daily 8.30am–3pm), beautifully situated at the end of the Phaestos ridge and overlooking the Bay of Messará. This ancient site was named after the small village of Aghía Triádha (the Holy Trinity), which has since vanished, and the small Byzantine chapel of the same name nearby, as there was no clue found on the site as to its original title. Although no-one knows the exact purpose of this palace, it is generally thought to have been the summer residence for the royalty of Phaestos (it is believed that it was situated by the sea in Minoan times). It could, however, have been the palace of a prince or a local landowner's mansion, although some scholars contend that it was only used for specific ceremonial purposes.

Whatever the true purpose was, it has been the site of remarkable finds, some of which are the most important of the Minoan civilisation. First excavated by the Italian School at the beginning of the 20th century, it has produced the fine, carved black steatic vases – the Harvesters' Vase, the Chieftan's Cup and the Rhyton of the Athletes as well as the famous painted sarcophagus (coffin),

BELOW: the Ida Mountains seen from Aghía Triádha.

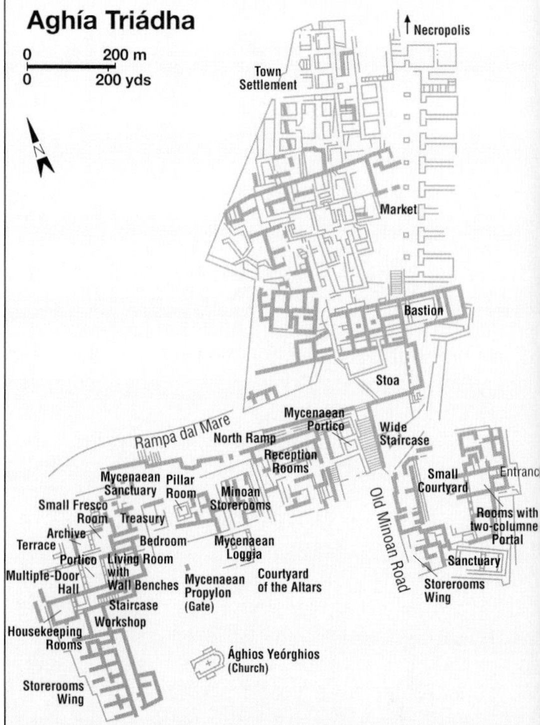

made of limestone, and discovered in a rectangular grave at the cemetery, 150 metres (165 yards) to the northwest. These are all now displayed in the Archaeological Museum of Iráklion.

Southwest of Phaestos is the site of **Kommós ⓬**, which once served as one of the palace's two ports. Although signs of Minoan occupation were first reported by Sir Arthur Evans, excavations did not begin until 1976 when the Canadian Joseph Sha, started to dig, under the auspices of the American School of Classical Studies. From what has been discovered so far, it has become obvious that this will become one of the major Minoan sites. Structures found to date include a 60-metre by 3-metre (200-ft by 10-ft) section of road, with ruts caused by cartwheels clearly visible, a 50-metre (165-ft) dressed-stone wall (the longest Minoan wall found so far in Crete) and, by the sea, an enclosed shipyard 30 metres (100 ft) long and 35 metres (115 ft) wide. There is also a temple to the west that the excavators believe was built by the Phoenicians, on the site of a 10th-century BC Dorian temple. Unfortunately, the site is not yet open to the public and remains fenced off, although much can be seen from the perimeter.

Mátala ⓭, the other port of Phaestos, is just 3 km (1½ miles) to the south. Once (in)famous for a community of travellers and hippies, who set up residence in the caves, it is now very much a tourist beach resort, with its full quota of bars, tavernas, travel agents and beach umbrellas. The main feature of Mátala is the sandstone cliffs, honeycombed with caves. No-one knows exactly by whom or when these hollows were hewn out of the rock-face. It appears that the first usage was as tombs during the Greco-Roman and early Christian periods. Much later, during World War II, the Germans found them to be useful as arms and ammunition dumps. ❑

Maps:
Area 136
Site 144

For relief from the hectic tourism of Mátala, there are twice-weekly boat trips to Préveli *(see page 166)*.

BELOW: Mátala beach viewed from one of the famous caves.

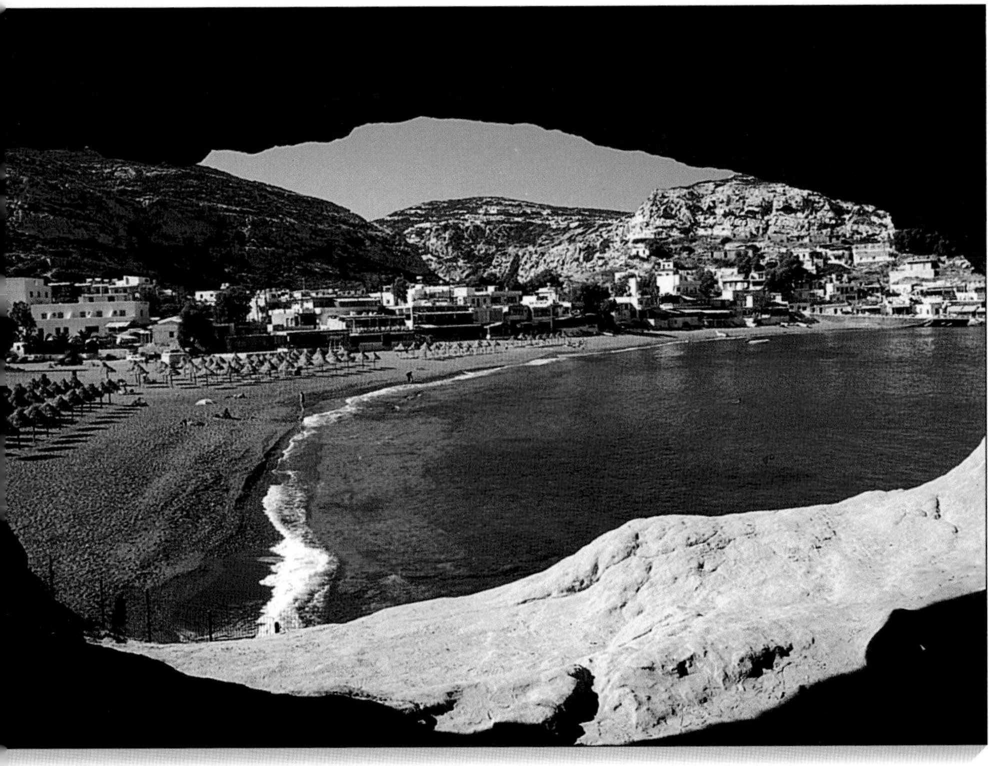

EVEREST
CAMPARI
CAMPARI
CAMPARI
CAMPARI
CAMPARI

RÉTHYMNON AND SURROUNDINGS

Maps: City 150 Area 155

A city full of relics from its Venetian and Turkish past, Réthymnon is the capital of a picturesque region that also contains Crete's most sacred shrine to independence

Initial impressions on entering **Réthymnon** ❶ are of dreary 20th-century concrete architecture, but leave the main road and turn seawards to find yourself in the fascinating old heart of the city. With a little imagination you can feel yourself transported back to the days of the Empire of Venice. The most interesting way in goes from the central crossroads at **Platía Tessáron Martýron** (Square of the Four Martyrs), through the beautiful Venetian **Porta Guora** Ⓐ (Megáli Pórta or Great Gate), and into narrow **Ethnikís Andistásis**, lined with small shops selling everything from medicinal herbs and hand-made lace to computer components and mobile phones.

Réthymnon (Réthimnon, Réthymno etc) is a city of many contrasts, legacies of the turbulent course of its history, of siege and occupation, and of fire, flood, plague and earthquake. The Fortezza, old harbour and Loggia serve as reminders of the days of Venetian rule. Memories of the Turkish occupation linger in the enclosed wooden balconies of the cramped streets, and in the mosques and minarets. To the east are the new suburbs of the city, with hotels, apartment blocks and restaurants in profusion. The summer season brings an enormous influx of visitors and the city is well placed for tourism. The huge beach starts right at the edge of the old city and extends 15 km (9 miles) to the east, though the bathing is better further away from the metropolis. There is much to keep the visitor engaged in this fascinating city.

PRECEDING PAGES: the inner harbour of Réthymnon.
LEFT: city rooftops and minarets.
BELOW: the Rimondi Fountain.

A long history

The area around Réthymnon was settled from the Late Minoan period or earlier. A rock grave of this era, found in the southern suburb of **Mastambá**, has revealed various artefacts now on display in the city's Archaeological Museum, although as yet no corresponding settlement of this period has been located. During the 4th and 3rd centuries BC an autonomous town named Rithimna flourished here, minting its own coins. The northern hill, where the Fortezza stands today, was once the Acropolis with a temple of Artemis and a shrine to the goddess Athena.

Crete was part of the Empire of Byzantium until the conquest of Constantinople by the crusaders in 1204, when the island was given to the crusader, Boniface of Montferrat, who quickly sold it on to the Venetians. With or without the treaty of sale, it took the Venetians a further five years to rid themselves of the Genoese, who had well-established and extensive trading contacts. Near the present day village of Monopári, 15 km (9 miles) to the southwest,

A handsome lighthouse stands on the tip of the Venetian harbour wall.

stand the remains of **Bonriparo** – one of 15 Genoese fortresses on the island.

By 1229 the Venetians had made the city more secure, concentrating on the western side of the little harbour. Following attacks by the pirate Barbarossa in 1538, Venice's greatest military architect, Michele Sanmicheli, designed more substantial fortifications. These were constructed, although not entirely to his plan, during the next 30 years. From this period, the Porta Guora and portions of the outer wall, parallel to today's Dhimakópoulou Street, can still be seen.

Venice regarded Crete as a crucial staging post in their overseas trade links to Asia, and expended much energy in maintaining its security. The Cretans regarded them as oppressors and strongly opposed Venetian moves for uniting the Eastern and Western Churches. The Venetians responded with savage and systematic brutality equalling any of the Turks' later activities.

New buildings sprang up, and others were completed, such as the Catholic churches of St Francis on Ethnikís Andistásis, St Mary and St Mary Magdalene. The Augustinian St Mary's on Vernárdhou was later converted by the Turks into the Gazi Huseïn Pasha Mosque, known as **Nerandzés** **B**, which today retains the city's highest minaret. St Mary Magdalene's at the far end of the same street, became the Angebút Ahmed Pasha Mosque, now the Greek Orthodox Church of **Kyrías ton Angélon** (Our Lady of the Angels). In a beautifully restored Venetian mansion between the sites of the two mosques, is the **Historical and Folk Art Museum** **C** (Mon–Sat 10am–2pm) which provides insights into life over the past five centuries.

In the small square at the end of Ethnikís Andistásis stands the **Rimondi Fountain** **D** of 1626–9 which, with other renovated fountains and wells, helped ameliorate the old city's water problems. The lions' heads between its Corinthian

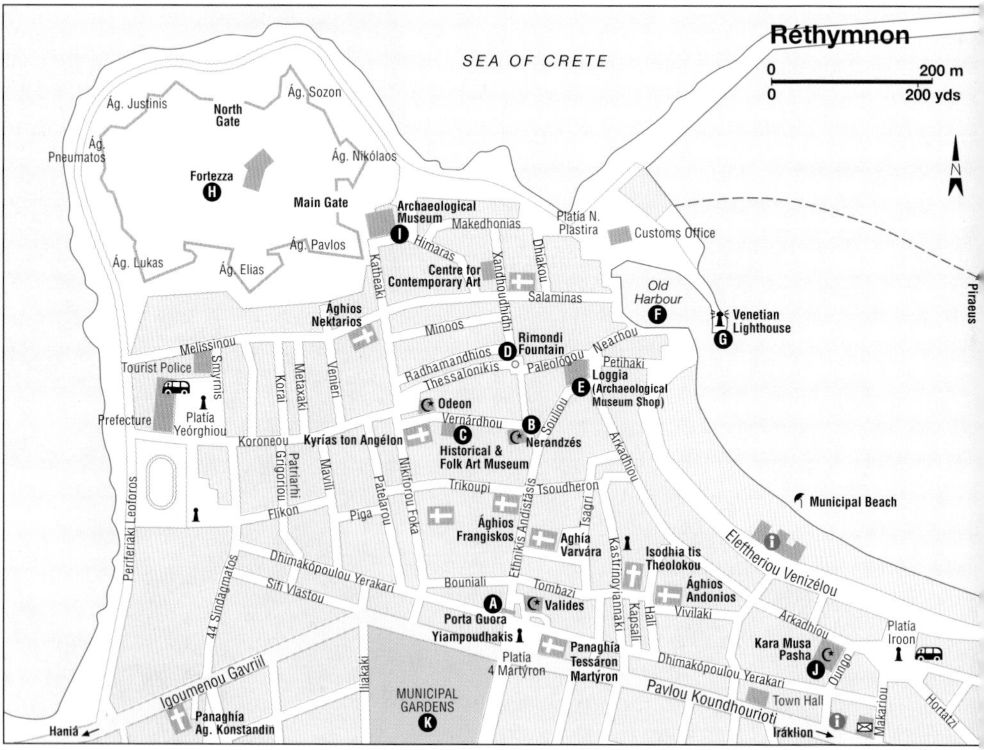

Réthymnon
0 200 m
0 200 yds
SEA OF CRETE
Ág. Justinis
North Gate
Ág. Sozon
Ág. Pneumatos
Ág. Nikólaos
Fortezza H
Main Gate
Ág. Lukas
Ág. Elias
Ág. Pavlos
Archaeological Museum I
Makedhonias
Plátia N. Plastira
Customs Office
Himaras
Katheaki
Centre for Contemporary Art
Xandhoudhidhi
Dhiakou
Salaminas
Old Harbour F
Venetian Lighthouse G
Piraeus
Ághios Nektarios
Minoos
Rimondi Fountain D
Nearhou
Melissinou
Tourist Police
Smyrnis
Radhamandhios
Thessalonikis
Paleológou
Petihaki
Loggia (Archaeological Museum Shop) E
Korai
Metaxaki
Venieri
Odeon
Plátia Yeórghiou
Prefecture
Vernárdhou
Soulíou
Nerandzés B
Koroneou
Kyrías ton Angélon
Historical & Folk Art Museum C
Arkadhiou
Patriarhi Grigoriou
Mavili
Nikiforou Foka
Patelarou
Trikoupi
Tsoudheron
Ethnikís Andistásis
Tsagri
Municipal Beach
Periferiaki Leoforos
Flikon
Piga
Ághios Frangiskos
Aghía Varvára
Isodhia tis Theolokou
Eleftheriou Venizélou
Dhimakópoulou Yerakari
Sifi Vlastou
Bouniali
Tombazi
Kastrinoyiannaki
Ághios Andonios
Vivilaki
44 Sindagmatos
Porta Guora A
Valides
Kapsali
Hali
Arkadhiou
Plátia Iroon
Yiampoudhakis
Plátia 4 Martýron
Panaghía Tessáron Martýron
Kara Musa Pasha J
Oungo
Igoumenou Gavriil
Iliakaki
Dhimakópoulou Yerakari
Pavlou Koundhourioti
Town Hall
Hortatzi
Makariou
MUNICIPAL GARDENS K
Panaghía Ag. Konstandin
Haniá
Iráklion

pillars have been aged by time, but the water still flows. Turn right just before the fountain, along **Paleológou**, to the **Loggia** Ⓔ. This was once the city's meeting hall for the land-owners of the town, and was probably designed by Sanmicheli. Today it houses the Archaeological Museum's gift shop. A short distance further leads to views of the **old harbour** Ⓕ and the old **lighthouse** Ⓖ. Much of the harbour follows the line of the Venetian reconstruction work of 1626, although the external shoreline has shifted considerably since then and the present-day fish tavernas on the south side stand on what was once the south pier. The lighthouse was added by the Turks.

Map on page 150

The Venetian commander Alvise Rimondi gave his name to the Rimondi Fountain, which is sometimes spelt "Arimondi" – after someone mistakenly added his initial to his surname.

Mighty citadel

Because of flaws in the earlier fortifications, shown up by a Turkish attack in 1571, work began in 1573 on the **Fortezza** Ⓗ (Fortétsa), often described as the "city within the city", and still dominating the area. A visit is essential (Tues–Sun, 8am–8pm). The historic ambience is tangible, the view an experience. You look out, over the massive walls – the total circumference is 1,307 metres (over ¾ mile) – towards the city, the distant mountains and to expanses of countryside and sea. There are four pentagonal bastions, and the whole structure follows the natural contours of the hill. The passageway of the eastern main gate was the only link with the town, and was therefore built high and wide for access.

The small north and west gates of the fort were used for delivering supplies and led down to sea moorings. In the southern part of the fort are barracks, warehouses and administrative buildings, with powder and food stores in the northern part, but perhaps the most obvious feature nowadays is the mosque of Sultan Ibrahim near the centre of the edifice. This was originally the Venetian

BELOW: the mighty Fortezza dominates the city.

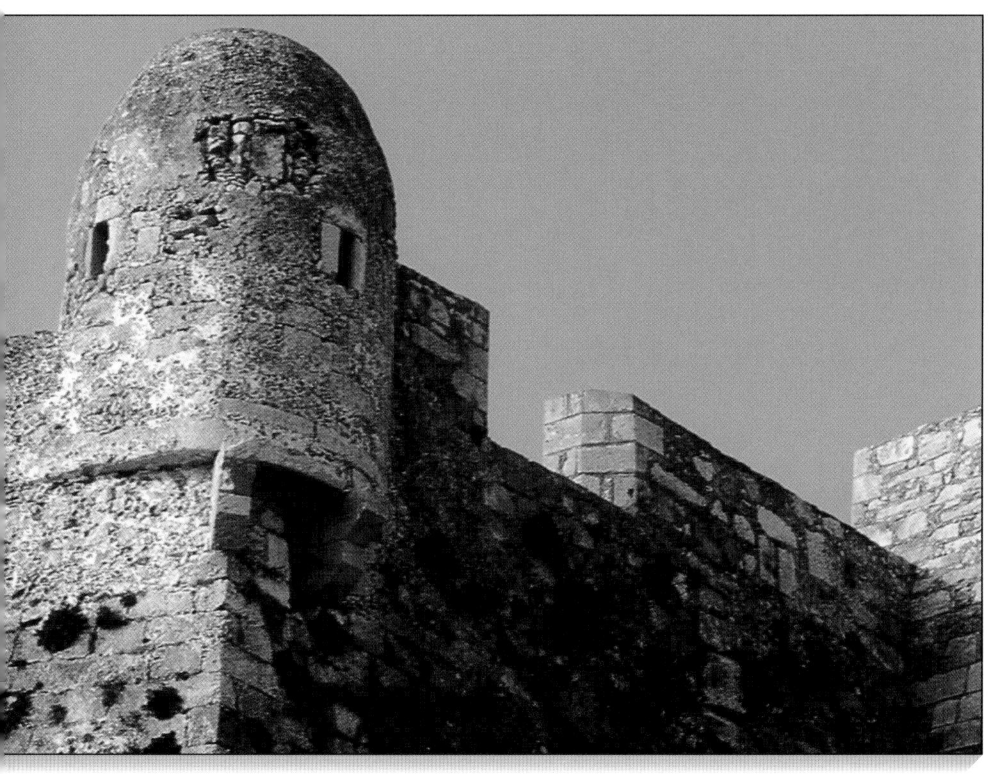

cathedral of St Nicholas, and was once surrounded by small private houses. The intention had been that all the citizens would move into the Fortezza and build their houses there inside the defences. However, once the immediate dangers had passed, the majority of residents of Réthymnon preferred to live outside, as before.

The harbour built for Réthymnon by the Venetians is prone to silting up and was inaccessible to large modern boats until recently. Now it is dredged constantly to allow a regular ferry service from Piraeus to dock here.

Opposite the entrance to the Fortezza is the **Archaeological Museum** ❶ (Tues–Sun, 8.30am–3pm). The building was erected by the Turks as an extra defence for the entrance, and was later used as a prison. Its interior has been modernised to provide cool, airy exhibition space for a collection of Minoan pottery and sarcophagi and many Roman finds, all from the Réthymnon area.

The Turkish takeover

When the attacking Turks appeared outside Réthymnon in 1646, the inhabitants hesitated for too long before retreating to the then unpopular Fortezza. Eventually, after a siege lasting 22 days, the city was taken and the residents were forced to take refuge within the castle. Bad weather prevented the relieving Venetian fleet from getting near. Three weeks later it became obvious that the fort too could not withstand the Turkish onslaught and it was surrendered to Huseïn Pasha.

Under Turkish control, Réthymnon retained its position as administrative centre, but its appearance was altered radically. The Christian Catholic churches were given minarets and new names, and converted into mosques, as was the Venetian Loggia. Even the Rimondi Fountain was given a traditional Turkish domed roof. The new rulers made the city look Ottoman, a clear statement of their dominance. They wanted to change the Greek Orthodox inhabitants of

BELOW: fresh fruit and vegetables in Réthymnon.

Crete in the same way, and they forced as many Cretans as they could to convert to Islam. Many did become Muslims, for pragmatic reasons, but others remained steadfast despite reprisals. As a warning to others, four of those who did resist were hanged in the square which is today known as Platía Tessáron Martýron (Square of the Four Martyrs).

Tension between the two groups came to a head in 1821, when the Turks unleashed a bloodbath among the Christians, partly in reprisal for the successes of the Greek Independence movement. By 1866, long after most of mainland Greece had attained self-rule, the Turks were still suppressing independence in Crete. Thousands of Resistance fighters, women and children took shelter behind the walls of the Monastery of Arkádhi. On the point of defeat, and determined not to fall into Turkish hands, they blew themselves up. It became a turning point in the outside world's perception of Crete, although it was another 32 years before Réthymnon was freed from Turkish rule. In 1897, Russian troops, as part of the Great Powers, occupied this part of Crete, and demolished most of the city's southern walls. Réthymnon suffered again, during World War II, when in May 1941 it was attacked by German paratroopers and became an occupied city. Bombing caused considerable damage to the Fortezza and elsewhere.

Along the seafront

From the old harbour you can stroll southeast along the broad seafront, lined with cafes, tavernas and palm-trees, or follow the parallel shopping street, Arkadhíou, one block inland. Near the end of Arkadhíou is the **Kara Musa Pasha mosque** ❶, once the monastery of St Barbara (Aghía Varvára).

As well as the buildings mentioned, the old city has many smaller delights to

Map on page 150

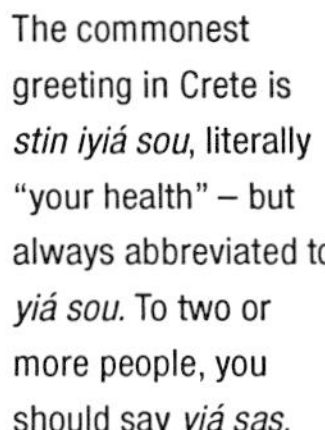

TIP

The commonest greeting in Crete is *stin iyiá sou*, literally "your health" – but always abbreviated to *yiá sou.* To two or more people, you should say *yiá sas.*

BELOW: handmade knives and worry-beads for sale.

Nougat made with Cretan almonds and thyme honey makes a tasty souvenir.

be found and enjoyed, in charming architectural fragments and features – particularly in house doorways. Return through the Porta Guora to Platía Tessáron Martýron and the **Cathedral**, the design of which is said to be based on that of the important Orthodox church of Evangelístria on the island of Tínos. The adjacent red belltower was built in 1889, with Russian Orthodox support, as a counterbalance to the recently erected minaret of the Nerandzes mosque.

In March or April, a flower festival is held in the shady **Municipal Gardens** **K**, which are just outside the old city and across the main road from Platía Tessáron Martýron. Within the park, which was the Turkish cemetery until the expulsion of the last Muslim population from the city in 1924, is a small and uninspiring zoo. Better known are the regular fruit and vegetable markets held opposite the park. The Wine Festival takes place in mid-July. During this lively festival, the low entrance fee will give you free wine for the evening, though you must provide your own glass. After that there is the Music Festival where dancers and groups from all over Greece, and further afield, come to perform. The proceeds of these events are used to pay for necessary maintenance work.

Even before the 1977 founding there of the University of Crete's Faculty of Philosophy, Réthymnon had the reputation of being an intellectual city, although the military dictatorship had provided severe constraints to public discussion. In the 14th and 15th centuries, many rich Cretans sent their offspring to Padua to study. The students returned with new concepts, bringing the ideas of the Italian Renaissance to Crete. The ensuing Cretan Renaissance, which followed in the 15th and 16th centuries, produced literature of a high standard, and the artists and intellectuals of Réthymnon played a prominent part. They included writers such as Yeórghios Hortátzis with *Erophíli*, Marínos Tzánes Bounialís with *The Cretan War*, and, probably the most admired of all, Vitzéntzos Kornáros with the verse drama *Erotókritos*. Emánuel Tzánes Bounialís, one of the most highly regarded of all icon painters, also came from Crete. While such cultural expressions were compatible with the ethos of the Venetian Empire, they were forcibly interrupted and suppressed for 230 years of Turkish rule. Réthymnon's outstanding literary figure in the 20th century was the historian Pandelís Preveläkis *(see page 73)*.

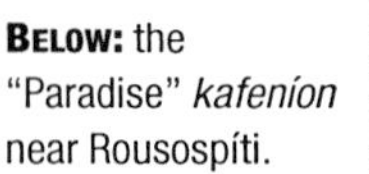

BELOW: the "Paradise" *kafeníon* near Rousospíti.

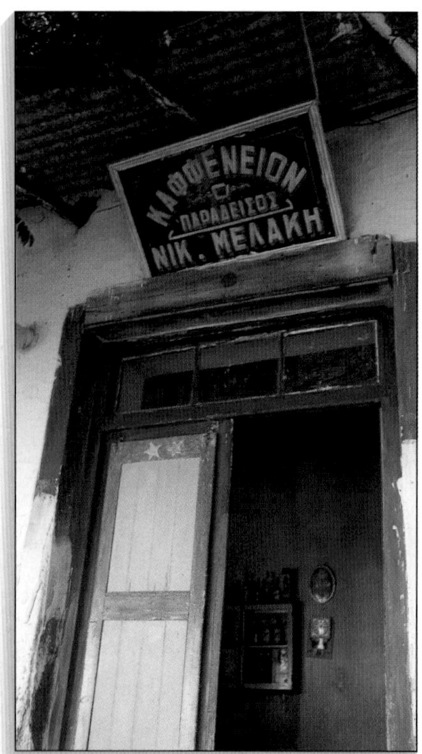

Touring the Réthymnon area

The city and immediate environs appear prosperous, but in fact Réthymnon province is the poorest of the four administrative regions in Crete. About a third of the city's population depends on earnings related to tourism, which is both seasonal and subject to wide fluctuation from year to year. But the real problem stems from the land itself. This is the most mountainous region in Crete, which makes life difficult indeed for the farmers. The Amári and Mylopótamos valleys are fertile and prosperous, but elsewhere olive growing, animal husbandry and milk production are not particularly profitable.

Heading south from Réthymnon, uphill above the motorway, you pass the dilapidated houses of the fortified settlement of **Mikrá Anóghia**. Seven kilometres (5 miles) south of Réthymnon, beyond the

Maps:
City 150
Area 155

village of **Aghía Iríni** ❷ (St Irene), you will see the ruins of a pre-Renaissance monastery of the same name. There is a basilica with three naves and a reservoir hewn out of the rocks.

The next village is **Rousospíti** ❸, where there are some well-preserved Venetian houses, a fountain and 15th-century frescoes in the church. From here, via the hamlet of **Kapedhianá**, you can set out southwards to climb the spring-studded **Mt Vrýsinas**. In a wonderful position, right on the summit at 858 metres (2,815 ft), is the church of **Ághios Pnévmatos** (Holy Spirit), where the celebration of Mass each Whitsun draws believers from all over the region. Clay idols were found here in 1938 which indicated that this was a peak-sanctuary in Minoan times. In 1973, further idols and votive offerings were found in clefts of the rocks.

The Greek word xénos *means both "foreigner" and "guest". As a visitor, you are both, and will automatically receive courtesy and hospitality.*

If you are interested in frescoes, return to Réthymnon via the village of **Chromonastíri** ❹. A couple of kilometres' walk to the northeast is the church of **Ághios Eftychíos** with 11th-century frescoes that are among the oldest in Crete, although unfortunately not well preserved.

The road descends from Chromonastíri through a gorge containing the fascinating ruined watermill village of **Mýli** ❺, abandoned because of earthquake and landslide danger. A further 5 km (3 miles) bring you down past the **Haleví monastery** (Moní Halevís) to coastal **Misíria**, an eastern tourist suburb of Réthymnon.

On the road to Amári, near the village of **Prasiés** ❻ with its old Venetian houses, there is the far larger **Prasianó Gorge**, although its 150-metre (492-ft) cliff walls are themselves dwarfed by the magnificent Samariá Gorge further west. You can only walk through the Prasianó Gorge in summer, as the gushing

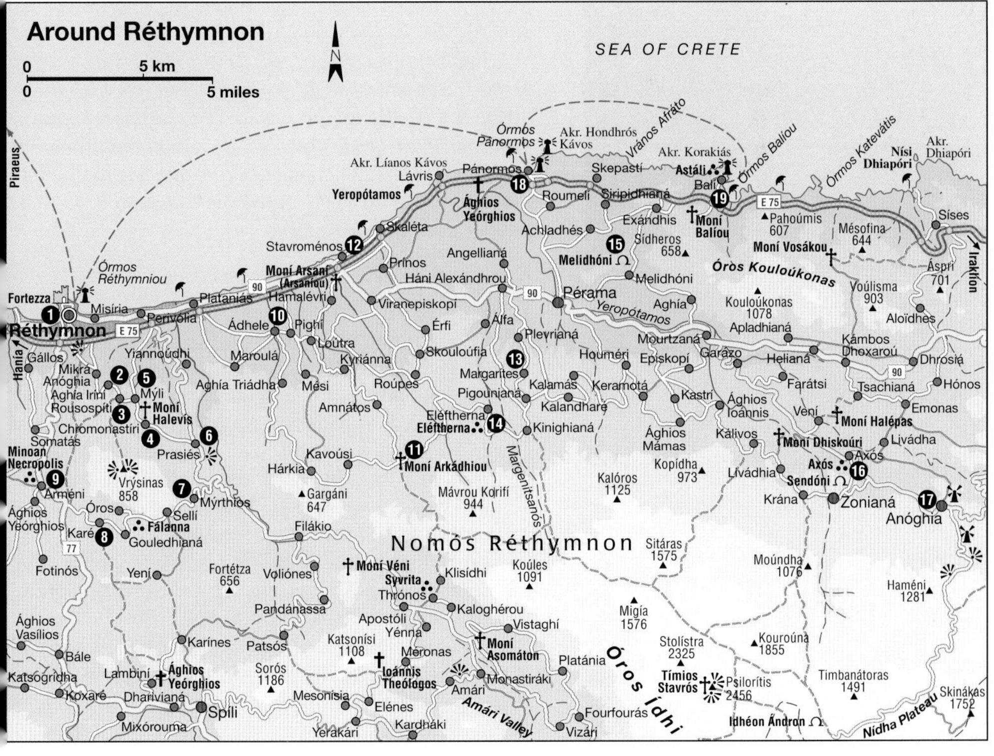

torrent of the River Plataniás fills it in winter and in spring. The walk through the gorge from the river mouth at Misíria takes around five hours. The beauty of the ravine lies in its lush vegetation – carob, plane trees and oleander grow here – as well as in its peaceful atmosphere, despite the proximity of Réthymnon. Until recently there has been little in the way of development around here, but a huge new dam and reservoir, under construction upstream, may change this landscape radically. The road, turning southwest to the village of **Mýrthios** ❼, where there are a couple of ruined 7th- and 8th-century houses, leads on to **Sellí** and **Karé** ❽, where you can see the remains of a basilica with a lovely mosaic floor. Then it's back north again to Réthymnon via **Arméni** ❾. You can also reach the **late Minoan necropolis** north of Arméni by the main south coast road from Réthymnon (8 km/5 miles) or on the minor road through the villages of Gállos and Somatás.

One of the most extraordinary finds in the graves at Arméni is a helmet made from boar's tusks.

The necropolis comprises more than 220 underground shaft tombs hacked out of the limestone. The larger ones can be reached by steps. Many of the finds unearthed in this cemetery, dated at between 1500 and 1200 BC, are displayed in the Archaeological Museum of Réthymnon. There are bones and clay sarcophagi, but also clay idols, ceramic pots, tools and weapons, often richly decorated with religious motifs and among some of the most valuable finds on the whole island. They also indicate the spread of Minoan culture – initially regarded as an eastern phenomenon – to the west of Crete.

One of the most impressive of the larger graves is probably that of a Minoan duke or king. The grand entrance area, 13 metres (43 ft) long, leads down 7 metres (23 ft) to the grave itself, which is about 4.5 sq metres (48 sq ft) in area. The scarabs on the steps are reminiscent of Egypt. Despite the technical capabilities of the time, the burial chamber is neither symmetrical nor, it would appear, designed according to any obvious geometrical principles.

BELOW: one of the 200-plus Minoan tombs at Arméni.

It has been suggested that the positioning of the graves had some kind of alignment, but it is extremely difficult to relate the graves to any kind of pattern or systematic arrangement. There must have been a settlement near such a large burial site, to provide the inhabitants for so many elaborate tombs, but this has not yet been located.

Monastery of martyrs

There are many little villages on the way to Arkádhi from Réthymnon, via **Ádhele** ❿ (birthplace of Konstantín Yiamboudhákis). They include **Pighí** – said to have Crete's largest olive plantation, with 1½ million trees – **Loútra**, **Kyriánna** and **Amnátos**, 340 metres (1,115 ft) above sea level in a fertile region of great contrast, with its slopes and steep-sided valleys. Here you will find colourful gorse bushes and olive trees, as well as cistus, wild roses and strawberry trees.

Twenty-three km (14 miles) from Réthymnon, the road reaches the **Monastery of Arkádhi** ⓫ (Moní Arkádhiou; daily 8am–8pm). Today it is a haven of peace, but that impression is at variance with its history. It has existed since at least the 14th century, but its appearance was completely restructured in the late 16th century, when it was the richest monastery in

Crete. The fortress-like enclosure extends for more than 5,200 sq metres (about 1¼ acres) and has entrances on all four sides.

The tragedy for which the monastery is famous took place on 8 and 9 November 1866. Earlier, in the May of that year, preparations were under way in Arkádhi for a rebellion. Since as many as 1,500 Cretans had met here, it was not surprising that the scheme was discovered by the Turks, and Abbot Gavriíl was ordered to disband the revolutionary committee. When he refused, the Turks attacked Réthymnon, whereupon about 700 women and children fled to Arkádhi to seek refuge. When Abbot Gavriíl ignored a second ultimatum, the 15,000 troops and 30 cannons of Mustafa Pasha attacked the monastery.

Despite only having a small cache of weapons at their disposal, the Cretans held off the first onslaught. But by the next morning the ammunition had run out. The survivors, mainly women and children, gathered in the powder storeroom. No one was to be taken alive by the Turks. Just as the Turks forced their way into the storeroom, someone – it is said to have been Konstantín Yiamboudhákis, with the agreement of Abbot Gavriíl – ignited the powder kegs. The explosion killed every Cretan in the storeroom, and many Turkish soldiers too.

Thirty-seven men survived the blast, either because they didn't make it to the storeroom, or because they disagreed with the suicide pact. They hid in the refectory, where they were later brutally murdered. Bullet marks and sword cuts can still be seen on the door of the refectory and on some of the tables. The monastery was set on fire.

In the ossuary just outside the monastery are laid the skulls of the victims, and an inscription honours the heroes. News of the tragedy of the Arkádhi Monastery was received with horror throughout the rest of Europe. The shock of the mass

Map on page 155

Legend has it that when Arkádhi Monastery exploded an infant girl was blown into a tree. She survived and later became a nun.

LEFT: a vaulted room within Arkádhi Monastery.
BELOW: the decorative facade of the monastery's church.

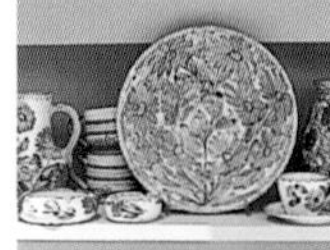

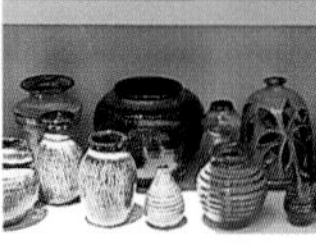

Pottery of all shapes, sizes and styles is for sale in Margarítes.

suicide and destruction of s[illegible] Now 8 November is the Na[tional] Day of [illegible] in memory of the [illegible] Arkádhi is the island's spiri[tual] centre.

The main entrance is in th[e west, rebuilt in 1872 after the damage of 1866 and] leads to the beautiful earl[y baroque facade of the church built in 1587. The] belltower – as elsewhere – [still shows traces of the 1866 fighting. The interior] of the church was refurbis[hed later. The altar wall was carved in 1927 out of] cypress wood and includes [parts of the original iconostasis. The west wing has] two storeys and the galler[ies have arched openings into the courtyard. The] monks' cells are almost exc[illegible] is the powder storeroom with a memorial tablet; in the north wing, are the guesthouse and refectory surrounded by kitchen rooms.

The museum is in the south wing. Apart from ecclesiastical manuscripts and religious relics, you can see memorabilia of 1866 and personal effects of the Abbot Gavriíl. You will also discover that the international arms trade began long ago – some of the Turks used Prussian firearms.

A potters' village

Go along the coast east from Réthymnon, and turn inland near the village of **Stavroménos ⓬**. About 5 km (3 miles) south of **Alexándhrou** is the pottery village of **Margarítes ⓭**, with workshops just above the village. Here, all kinds of pots are still handmade, in particular the large storage *píthi* which are known from Minoan times. There are ovens made from oil barrels, used for firing smaller objects, but next to these are the walled ovens, several metres high, for the *píthi*.

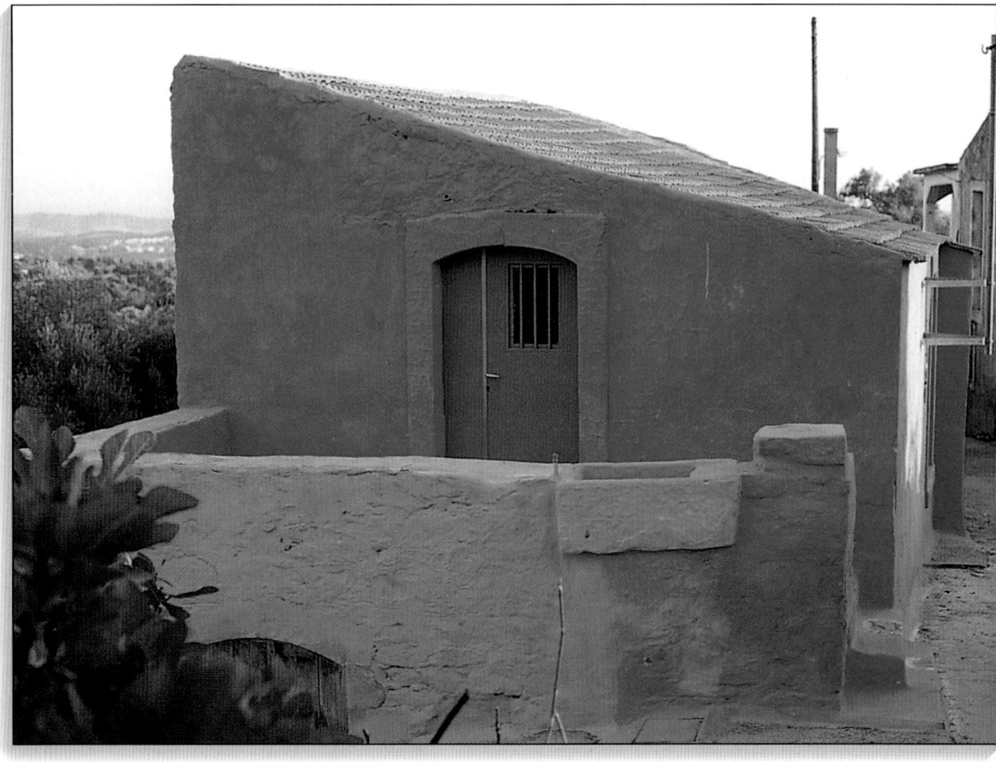

As you wander through the lovely village, stop to have a look in the former

BELOW: colourful house, Margarítes.

monastery church of **Ághios Ioánnis Prodhrómos** (John the Baptist). The architecture of the church and the well preserved 12th-century frescoes are most interesting. The nearby church of **Ághios Yeórghios** has a most expressive painting of the Virgin Mary.

Map on page 155

Situated to the southwest of Margarítes are the ruins of the Dorian city of **Eléftherna** ⓮, important right up to the Byzantine era, then destroyed by the Saracens. Remains spanning 1,500 years of use of the site include a 9th-century BC cemetery, a triangular-arched Hellenistic bridge, Roman cisterns and an early Christian basilica. Recent excavations below the acropolis to the east have revealed more of Hellenistic and Roman Eléftherna, including the remains of a fine Roman villa.

According to legend, the Melidhóni Cave was the home of Talos, a bronze giant who protected Crete by marching round the island three times a day, hurling rocks at unfriendly ships.

Return to Alexándhrou via Margarítes, and from there a wide but winding road leads east via Pérama towards Anóghia. Accessed by a side road 6 km (4 miles) from Pérama is the **Melidhóni Cave** ⓯ (Spílio Melidhóni), or Yéros Spílios, where long ago Hermes was worshipped in stalactite-filled hollows. However, the altar there now is a reminder of more recent events. In 1824 some 370 Cretans had used the cave for three months as a hide-out. But the Turks discovered this and lit a fire at the cave entrance. All those inside were asphyxiated by the smoke.

Axós ⓰, 21 km (13 miles) from Pérama, was founded according to myth by Oaxon, a grandson of Minos, but was certainly inhabited from late Minoan times. Ruins of an acropolis indicate a period of glory in the past, and later historical indications are reflected in various Byzantine churches. During the 13th century the inhabitants were driven out for their resistance to the Venetians. They moved 8 km (5 miles) southeast to settle at Anóghia, which had escaped destruction.

The village of **Anóghia** ⓱ is 790 metres (2,590 ft) up in the northern foothills of the Ida (Ídhi) Mountains, on the borderline between the fertile lowland valleys and the arid uplands only suitable for rough grazing. The Turks destroyed the village twice after insurrections, once in 1821 and again in 1866, but it was rebuilt each time. Ironically, two centuries before this, it had been the birthplace of the queen-mother of the Ottoman sultans Mustafa II and Ahmed III.

The cycle of resistance and destruction was repeated during World War II when, on 15 August 1944, following the abduction of the German General Kreipe, all the men and boys of the village were shot, and the place destroyed. Unimaginative postwar reconstruction in concrete left the village austere, but despite or perhaps because of that, the character of Anóghia remains unique. The people here are hospitable but cautious of outsiders, with a distinct, relict dialect. Speech, however, is quite unnecessary to appreciate their wonderful music and dance which is performed in their national costume.

BELOW: local pottery adorns a Margarítes house.

The heights of Ídhi

Anóghia is a good point from which to set off into the Ídhi (Ida) Mountains, also known as Psiloritis. There is a 21-km (13-mile) road, surfaced for the first two-thirds, to the **Nídha Plateau** at 1,360 metres (4,460 ft). In early summer the shepherds of Anóghia

gather up here with their flocks and make cheese in small huts; in winter the skiers of Iráklion pass en route to the ski centre. Above the western edge of the plateau, in a rugged, wild landscape, lies the **Ida Cave** (Idhéon Ándron), once home to the infant Zeus. In this extraordinary vault, currently closed for research, bronze shields, gold jewellery, hand drums, Minoan sealstones and many other objects have been found. An altar was discovered too, making this one of the oldest places of worship on Crete.

The landscape and climate – perhaps the people too – have hardly changed since mythical times. The shepherds still keep bees on the Nídha Plateau and live in stone summer-houses, called *mitáta*, built on the same principles as the Minoan dome graves. The plateau is a good starting place for longer walks into the Ídhi Mountains. **Tímios Stavrós** at 2,456 metres (8,056 ft) is the highest summit of the Psiloritis ridge, and the waymarked walk to the top from Nídha takes 3–5 hours. Once there, the view of the island from Crete's loftiest peak is magnificent. On 14 September you may find yourself with numerous locals making their way to the summit chapel for its name-day celebrations. A month later, however, the first snows of winter may be falling here.

If you are robbed in Crete (very unlikely) contact the Tourist Police: see Travel Tips for details.

East from Réthymnon

Réthymnon has been blessed with beautiful beaches. Nowadays this only means one thing – increasing numbers of new hotels and more mass tourism. As so often happens, this changes the character of a place. **Misíria**, **Plataniás**, **Ádhele**, **Stavroménos** and **Skaléta**, built alongside the longest sandy beach in Crete, stretching more than 15 km (9 miles) east of Réthymnon, have managed to preserve a friendly atmosphere, although little individuality. Unfortunately, the loggerhead turtles that once nested along this beach are rarely seen now.

BELOW: sunset on the sandy beach east of Réthymnon.

Behind Stavroménos the road leads through the delta of the Mylopótamos, a fertile area of intense fruit and vegetable cultivation. The pretty little village of **Pánormos** ⓲ has only a small beach and is thus unable to compete with its neighbours in the package tourism market. It has declined considerably since Byzantine times when it was a bustling port for ancient Eléftherna, but small remnants of its former days of glory are the ruins of the old harbour walls and parts of the 5th-century Byzantine basilica. Nothing survives of an enormous Venetian castle that once stood here.

To the east of Pánormos is the village of **Balí** ⓳, which is set around a series of small coves, and considered by some to be one of the most beautiful places in northern Crete. The motorway access and the tourist industry have robbed Balí of some of its isolated charm and it is on the way to becoming the Kritsá of fishing villages, although thankfully the small beaches discourage mass tourism. Experts think this was the site of another ancient town, Astáli, the port of the city of Axós.

The **Monastery of Ághios Ioánnis**, situated about five minutes west of the resort (by car) in the foothills of the Kouloúkonas mountain ridge, has some late frescoes and is well worth a visit. ❑

The Blessed Tree

Evidence shows that olive trees have been grown on Crete at least since Mycenaean times. Locals call it the blessed tree because everything from it is precious: the fruit, the leaves and the wood.

As one can make use of its components for food, soap and medicines, and the tree seems so tailor-made for man, it is small wonder that it has taken on such a religious significance. According to Homer, the gods rubbed themselves with perfumed olive oil.

The olive propagates easily. A new tree will grow from an olive stone or a piece of root. To "domesticate" the tree is more difficult. The wild tree must be three years old before it is transplanted to a convenient place for cultivation. The next few years are nothing but hard work for the farmer: grafting, transplanting, digging, fertilising, watering and protecting the tree from parasites. The trees, spaced 10–12 metres (33–40 ft) apart grow quickly, but it is still 15 to 18 years before the olive tree is profitable.

Different Mediterranean countries utilise varying methods of cultivation. In Spain three trunks are grown, but the Greeks prefer a single tall trunk. The tree flowers in April, and by May the first fruit is visible. It is a local belief that 20 May – Prophet Elijah's Day – is when the oil is formed.

Olive trees do need water, and in winter ditches are dug around the trees to catch every drop. In the hot Cretan summer, wells, ditches, pumps and hoses, all expensive ways of watering, have to be used. Olive groves have to be watered at least once a week. On watering days, the trees have absolute priority. Houses set in the groves have no running water, however hot the day.

In October, nets are spread out under the trees; from the beginning of November onwards, the ripe olives fall. Every three weeks the fruit is collected and sold in the market, or taken to the oil mill. Some types are harvested directly from the trees, using monstrous comb-like implements or compressed-air machines. The harvest varies from year to year. A good harvest exhausts the tree, so that in the following year it will not yield much.

As in all Mediterranean countries, people in Crete cook with plenty of olive oil. The top-grade oil is from the first pressing; middle-grade oil from the second hot pressing is used for soap, creams and fuel. Oil presses used to be enormous vats in which a round stone was turned by hand. Nowadays, the olives are pulverised by machine, and the oil extracted with hydraulic presses.

There are no black and green olives; green olives are simply unripe black ones. However, there are different kinds of olives, and they are quite easy to tell apart. The large, almost round Koroliá-Etonicholiá yield about 125 per kilo. The longer sort, Ladoliá, which are rich in oil, are about 1,000 to the kilo. There are some 500 other species of this *dicotyledonous Oleanceae* family, among them ash, jasmine, privet and, in a few corners of southern Europe and East Asia, forsythia and elder. Of all the souvenirs available on Crete, pure olive oil in tins is one of the finest. ❑

RIGHT: harvesting olives by striking the tree and collecting the fruit in nets on the ground.

SOUTH OF RÉTHYMNON

This journey through the centre of the island takes in fertile valleys and dramatic gorges, Byzantine churches and famous monasteries – and some delightful beach resorts

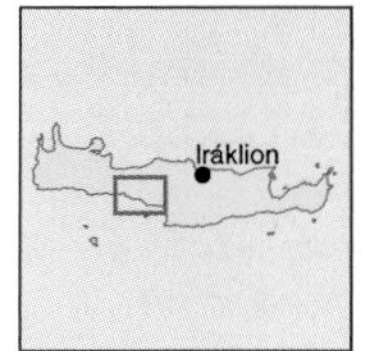

On the western outskirts of Réthymnon, join the Old National Road and head inland via **Atsipópoulo** and **Prinés**. Once the busy main north coast route, but now little used, this winding road takes you through an Arcadian countryside of small villages, chapels, streams, meadows and groves of oak trees. To reach the village of **Arghyroúpoli ❶**, turn off the road at **Episkopí**, 20 km (14 miles) from Réthymnon and head 6 km (4 miles) to the south. The village was built near the ruins of the Dorian settlement of Láppa, which was completely destroyed by the Romans. However, Láppa was rebuilt by Octavius, later Augustus Caesar, in recognition of the support of the city against Mark Antony.

Near Arghyroúpoli, locals discovered a burial site composed of five chambers. They believed it to have been the burial place of the five holy women who died as Christian martyrs during the Roman occupation, but archaeological research indicates that the grave is in fact older. Two children and two adults lie buried around a central room, which appears to have been used for sacrifices. The two statues of Artemis Vritómartis and Aphrodite found nearby are displayed in the Archaeological Museum of Réthymnon.

Arghyroúpoli, as a centre of resistance, must have incurred the particular wrath of the Turks, for in 1867 it was subjected to an especially brutal campaign of revenge. Houses were razed to the ground, orange and olive trees felled, and even the graves were opened and the remains of the dead strewn about.

Today, the village benefits from tourism and is relatively prosperous. It lies between two rivers, and maize, cereal and fruit trees grow well, while cattle graze in the green meadows. Just to the west, in a lush corner of the road to **Así Goniá**, are a remarkable line of springs, which once powered a series of watermills and which now supply Réthymnon. At the end of the surfaced road, 6 km (4 miles) beyond Arghyroúpoli, lies the village of **Myriokéfala ❷** at a height of 500 metres (1,640 ft), on an eastern outlier of the Lefká Óri (White Mountains). The Panaghía monastery, founded in the 11th century by Kyriánni the Hermit, was burned down by the Turks in 1821; only the church, with frescoes from the 11th and 12th centuries, withstood the fire.

Monasteries and gorges

If you take the main road south from Réthymnon, in 22 km (14 miles) you reach first the intersection near **Koxaré ❸** and then the magnificent **Kourtaliótis Gorge ❹**. The road goes through the gorge, and a stop here allows you to appreciate the depth and drama of this remarkable chasm. A flight of several hundred steps lead down to chapel of **Ághios Nikólaos** (St Nicholas), which commemorates nearby

PRECEDING PAGES: a goatherd tends his flock near Spíli. **LEFT:** the new Monastery of Píso Préveli. **BELOW:** Palm Beach, near Préveli.

Snails, a Cretan delicacy, are collected after a shower of rain.

moss-encrusted springs, known locally as the "Blessing of the Lord". The five holes from which the water pours forth are said to symbolise where the saint's fingers touched the rock when his companions were suffering from thirst. These springs never dry up, even during the hottest summer, evidence of the centuries of rainfall stored in the surrounding limestone.

Six kilometres (4 miles) to the south, just after a gorgeous Venetian-style bridge (1850–52) spanning the river, there is a dilapidated cluster of buildings by the modern road. Although it does not look impressive, it is worth a visit. Above one of the doors is a plaque dated 1795. There is a stable too, with room for more than 20 cattle, and quite a few smaller rooms, most of them reasonably well kept and some decorated with murals. A well house with a dome, dated 1865, had been constructed over a spring. On the church wall is a plaque commemorating the destruction of the settlement by the Turks in 1821. These ruins are the remains of the Lower Monastery of Préveli, **Káto Préveli** ❺ which was rebuilt, but destroyed again in 1867. Strategically, it appears badly positioned, and location was usually an important consideration for Cretan monastery-builders. It is possible that access was once far more difficult, or that too much reliance was placed on the gorge as a defensive barrier.

Whatever the explanation, the fact is that Upper Préveli, or **Píso Préveli** ❻, 3 km (2 miles) further along, was the more important structure, and this is what is generally meant by the **Monastery of Préveli** (daily, 9am–1pm, 5–7pm). Its location is quite superb, 170 metres (558 ft) above sea level, facing southeast. It is not known when the monastery was built, and since the old monastery church, where one might have expected to find clues, was abruptly demolished in 1835 when the new one was built, there seems little chance of discovering

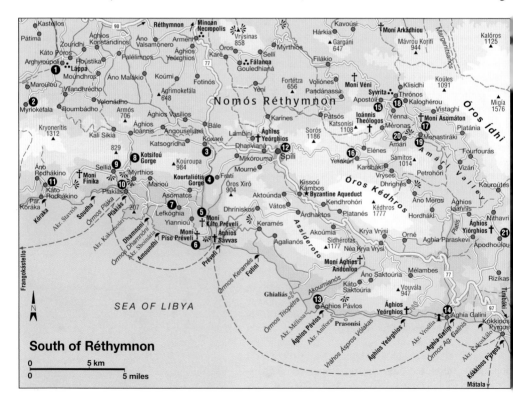

South of Réthymnon

0 5 km

0 5 miles

more now. Some chroniclers believe that circumstantial evidence points to a construction date of about 980.

Nowadays, there are few monks, but until the early 20th century Préveli was a centre of solidarity and national resistance, particularly during the years of oppression. Although not of the same political significance as Arkádhi (see page 156), it was far more important in economic terms to the area. In its heyday, the monastery was incredibly rich. Gifts, generous donations and transfers by means of which wealthy Cretans kept their possessions out of Turkish hands, brought huge areas of land under the protection of the monastery.

The olive harvest brought in about 130,000 litres (29,000 gallons) of oil per year. Then there were 80 tonnes of cereals, 120 tonnes of carob, as well as large amounts of fruit and vegetables. About 2,000 goats and sheep grazed in the meadows, and there were pigs, cattle and mules. In addition, the monks kept bees and silkworms. Préveli was like a prosperous estate which invested in community projects and social progress. Churches, schools, hospitals and many other establishments were founded or aided with the money from Préveli, so it is not surprising that there are valuable icons here, as well as an interesting library.

The most important item in the monastery is a **gilded cross** set with precious stones, in which is kept what is reputed to be a splinter of the True Cross of Jesus. It was a donation of the former abbot (1755–75), Efraím Prévelis, a direct descendant of the presumed founder of the monastery, Akákios Prévelis. The cross is said to heal eye disorders, and is even supposed to have restored sight to the blind. There are many tales concerning the powers of this miraculous cross. One relates to the German occupation during World War II, when the monastery hid many Britons and New Zealanders and assisted their escape in

Out of courtesy, you should not enter an Orthodox church or monastery wearing shorts. Women should also keep their shoulders and upper arms covered. No head covering is required.

BELOW: the mountain road from Préveli to Plakiás.

Palm Beach, below Préveli, is a delightful spot that gets uncomfortably crowded in summer. It was from here that the Allied troops who sought refuge at the monastery were eventually evacuated by submarine.

Allied ships. As punishment for these and Resistance activities centred on Préveli, the Germans wanted to weaken the economic power of the monastery. They robbed the monastery of its domestic animals, cereal crops and treasures – including the miraculous cross. Three times the Germans attempted to take the cross to Germany, but each time they loaded it on an aircraft, the engines failed to start, even though they had been in perfect working order. In the end the Germans gave up, and returned the cross to where it belonged.

In the lowest part of the monastery yard is a fountain, dated 1701, with an anagrammatic inscription meaning: wash not only your face, but also your sins. Beside it is a small museum containing a collection of ecclesiastical and historic items, including the portrait and medieval-looking firearms of a warrior-priest from the monastery, who in fact died in the early 20th century.

A little further eastwards is the small beach of Préveli. As you come away from the monastery, turn right into a side road which takes you 1km (½ mile) down to a viewpoint overlooking the beach. Behind the beach is a deep gorge, containing the palm-fringed canal-like lagoon of the Megapótamos River. A stony zigzag path, steep in places, leads down from the viewpoint to the beach.

Call of the wild

In addition to the Monastery of Préveli, there are interesting villages south of the mountains in the district of **Ághios Vasílios** (St Basil). They can be reached either on the main road from Koxaré by way of the agricultural village of **Lefkóghia** ❼, below its sugar-cone mountain Tímeos Stavrós, or through **Angouselianá** and the **Kotsifoú Gorge** ❽ – a botanist's and birdwatcher's delight. South of this dramatic windswept gorge are the villages of **Selliá** ❾ at

BELOW: Selliá, overlooking the Libyan Sea.

an altitude of 300 metres (984 ft) and its twin, **Mýrthios**, slightly lower across the valley. To the northwest, Selliá is protected by the massif of **Kryonerítis**, and to the south, olive groves stretch away down to the Libyan Sea.

The better-known **Plakiás ❿**, a former fishing village, belongs to the same district. Its mild climate, wonderful beaches, mountain backdrop and proximity to the gorges of Kotsifoú and Kourtaliótis, make it a worthwhile stop on any itinerary. Plakiás is a typical example of the expansion that can happen when a place turns to tourism as its main source of revenue. It used to be an insignificant little settlement, but due to its natural beauty and huge beach, it has experienced an economic upsurge leading to a surfeit of accommodation and tavernas.

Further west, almost in the rural district of Sfakiá, renowned for its lawless and independent fighting men, are the villages of **Áno Rodhákino** and **Káto Rodhákino ⓫**. Long ago the feuding families Papadhópouli and Páteri lived here. For years, violent acts of revenge perpetrated by these families on each other in their long-drawn-out vendetta led to the deaths of so many of them that they finally buried the hatchet and made peace. Much has been written about the islanders' violent characters and thirst for vengeance, but here is one example of Cretan pragmatism. Nowadays, most visitors head south from the village, on the side road to **Kóraka** beach – but continue beyond the taverna and headland to find one of Crete's largest, and sometimes emptiest, beaches.

East of Koxaré

Spíli ⓬, 29 km (20 miles) southeast of Réthymnon, is a lovely place in a gorgeous position, sheltered by the craggy mass of Mt Kédhros. Tourists are always passing through, usually to or from Aghía Galíni, Mátala or Phaestos. Yet Spíli has

The countryside around Plakiás is the most botanically rich coastal region of Crete, with a huge variety of plants, and one of the best areas for walkers.

BELOW: Spíli's famous fountains.

To use a phone booth with a blue band, you need to buy a tilekárta *(phone card), available from kiosks.*

BELOW: Aghía Galíni harbour.

far more to offer than just the refreshing spring water from the row of Venetian lion-headed fountains that are the popular attraction of the town. The old churches, comfortable tavernas and old-fashioned shops should not be overlooked. Stop and sit a while under the plane trees. From Spíli, a surfaced road leads over the plateau to the east, where fields are covered with red tulips in spring, to **Yerakári** and the **Amári Valley**.

Head 16 km (10 miles) south from Spíli, and turn right beyond **Krýa Vrýsi** for the road to **Saktoúria**. Continue through the village to **Ághios Pávlos** ⓭ above the beautiful beach at **Akrotíri Mélissa**. Ághios Pávlos itself is a collection of fish tavernas, overlooking the sea and a popular lunch or dinner venue for the city folk of Réthymnon.

Back near Krýa Vrýsi, and another 11-km (7-mile) drive brings you to **Aghía Galíni** ⓮ ("Holy Serenity"). Arriving in the evening, which is the loveliest time, is like wandering into a dreamland. Terraces of coloured lights on the steep hillsides around seem to hang in the velvet sky. From the breakwater in the harbour one can see the lights of Mátala twinkling in the distance over the dusky water.

The harbour car park is usually packed and the narrow pedestrian streets are crowded with people. It doesn't sound very cosy, but don't be put off by first impressions – the centre of Aghía Galíni can be both delightful and exhilarating. It is obvious what visitors of all age groups come here for – sun, sea, sand and scenery but above all, a great social life. The inhabitants of the village are rumoured to have been successful smugglers before they turned their attention to tourism. It may be true, for there is no denying a distinct and charming rakishness in their manner. Aghía Galíni is a good place to party.

The Valley of Amári

The incomparably lush **Amári Valley**, 32 km (22 miles) from Réthymnon, is reached by turning south at Misíria and continuing through Prasiés. Even if you have resisted all the other cultural points of interest, you should not exclude this delightful area, which lies between the mountains Psiloritis and Kédhros. In the countryside around the little hillside villages, it has many frescoed Byzantine chapels and churches. The main agricultural crops are olives and fruit, particularly cherries, and trees alternate with a profusion of wild spring flowers, including wild chrysanthemums, pink gladioli and blue chicory. You will enter the valley through **Apostóli** ⓯, where you should pause awhile to admire the 14th-century church and, from its terrace, the splendid views of the Amári Valley, with the Ida Mountains to the east and Mt Kédhros to the south.

The Asomáton Monastery, now a college, is not officially open to the public – but you will not be challenged if you stroll in to have a look around.

A little further on is the hamlet of **Aghía Fotiní**, which offers a view of the whole valley and a choice of routes to **Níthavri.** The roads go either side of **Mount Samítos**, which stands 1,014 metres (3,326 ft) high right in the middle of the valley. Turn right at Aghía Fotiní for the route round the western side, below the fortress of **Méronas**, to **Yerakári** ⓰. This village was another resistance centre in both the 19th and 20th centuries and was destroyed by the Germans in 1944. The post war concrete houses and memorial lend a melancholy air to the place and the attitude to tourists can be cautious, leaving one to ponder one's presence there. It takes from four to five hours to climb 1,777-metre (5,829-ft) **Mt Kédhros** from Yerakári, from Áno Méros to the south, or from Krýa Vrýsi on the far side.

The left turn at the Aghía Fotiní junction takes you east 5 km (3 miles) to the 17th-century buildings of the **Asomáton Monastery** ⓱ (Moní Asomáton), which now house an agricultural college. Between the two, a side road leads northeast up to the village of **Thrónos** ⓲, where the 14th-century Panaghía Church – built on top of a basilica 800 years older – has well-preserved frescoes. Above the village are the ruined walls of the Greco-Roman Syvrita, a settlement for which Aghía Galíni was the port.

Beyond Asomáton, close to **Monastiráki** ⓳, a Minoan palatial settlement and religious site of around 1950–1700 BC was discovered. The storage jars from this excavation are exhibited in the Archaeological Museum of Réthymnon. From here you can divert to **Amári** ⓴, an exceptionally pretty village, with the 13th-century frescoed church of Aghía Ánna. The village is at least 1,500 years old, and was the main centre of the district, even in Venetian times.

From Monastiráki, continue for 14 km (9 miles) through the villages of **Fourfourás** and **Kouroútes**, to Níthavri, from where the road circles back 31 km (21 miles) to Apostóli. Alternatively proceed south to **Apodhoúlou** ㉑, where you can see 13th-century frescoes in the Ághios Yeórghios Church. A Minoan building complex (Tues–Sun, 8.30am–3pm) of around 1950–1700 BC, and some tholos tombs dating from 1380–1200 BC, have been excavated near the village. Four sarcophagi are housed in the Archaeological Museum of Réthymnon. Beyond Apodhoúlou are roads to Aghía Galíni or Zarós. ❑

Below: the ancient village of Amári.

AN ISLAND IN RIOTOUS BLOOM

The Cretan landscape is at its most abundant in spring and early summer, when every hillside and valley bursts into glorious colour

A mild winter climate, a broad variety of habitats, the island's long isolation, and the relative proximity of Asia and Africa have all been factors in the evolution of Crete's unique flora. April is the prime period to see botanical Crete performing at its best. The flowering season produces waves of colour, starting with a predominance of yellow and white, followed, as the island heats up, by shades of the reds, purples and blues that attract bees and butterflies. Most plants are dormant during the scorching summer then, after the first rains, the sparser autumn flowering is a less co-ordinated mixture of purple, pink, yellow and white, combined with the fresh green of seedlings and new shoots.

With almost one in 10 plant species here being island endemics, found wild only on Crete, first-time visitors will find much that is new to them. Many only see the coastal areas around their resort, plus a few well-worn inland tourist routes, but the interior has much to offer. A short stroll down that unmarked dirt track, or into that unremarkable valley, may reveal something completely new. Even experts who have devoted a lifetime to Crete's now well-studied flora add a remarkable average of six species each year to the island's plant list.

In contrast to the enthusiasm of foreign visitors, Cretans show a lack of interest in their native flowers, although wild anemones (above) are picked for local markets. For their gardens, they tend to prefer introduced subtropical plants.

▷ **BEE IMITATOR**
Of Crete's 67 orchids, *Ophrys heldreichii* is one of the largest of those that mimic insects for pollination.

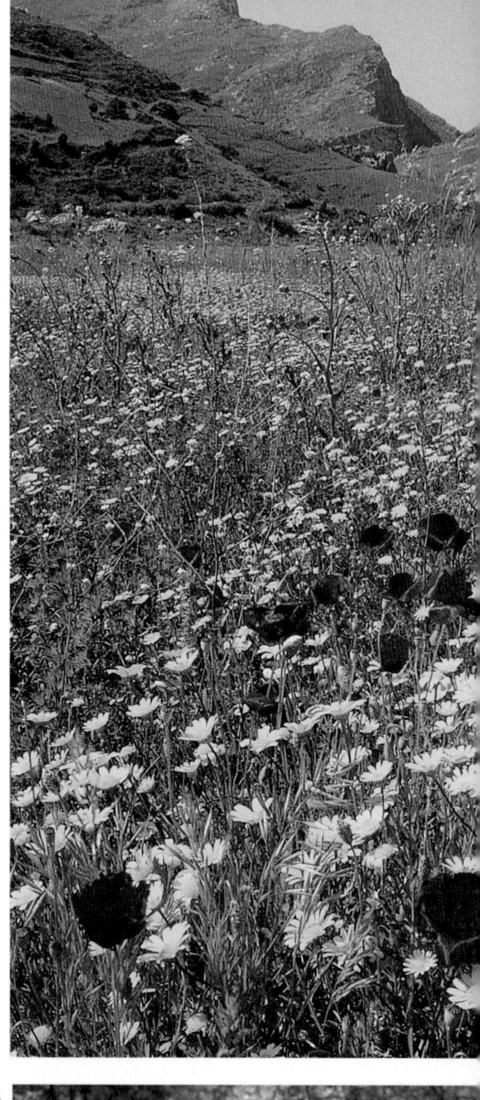

△ **FIELDS OF GOLD**
Corn marigolds and poppies light up a field below the Ida Mountains. Crete in April is a treasury of colour, whether on remote hillsides or a city waste ground.

◁ **LOCAL SPECIALITY**
Found nowhere else but on Cretan walls and cliffs, and with no close relations, *Petromarula pinnata* has spikes of star-shaped blue, white or grey flowers.

△ **GORGE-OUS**
The golden drop, *Onosma erecta*, is a jewel of the mountains, particularly on the rocks and screes of the upper Samariá Gorge.

▽ **ROADSIDE PINK**
Confined to the island but plentiful here, Cretan ebony forms swathes of pink on hilly slopes, and often colonises road cuttings.

▽ **EARLY STARTER**
The delicate Cretan iris flowers on hillsides in early spring, before most tourists arrive. Later, the clumps of tiny leaves are easily mistaken for grass.

▽ **EDIBLE TULIP**
One of Crete's five species of wild tulip, *Tulipa saxatilis* grows around upland rocks and stream banks. Its bulbs were a source of food for the island's early settlers.

A NATURAL HERB GARDEN

Cretan dittany (above) is perhaps the most famous of the island's medicinal herbs, growing wild on inaccessible cliffs, though nowadays cultivated commercially in Lassíthi olive groves. It was believed to cure wounds, particularly those from arrows, and injured wild goats were said to seek it out. Recommended by several classical writers for various purposes, it was one of Crete's earliest recorded exports.

The island's arid climate produces a surfeit of other small but strongly aromatic wild herbs, including sages and *malótira* from which mountain teas are made. Ironically, their strong flavours and scents evolved originally to discourage grazing animals, but have attracted the attention of the human palate. Other native herbs such as thyme, savory, fennel, and several types of marjoram are popular both with local cooks and with bees when flowering. A variety of wild garlics are used in the same way as shop-bought bulbs. In Crete's more sheltered, humid valleys grow bay trees, and their fragrant, spicy leaves are much gathered for drying.

ΠΑΡΟΔΟΣ 1:
Χ ΜΙΧ. ΝΤΑΛΙΑΝΗ

HANIÁ AND SURROUNDINGS

Crete's second city – until recently its capital – has the intimacy and charm of a village. The surrounding region is rich in reminders of Crete's history, ancient and modern

Maps: City 178 Area 182

As visually attractive as it is historically fascinating, **Haniá** ❶ is an evocative town. There is the theatrical backdrop of the Lefká Óri (White Mountains), snow-covered for half the year, rising to over 2,450 metres (8,000 ft); the sapphire Sea of Crete lapping against the harbour and foreshore; the subtle earth colours of painted walls and woodwork – terracottas, ochres, washed blues and faded apricot; the murmur of Cretans at the outdoor cafes with the constant clicking of their worry beads; and the aromas – a blend of herbs, spices, cheeses, freshly baked bread and the flowers.

Haniá (Chaniá, Khaniá, etc) has been home to many differing races throughout its 6,000 years of existence. There are few places in the world that can claim such a long period of continuous occupation by man. In and around the city, the influences of Neolithic, Minoan, Mycenaean, Dorian, Classical and Hellenistic Greek, Roman, Byzantine, Arab, Venetian, Turkish and modern Greek are exposed like a slice of multi-layered history cake; a true kaleidoscope of architectural styles and building techniques.

Though Iráklion is the present-day capital of Crete, Haniá enjoyed the honour from 1849 to 1971. Today it is the island's second largest city with a population of 70,000. Surprisingly, it remains relatively unspoilt by the advent of foreign holiday-makers. Today, the real town is easily discernable beneath the veneer of recent tourism. You only have to look beyond the colourful awnings of the harbourside tavernas and the adjacent souvenir shops to see what Haniá is really all about.

PRECEDING PAGES: Haniá, the "Venice of the East".
LEFT: one of the city's two surviving minarets.
BELOW: Haniá is renowned for leather goods.

A walking tour

Your tour of the town should begin with a visit to the Tourist Information Office (EOT) located at Kriári 40, near **Platía 1866** (the square commemorates the uprisings against the Turks during their 253 years of occupation of this city and the great revolt of that year). Here you can obtain a free map of the town and other useful literature regarding accommodation, transport, excursions, forthcoming events, etc.

The legendary founder of the city was King Kydon, the son of Queen Pasiphae (wife of King Minos) and one of her extra-marital lovers, Apollo. The oldest part of the original town of Kydonía is contained on the acropolis – known as the area of **Kastélli** Ⓐ (the Venetian word for castle). On this hill is evidence of Neolithic man from 4,000 BC. In Kaneváro Street a large excavation of the Minoan settlement has been left exposed. The Minoan houses here date from 1700 BC, all destroyed in 1450 BC by the volcanic eruption of Santoríni and some rebuilt around 1200 BC.

The **defensive walls** around this inner city are staggering. The Byzantines lost the island to Arab pirates

When the Muslim Egyptians rebuilt the original lighthouse they did so in the form of a minaret.

in AD 824 and did not regain it again until 961. They were so afraid of losing the city to the Saracens again that they seem to have torn down every remaining Greek and Roman building and used the materials to enhance the original city wall. Marble and limestone column drums, blocks of stone from palaces, temples, large administrative buildings and the like are all to be seen. In 1941, these walls were still intact with their towers, battlements, gates and so on: the ruins you see today are the result of the German bombing in May of that year.

The Venetians made Haniá a centre for the western end of the island and, with the building of many fine private and public structures, the town became known as the "Venice of the East". All that remains of the grand 17th-century **Rector's Palace** B is the Treasury House and the archives section, with a very interesting doorway dated 1624.

The Venetians had great plans to make the harbour the finest docks and port in the eastern Mediterranean. But no matter how much they dredged the harbour, it was never really successful. On top of the natural barrier reef, they built an immense breakwater – a harbour wall/mole – and at the end erected a lighthouse. The present structure is much more recent, dating from 1824–32 when Egyptian troops were here as part of the Ottoman Empire.

The harbour had a capacity for 40 galleys and the infrastructure to support all this naval activity was the construction of 20 colossal **Arsenáli** (or **Neória**) C – dry docks or shipbuilding yards. Unfortunately only nine of these immense, barrel-vaulted structures survived the blitz of 1941.

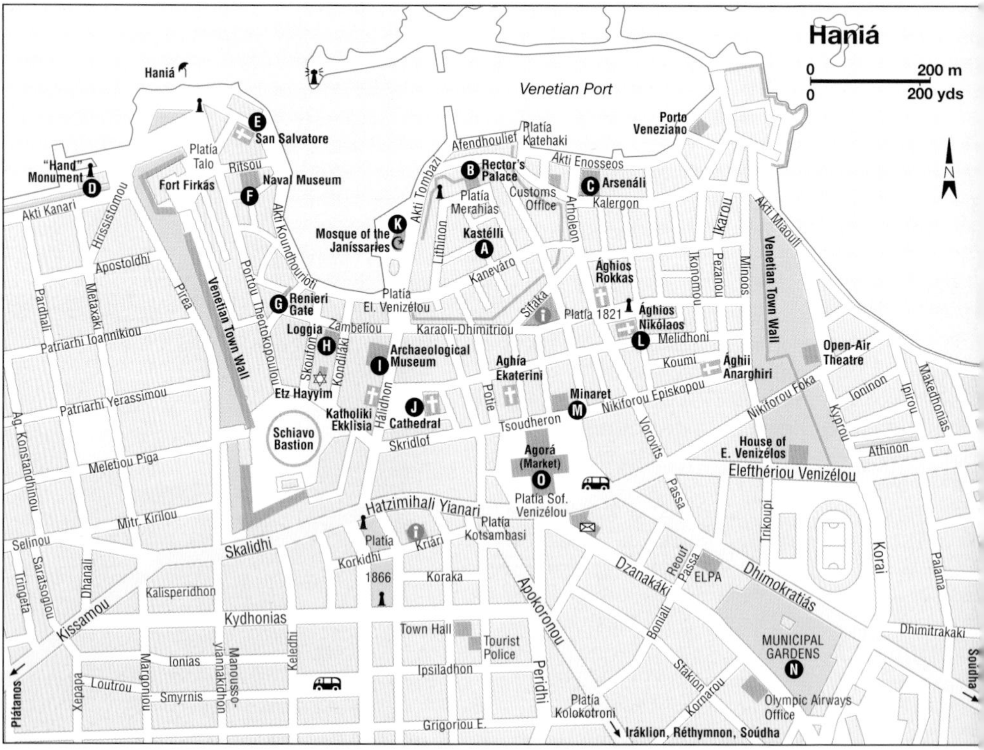

The huge **fortifications** enclosing the Old Town were designed in 1536 by the renowned Venetian military engineer/architect Michele Sanmicheli and were completed 12 years later using a regular labour force of 30,000 men. Enhanced by four great bastions, these defences epitomise the height of Renaissance military architecture, displaying great technical ingenuity and geometric beauty.

The Venetians considered the town to be impregnable, but when the Turks invaded Crete in 1645, Haniá surrendered after a siege of only 57 days. The best preserved sections of the walls and the moat are on the western side, next to the **"Hand" Monument** D below the Xenía Hotel and the San Dometrio bastion which forms part of the **Firkás** fortress. Adjacent to the bastion which is still in ruins from the Turkish bombardment, is the recently restored church of **San Salvatore** E (Tues–Sun 8.30am–2pm). Converted into a mosque in 1645 by Hassan Aga, it was originally the chapel of the Venetian Monastery. The church has been superbly renovated and now houses a beautifully displayed collection of Byzantine and post-Byzantine art from the *nomós* (province) of Haniá.

After 2,000 years of subjugation by foreign powers, *Énosis* (Union with the Motherland) was eventually achieved on 1 December 1913 when the Greek flag was raised for the first time on Crete by King Constantine (Konstantínos) and Elefthérios Venizélos. This was in Haniá, at the flagpole in the fortress known as the Firkás, which makes this a much revered spot. The exquisite models in the **Naval Museum** F (daily 10am–4pm, closed public holidays) adjoining the Firkas clearly illustrate the extent of Venetian engineering achievements. The museum also contains a display of maritime history, together with an interesting and highly emotive exhibition of the "Battle for Crete" in May 1941.

South of here, in the **Topanás** area (Turkish for gunpowder or cannons), there are still some excellent Venetian patrician houses, the **Renieri Gate** G (1609) and many examples of the later Turkish architectural features such as the projecting timber upper storeys and balconies. Probably once the finest of the

Map on page 178

The "Hand" Monument is a moving piece of modern sculpture commemorating a disaster in 1966 when the Piraeus ferry went down and all those aboard were drowned.

BELOW: the moon rises over the harbour.

The central part of the Mosque of the Janissaries is Crete's oldest Ottoman building.

Venetian buildings was the **Loggia** (H) or "Gentleman's Club" in Zambelíou, with its dressed stonework around window and door openings and its motto and coat of arms.

Considered to be the most outstanding example of Venetian ecclesiastical architecture on the island, is the monastery church of **St Francis** (San Francesco), the largest of the 23 churches built by the Venetians in Haniá. This is located in Hálidhon Street and now houses the **Archaeological Museum** (I) (Tues–Sun 8.30am–3pm). This building was also a mosque in the Turkish period and there is a very fine example of an octagonal Turkish fountain house in the garden. Directly opposite the museum is Haniá's **cathedral** (J), the Church of the Trimártyri.

When the Turks captured Haniá in 1645, the first structure they erected was the multi-domed **Mosque of the Janíssaries** (K) (or Djamissi Mosque or Shore Mosque) on the most prominent spot on the harbour. The central large dome is the oldest Ottoman building in Crete. The smaller domes were added in the neoclassical period (1880s) and there was a minaret at the side which disappeared in the bombing of 1941. Due south of the mosque is **Platía El. Venizélou**, an expanse of cafés, restaurants and tourist shops formerly known as Platía Sindriváni (Turkish for "fountain"). One of the fountains still exists, lost behind the tables and cushioned chairs of the Cafe Remezo.

The largest of the two remaining minarets in the town has been completely rebuilt and is attached to the church of **Ághios Nikólaos** (L) (San Nicolo) located in Splántzia, which was once the completely Turkish part of the town. In **Platía 1821** (named to commemorate another of the great Cretan uprisings), the Turks hanged the Bishop of Kísamos and several other clerics from the nearby plane tree, under which there is a memorial tablet. The other **minaret** (M), once part of the Aga Mosque, is just off Dhaskologhiánni Street, and still in good condition despite a fire. The tower is topped with the crescent moon and retains its balcony where the *muezzin* would call the faithful to prayer.

BELOW: plenty of rooms to let in the old town.

Because the Koran places such emphasis on personal hygiene and condemns any form of alcohol, drinking fountains and *hammans* (steam baths) featured importantly in Turkish life in the city. Three of the Turkish bath-houses still exist, but none of them are operational today. The one in Zambelíou contains some elegant round-headed windows through which can be seen the domes and the vent holes. Next door to it is the Tamam taverna, which was the original cold plunge pool. The other examples of steam baths are the recently restored complex situated opposite the Archaeological Museum and the one above road level in Katrí.

In a lane just off Kondiláki Street is the **Etz Hayyim Synagogue**. The portion of the building to the left-hand side was originally a Venetian church, given to the Jews by the Turks to be used as their place of worship. It is one of the oldest surviving synagogues in Greece, along with that of Rhodes. The area is known as the Evraikí and was the Jewish quarter until 1944 when the Nazis deported the entire Jewish population. The synagogue has been beautifully restored in recent years due to the untiring energy and perseverance of Nicholas Stavroulákis-Hannan.

The shady and pleasant **municipal gardens** Ⓝ, between the streets of Dzanakáki and Andréa Papandréou (Dhimokratiás), were originally laid out in 1870 by a Turkish Pasha. They now incorporate a tiny zoo, a playground, a cafe and an open-air cinema. Close to this area are the **Historical Archives** (Mon–Fri 9am–1pm) on Sfakianáki Street and the **War Museum** (Tues–Sat 9.30am–1pm) on Dzanakáki Street.

The large, neoclassical style **Agorá** Ⓞ is a Market Hall dating from 1913 (it was opened by Elefthérios Venizélos). Its cruciform shape is modelled on the market hall in Marseille, France. The covered lofty space with its clerestory windows provides a cool and airy atmosphere, but the scents of aromatic herbs, cheeses, meats, vegetables, nuts, fish, oils, wines and other products combine to create a heady experience. In the small eating places, or *estiatória*, you can sit with the locals and sample the delicacies of traditional Cretan cuisine.

Nearby is **Odhós Skridlof**, Haniá's "Leather Lane"or *Stivanádhika*, named after the cobblers who make the *stivánia,* the traditional tall Cretan boots. Today, it is still possible to order a pair of boots made to measure and watch the cobbler at his work. On Saturdays there is a colourful open-air market in **Mínoos Street** where a vast assembly of farmers display a wide range of local produce.

The beaches

The *Nomós* (county) of Haniá has many wonderful beaches and those nearest to the town itself are generally to the west. These are clean and sandy and you can relax beside a refreshing, clear sea in the company of both locals and visitors.

Map on page 178

Canea is second Citie of Crete, called auncientlу Cydon, being exceedingly populous, well walled, and fortified with Bulwarkes. It hath a large Castle, containing ninety seaven pallaces in which the Rector and other Venetian Gentlemen dwell.

– SCOTTISH TRAVELLER WILLIAM LITHGOW, 1613

BELOW: wedding cakes for sale in Haniá market.

The town beach at **Néa Hóra** is only a 10-minute walk away, west from the Venetian harbour. This provides safe swimming and plenty of watersports with speedboats, jet-skis and canoes, as well as sunbeds, umbrellas and the like. One of your best choices in the immediate vicinity is 5 km (3 miles) away at **Chrissí Aktí** (Golden Coast), a large expanse of sand that is never overcrowded.

Beyond this headland is the promontory of **Ághii Apóstoli** and then a long curve of beach with sections named after local cafés or restaurants, such as Óasis and Gláros. It ends up at **Kalamáki**, which is sometimes crowded but has probably the best swimming in the area, with a gently sloping, sandy bottom and a rocky reef that breaks up the stronger waves.

Akrotíri Pensinsula is tautological: the word akrotíri *(abbreviated to Ak. on maps) actually means "peninsula".*

Zorba's Peninsula

The **Akrotíri Peninsula** lies northeast of Haniá and is best explored by car or bike, as the local bus service is somewhat minimal. (If the bus is your only option, you should check at the central bus station in Haniá, KTEL, for the current timetable.) The road to the airport climbs a hill and at the top you turn left to the **Venizélos Graves ❷**. On this historic spot are buried Elefthérios Venizélos (1864–1936) and his son Sofoklís (1896–1964). It was here in 1897 that the Revolutionary Committee, under the leadership of Venizélos, met in the **Monastery of Profítis Ilías** (Prophet Elijah) and hoisted the Flag of Independence. However, it was not until 1913 that the demand for *Énosis* was granted. All that remains of the monastery today is the small church. The view overlooking Haniá, the island of Ághii Theódhori and the Rodhopoú Peninsula is spectacular.

Just down the road (2 km/1¼ miles) towards the airport is a turning to the village of **Korakiés ❸**, where the **Convent of Ághios Ioánnis Pródhromos** (daily

BELOW: the town beach at Néa Hóra.

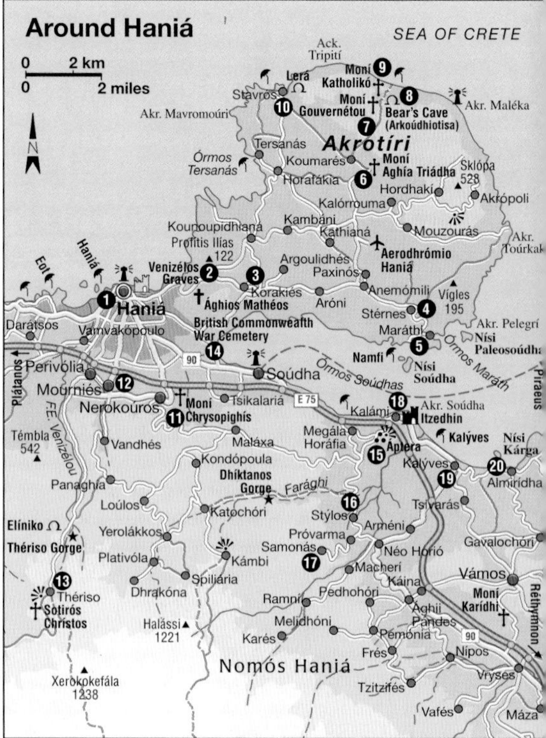

10.30–11.30am, 5.30–6.30pm) – literally the "Forerunner", ie John the Baptist – is situated. Although it is not known exactly when the original convent was built during Byzantine times, it survived during Venetian rule. But it was destroyed by the Turks in 1821 and it was not until 1840 that three nuns rebuilt three of the cells and started to recite the liturgy in the church again. During both the Venetian and Turkish occupations it was used as an asylum for young virgins. In the late 19th century Lady Egerton, the wife of the British ambassador in Athens, invited a nun to study embroidery and to this day this craft has secured their livelihood and the survival of the convent.

Now double back and follow the road for 6 km (4 miles) past the airport turn, to the old village of **Stérnes** ❹, where you will find a ruined Venetian country house and the remains of a 6th-century Byzantine church.

Continue eastwards down a twisty and badly signposted road and after 4 km (2½ miles) you eventually arrive at the much favoured little harbour and beach of **Maráthi** ❺, situated at the entrance to **Soúdha Bay**. It is a stunning location and offers excellent bathing in clear, turquoise waters. There are *kantínas* (literally "canteens", often converted caravans) selling soft drinks, beers, *oúzo* and snacks, as well as two or three restaurants that operate in the summer months. Go back the way you came through Stérnes and after 1 km (½ mile) turn right to **Paxinós**. In the centre of this small village, you will find Sífis taverna, which serves excellent home cooking at lunchtimes. Kyría Andonía still fries her potatoes on a wood fire.

Rejoin the airport road, but just by the airport turning, turn left, then right and after a few hundred metres you will see a left turn to **Aghía Triádha** ❻ (daily 6am–2pm, 5–7pm), about 2 km (1 mile) further on. Aghía Triádha (the Holy

At the beginning of the 20th century, there were only 8 km (5 miles) of paved roads on the whole of Crete.

BELOW: a few monks still live in Aghía Triádha Monastery.

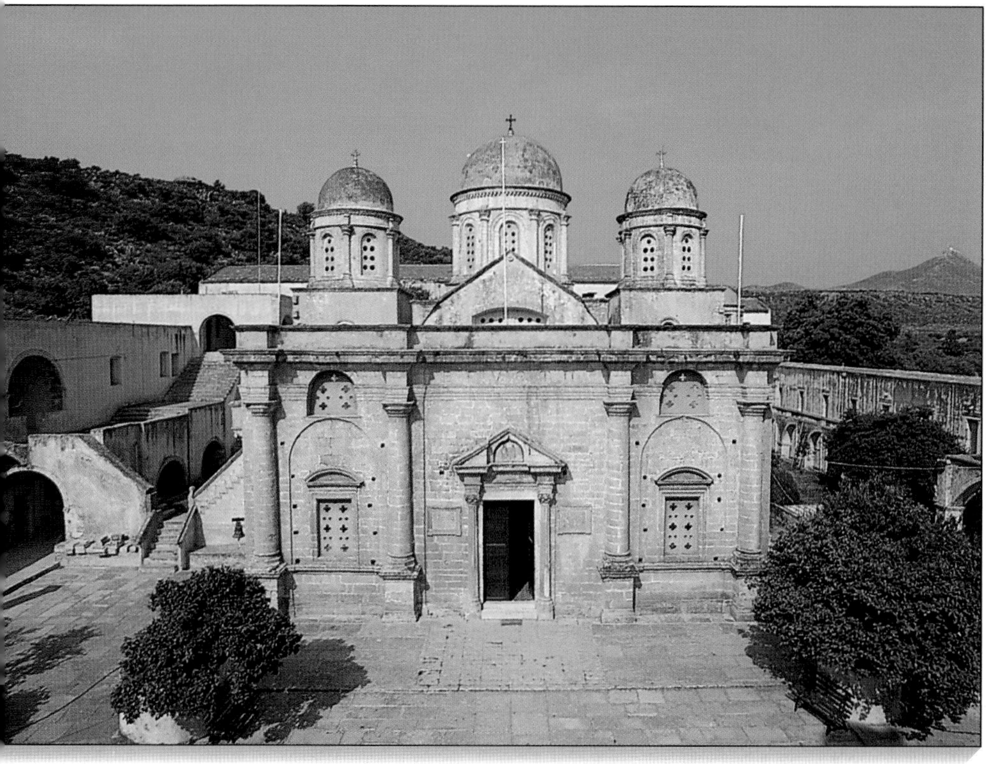

Elefthérios Venizélos – later Greece's first Prime Minister – summoned an illegal Revolutionary Assembly in Thériso in 1905.

Trinity), a 17th-century monastery is the most impressive sight on Akrotíri. Originally built by a Venetian merchant family, Tzangaróli, it is also known by this name. A handful of monks currently live here, keeping the surrounding olive groves and vineyards in excellent order. It was always a rich monastery due to the efforts of its own workforce. In 1821 the Turks laid it to waste, but it was rebuilt in 1830 and managed to regain its wealth.

The massive, somewhat severe, building is impressive, and houses a library of more than 700 volumes, some extremely old. You will also find icons by the Byzantine artist Skordíli. Though many of the treasures were saved from destruction, the only icons on view in the church nowadays are those from the 18th and 19th centuries. An excellent, historical guide by Michális Andrianákis is available from the monastery.

About 4 km (2½ miles) to the north of Aghía Triádha is the 16th-century **Monastery of Gouvernéto** ❼ (Moní Gouvernétou; daily 8am–12.30pm, 4.30–7.30pm). The monks' cells, mostly uninhabited now, are grouped around an inner courtyard. In 1821, a year of terror, most of the monks were murdered and the monastery was razed to the ground by the Turks. The library and icon collection were completely destroyed by fire, so there are no art treasures to attract the visitor today. Sculptures of mythical beasts, seemingly carved by a soul-mate of Hieronymous Bosch, decorate the church portal. Unfortunately, the soft sandstone used by the sculptor is eroding away.

Further to the north, slightly downhill, a path leads to the so-called **Bear's Cave** ❽ (Spílio Arkoúdhiotisa). The name comes from a huge stalagmite, larger than a man, in the shape of a bear. Findings confirm that this cave was a place of worship in Neolithic and late Minoan times. There is a tiny Lady Chapel here now, just near the entrance under the overhanging rocks, which was built during the 16th and 17th centuries. On 6–7 October each year, processions and services are held here in memory of Ághios Ioánnis Xénos (St John the Stranger), later known as Erimítis (the Hermit), who was accidentally killed by a shepherd's arrow on 6 October 1042. By walking for about 40 minutes down a path, which ends in a flight of steps in the rocks, you arrive at the cave of St John. It apparently goes 135 metres (450 ft) back into the mountain.

BELOW: down the steps of Moní Katholikó.

The legendary **Katholikó Monastery** ❾ (Moní Katholikó), which dates from the 10th and 11th centuries, is close by. The founder was none other than St John the Stranger himself, and the monastery is possibly the oldest in Crete. The church, the bell-tower and other additions came into being much later in the 16th century. Pirate attacks forced the monks to move up to Gouvernéto.

From Aghía Triádha it is about 5 km (3 miles) to **Horafákia**, where there is an excellent taverna run by Kyría Iríni (Mrs Irene) that is very popular with the Haniótes, as the residents of Haniá are known. Another 3 km (1½ miles) further on are the beaches of **Stavrós** ❿. The eastern beach, more of a cove really, is a popular tourist area with a tiny harbour, small hotels, bungalows and restaurants. It is situated opposite the slope where the cable contraption was erected for the filming of *Zorba the Greek*. The northern beach is long, unspoilt, undeveloped and virtually deserted, although there is a small beach bar.

To return to Haniá you must go back to Horafákia, where you can either make a detour to the delightful cove at **Tersanás** or turn right to **Kalathás**, 2 km (1½ miles) further on. This is another charming sandy beach area with beach bars, cafeterias and a restaurant which is popular with Haniótes as well as personnel from the US base, who hold volleyball competitions there. Returning to Haniá you go back via the Venizélos Graves and down the hill, a journey of 6 km (4 miles).

Map on page 182

The hill that towers over Stavrós beach is known locally as "Zorba's mountain", after the major role it played in the film.

South of Haniá

The area around Haniá can easily be explored by bus, taxi or even on foot. About 3 km (1¾ miles) along the road towards Soúdha is a turning on the right, which takes you down an avenue lined with trees, to the **Monastery of Chrysopighí** ⓫ (Moní Chrysopighís; daily 8am–12.30pm, 4–6pm). Built in 1560 by the physician Ioánnis Hartofílakas, its main entrance bears his family's coat of arms. The triple-apsed church, with its three domes, contains icons and a remarkable wood-carved iconostasis. The churchyard has many trees and is surrounded on all sides by stone walls. The monastery owns the fields adjoining it, where vines, fruit and vegetables are cultivated. Nowadays it is a convent.

Mourniés ⓬, the birthplace of Elefthérios Venizélos, is only 6 km (4 miles) south of the city. Though a humble place today, Mourniés once played an important role, at great cost to itself, in the history of the island. When the Turkish commander Mustapha Pasha raised the level of taxation beyond the endurance of the people, he caused an armed demonstration in Mourniés. During the course of the action most of the Cretan peasants were captured by Turkish soldiers, then hanged from mulberry trees.

The village also suffered during the German occupation. After an attack on German headquarters, when the culprits could not be found, "punitive action" was immediately taken: all males between the ages of 15 and 50 were assembled under an old plane tree, which is still the centre of the village, and shot. These gruesome events are still talked about by locals.

Thériso ⓭ (Thérisso), 16 km (10 miles) from Haniá, is accessible through the gorge of the same name (also known as the Venizélos Gorge). Its strategic position, 580 metres (1,935 ft) above sea level, made it an excellent base in the struggle against the Turks. Moreover, it was the home town of Elefthérios Venizélos' mother. It was here, in 1905, that Venizélos and his committee held the Revolutionary Assembly that led to the fall of Prince George and ultimately to union with Greece. Many Cretans, including busloads of schoolchildren, make the pilgrimage to see the little house. Thériso is an ideal place from which to set out on tours to Mesklá and Zoúrva, or for climbing **Páchnes**, at 2,454 metres (8,051 ft) the highest peak of the Lefká Óri.

BELOW: a fishing boat in Soúdha Bay.

Sailors and saints

Soúdha Bay (Órmos Soúdhas), 6 km (4 miles) east of Haniá, embraces one of the largest natural harbours in the Mediterranean. Its perimeter is some 19 km (12 miles) and it is between 3 and 6 km (1¾–4 miles) wide. This is a Greek and NATO naval base and the ferry port for Haniá. The mouth of the bay is blocked by three small islets. In 1560, the Venetians built extensive fortifications on the islet of **Soúdha** to protect the bay from enemy attacks, mostly by pirates. This fortress island did not fall into Turkish hands until 1715 (70 years after the fall of Haniá).

The name Soudha means "trench", referring to the narrow entrance to the bay.

An unusual event took place on 23 April 1913 on the feast day of St George. The little church of Ághios Nikólaos (St Nicholas) on the island was to change its name to Ághios Yeórghios (St George), in memory of King George I who had been assassinated in Thessaloník the previous month. But when a boat that was sailing to the small island was overturned and six out of the 11 people in it were drowned local inhabitants decided the tragedy was due to the anger of St Nicholas because "his" church was being given to another saint. It therefore remains consecrated to Nikólaos.

In 1941, the anchorage played an important role, first during the evacuation of the Allied Expeditionary Force from the mainland of Greece and then in supplying the garrison during preparations for the Battle of Crete.

A short distance from Soúdha town is the **British Commonwealth War Cemetery** ⓮ (Allied War Cemetery). Beautifully laid out and cared for, it is located close to the tranquil waters of the bay. Under the simple, carved headstone tributes, 1,527 servicemen are interred there (862 British, 446 New Zealand, 197 Australians and 22 from other Commonwealth countries). In 1963, 19 World War I graves were transferred here from the Consular Cemetery, as were 51 others dating back to 1897.

Grave 10E on the cemetery's northern side contains the remains of the distinguished archaeologist John Pendlebury, who in 1929 took over as curator of Knossós when Sir Arthur Evans retired. He was shot by the Germans on 22 May 1941 as a member of British Intelligence, fighting alongside the Cretans during the German assault on Iráklion. After the war the people of Iráklion held a memorial service for him and an address given by the eminent Greek archaeologist Dr N. Platon included the eulogy: " Dear friend, Crete will preserve your memory among her most sacred treasures. The soil which you excavated with the archaeologist's pick and enriched with a warrior's blood will shelter you with eternal gratitude."

BELOW: the British Commonwealth War Cemetery beside Soúdha Bay.

Past prosperity

Leave the Haniá-Iráklion highway about 10 km (6 miles) east of Haniá, and take a left turn at Megála Horáfia to find the ruins of **Áptera** ⓯. This was the great ancient city in this part of the island, inhabited from about 1000 BC, and undoubtedly one of the most prosperous cities of its day. It was situated on a plateau and surrounded by a wall almost 4 km (2½ miles) long, of which about 600 metres (1,970 ft) survive. It was destroyed by an earthquake in AD 700 and most of the survivors were forced to leave the area. As a result it was not difficult for the Saracens to take the city in 824.

Sadly, Áptera was plundered before being put under archaeological protection by the authorities. Since World War II, however, more statues, clay tablets and

vessels have been found and these are now exhibited in the Archaeological Museum of Haniá. In the area of ancient Áptera, remains of a Doric and Hellenistic temple, Roman cisterns, rock graves, a small theatre, Byzantine ruins and the Venetian monastic settlement can be seen. At the villages of **Stýlos** ⓰ (Stílos) and **Samonás** ⓱, a few kilometres to the south, there is evidence of Minoan sites including a good example of a late Minoan/Mycenaean *tholos* tomb near Stýlos.

Back on the coast, about 14 km (9 miles) from Haniá, overlooking Soúdha Bay, is the small hamlet of **Kalámi** ⓲ (literally "bamboo") which has a popular taverna and an inviting *kafeníon* overlooked by one of the best preserved Turkish forts in Crete, **Itzedin**. Originally there was a tower built by the Turks in 1646, but between 1867 and 1872 Reouf Pasha enlarged it into a fortress and named it after his favourite son. It was used as a prison until the 1970s and is now occupied by the Greek Navy.

Olive oil and tinned olives make a tasteful souvenir of Crete.

Sandy beaches and Byzantine remains

Just over 3 km (2 miles) further on is the village of **Kalýves** ⓳ (Kalíves), situated in the southeast corner of Soúdha Bay in a well cultivated area, with an extensive sandy beach. This fishing village and agricultural market centre has an imposing modern church, a tree-lined square and many old stone buildings with red tile roofs as well as the River Xidés running through the centre, with caïques and other fishing vessels moored by the bridge.

Kalýves is the Greek word for shelters made from bamboo or palm fronds, and the village probably takes its name from the time of the Arab landings in AD 824, when the invaders camped hereabouts. Another explanation that has been put forward is that the farmers of surrounding mountain villages decided to use this area as a base for their crop production. The flat wide plain, with its five rivers, running with water even during the hot dry summers, was ideal for agriculture. Instead of travelling back to their villages at the end of each day, the farmers would spend the nights in small bamboo shelters that they built close by.

To the east of the village is a cove with a small fishing harbour and a tavernas. Above are the ruins of the Venetian fort of Castel Apicorno, which is probably also the site of the ancient town of Ippokoronion, one of Áptera's two harbours.

Almirídha ⓴, 19 km (12 miles) east of Haniá, is a fishermen's village above a sheltered bay with a good sandy beach, a shallow sea suitable for children, and plenty of tavernas and fish restaurants. Tradition has it that the people from the now deserted village of Ághios Vasílis built the first houses here. At the western entrance to the village, on the left hand side of the road, you can see the remains of a Byzantine basilica-style church (5th–6th century) which has some intricate mosaic floors in situ. These remains were uncovered in 1973 when builders were digging the foundations for a new family house. Next-door to the church are the grave pits of the priests and bishops, and at the eastern side of the village there is a small caïque harbour. ❑

BELOW: still life at a harbourside taverna.

WESTERN CRETE

Map on pages 192–3

Wild and undeveloped, this part of the island has some of Crete's most spectacular sights – the mighty Samariá Gorge, the soaring White Mountains and the rocky southern coast

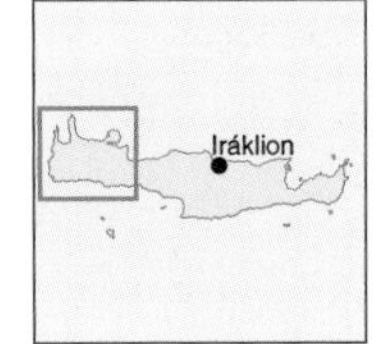

The picturesque journey south from Haniá to Omalós and the Samariá Gorge takes you through lush gardens, eucalyptus woods and orange groves. A bus leaves the long-distance depot in Haniá every hour. If you are driving, take the main road to the west of Haniá and take a left turn for Omalós after 1½ km (1 mile). Pass under the new motorway bridge and 9 km (5½ miles) later, you arrive at the village of **Aghiá** ❶ which was founded under Arab rule (AD 824–961) and probably takes its name from *aia*, the Arabic word for water, due to its springs and reservoir. The latter is of special interest to birdwatchers as the lake is a stop-over for migratory birds and a breeding area visited by terns, herons, warblers and swallows, among others.

On the outskirts of the village are the remains of a Byzantine church dedicated to Panaghía (the Virgin Mary). This was built on the site of an earlier Byzantine church which had three naves separated by two rows of red marble and granite columns – one of the few examples in the whole of Greece. Close to the village is the local prison: the area was nicknamed "prison valley" during the Battle of Crete. A further 3 km (1¾ miles) through the orange groves is the village of **Alikianós** ❷, close to which is a memorial to hundreds of partisans executed by the Germans during World War II.

PRECEDING PAGES: dawn on the south coast.
LEFT: walking the Samariá Gorge.
BELOW: church bell without a church.

There are also two churches of note in the area. The older, dedicated to St John the Hermit dates from the 10th–11th centuries and has interesting murals and mosaics, while the later one (AD 1243), dedicated to Ághios Yeórghios (St George), has some well-preserved frescoes.

The road continues through **Fournés** ❸, 25 km (16 miles) from Haniá, where the cave of **Hiróspilios** is situated close by. A turning leads to **Mesklá** ❹, a beautiful village on a fast-flowing brook. It is built on the ruins of what some believe to be the site of the Dorian city of Rizinia (circa 400 BC). The road then winds its way up, via the village of **Lákki** ❺ with its stunning views, to the **Omalós Plateau**, 1,100 metres (3,667 ft) above sea-level.

Here the soil is extremely fertile and cereals, potatoes and tomatoes are cultivated. Sheep and goats are also in abundance. In winter, when it's not covered in snow, the plateau is flooded by water from the surrounding mountains, although fortunately the water can drain into the 2.5-km (1½-mile) long Dzanís Cave. Legend has it that on moonless nights, a shepherd, enchanted by a water nymph, plays his *lýra* and sings of his sorrow at the mouth of the cave.

The geographical position of the plateau made it an ideal base for Cretan resistance to the Ottoman Turks, and on one side are the house and grave of Hadzí Micháli Yiánnari, a 19th-century freedom fighter. If

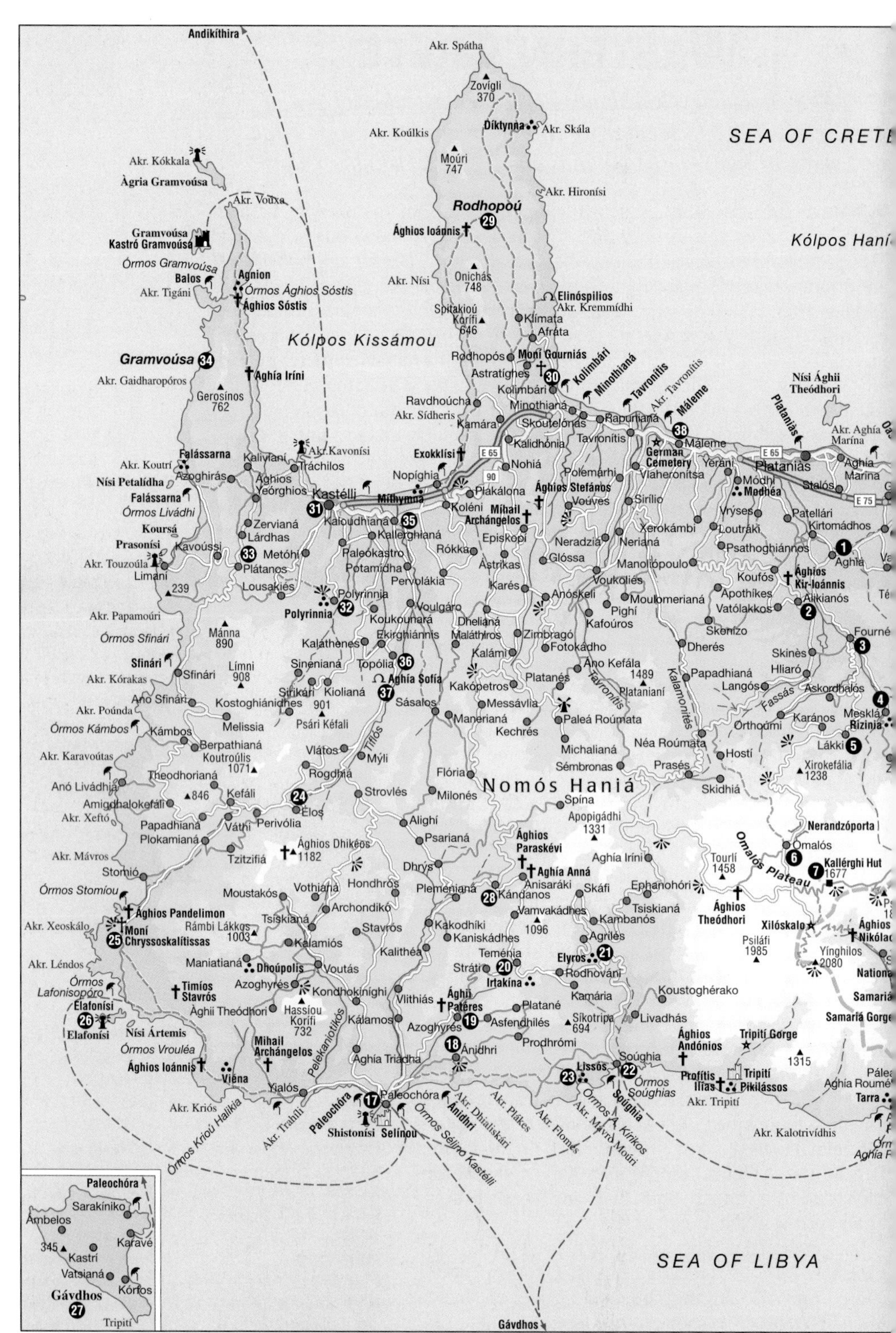
SEA OF CRETE
Kólpos Haniá
Kólpos Kissámou
SEA OF LIBYA
Nomós Haniá
Andikíthira
Akr. Spátha
Zovígli 370
Díktynna
Akr. Skála
Akr. Koúlkis
Moúri 747
Akr. Hironísi
Rodhopoú
29
Ághios Ioánnis
Onichás 748
Akr. Nísi
Elinóspilios
Akr. Kremmídhi
Spitakioú Korífi 646
Klímata
Afráta
Rodhopós
Moní Gourniás
Astratíghes
30
Kolimbári
Minothianá
Tavronítis
Akr. Tavronítis
Máleme
38
Akr. Kókkala
Àgria Gramvoúsa
Akr. Voúxa
Gramvoúsa
Kastró Gramvoúsa
Órmos Gramvoúsa
Agnion
Órmos Ághios Sóstis
Ághios Sóstis
Balos
Akr. Tigáni
Gramvoúsa 34
Akr. Gaidharopóros
Ághía Iríni
Gerosínos 762
Falássarna
Akr. Koutrí
Nísi Petalídha
Kaliviani
Akr. Kavonísi
Tráchilos
Azoghirás
Ághios Yeórghios
Kastélli 31
Falássarna
Órmos Livádhi
Koursá
Prasonísi
Akr. Touzoúla
Limáni
Zerviana
Lárdhas
Kavoússi
33
Metóhi
Plátanos
Lousakiés
239
Polyrinnia 32
Exokklísi
Nopíghia
Míthymna
E 65
90
Plakálona
Koléni
Kaloudhianá 35
Kallerghianá
Paleókastro
Potamídha
Pervolákia
Voulgáro
Koukounará
Ekirghiánnis
Kalathenes
Sineniana
Topólia 36
Aghía Sofía 37
Sirikári
Kioliana
Kostoghiánidhes
901
Psári Kéfali
Sásalos
Akr. Papamoúri
Órmos Sfinári
Mánna 890
Sfinári
Límni 908
Akr. Kórakas
Ano Sfinári
Akr. Poúnda
Órmos Kámbos
Kámbos
Melissia
Berpathianá
Koutroúlis 1071
Akr. Karavoútas
Theodhorianá
Anó Livádhia
846
Kefáli
Amigdhalokefáli
Akr. Xeftó
Papadhianá
Váthi
Perivólia
Plokamianá
Tzitzifiá
Akr. Mávros
Stomió
Órmos Stomíou
Ághios Pandelímon
Akr. Xeoskálo
Moní Chryssoskalítissas 25
Rámbi Lákkos 1003
Akr. Léndos
Maniatianá
Dhoúpolis
Órmos Lafonisopóro
Elafonísi 26
Elafonísi
Nísi Ártemis
Órmos Vrouléa
Ághios Ioánnis
Timíos Stavrós
Àghii Theódhori
Hassíou Korífi 732
Mihail Archángelos
Viéna
Akr. Kriós
Órmos Krioú Halikia
Akr. Trahíli
Paleochóra 17
Shistonísi
Selínou
Ravdhoúcha
Akr. Sídheris
Kamára
Skoutelónas
Kalidhónia
Nohiá
Rapaniana
Tavronítis
German Cemetery
Polemárhi
Vlaherónitsa
Ághios Stéfanos
Mihail Archángelos
Voúves
Episkopí
Neradzia
Neriana
Sirilio
Xerokámbi
Rókka
Glóssa
Manolópoulo
Ástrikas
Voukolies
Karés
Anóskeli
Moulomerianá
Pighí
Kafoúros
Dheliana
Maláthiros
Zimbragó
Fotokádho
Kalámi
Áno Kefála 1489
Platanés
Kakópetros
Messávlia
Plataniani
Paleá Roúmata
Manerianá
Kechrés
Michalianá
Sémbronas
Tavronitis
Kalamonites
Néa Roúmata
Vlátos
Mýli
Tiflós
Rogdhiá
Flória
Strovlés
Milonés
24
Élos
Spína
Apopigádhi 1331
Alighí
Psarianá
Ághios Dhikéos 1182
Ághios Paraskévi
Aghía Anná
Aghía Iríni
Dhrýs
Anisaráki
Skáfi
Plemenianá
Kándanos 28
Hondhrós
Vothianá
Moustakós
Archondikó
Tsiskianá
Vamvakádhes
1096
Kambanós
Kakodhíki
Kaniskádhes
Stavrós
Kalamiós
Kalithéa
Teménia
Stráti 20
Irtakína
Elyros 21
Agrilés
Rodhováni
Voutás
Azoghyrés
Kondhokinighi
Vlithiás
Ághii Patéres 19
Kamária
Plataně
Síkotripa 694
Kálamos
Azoghyrés
Asfendhilés
Pelekaniotikos
Ánidhri 18
Prodhrómi
Aghía Triádha
Yialós
Paleochóra
Akr. Dhialiskári
Anidhri
Akr. Plákes
Akr. Flomés
Órmos Sélino Kastélli
Lissós 23
Soúghia 22
Órmos Soúghias
Órmos A. Kirikos
Akr. Mávro Moúri
Soúghia
Gávdhos
Nísi Ághii Theódhori
Platanias
Akr. Aghía Marína
Aghía Marína
Máleme
Yeráni
Platanías
E 65
Stalós
E 75
Módhi
Modhéa
Vrýses
Patellári
Kirtomádhos
Loutráki
Psathoghiánnos
1
Aghiá
Koufós
Ághios Kir-Ioánnis
Apothíkes
Alikianós
Vatólakkos 2
Skonizo
Fourné 3
Dheres
Skinès
Papadhianá
Hliaró
Langós
Fassás
Askordhalós
4
Mesklá
Rizinia
Orthoúni
Karános
Lákki 5
Hostí
Prasés
Xirokefália 1238
Skidhiá
Nerandzóporta
Omalós Plateau
Omalós 6
Tourlí 1458
Kallérghi Hut 1677 7
Ephanohóri
Tsiskianá
Ághios Theódhori
Xilóskalo
Ághios Nikólaos
Psiláfi 1985
Yínghilos 2080
Koustogherako
Livadhás
Ághios Andónios
Tripití Gorge
1315
Profítis Ilías
Tripiti
Pikilássos
Akr. Tripití
Akr. Kalotrivídhis
Tarra
Aghía Roumélí
Samariá Gorge
Samariá
National
Paleochóra
Sarakíniko
Ámbelos
345
Kastrí
Karavé
Vatsianá
Kórfos
Gávdhos 27
Tripití

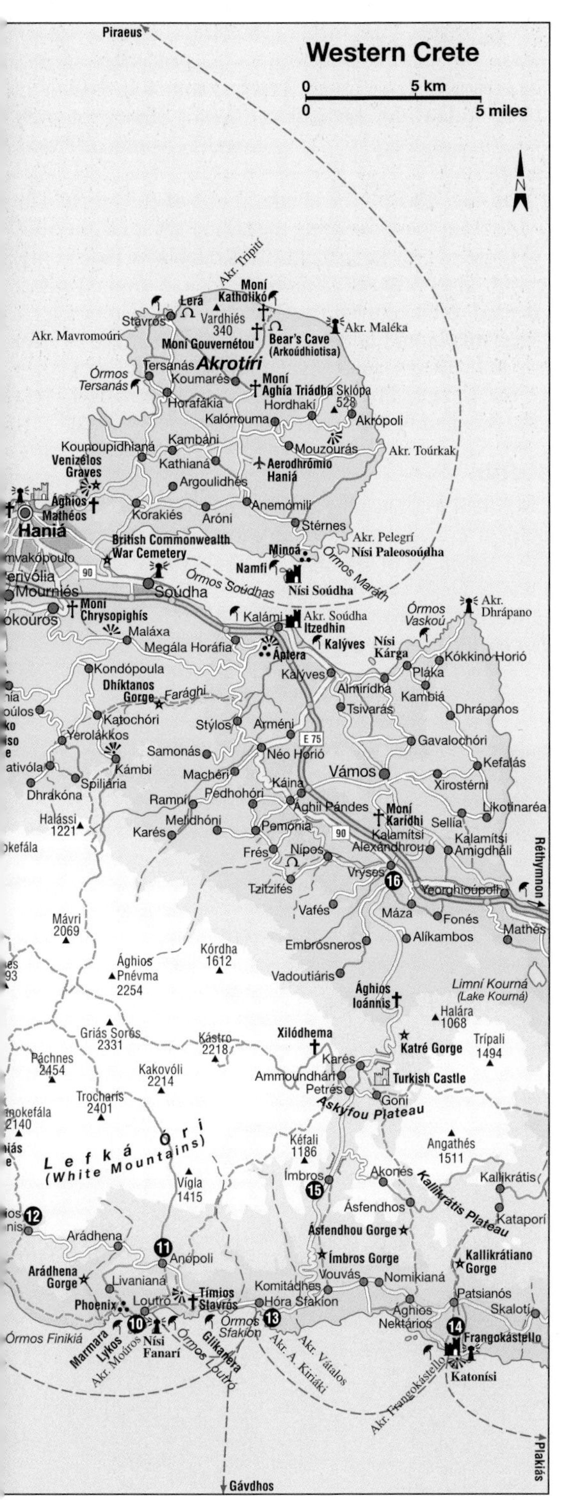

you wish to stay overnight on the way to the Samariá Gorge there are now a number of small hotels, pensions and restaurants in the village of **Omalós** ❻. From here it is 4 km (2½ miles) to the entrance to the gorge. Just before the descent begins there is a path leading to **Kallérghi Hut** ❼, the retreat managed by the Greek Mountaineering Club (EOS); it stands at an altitude of 1,677 metres (5,501 ft) and can serve as a starting-point for mountain treks.

A walk down the gorge

You enter the **Samariá Gorge** ❽ itself via the Xilóskalo (literally, wooden staircase) made from tree trunks. The name is a reminder of the days when the only access to the gorge was by ladders.

Botanically speaking, this is a fascinating place with cypresses, kermes oaks, pines, plane trees, the Greek yellow tongue, Cretan corymb and Cretan campanula growing here. The area was designated a National Park in 1962 and is home to a number of endangered species including the golden eagle, the *zourídha* (Cretan polecat) and the *agrími*, the Cretan ibex which in recent years has been nicknamed the *krí-krí*.

You come to the church of **Ághios Nikólaos** (St Nicholas) after about 4 km (2½ miles) and a little further down is the village of **Samariá** with its half-dozen houses that were occupied up until 1965. There is a Venetian church in the Byzantine style with an engraving on the lintel dating it to 1379. It is the church of Osías Marías Tis Eghiptiás (St Mary of Egypt), which was later shortened to Sía María, which became Samariá. There is another theory, however, that Samariá is a derivation of the word *samári* (saddle), as a donkey was the only possible form of transportation.

There is a spring to refresh tired travellers and an underground stream emerges soon after the village. This stream, which has to be crossed 47 times on the descent, is the reason the gorge is closed in the winter months, when it becomes a torrent. The last 4 km (2½ miles) are the most interesting, as you pass between the high

Frappé (iced coffee) is a refreshing drink available everywhere.

cliffs where all sounds are magnified. When the wind howls through the narrow **Sidheróportes** (Iron Gates) you can understand how tales of water sprites, demons and other strange creatures came about. The last stretch is extremely narrow, only 3 metres (10 ft) wide with 500 metres (1,660 ft) of vertical cliffs towering above. You look through the gap to a wide valley which stretches right down to the Libyan Sea.

The village of **Aghía Rouméli** 9 is at the southern end of the gorge. The inhabitants make their living from tourism during the hiking period from April to October, and the rest of the year they keep themselves busy with their cattle, goats, sheep and beekeeping. They also sell *dhíktamos*, Cretan dittany, which grows in the gorge and is used to make what the Cretans call "mountain tea".

Recently, a Samariá "Lazyway" tour has been organised. You arrive by boat at Aghía Rouméli, walk up to the Iron Gates (about 45 minutes) and back, then leave again. The village is connected by regular boats to Loutró and Hóra Sfakíon to the east and Soúghia and Paleochóra to the west.

East to Frangokástello

Near what is now Aghía Rouméli was once the ancient city of **Tarra**. The finds, which include a stone tablet inscribed with the double axe, are displayed in the Archaeological Museum of Haniá. In mythology, Apollo is said to have come to Tarra and some evidence suggests that there may have been a sacred building here before the basilica, in the shape of a Hellenistic temple to Apollo. Today, on top of the earlier basilica is the Panaghía Church, built in the 12th and 13th centuries. The coins from Tarra show the head of a goat and a bee, very similar to coins from other towns in the Cretan League of Cities, to which Lissós,

BELOW: the snow-capped Lefká Óri.

Élyros, Syía, Poikílassos and Irtakína also belonged around 300 BC. In AD 66 an earthquake destroyed Tarra, and it was never rebuilt.

It is possible to walk to **Loutró** ⓾ from Aghía Rouméli, but is not easy, as it takes about five hours and there is very little shade. Once known as Phoenix (Fínix), the town was important in ancient times as the port for Anopolis, and can still only be reached by boat or by foot along the ancient trails. Together the two towns probably had 60,000 inhabitants and west of the village are a few scattered ancient ruins. In Byzantine times Loutró was the seat of a bishopric. The Sotíros Christoú Chapel with frescoes from the 14th and 15th centuries is of particular interest.

The English naval captain T.A.B. Spratt remarked that Loutró was the only harbour on the entire south coast where ships could be moored with complete safety all year round. Although there was a fleet of small trading ships until the beginning of the 19th century, this has dwindled to a couple of boats today, and there are hardly any fishermen left in Loutró. As in so many coastal villages, tourism is now the mainstay. Hotels and rooms are available, and there are many tavernas to choose from.

Anópoli ⓫ lies north of Loutró, some 600 metres (2,000 ft) up, at the foot of 2,218-metre (7,393-ft) Mount Kastró. Ioánnis Vláchos, one of the most famous of all Crete's freedom fighters, was born here. His wide education earned him the nickname Dhaskaloghiánnis, or Teacher John. It was he who led the rebellion of 1770. Anopolis was one of the most important of the ancient settlements. It was burned to the ground in 1365 for resisting the Venetians, and it suffered the same fate again in 1867, this time at the hands of the Turks.

A few kilometres west of Anópoli there is a 70-metre (235-ft) long bridge

Map on pages 192–3

In a cave in the cliffs east of Loutró the freedom fighter Dhaskaloghiánnis set up a mint to produce revolutionary coinage. You can visit it by boat from Hóra Sfakíon.

BELOW: the road winds down to Hóra Sfakíon.

Windsurfing in the Libyan Sea: boards may be hired at Frangokástello.

crossing the **Arádhena Gorge**, one of the most beautiful in Crete. Until recent times the only access to the villages of **Arádhena**, situated on the site of ancient Aradin, and **Ághios Ioánnis** ⓬ involved a descent of 130 metres (435 ft) and a climb up the other side. The cost of constructing the bridge (40 million drachmas in 1986) was borne by the company run by the Vardhinoghiánnis family, whose roots are in Ághios Ioánnis. Here, at an altitude of 780 metres (2,600 ft) on the southern slopes of Páchnes (2,454 metres/8,051 ft), are two old churches, Ághios Ioánnis and Panaghía, which both have rare frescoes.

To the east, 16 km (10 miles) from Loutró, is **Hóra Sfakíon** ⓭, the capital of the Sfakiá region which has always been famous for its fierce fighters. The buildings are arranged around the harbour like a Greek theatre, with many hotels, pensions and tavernas. Until the last century, the harbour was visited by boats from North Africa, bringing merchandise that was transported by pack animals to Réthymnon and Haniá. These days there is a regular bus service to Haniá as well as boat connections along the south coast to both the east and the west, and to the island of Gávdhos (see page 201), which makes it something of a transit village.

About 8 km (5 miles) to the east is **Frangokástello** ⓮ (Frankokástelo). This Venetian castle, built in 1340, was originally named after the neighbouring church of Ághios Nikíta, but to stress its foreign nature, the Cretans called it Castle of the "Franks", a generic local term for "foreigners from Europe". On 17 May 1828 there was a bloody battle here between 385 Cretan rebels led by Hadzí Micháli Daliáni and 800 Turks under Mustafa Bey. Daliáni made his last stand at the fort, but was killed along with all his followers.

North of Hóra Sfakíon, high on a plateau, is the village of **Ímbros** ⓯, where

BELOW: the "Franks' castle", Frangokástello.

EARLY-MORNING WALK

Each year, on a morning between 17 and 30 May, a strange phenomenon is said to take place in Frangokástello, an event immortalised in legend and guidebooks of the 19th century. Just before sunrise a shadowy procession leaves the ruins of Ághios Harálambos, and for about 10 minutes columns of armed black figures march along the castle walls. The locals believe that these ghosts, who return each year, are the souls of Hadzí Micháli Daliáni and his rebels, slaughtered in 1828. Because they appear in the damp early morning air, they are known as *dhrosoulítes*, or "dew men".

The phenomenon has been confirmed by a number of independent observers. Scientists have looked into the matter and their conclusion is that the apparition is merely a mirage from Libya, perhaps brought about by an unusual refraction or reflection of light that happens only in certain atmospheric conditions.

If you want to see the dew men, you will need luck and patience. Luck, because the sea must be calm and the humidity just right, and patience because no-one knows exactly when the procession will appear – and there are apparently only 10 minutes when conditions are just right for the phenomenon.

one of Crete's most beautiful gorges begins. It is just 7 km (4½ miles) long, and its walls reach heights of up to 300 metres (1,000 ft), closing into a gap of no more than 2 metres (6 ft 6 ins) at the narrowest point. This was the route taken by the retreating British Commonwealth forces in World War II, prior to evacuation. The **Ímbros Gorge** is an excellent (and somewhat easier) alternative to the Samariá Gorge, if you don't have time for both.

From Ímbros the road leads north through the fertile plain of **Askýfou**, believed to have once been a lake, where vineyards, potatoes, fruits and nuts are cultivated. The plain is dominated by a Turkish castle. Nearby is a small, private museum with a vast array of weapons and other military paraphernalia relating to the Turkish and German campaigns. Dropping down 16 km (10 miles) to the village of **Vrýses** ⓰ (Vrísses), you can fortify yourself for the 33-km (20-mile) journey to Haniá with freshly-made sheep's yoghurt and honey eaten under the plane trees by the river.

The Southwest

The town of **Paleochóra** ⓱, with about 2,000 inhabitants, lies on a peninsula jutting out into the Libyan Sea. Its geographic location means that there are two beaches, a long sandy one to the southwest, and a pebbly stretch in the east. Sometimes the latter offers a welcome alternative, as the sandy beach is often too windy for comfort. Paleochóra has a small jetty used by excursion boats and ferries which link it to other ports in the south. A projected new harbour will be able to accommodate large car ferries and facilitate motor access to some of the interesting villages in the area, which are still difficult or even impossible to reach by bus.

The easiest way to tackle the Ímbros Gorge is to leave your car at Komitádhes, at the bottom of the ravine, and ask the taverna there to call a taxi to take you to Ímbros, at the top. The walk down the gorge to Komitádhes takes about three hours.

BELOW: Paleochóra, the top town on the southwest coast.

Several companies in Paleochóra run dolphin-spotting boat trips. Perhaps the most reputable (and a member of International Dolphin Watch) is E-Motion Travel, located at the Old Harbour; Tel/fax: (0823) 41755.

The new houses that have replaced the old in recent years have fortunately not spoiled the centre of the village of Paleochóra. Behind the harbour the little streets are still much as they were before the advent of tourists, with the old women still sitting doing their needlework, looking as if progress has completely passed them by. The people of Paleochóra are friendly and you can win their affection, but you should first learn to speak a little Greek. Go through the old part of the town bordering on the Panaghía (Virgin Mary) Church, which has a bell-tower, and you will come to the ruins of a Venetian castle, built in 1282, called Selínou. Nowadays, this is the name given to the whole region. If you are in Crete in March, don't miss the festival of the Annunciation of the Virgin Mary here.

Paleochóra is the most important town on the southwestern coast, with all the necessary civic amenities. Most people here manage to make a living from fishing and raising sheep and goats, and supplement their income in the summer with the profits of tourism. During the winter they grow vegetables (tomatoes and cucumbers) in the greenhouses. The vegetable season starts in September and continues until May–June of the following year.

Paleochóra earned a reputation as a hippy hangout in the 1960s, but times have changed. In the summer season the main street is closed to traffic after 6pm, and it is then that the evening *volta* (stroll) begins. In the cafes, restaurants and tavernas, tourists and locals mingle until the early hours.

From Paleochóra

There are several interesting trips which you can make from Paleochóra. One is to the village of **Ánidhri** ⓲, which lies just 5 km (3 miles) to the northeast. Here stands the beautiful Ághios Yeórghios church, which was decorated with

BELOW: Paleochóra fishing family.

paintings by Yoánnis Pagoménos in 1323. About 2 km (1 mile) to the north is **Azoghyrés** ⓳ (Azogirés), a village whose population has dwindled from 400 in 1971 to only 40 today. Just outside the village, next to the oil press, there is an enormous plane tree, the leaves of which remain green even in winter. Legend has it that the tree was planted by the 99 Holy Fathers. Scientific examinations have so far failed to come up with any explanation for this wonder of nature. The church, dedicated to the Holy Fathers (Ághii Patéres), is built into the rock face, just outside the village. A tour of the church and the little folk museum is conducted by a friendly custodian. You will have to ask for him in one of the tavernas and he will take you around. Weapons, pots, books, clothing and other objects provide visitors with a lively picture of life in Crete in the 19th century and there is also a section devoted to the Battle of Crete in World War II.

Map on pages 192–3

The road to the **Zoures Cave**, where the 99 Holy Fathers lived in the 11th century, winds its way up into the open countryside. Through a small gate in the wire fence (right fork at the top), you reach a path which leads downhill first, then up again. A black cross marked on a rock indicates the entrance to the cave. There are three iron ladders to enable you to get down about 15 metres (50 ft) to the floor of the sacred cave. It is quite cold down there, and you get a strong feeling of the ascetic environment of the hermits' life. You have to feel your way forward with the help of a rope. The cave goes back about 70 metres (230 ft) and slightly uphill into the mountain. Further up, the path becomes oppressively narrow. If you want to go right to the far end, you need a torch or two.

St John the Hermit was the leader of the 99 Holy Fathers. Legend has it that when St John left the group to live on Akrotíri, the remaining 98 monks agreed that if one of their members should die, they all would. Some time later, St John was accidentally shot with an arrow by a shepherd who mistook him for an animal, as he wore furs and skins rather than normal garments. He died from the wound and that very same evening the remaining 98 monks also died, apparently from natural causes. They were discovered by the villagers the following morning.

BELOW: a lamb is killed for Easter Sunday's feast.

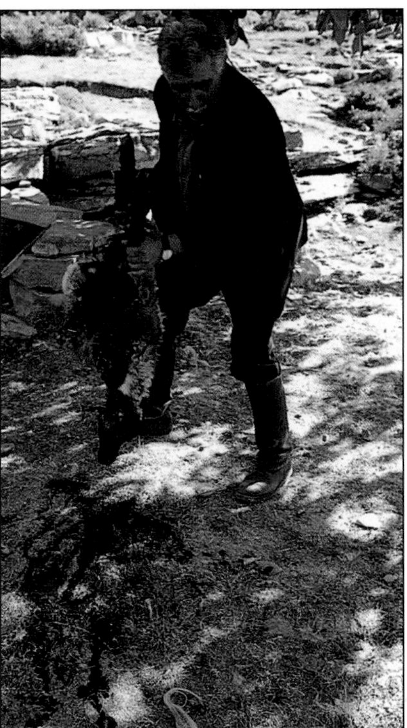

Then on to **Teménia** ⓴, 17 km (10½ miles) from Paleochóra, a village which supplies a good part of western Crete with mineral water and bottles excellent soft drinks. Nearby are the ruins of the site of ancient **Irtakína**, which was one of the major Dorian cities. Remains of cisterns, buildings and fortifications can still be found in the undergrowth as well as rock-cut tombs. Irtakína, like others in the League of Cities, minted its own coins. The dolphin and stars depicted on these coins indicate the seafaring tradition. For years, no-one bothered about this place; people just took the debris from the ruins and used it to build their own houses. However, a 3rd–4th century BC headless statue of Pan was excavated and is now displayed in the Archaeological Museum of Haniá.

After passing through **Rodhováni** a few kilometres further on, there is the small cave of **Skotiní** in which ceramic remains from the Classical/Hellenistic periods (550–67 BC) have been found. Close by are the ruins of the Dorian city of **Elyros** ㉑, with a view of the harbour of Soúghia. In the Greco-Roman period it was one of the most powerful city states. Ruins of a 6th-century

This black head scarf is the traditional headgear of the fighting men of Sfakiá. The droplets represent their tears for freedom.

basilica church, the seat of a bishop, are visible under the large modern church of the Virgin Mary. The city was eventually destroyed by the Saracens.

About 11 km (7 miles) southeast of Rodhováni, you come to **Soúghia** ㉒, a village with a broad pebble beach, which is now definitely on the tourist map. Here lay ancient Syía and in the church built in 1875 there was a beautiful mosaic floor which had originally belonged to a 6th-century basilica. This has since been removed for safe keeping to the Archaeological Museum in Haniá. To the east of the village is the mouth of the 7-km (4-mile) long **Gorge of Aghía Iríni** (St Irene).

Behind the harbour at the western end of Soúghia beach you can walk through the rugged ravine, up over the hill and down into the valley on the other side to the site of the ancient Dorian city of **Lissós** ㉓ (a 1½-hour walk). During its heyday in the Roman epoch, the town was so wealthy that it could afford to mint coins in gold. Only Irtakína was comparably affluent. Lissós also became famous for its mineral springs, and remains of bath chambers show that this place was a spa in ancient times. Most impressive of all is the Temple of Asklepiós, the god of healing. Everywhere you look are ruins of houses, theatres and public buildings. Various statues discovered on the site are on display in the Archaeological Museum of Haniá.

From Paleochóra to Elafonísi

Drive in the direction of Haniá, turning left at **Plemenianá**, and go through the *kastanochória* (chestnut villages) of **Dhrýs** (Drís), **Strovlés** and **Élos** ㉔, a larger village where a chestnut festival is held every October. The last stage of the journey is through **Vathí**, 28 km (17 miles) from Paleochóra. A 5-km (3 mile) detour north between Strovlés and Élos brings you to the hamlet of **Mýli** which, with the aid of an EU grant, has renovated traditional stone houses. Furnished in the Cretan style, but without electricity, it acts as a peaceful retreat.

Below: a priest summons the faithful to worship.

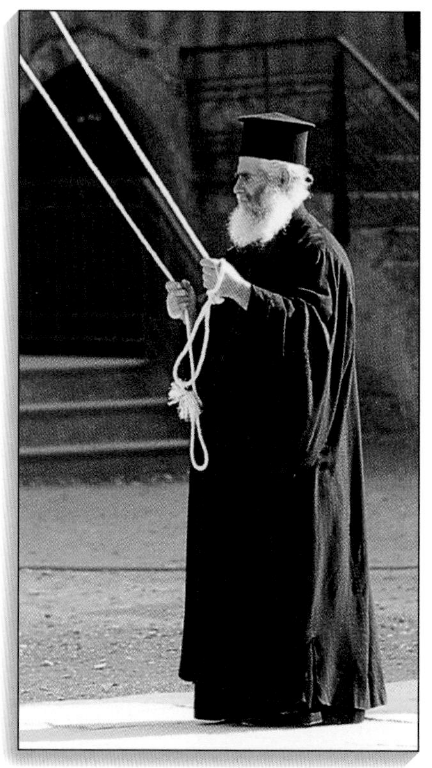

The **Convent of Chryssoskalítissa** ㉕ (Moní Chryssoskalítissas; daily 7am–sunset) is set high on a cliff on the west coast. The name means "Virgin of the Golden Step". One of the 90 steps up to the convent is said to have been fashioned from gold which can only be seen by a pure, sinless person. In Easter of 1824, a terrible slaughter took place here. Many Cretan women and children had fled from Ibrahim Pasha Messez and his followers. The Turks found their hiding place and killed 850 people. After the massacre, the soldiers prepared to plunder the convent, but beekeepers living there set upon them and put them to flight. The convent was thus spared from destruction.

The island of **Elafonísi** ㉖ is 6 km (4 miles) to the south of the convent. This area has been developed in recent years with an asphalt road, tavernas, *kantínas* and water supply. In the summer months it is a popular destination for tourist coaches.

South Sea Island

During the summer season, boat services from Paleochóra, Soúghia and Hóra Sfakíon connect you to the island of **Gávdhos** ㉗, the southernmost point of

Europe. Depending where you leave from, the journey is about 30 nautical miles (the boat from Hóra Sfakíon takes 2½ hours). In spring and autumn, however, the sudden and unpredictable storms can cause visitors to be stranded for several weeks on the island. You arrive in the small harbour of **Karavé** but the loveliest beach near there is **Sarakíniko** to the north of the harbour, where rooms are available and visitors can stay to get away from it all. The island is really only for those prepared to rough it, with limited fresh water and electricity supplied by generators. Gávdhos is tiny, but it still takes two days to walk around the 37 sq. km (14 sq. mile) island. The path is rough but not dangerous; so long as you are careful, it should not present any problems.

Ancient settlements on Gávdhos remain as yet unexcavated. Apparently it was densely populated during the Byzantine epoch, with some estimates putting its population as high as 8,000. In those days it even had its own bishop. Later, in Venetian times, Gávdhos was a pirate hideout. However, during the period of Turkish domination, it became one of the most important refuges of the Resistance fighters. Today there are very few permanent inhabitants on the island (at the time of writing, only 44), most of whom reside in the principal town of **Kastrí** and in the villages of **Ámbelos** and **Vatsianá**. On the island is the cave that was home to the nymph Calypso, who detained Odysseus for a period of seven years.

On the way to Kastrí from the harbour you pass the Panaghía church, the bell of which once belonged to a ship that was wrecked on the rocks near Gávdhos during a storm. Later, one of the islanders saw the bell deep in the water and managed to dive down and salvage it. Diving to such depths, however, caused him to lose his hearing so that he became known as Koufidhákis (the deaf one).

Gávdhopoúla, the islet northwest of Gávdhos, is deserted except for a few shepherds in summer. If you want to visit it, make arrangements with a Gávdhos fisherman.

BELOW: the Convent of Chryssoskalítissa.

Avocados are grown in the fruitful area around Kándanos.

There have been many attempts to remove the bell from the island, all mysteriously thwarted, and so it remains. When German soldiers were stationed on Gávdhos during World War II, they mined the island, which led to numerous casualties among the civilian population. Many fishermen and farmers left their homes and moved to safety in Paleochóra.

Fruitful fields

On the way back to Haniá, 16 km (10 miles) from Paleochóra is the town of **Kándanos** ㉘. As this area has the highest rainfall in Crete, the vegetation is lush, with olives, chestnuts, fruit trees and vineyards growing in profusion and the rich meadows are ideal for grazing. The River Kándanos is narrow but has the great advantage that it does not dry up in summer. Being a market town, Kándanos has become a centre for the 15 surrounding villages, many of which are famed for their frescoed Byzantine churches.

The town's history goes back a long way. A little to the south lay the ancient city of Kadros, which was situated on two acropoli, possibly one hill split in two by an earthquake, and here there are some good examples of Dorian rock-cut chamber tombs. The area is also rich in old churches with good examples of Byzantine art, such as that in the Panaghía Dzivremianá church.

After the Germans invaded Crete in May 1941, they heard that Allied reinforcements were being landed on the south coast, and quickly dispatched a 16-strong reconnaissance group into the mountains, but the brave Cretans ambushed them at Flória and the group were wiped out, with a number of partisans also being killed. On 3 June, the Germans took retribution on the nearest large town, which was Kándanos. They cordoned off the town, killed all the domestic ani-

BELOW: Kolimbári's pretty harbour.

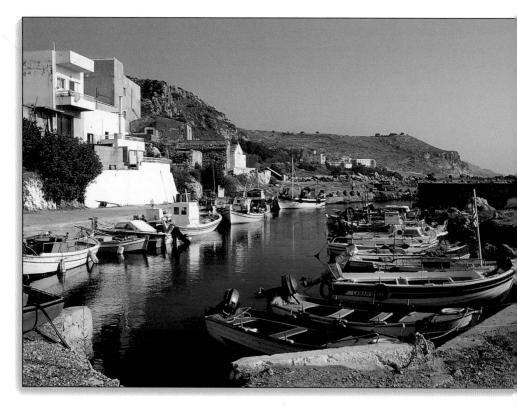

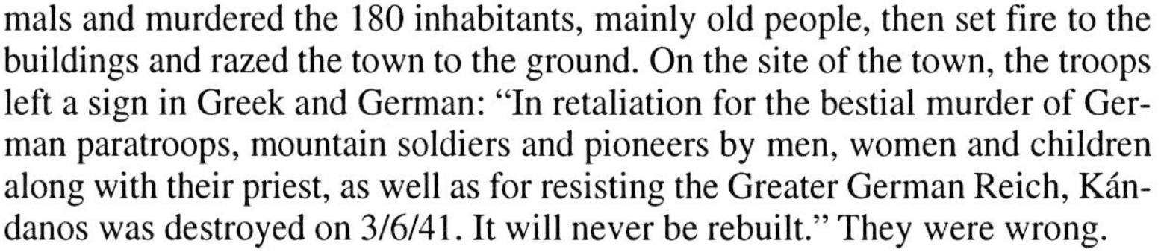

mals and murdered the 180 inhabitants, mainly old people, then set fire to the buildings and razed the town to the ground. On the site of the town, the troops left a sign in Greek and German: "In retaliation for the bestial murder of German paratroops, mountain soldiers and pioneers by men, women and children along with their priest, as well as for resisting the Greater German Reich, Kándanos was destroyed on 3/6/41. It will never be rebuilt." They were wrong.

Map on pages 192–3

An empty peninsula

The **Rodhopoú Peninsula** ㉙ is one of the most beautiful parts of Crete, although it isn't easy to get to. The peninsula begins at **Kolimbári** ㉚, a peaceful fishing village 24 km (15 miles) west of Haniá, with hotels, rooms, restaurants and a long pebble beach. North of the village, also on the coast is the **Monastery of Goniá** (Moní Goniás; Sun–Fri 8am–noon, 4–8pm, Sat 4–8pm). There is a pottery school here as well as a large library and a notable collection of icons. Behind the monastery is the Orthodox Academy of Crete and its architecturally contrasting modern conference centre.

The Orthodox Academy of Crete does not just give instruction in theological matters but also in modern farming techniques – useful for self-sufficient monks.

The asphalt roads end suddenly at either **Afráta** or **Rodhopós** and proceeding north by car becomes very difficult. Not far north of Afráta, on the east coast, is the fascinating cave of **Elinóspilios** which can only be reached by sea. It is 165 metres (550 ft) long, stunning and archaeologically important. Human and animal remains were found here, as well as ceramic fragments, some dating from the early Neolithic period (6000 BC). In the north of the peninsula near Akrotíri Skála is the **Díktynna** (Diktíneon). Originally there was a 7th-century Doric temple here, dedicated to the nymph Díktynna. The nymph, identified with the Cretan goddess Vritómartis, is said to have leapt into the sea

BELOW: Goniá Monastery.

here to escape the attentions of King Mínos. She was saved from drowning by fishermen with their nets. Emperor Hadrian is reputed to have ordered a new temple to be built here after his visit to Crete.

From Rodhopós there is a road leading to the church of **Ághios Ioánnis**. There are many turnings and no signposts, so remember to turn right at the cistern. Soon you reach a point where you can see the church lying deep in the valley. On 29 August thousands of believers come here to commemorate the beheading of St John the Baptist. It is one of major festivals of the Cretan religious calendar, and involves a mass baptism of boys called Ioánnis (John).

Binoculars are a great asset on Rodhopoú, as there are so many birds of prey to watch. It is so peaceful here that a day on Rodhopoú is definitely preferable to a visit to the Samariá Gorge if you really want to get away from it all.

TIP

While it is not true that "all Cretans are liars", you should not always believe their answers to your questions – "No, it is not far from here," "Yes, the weather will be fine tomorrow," etc. They do not like to disappoint tourists, so they are telling you what you want to hear.

Kastélli and Gramvoúsa

Kastélli ㉛, sometimes called **Kíssamos** after the region it dominates, lies between the two peninsulas of Rodhopoú and Gramvoúsa, 42 km (26 miles) west of Haniá. The little harbour, from which ferries leave regularly for the Peloponnese, has made the town a trading centre of western Crete. The inhabitants are fishermen, farmers and merchants, and the favourable climate and abundant supply of water here give rise to a wonderfully green environment. As there are also lovely beaches, with hotels, pensions and tavernas, Kastélli is gradually becoming a tourist destination.

This area has been inhabited since very early times. There was a late Minoan settlement here called Kisamos, which was the independent port city of ancient Polyrrinia. Above the modern village of **Polyrrinía** ㉜, 6 km (4 miles) from

BELOW: grazing in the olive grove.

Kastélli, noted for its wild flowers in spring and the excellent Odysséus taverna, are the ruins of the city of that name. It was founded around 800 BC and destroyed by the Saracens in the 9th century AD. It was one of the most important Dorian city states in western Crete, being a well-fortified settlement in the hills within sight of a port. Apart from the remains of a temple, cisterns and burial chambers, there are also the ruins of fortifications which were rebuilt in Byzantine times.

Map on pages 192–3

From Kastélli you can take a bus or taxi to the peaceful village of **Plátanos** ㉝. In the church are some interesting icons, among them one depicting the 99 Holy Fathers. From here you can visit the ancient city of Falássarna, which was one of the ports for Polyrrinia. The Greek and Roman port became silted up, but recent excavations are revealing extensive remains. The destruction of the harbour was caused by the island's continuous tilting on its axis from west to east. The Englishman Captain Spratt was the first person to recognise that the prehistoric wave notch around the cliffs on the west coast was the result of this action. The sandy beach itself is expansive (about 3 km/1¾ miles) and in recent years the tavernas and rooms available have increased in number. The plain behind the beaches is an important area for the growing of tomatoes and bananas under acres of plastic greenhouses, and there is an annual tomato festival.

The two islands off the Gramvoúsa Peninsula both take its name – Ímeri (Tame) and Ágria (Wild) Gramvoúsa.

The ancient city of Agnion, famous for its temple of Apollo, lay on the north-east end of the **Gramvoúsa Peninsula** ㉞. Now the peninsula is uninhabited, a good place for walking and watching vultures and other birds of prey. From Kastélli you can take a boat to the island of Ímeri Gramvoúsa, one of the oldest pirate haunts in the Mediterranean, complete with a lagoon, a mist-topped mountain and a Venetian fortress that was built around 1580. Being 137 metres

LEFT: giant fennel in bloom.
BELOW: buzzards breed on the Gramvoúsa Peninsula.

Map on pages 192–3

(455 ft) above sea level, it proved impregnable to the Turks. There is also the rusting hulk of a trawler whose skipper did not know these waters.

The road back to Haniá

From Kastélli, take the old road to Haniá and after about 2 km (1¼ miles) you pass through the village of **Kaloudhianá** ㉟. It is worth making a small detour to the **Villa Trevizan**. Rather than taking the turn to the right for Topólia, proceed straight on for 1 km (½ mile), where you will find, signposted to the left, a dirt road leading to the villa nestling in the olive groves. This 17th-century villa is a fine example of the style of country house favoured by the Venetians and is based on a plan by Palladio. The ground floor was reserved for storerooms and an external staircase on the front elevation leads to the main entrance. The pediment is decorated with the Trevizan family's coat of arms, carved in stone. Unfortunately today this superb building is in a deplorable state of disrepair.

Graviéra, made from goat's milk, is Crete's most popular cheese.

Below: a Sfakiot shepherd. **Right:** the road to the west.

Close by is the site of the ancient city of **Míthymna**, where you can see the hill known as Rókka. Looking like a volcano-shaped cone, this isolated pillar of rock was inhabited by the Dorians and is a good example of a hilltop refuge town of that period.

Back in Kaloudhianá is a sign for **Topólia** ㊱, a village 10 km (6 miles) from Kastélli, which straddles the hillside. It is renowned for its mineral springs as well as its unusual Italianate bell-tower at the church of Aghía Paraskeví (a 2nd-century martyr, the healer of the blind) which also has late Byzantine period frescoes. After the village is the **Topólia Gorge**, an impressive ravine 1½ km (1 mile) long with vertical cliffs rising up to 300 metres (1,000 ft) and a width of 5–10 metres (15–33 ft) at the river bed. The road is extremely narrow and twisting and at one point disappears into a single lane tunnel carved into the rock.

Soon after, you come to a stairway leading up to the cave of **Aghía Sofía** ㊲, a cathedral-like space full of stalagmites and stalactites. There is a small chapel and, from remains found on the site, there is evidence of occupation dating back to the Neolithic age. It was also used in Greek and Roman times as a place of worship and even today, on the feast day of St Sofía, numerous local people congregate here for a religious service.

Máleme ㊳, 16 km (10 miles) west of Haniá, is where a beehive-shaped (*tholos*) tomb with an unusually long (13.8m/46 ft) *drómos* (approach road) was excavated in 1966 by the Greek archaeologist C. Davarás. Unfortunately, by this time the tomb had already been robbed. In World War II, Haniá airport was located here, and in 1941, after heavy fighting, it was captured by German airborne troops. There are 4,465 graves in the German cemetery of Máleme, mainly of very young men. Most of them lost their lives on 20 May 1941, the day they landed. Their remains were kept in the Monastery of Goniá until the cemetery was created in 1973. For many years there has been a celebration by Cretan and British commonwealth veterans to commemorate the anniversary of the Battle of Crete, not just here but in other parts of the island as well. ❑

LIP STICK
DANCING BAR

ÁGHIOS NIKÓLAOS AND SURROUNDINGS

Maps:
Town 212
Area 214

Although "Ag Nik" thrives on tourism, the attractive little port is very appealing. The surrounding region offers well-preserved ancient sites, attractive villages and stunning coastal scenery

Capital of the province of Lassíthi, **Aghios Nikólaos** ❶ is the largest town in the east of the xisland. Its permanent population is about 10,000, which multiplies several-fold in the summer. "Ag Nik", the diminutive used by tourists (the locals call it Águios), owes its popularity to its glorious situation on the southwest of the Gulf of Mirabéllo and to the fact that it is strategically situated for excursions into the surrounding countryside. It most certainly does not owe its fame to its beaches.

These are the **municipal beach** Ⓐ, which is immediately south of the bus station and stadium; **Kitroplatía beach** Ⓑ, north of the harbour; and **Ammoúdi beach**, which is on the road to Eloúnda. The best of a poor lot is at **Almyrós**, about 2 km (1¼ miles) out of town, southwards on the Sitía road. It attracts naturists. Otherwise there is bathing in town from **Aktí Koundoúrou** Ⓒ, the rocks below the shoreline road.

In the main square, **Platía El. Venizélou** Ⓓ, stands a monument honouring 400 people shot by the German forces in the southwest of the city in 1943. From the square, two short, steep, parallel, shop-lined streets – Koundoúrou and 29 Octovríou – lead down to the small boat harbour. This, and the lake, where every available spot is crowded with cafe and taverna tables, are the social centres of the town.

Face the small boat harbour and the road to the right leads to a long quay, at the end of which stands a lighthouse. It is from here that excursion boats leave for Spinalónga and Psíra and the occasional passenger ship – from Piraeus, from Sitía or from Rhodes – ties up. Behind this quay is the workaday part of the town, a new marina and the bus station.

If you turn left from the harbour, you come to a bridge that crosses a short narrow canal connecting the waters of the harbour with those of **Lake Voulisméni** Ⓔ. Legend has it that the lake is bottomless, and the home of spirits. The goddesses Athena and Vritomartis, the Cretan Artemis, are said to have bathed here. Less romantic modern surveyors have found that Voulisméni is in fact 64 metres (210 ft) deep, and fed by an underground river.

On crossing the bridge resist the temptation – at least for the time being – to join the sybarites seated at tables all around the lake. Rather, a half-left leads to **Odhós Paleólogou**, a steepish hill, at the foot of which stands the **Folk Museum** Ⓕ (Sun–Fri 10am–1.30pm, 6–9.30pm). It houses a well-displayed collection of traditional hand-woven textiles, costumes and wood carvings.

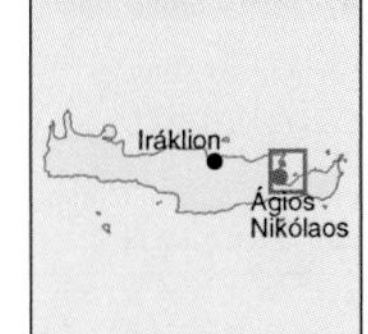

PRECEDING PAGES: Ághios Nikólaos by night.
LEFT: catching the breeze, Ag Nik.
BELOW: a seller of sponges.

The Minos Beach Hotel in Ag Nik was Greece's first five-star resort hotel.

Near the brow of the hill is the **Archaeological Museum** **G** (Tues–Sun 8.30am–3pm, extended to 5pm Aug–Sep) which houses finds, roughly in chronological order, uncovered from sites in Eastern Crete and dating from the Neolithic, Minoan, Post-Minoan and Roman eras. The outstanding item is the Goddess of Mýrtos, an unusual clay libation vase considered worthy of a case to itself. Other highlights are a Neolithic phallus-shaped idol, Middle-Minoan vases from a shipwreck, gold jewellery and a skull decorated with a wreath of gold leaves and, alongside it, formerly in its mouth, the silver coin that was the ferry fare across the River Styx to Hades.

From the museum backtrack down Odhós Paleólogou then turn right on Solomoú. An immediate left turn places you above the lake from where you can enjoy splendid views. Steps cut in the hillside permit descent to the lake for a well-earned break.

From the bridge follow the shoreline (Aktí Koundoúrou) and soon pass the **Aquarium** and then the entrance to the Minos Beach Hotel, the first five-star resort hotel not only in Crete, but in all Greece. Immediately after this, a secondary road to the right passes the church of **Ághios Nikólaos** **H**. The undistinguished simple church lays claim to being the oldest in Crete. The basis for this claim is that the underlayer of frescoes in the church – two layers were found – consists of geometric designs suggesting that the church dates from the time of the Iconoclasts (8th–9th century) who banned the representation of the divine or saintly form in religious art. The church is usually closed; for the key enquire at the reception desk of the Minos Palace Hotel in whose grounds the church stands. The road beyond it leads to a raised promontory, a pleasant place to relax far from the madding crowd.

BELOW: a local woman and a tourist shop.

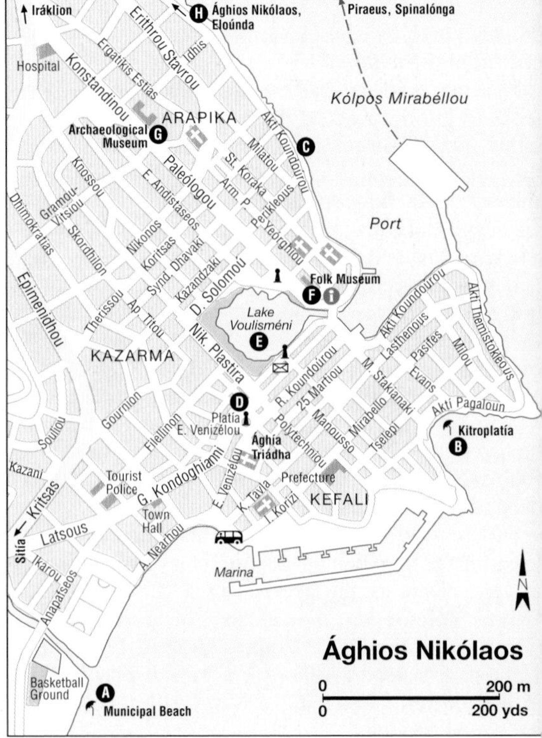

North to Spinalónga

An 11-km (7-mile) road climbs north from Ághios Nikólaos and then descends to Eloúnda. At the brow of the road stands a small chapel, from which you can enjoy magnificent views over the **Gulf of Mirabéllo**. As you proceed towards Eloúnda the long peninsula of Spinalónga extends outwards from the narrow isthmus of Póros and runs parallel to the coast for about 4 km (2½ miles) to form an inlet of the sea that is virtually a salt lake, its narrow entrance partially blocked by a tiny island, also called Spinalónga.

As you approach Eloúnda, a sign points to ancient "submerged city" of **Oloús** to the right. A track runs along the shore passing salt pans that were built by the Venetians and in use until recently. This soon leads to a causeway above an isthmus which is interrupted by a small bridge in the lee of three disused windmills. The bridge spans a canal dug by the French to open up to the sea the south end of the natural sheltered harbour of Eloúnda.

When the waters around the causeway are calm the scanty remains of the Minoan port of Oloús may be seen under the sea on the right. Here, the moon goddess Artemis Vritomartis, inventor of the fishing net, was worshipped. Legend has it that she turned into a fish to escape the amorous embraces of King Minos. Further along the causeway is a 4th-century Byzantine basilica with a black and white mosaic floor enlivened by dolphins. Birdwatchers will wish to reach the peninsula – best done by boat. It and the waters on either side of the causeway are popular with swimmers, but beware sea urchins.

And so to **Eloúnda** ❷, a more subdued beach resort than Ag Nik, which contains some glorious hotels. Life in the village centres on the pleasant large central square overlooking the sea. Five kilometres (3 miles) north of Eloúnda

Maps: Town 212 Area 214

Oloús was still a flourishing city in the 2nd century AD, according to the Greek geographer Pausanias. It probably sank beneath the waves during tectonic upheavals in the 4th century.

BELOW: relaxing by Ag Nik harbour.

The ruins of the former leper colony Spinalónga.

is the quiet resort of **Pláka** ❸, a former fishing village with a crescent-shaped pebble beach, good windsurfing and a few tavernas. Pleasure boats leave from here (also from Eloúnda and Ághios Nikólaos) for the short voyage to the island of **Spinalónga** ❹.

Spinalónga's fortress, built by the Venetians in 1579 in order to defend the approach to the Gulf, was one of the strongest in all Crete. Throughout the 17th century the fortress remained in Venetian hands and was a refuge for Christians fleeing from the Turks. But in 1715, as the result of a treaty, it was handed over to the Turks who remained until driven out of Crete in 1903. It then became a leper colony – practically a prison – and remained one, the last in Europe until it closed in 1957, when word finally reached Crete that leprosy (by now called Hansen's Disease) was not contagious. Among the locals it was known as "the island of the living dead".

After landing at the south end of Spinalónga, turn left through a long vaulted tunnel which leads to the ruins of the town. The remains of a church and the doctors' hall can be seen, as well as the shells of houses. The cemetery, with open graves, is a particularly gruesome spot. Climb to the top of the island to view the crumbling fortifications and to enjoy a splendid view of the mountains.

Famous frescoes

As you travel southwest from Ághios Nikólaos, up in the hills just before Kritsá you reach the renowned church of **Panaghía Kerá** ❺ (Our Lady of Kerá; Mon–Sat 9am–3pm, Sun 9am–2pm; entrance fee), sitting in a grove of cypresses and pines. The church, the earliest part of which dates from the 13th century, the latest from the 14th, has three aisles. Although dedicated to the Virgin Mary it

BELOW: one of the many images of Christ in Panaghía Kéra's frescoes.

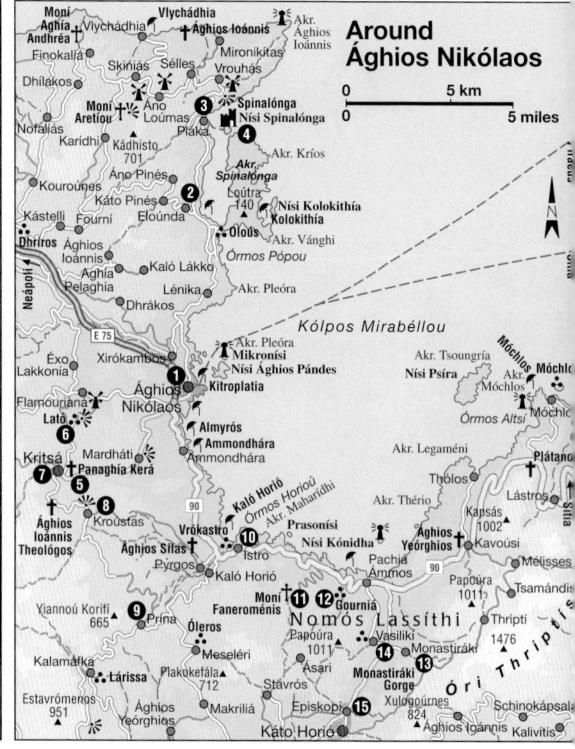

houses two more saints – St Anne, mother of the Holy Virgin, and St Anthony. The entire interior is a picture-book bible composed of splendidly preserved 13th- and 14th-century frescoes. Until not too long ago Panaghía Kerá was a functioning church: now, it is a museum.

Enter the church by the south aisle door and you are immediately faced by a sea of frescoes. This is the most glorious Byzantine fresco cycle in all Crete. The south aisle is dedicated to St Anne, who looks down from the rear of the apse. Scenes from the life of the Virgin, arranged in pairs on either side of the vault, end in the journey to Bethlehem and Mary triumphant with the Infant Jesus encircled above a closed gate.

The story of Mary is continued in the centre aisle which also has scenes from the life of Christ, including the nativity, Herod's banquet and the Last Supper. The dome does not have the customary Christ Pantokrátor painting but instead has four gospel scenes – Christ in the Temple, the Baptism of Christ, the Raising of Lazarus and the Entry into Jerusalem.

In the north aisle, dedicated to St Anthony, the main iconography depicts the Second Coming of Christ. High on the west wall the Archangel Michael sounds the last trumpet call which proclaims that coming, while the painting of Christ Pantokrátor is at the rear of the apse. Also painted in this aisle are a vision of Paradise and a walled garden in which the seated Virgin, surrounded by the Patriarchs Abraham, Isaac and Jacob, protects the souls of the just.

Among all these biblical scenes in the north aisle you might wish to search for the portrait of the donor, Yeórghios Azizánis and his wife and child: it is in the northwest corner. Back in the south aisle, on the west wall, is an inscription naming the donor, Antónios Lámeras, and the village of "Kritzea".

The Panaghía Kerá frescoes have been retouched and restored so often over the centuries that it is impossible to say with certainty which are the oldest.

BELOW: sailing past Spinalónga island.

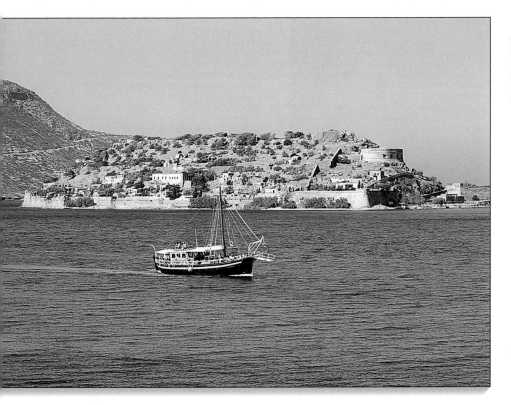

Experts will be able to distinguish the different styles of fresco painting (the 13th-century "archaising linear style" and the more natural 14th-century Palaeologan style) but for the average visitor it is not the different styles but the sheer, overwhelming mass of dazzling iconography that fascinates.

A number of other frescoed churches can be found close to Panaghía Kerá, whose custodian can supply the keys if you are interested in visiting them (they are invariably locked).

Sometimes the custodian at the Lató site leaves the gate open well after the official closing time – and at other times he locks up when visitors are still inside. But it is not difficult to climb out.

Post-Minoan city

Just up the hill from Panaghía Kerá a right turn leads, after 3 km (1¾ miles), to the ruins of **Lató** ❻ (Tues–Sun 8.30am–3pm). A path also leads directly from the church to the ruins. The city was founded in the post-Minoan period, probably at the time of the Doric migration to Crete during the Dark Ages of the Greek world. Lató became the dominant city in the region during the Archaic period and continued to flourish through the Classical and Hellenistic eras. Most of its scanty ruins, spread out over twin peaks and the saddle between them, date from the 7th–4th centuries BC.

Enter the ruins by the original city gate, about 100 metres (110 yds) downhill from where the road ends. Immediately turn right and walk up a cobbled street past houses and shops, including a miller's with a stone hand-mill, to reach the irregular-shaped *agora*. This was the town meeting-place and a cult centre. On the northern side of the *agora* a broad flight of steps flanked by the remains of two towers leads to the *prytaneion* (Town Hall) while on the west side of the *agora a stoa* (colonnaded walkway) with stone benches offered shelter to the citizens. On a terrace, about 100 metres to the southeast, stand the well-preserved

BELOW: Classical steps, Lató.

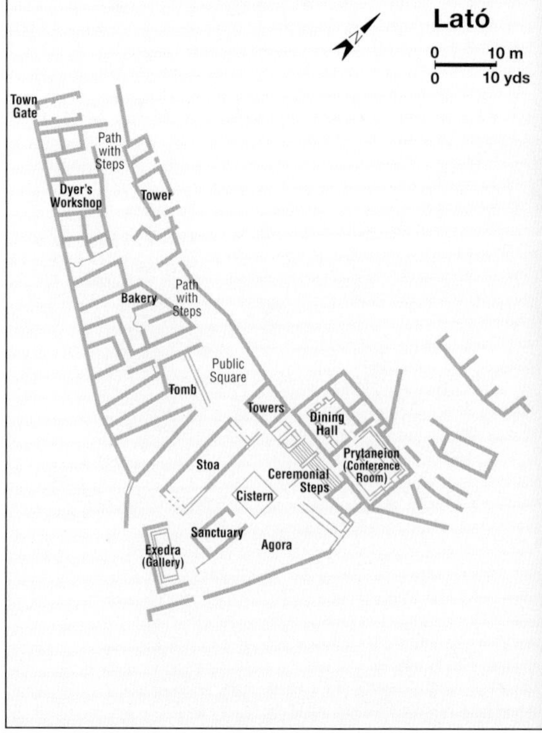

remains of the lower courses of a rectangular temple. Here, too, are the remains of what is believed to have been a small theatre.

The pleasure of Lató lies not so much in the Greco-Roman mute stones but in superb views from the upper acropolis across a plain covered with olive and almond trees as far as the coast and Ághios Nikólaos (in ancient days the port for Lató), and beyond to the Gulf of Mirabéllo and the Sitía mountains. To sit here and to absorb the view with background music provided by the bells of unseen sheep is to feel completely chaste.

Maps:
Area 214
Site 216

Kritsá was used as a location for He Who Must Die*, the 1956 film version of Kazantzákis' novel* Christ Recrucified. *Many of the villagers appeared as extras.*

Most beautiful

And so to **Kritsá ❼**, 11 km (7 miles) from Ághios Nikólaos, which is said to be the largest village in Crete and is claimed (by the Greek National Tourist Office, but with some justification) to be the most beautiful. It hangs suspended on the mountainside 300 metres (1,000 feet) above Ag Nik. Just before the village is the the church of Ághios Yeórghios Kavousiótis which contains two interesting frescoes dating from the 13th and 14th centuries. A kilometre (½ mile) further, on the Kroústas road, is the triple-aisled church of Ághios Ioánnis Theológos which once belonged to Toploú Monastery. It contains a magnificent iconostasis. Then there is the church of Ághios Konstantínos with its mid-14th century frescoes, and the cemetery church of Ághios Ioánnis whose frescoes have a dedicatory inscription dated 1370.

Visitors are greeted at the entrance to Kritsá by a bronze statue of Kritsotópoula, "The Maid of Kritsá". She is revered as a freedom fighter against the Turkish oppressors. The Turkish Pasha Husein had chosen this daughter of the priest of Kritsá as his mistress. On her first night with him she stabbed the

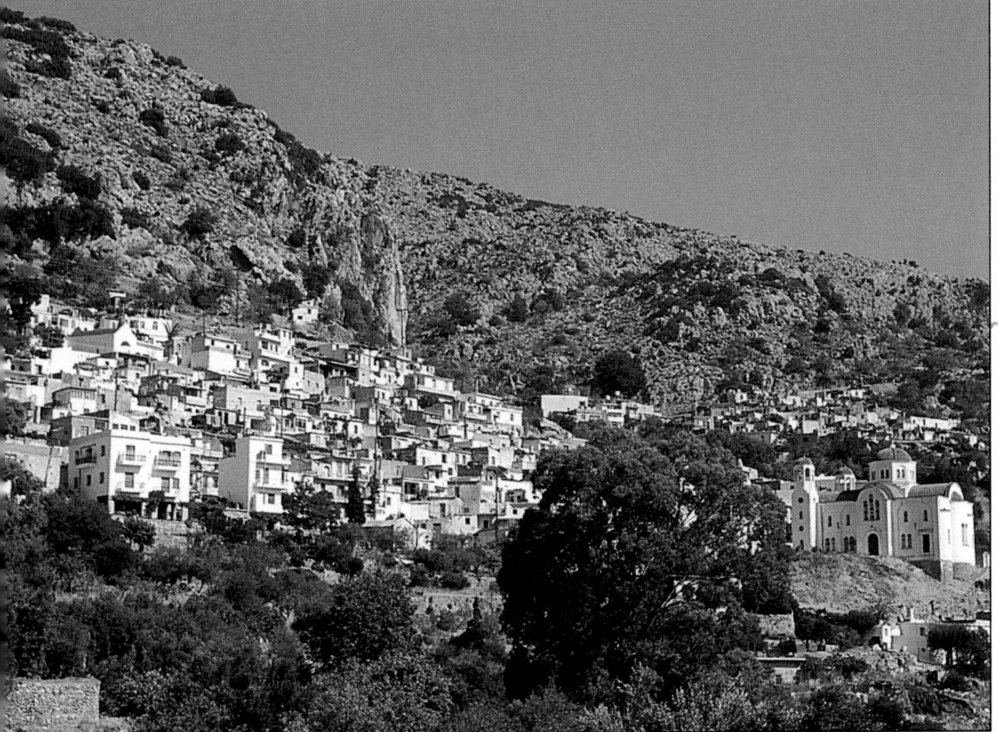

Below: Kritsá, the largest village on Crete.

Pasha, dressed herself as a man, and joined the freedom fighters on the Lassíthi Plateau. Not until she was fatally wounded did her comrades discover that brave Kritsotópoula was a woman.

On the narrow whitewashed streets of Kritsá, among the throngs of tourists, the men of the village can be seen dressed in traditional Cretan clothing – baggy pants, knee-high leather boots and a bandana round their head – while the women, dressed in black, conduct the business of the village. And that is largely selling the leather goods, embroidery and elaborately woven rugs for which Kritsá is renowned. During the summer, joyous mock weddings are celebrated for the edification of (paying) tourists.

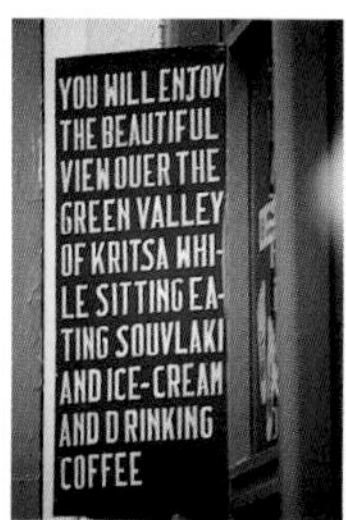

An invitation to linger that is hard to resist.

Sheep climbing over the rocky landscapes around provide the wool for the weaving of brilliant orange and crimson rugs and blankets which hang, after dyeing, together with hanks of wool, over balconies and garden walls throughout the village. The views from these balconies and terraces, especially at the far end of the village, over the valley to the Gulf of Mirabéllo are superb. The red soil is covered with well-manicured groves of thousands of olive trees and scattered among these are carob and almond trees.

The much quieter yet still lovely village of **Kroústas** ❽ is reached after 6 km (4 miles) by turning left at the entrance to Kritsá. Those with an adventurous spirit may wish to continue on a rough road for 8 km (5 miles) to the small flower-bedecked unspoilt village of **Prína** ❾, from where magnificent views may be enjoyed, and then circle back to Ághios Nikólaos via **Kaló Horió** (Kaló Chorió). To achieve this, take a left at Prína on to a sealed road and after 8 km (5 miles) you reach the main road, from where it is 11 km (7 miles) to Ághios Nikólaos.

From the other end of Kritsá village a dirt road climbs for 16 km (10 miles)

BELOW: cool shade in Kritsá.

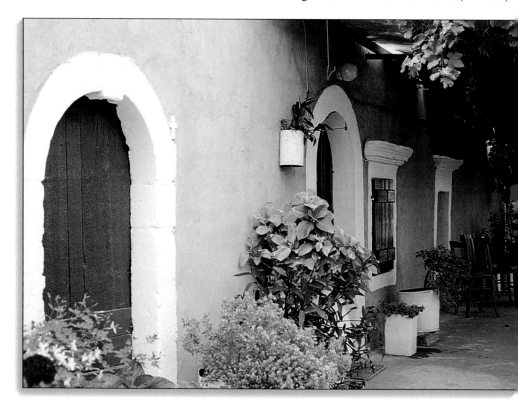

to the isolated **Katharó Plateau**, a glorious circular carpet of vegetable plots and orchards enclosed by mountain peaks dominated by **Mt Lázaros** (2,085 metres/ 6,560 ft). The plateau, at an altitude of 1,100 metres (3,830 ft), through which the Lasíthiou River flows, is 8 km (5 miles) long and 2 km (1¼ miles) wide. On 20 May the horticulturists, the wine and *rakí* makers abandon Kritsá and make for their simple houses on the plateau where they remain until the autumn. During the winter the plateau is desolate and abandoned.

Maps: Area 214 Site 220

Ancient streets

Twelve kilometres (8 miles) southeast of Ághios Nikólaos on the road to Sitía lies the relatively new beach resort of **Ístro** ❿, around which are two or three decent sandy coves. Travel for a further 6 km (4 miles) and a dirt road to the right dizzily zigzags for nearly 7 km (4 miles) to reach **Faneroméni Monastery** ⓫ (Moní Faneroménis), built in the middle of the 15th century and dedicated to the Virgin Mary whose icon manifested itself in a small cave on this spot. However, it is not for ecclesiastic excitement that one makes this detour but for breathtaking views down to the Gulf of Mirabéllo.

Although Moní Faneroméni has no official opening times, if you knock loudly you will be admitted and shown the grotto/chapel where the icon of the Madonna was found.

Back on the main road, 19 km (12 miles) from Ághios Nikólaos, the extensive remains of **Gourniá** ⓬ spread over a low ridge, come into sight. This is the most completely preserved of all Minoan towns. Gourniá flourished around 1600 BC and continued to flourish until it was destroyed in about 1450 BC in the same catastrophe that brought down Knossós and the other great Minoan centres. Especially in spring, when the site is covered with a riot of flowers and perfume fills the air, even those bored with old stones will be delighted.

When you enter Gourniá you are immediately faced by a labyrinth of narrow

BELOW: taking a break from the olive harvest.

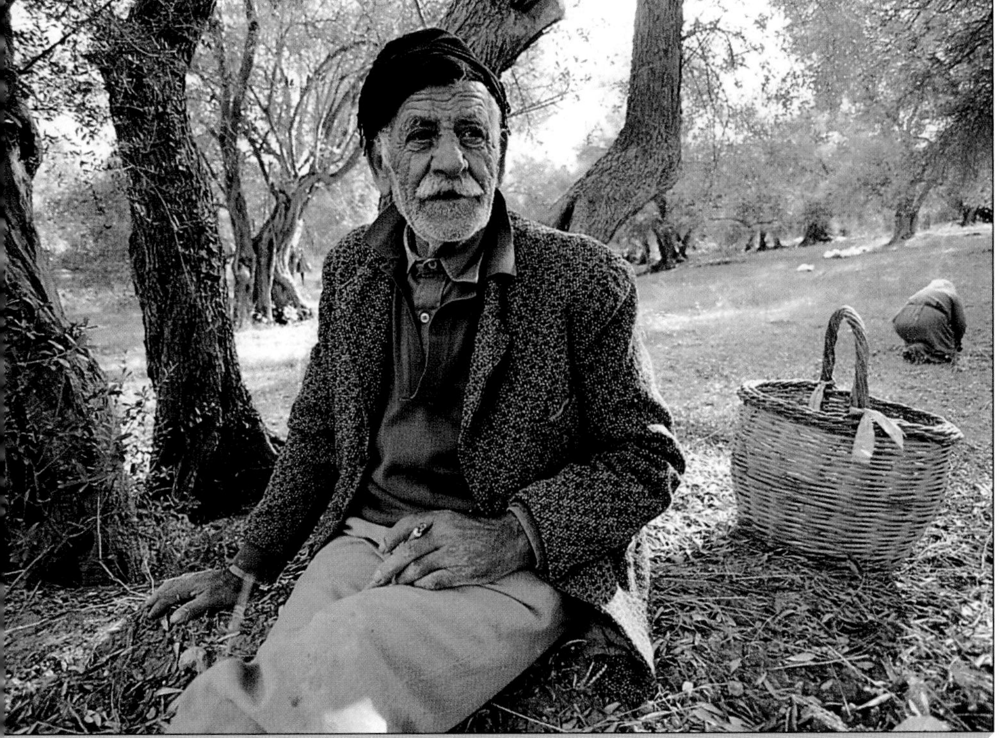

The Gourniá site was excavated in 1901–4 by a team led by a young American, Harriet Boyd Hawes. The discoveries made her reputation as an archaeologist.

cobbled streets, each a mere metre (3 ft) wide, bordered on both sides by ruined homes and workshops. If you have visited any contemporary Cretan mountain village, you will experience a *déjà vu*. These ancient lanes divide Gourniá into four unequal and irregular quarters. The buildings, some of whose walls still stand to shoulder height, are believed to have had two storeys – stairways have been found – basements or semi-basements containing work rooms and/or storage space, and living quarters on the upper floor.

The main interest at Gourniá is the light that the contents of these buildings shed on everyday domestic life. A great number of common or garden objects were unearthed, including tools and implements relating to activities such as agriculture, fishing, weaving and pottery. The artefacts found in some dwellings to the north and to the east have enabled identification of the trade of the occupant – a carpenter, a potter, a smith. Stroll along the street which runs south and then curves to the right to arrive at a large open space which was probably the town's *agora* (market place). At the north side of this court are circular stones with depressions which were perhaps used for ritual offerings. At the northwest corner a series of steps leads to the palace area. The relatively small palace, a complex of corridors and stairways leading to apartments, halls and storerooms, was probably occupied by an overlord rather than a king. It is a smaller, less ostentatious than the palaces of Knossós and Phaestos.

About 20 metres north of the palace, reached by a path paved with cobblestones and a flight of three steps, is the Shrine of the Minoan Snake Goddess. A small room contains a shelf on which terracotta goddesses with raised arms, snake totems and other cult objects were found. (These are now in the Archaeological Museum of Iráklion.) From here descend the hill to more houses and workshops.

BELOW: ancient Gourniá overlooks the Sea of Crete.

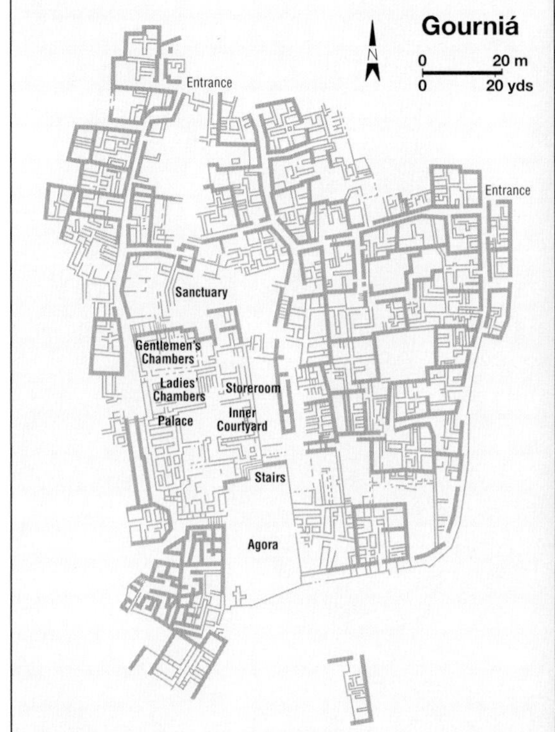

Two kilometres (1¼ miles) after leaving Gourniá you will reach the village of **Pachiá Ámmos** (Pahiá Ámmos), which in days gone by had an attractive harbour. Now, it is a rather sad resort. In another 2 km (1¼ miles), to the right, is the road to Ierápetra on the south coast. This road is dominated to the east by the massive Thryptí range. This is Crete's "waist": at this point the island is at its narrowest, a mere 14 km (9 miles) of land separating the Sea of Crete to the north from the Libyan Sea to the south, a topographical fact that may well have prompted the founding of Gourniá.

To the left, about 5 km (3 miles) along the Ierápetra road, a dramatic, wedge-shaped cleft in the Thryptí mountains – the **Monastiráki Gorge** ⓭ – can be seen. To the right, a secondary road leads to **Vasilikí** ⓮, a Pre-Palace Minoan settlement (2600–2000 BC) renowned for a distinctive style of pottery, known as Vasilikí ware. The site, which was destroyed by fire, is of great importance for the information it yields on the Pre-Palace Period, the first Minoan era. Like Gourniá, it includes the remains of houses with basements.

Plans are afoot to build a new international airport south of Vasilikí, to make the east of the island more accessible to mass tourism. But the objections of archaeologists, worried about potential damage to as yet undiscovered sites, have so far held back the earth-moving machinery.

Back on the main Ierápetra road, the village of **Episkopí** ⓯, noted for its blue-domed church in the shape of a cross, is soon seen below the road on the left. It is often locked, but it is its exterior that makes it unique in Crete. The church has a double dedication and an unusual ground plan. The Venetian south nave is dedicated to Ághios Harálambos, while the earlier (12th- or 13th-century) north nave, with an arched, blue-tiled drum dome, is dedicated to Ághios Yeórghios. ❐

Maps: Area 214 Site 220

The unusual clay vases found at Vasilikí have elongated spouts, like a teapot, and a semi-lustrous red and black mottled surface. There are examples in the Iráklion and Ághios Nikólaos Archaeological Museums.

BELOW: gathering *hórta* (wild greens) in an olive grove.

FASCINATION FOR ORNITHOLOGISTS

Crete's riot of spring flowers, and the insects they support, supply the island's varied bird life with abundant food for most of the year

Bird-watchers will find much to delight them throughout Crete. Hoopoes, rollers, bee-eaters and golden orioles provide the brightest colours, but stop and listen in any olive grove, and you will hear the constant background of birdcalls from the unseen majority, small birds leading undramatic lives. Look to the skies and there are swifts, swallows, martins and buzzards or larger raptors. Waste ground feeds sparrows, finches, warblers, wagtails and larks. One of the commonest is the sociable and melodious crested lark (above).

Unlike many other Greek islands, the shooting (and eating) of small birds is comparatively limited on Crete. The hunters' main quarry today are partridge or quail, although griffon vultures were a frequent target in the past, to judge by the sad and dusty stuffed specimens languishing in country tavernas. There are few four-legged predators, although stone martens may raid nests.

PASSING THROUGH

In spring, migrants from Africa pause in Crete before they head on further north, resting for a while in sheltered bays on the south coast, or small patches of fresh water and fertile land. The island's many gorges provide both nesting sites for raptors and gateways through the mountains for lower-flying migrants. Autumn sees migrants heading south again – and some get no further, such as the famous swallows that overwinter in Ierápetra. Occasional rarities from Asia Minor appear, such as the pied kingfisher, palm dove and blue-cheeked bee-eater.

▷ HIDDEN GOLD
Gloriously coloured, golden orioles are surprisingly hard to see, except when they break cover and fly fast between trees. Listen for their blackbird-like song.

△ AERIAL HUNTERS
The chatter of high-flying groups of insect-hunting bee-eaters is usually the first indication of their presence. Their voices can be heard almost anywhere.

△ AUTUMN BREEDER
The rare Eleanora's falcon nests on coastal cliffs at the end of summer, breeding to coincide with the passage of the small migrating birds on which it feeds its young.

◁ UNIQUE BLUEBIRD
The male blue rock thrush, uniquely coloured among Mediterranean birds, is a distinctive sight, though it rarely stays around for closer inspection.

▽ SMALL SONGSTER
The Sardinian warbler can be distinguished from other warblers by its red-ringed eyes and a black cap. Other warblers are often best identified by their song.

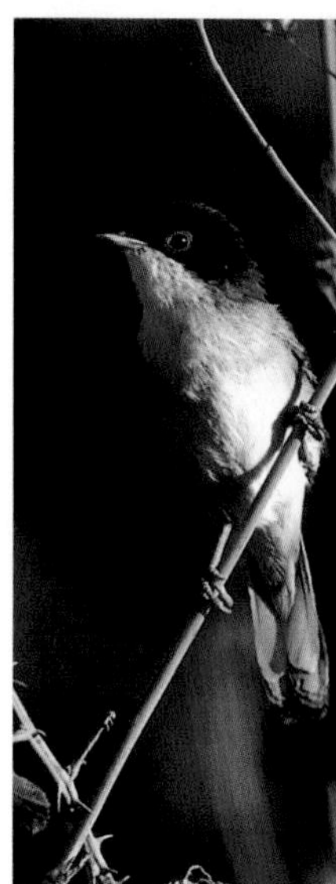

A SCAVENGER UNDER THREAT

The extraordinary lammergeier, or bearded vulture, is one of Crete's rarest residents. The nine or 10 pairs that survive in the remotest mountains of the island are the only viable breeding population left in Greece or the Balkans. One pair will patrol a territory of 200–400 sq. km (75–150 sq. miles) so, even under ideal conditions, Crete could probably never support more than 20–25 pairs.

Almost uniquely, the lammergeier feeds mainly on animal bones. Larger bones are repeatedly dropped onto sharp rocks until they break to reveal the marrow, while smaller bones are swallowed whole and digested by powerful gastric juices.

The main threats to the lammergeier in Crete are from illegal shooting and from poisoned bait put out for crows. At the same time, a decrease in stock-breeding has reduced the amount of food available.

A programme initiated by the Iráklion Natural History Museum and the Greek Ornithological Union is aimed at protecting seven strategic mountainous areas and improving public awareness of the plight of this rare and unusual bird.

▷ NOCTURNAL PEEPS
ounding like the ping of a ubmarine's sonar, the call f the tiny Scops owl, is ndlessly repeated through he night. Pairs of birds ometimes call in duet.

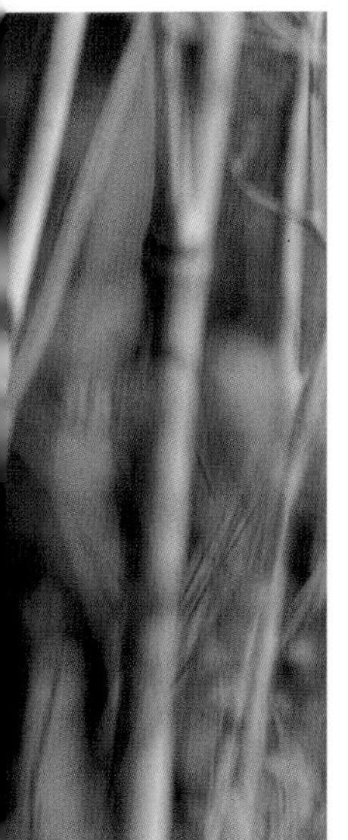

◁ SPRING VISIT
Migrating squacco herons pass through on their way to breeding grounds further north.

▷ HIGH FLIER
Griffon vultures, Crete's commonest vulture, favour upland areas, steep slopes or gorges which provide the uplifting thermals they need.

EASTERN CRETE

This part of the island includes the fertile Lassíthi Plateau, a spectacular coast road leading to the eastern tip, the near-deserted far southeast, and the southernmost town in Europe

Map on page 228

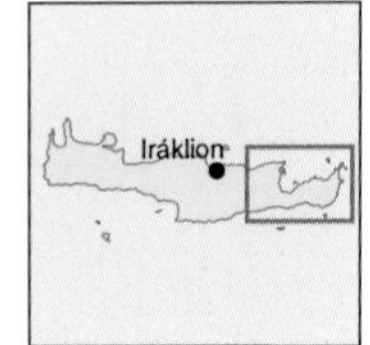

To reach the Lassíthi Plateau, one of Crete's outstanding attractions, you leave the main road from Iráklion to Ághios Nikólaos at the market town of **Neápoli** ❶. The place was founded in the 16th century under the name of Neochorió (New Village). In 1870 the Turkish prefect Kostis Pasha moved the district administration and bishopric here, which meant the name was no longer adequate. It was changed from New Village to New Town: Neápolis. But today, apart from the district court and the bishopric, all the important offices of Lassíthi are situated on the coast in Ághios Nikólaos.

A winding road climbs 31 km (19 miles) into the mountains, passing through the villages of **Vrýses** (Vrísses), **Zénia** and **Éxo Potamí**, then along a river valley lined with oaks and fruit trees to **Mésa Potamí** and upwards to a pass at 1,100 metres (3,830 ft) from where there are glorious vistas. The road now descends again, and spread out in front of you is a breathtaking scene: a huge intensely-farmed basin surrounded by some of the highest peaks of the Dhíkti range. The average elevation is 866 metres (2,882 ft), and the basin measures 12 km (8 miles) east to west and 6 km (4 miles) from north to south.

The **Lassíthi Plateau** ❷, the best known upland plain on the island, is a vast cornucopia as far as the eye can see. Impeccably cultivated tiny fields, laid out like a patchwork quilt, are enclosed by the bare flanks of mountains. The rich soil supports potatoes and cucumbers, grain crops, apples and pears and an abundance of almonds. The visitor can well believe that Crete was the granary of Rome and will recall Pliny's statement that whatever is produced in Crete is incomparably better than that which is produced in other parts. However, rare is the day – best opportunities are in late summer – when you will see the unfurled white sails of any of the 10,000 windmills installed to irrigate the rich alluvial soil. Indeed, many of the rusted pumps have now collapsed.

During the Venetian occupation the Lassíthi Plateau was a centre for revolutionary activity. In 1263 the Venetians savagely suppressed the revolts by executing the rebels, destroying the villages, cutting down the orchards and issuing an edict forbidding anyone to farm or to graze their flocks under pain of dismemberment or death. In 1463, grain shortage forced the Venetians to permit cultivation, construct irrigation systems and introduce the famous windmills. By the 16th century new villages had arisen. In the struggle for independence from the Turks, the plain was again a revolutionary hotbed and Turkish armies wreaked vengeful havoc in 1823 and in 1866. During World War II the Germans carried out reprisals against the plain's Resistance movement.

Proceed clockwise around the plateau, passing the

PRECEDING PAGES: windmills on the Lassíthi Plateau.
LEFT: a harvest of tomatoes.
BELOW: Lassíthi is extensively farmed.

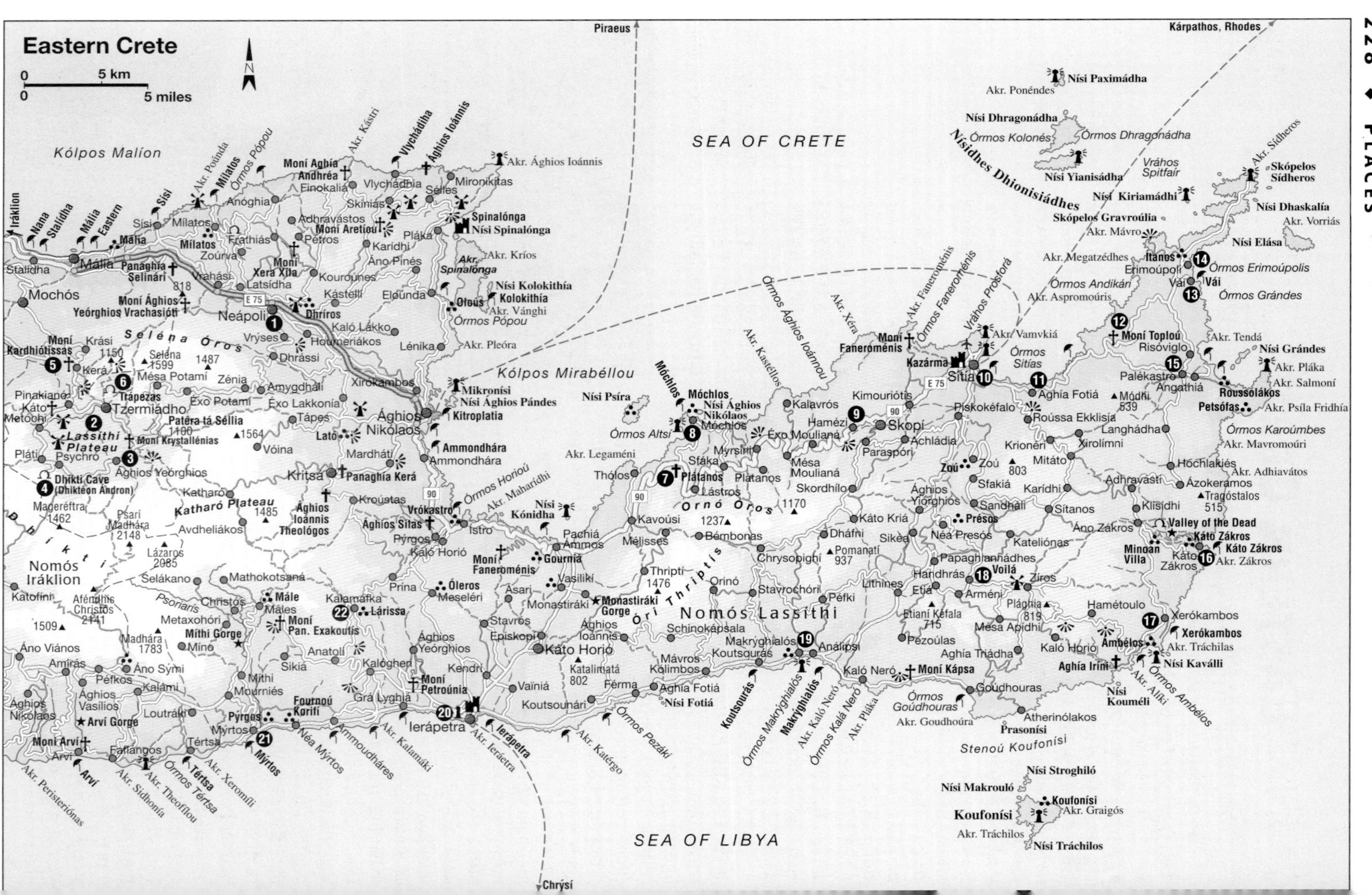
Eastern Crete
0 5 km
0 5 miles
SEA OF CRETE
SEA OF LIBYA
Kólpos Malíon
Kólpos Mirabéllou
Nomós Lassithi
Nomós Iráklion
Piraeus
Kárpathos, Rhodes
Chrysí
Iráklion
Nana
Stalídha
Mália
Eastern
Sísi
Mílatos
Neápoli
Dhríros
Spinalónga
Nísi Spinalónga
Eloúnda
Olous
Nísi Kolokithía
Ághios Nikólaos
Kitroplatia
Mikronísi
Nísi Ághios Pándes
Ammondhára
Latô
Kritsá
Panaghía Kerá
Tzermiádho
Lassíthi Plateau
Moní Krystallénias
Psychro
Dhiktí Cave (Dhiktéon Ándron)
Katharó Plateau
Vrókastro
Gourniá
Moní Faneroménis
Nísi Kónidha
Móchlos
Nísi Psíra
Pláitanos
Ornó Óros
Óri Thriptís
Monastiráki Gorge
Kató Horió
Ierápetra
Moní Petroúnia
Lárissa
Máles
Moní Pan. Exakoutís
Míthi Gorge
Mýrtos
Pýrgos
Fournoú Korifí
Arví Gorge
Moní Arví
Makrýghialós
Koutsourás
Nísi Fotiá
Skopí
Moní Faneroménis
Kazárma
Sitía
Aghía Fotiá
Moní Toploú
Palékastro
Roussolákos
Petsófas
Vái
Ítanos
Zou
Présos
Voilá
Zíros
Moní Kápsa
Valley of the Dead
Minoan Villa
Káto Zákros
Xerókambos
Ambélos
Aghía Iríni
Nísi Kouméli
Nísi Kaválli
Nísi Paximádha
Nísi Dhragonádha
Nísi Yianisádha
Nísidhes Dhionisiádhes
Nísi Kiriamádhi
Skópelos Gravroúlia
Skópelos Sídheros
Nísi Dhaskalía
Nísi Elása
Nísi Grándes
Stenoú Koufonísi
Prasonísi
Nísi Stroghiló
Nísi Makrouló
Koufonísi
Nísi Tráchilos
Akr. Sídheros
Órmos Erimoúpolis
Órmos Grándes
Órmos Karoúmbes
Órmos Ághios Ioánnou
Ormos Makrýghialós
Ormos Pezáki
Ormos Tértsa
Sélena Óros
Dhíkti
1 2 3 4 5 6 7 8 9 10 11 12 13 14 15 16 17 18 19 20 21 22

Krystallénia Monastery (**Moní Krystallénias**) and villages offering embroidery and weaving, fluttering gaily on clothes-lines, until you reach the village of **Águios Yeórghios** ❸. It contains an excellent **folklore museum** (summer only, 10am–4pm) in a village house furnished in traditional style.

Map on page 228

Birthplace of Zeus

Next is **Psychró** (Psichró), the starting point for the descent to the giant **Dhíkti Cave** (**Dhiktéon Ándron**) ❹, supposedly the birthplace of Zeus. Guides here can be as irritating as those at the Pyramids of Giza – but without one, how will you be able to distinguish the nipples upon which Zeus suckled from all the other stalactites and stalagmites? Donkeys are available for the 1-km (½-mile) uphill journey to the entrance to the cave. Non-slip shoes are necessary for the descent into the yawning chasm.

There are more than 3,000 caves in Crete – approximately half of all the caves in Greece. This is due to the crystalline nature of the island's limestone crust.

According to legend it was here that Zeus was born to Rhea. (The Idhean Cave also lays claim to this honour. With a wisdom of which Solomon would be proud, the Cretans have designated Dhíkti as the birthplace, Ídhi as the nursery.) Kronos, the husband of Rhea, had been warned that he would be overthrown by his son and accordingly ate all his offspring. However, when Zeus was born, Rhea gave Kronos a stone to eat and left the baby in the cave protected by the *koúretes* who beat their shields to disguise his cries. The nanny goat Amaltheia nursed him while Rhea spurted her own breast into the heavens creating the Milky Way.

The main cavern, reached through a narrow entrance, is 85 metres (283 ft) long, 40 metres (133 ft) wide and up to 20 metres (67 ft) high. On the right side of the upper cave is a sacred precinct where an altar and pottery offerings was found. On the left, a passage leads to the lower cave where wondrous stalactites and stalagmites grow. Many votive offerings were found here. On the left is a small chamber where Zeus was supposedly born.

Before you complete your circuit of the plateau and return to Neápoli, a short side trip is rewarding. At the **Pinakianó** crossroads, continue north for 3 km (1¾ miles) to the pass of Selí Ambeloú, from which there are breathtaking views in all directions. On a clear day you can see the island of Santoríni. A further 3 km (1¾ miles) leads to the village of **Kerá** and just beyond this is the **Monastery of Kardhiótissa** (**Moní Kardhiótissas**) ❺. Frescoes from the 14th-century adorn its walls but the church's renown is based on a miracle-working icon of the Virgin (Kardhiótissa means Our Lady of the Heart) which thrice was taken to Constantinople but returned to Kerá of its own accord. Legend has it that the icon was then chained to the column which still stands in the church courtyard. In spite of this, in 1498 the icon was removed to Rome, where it remains.

Rather than continuing on this road, which leads to the Águios Nikólaos–Iráklion road, backtrack to Pinakianó and turn left to continue the clockwise circuit of the plateau. You soon reach **Tzermiádho**, the largest and most important of a score of villages dotted around the periphery of the plain. North of the village is the **Trápeza Cave** (**Spílio tis Trápezas**) ❻,

BELOW: a roadside shrine, with oil lamp and offerings.

discovered by Arthur Evans and explored by Pendlebury, who ascertained that it was used as a burial place in Neolithic times.

East to Sitía

The municipality of Sitía holds an annual festival in the third week of August in celebration of the soultanína grape grown there.

The 77 km (48 miles) of route E75 which links Ághios Nikólaos and Sitía is lauded as one of the most scenic roads on Crete. It passes through a jagged and precipitous coast without ever quite running alongside the sea. Indeed, in its latter part, you seldom see the water but, as compensation, the road is lined with a profusion of pink and white oleanders.

The first stretch of the journey, through **Ístro**, **Gourniá** and **Pachiá Ámmos**, is described in the previous chapter *(see pages 219–21)*. After Pachiá Ámmos, the road climbs into the mountains until, 31 km (19 miles) from Ághios Nikólaos, you reach **Plátanos** ❼. This is a mandatory stopping place for glorious views of Psíra island and back across the Gulf of Mirabéllo.

The road now zigzags as it runs further inland and soon several signposted roads lead down to the small seaside village of **Móchlos** ❽. Best to take the road at **Sfáka**. (Excursion boats from Ághios Nikólaos also sail to Móchlos.) The tiny islet at the far end of the bay can be reached by swimming but take care to protect your feet as the waters are rich in sea urchins, which are collected and sold by divers. The island was probably once attached to the mainland by a narrow isthmus, and was an important settlement in the Early and Late Minoan eras (contemporary with Gourniá). The most important finds have been tombs containing a rich collection of stone vases, jewellery, seal stones and other funerary objects. There are also Roman fortifications above the northern cliff.

About 2 km (1¼ miles) offshore lies the larger island of **Psíra** (Pseíra), which

BELOW: a welcoming Cretan. **RIGHT:** inside Moní Faneroméni.

was also a Minoan port. The remains here are of a town built around a good natural harbour. Later, the Romans used the island for strategic and navigational purposes and their lighthouse and military settlement can be discerned on the island's peak. You can take boat trips to Psíra from either Ag Nik or Móchlos.

Back on the main road, 44 km (27 miles) from Ághios Nikólaos, is **Myrsíni**, where lovely views can be enjoyed from the terrace of a well restored Venetian church. Nearby are Minoan tombs. Just before the village of **Hamézi** ❾, high above Sitía, two ruined stone windmills are a striking landmark. A track to the right of these leads in 2 km (1¼ miles) to the ruins of a unique Middle Minoan house – the only known Minoan building to have an oval ground plan – on the crest of a conical hill. A wall encircles rooms and a small central courtyard in which is a deep cistern. Hamézi itself contains the **Cretan House Museum**, a local folk museum with ancient farm implements and rooms filled with furniture and utensils. If the museum is closed, enquire at the nearby *kafeníon* for the key.

A short distance further on, at the village of **Skopí**, an inferior winding road to the left leads in 6 km (4 miles) to the **Monastery of Faneroméni** (**Moní Faneroménis**, not to be confused with the monastery of the same name close to Gourniá) which offers splendid views across to Sitía. A small frescoed church perched on the edge of a ravine and overlooking the sea stands above a cave in which an icon of the Virgin Mary appeared in the 15th century. Each time the church was plundered and the icon taken away, it miraculously returned.

As you near Sitía, vineyards come into view. This region produces some of Crete's best wines yet most grapes are made into sultanas. In late summer when the grapes are laid out to dry they form an attractive picture with colours ranging from green through brown to gold.

The Rural Tourism Office at 5 Anthéon St, Sitía (Tel:0843 25967) is the best on the island. Run by the enthusiastic Mrs Georgia Stavrakáki, it can supply a wealth of information and maps, and organises various one-week tours for groups of 8–15 people.

BELOW: Sitía harbour.

Moní Toploú is a treasure-house of beautiful icons.

Sitía ⑩, the most eastern town in Crete, placed in an amphitheatre among gentle mountain scenery and lush vineyards, is a laid-back place with a population of about 8,000. Tier upon tier of colour-washed houses rise from the tree-lined waterfront where visitors are greeted by Níkos, the town's pet pelican. The stepped and cobbled streets of the old town, centred around the church of Aghía Ekateríni, wind their way up from the harbour to the northeast, while a long narrow sandy beach occupies the town's southern end. (Better beaches are found further east towards Aghía Fotiá.)

The harbour is dominated by a Venetian fort known as the **Kazárma** (from *casa di arma,* or House of Arms). From here there are splendid views of the Bay of Sitía and the hills of Eastern Crete. The fort sometimes serves as an open-air theatre. Below it, close to the pier, are rock-cut Roman fish tanks. The **Archaeological Museum** (Tues–Sun 8.30am–2.30pm) contains a well displayed collection of local finds including a case full of rare Linear-A tablets. Completing the cultural attractions is a **Folk Museum** (Tues–Sun 9.30am–2.30pm, also 6–8pm Tues and Thur), which has an excellent collection of weaving and embroideries displayed in rooms furnished in traditional Cretan style.

About 5 km (3 miles) after leaving Sitía the highway passes the village of **Aghía Fotiá** ⑪ where a Minoan necropolis was uncovered in 1971. More than 250 tombs, many with multiple burials, yielded a rich harvest of grave offerings which may be seen in the Ághios Nikólaos and Sitía museums.

Religious riches

About 7 km (4¼ miles) further on, where the highway turns south at the eastern end of Sitía Bay, a road sets off to the left through a barren landscape. Soon, the 16th-century Italianate belltower of **Toploú Monastery (Moní Toploú)** ⑫, beckoning like the minaret of a mosque, comes into view. The monastery, which is fronted by a windmill, stands in splendid isolation. An impressive edifice, it is reputed to be one of the richest monasteries in Crete, which permits the monks to make many improvements, some of which border on kitsch.

BELOW: Níkos, Sitía's best-known resident.

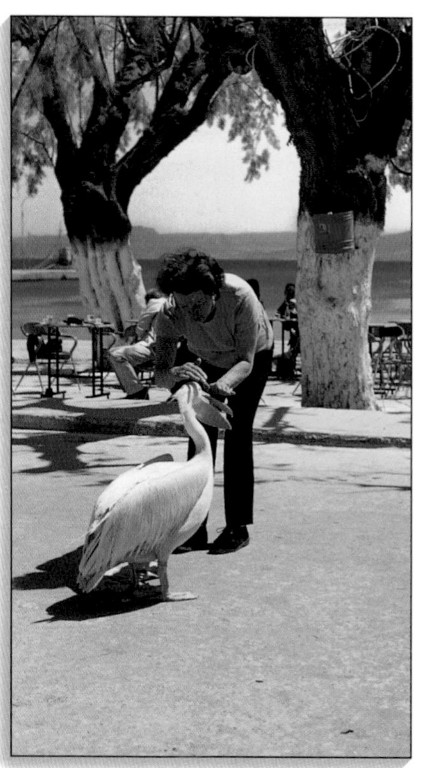

Founded in the 14th century, Toploú was destroyed several times and successive reconstruction has resulted in a square fortress-like appearance with high walls pierced by tiny windows. Inside the inner gateway the central flower-decked courtyard is patterned with myriad small pebbles and the monks' cells and offices rise all around to a height of three storeys.

The monastery derives its name from a famous cannon (*toplou* is Turkish for cannonball) which once defended it. The monks also had other methods of protecting themselves: observe the hole above the gate through which they poured hot oil over their assailants. They needed these defences. In 1821 during the War of Independence the Turkish forces hung 12 monks over the gate; and a memorial near the entrance honours the abbot and monks who were shot during World War II as a reprisal for sheltering the British and for possessing an underground radio transmitter.

Within the monastery stands the 14th-century church of Panaghía Akrotiriáni, the monastery's proper name. In the north aisle, together with 14th-century frescoes, is a superb icon created in 1770 by Ioánnis Kornáros. Painted on it are 61 miniature scenes each of which is inspired by a phrase from the Greek orthodox prayer, "Lord, Thou art great". One of several stone tablets embedded in the church walls records the arbitration of Magnesia in a dispute between the ancient cities of Itanos and Ierapythna.

Map on page 228

The eastern shores

The road continues across moorland for 6 km (4 miles) to a T-junction. Turn left and after 2 km (1¼ miles) right, and you are facing the famous beach of **Vái** ⓭, renowned for its stunning setting, myriad palm trees and an expanse of pink-white sands from where children can bathe in perfect safety, although the fish have a fondness for biting. The palm trees are Europe's only wild palms, a species called *Phoenix theophrasti*. Vái's beach is usually choc-a-bloc with bodies and consequently, except in the very early morning and late afternoon, not for those who dream of a palm-fringed desert island.

For quieter bathing, continue past the Vái turn-off for a couple of kilometres (just over a mile), or alternatively walk along the shore for 30 minutes, to reach palm-free **Erimoúpoli** ⓮, where there are three quiet, delightful small beaches with coarse sands. This is the site of ancient **Itanos** which flourished in the Greek and Roman eras when it competed with Ierapythna (today's Ierápetra) for control of eastern Crete. The settlement remained prosperous until the Byzantine era when it was destroyed, probably by Saracen pirates. Exiguous ruins abound and the view of the serpentine peninsula wriggling northwards to end in Cape Síderos is spectacular.

Although the palms that grow in Vái are closely related to the Egyptian date palm, their fruit is inedible.

BELOW: the palm-fringed beach at Vái.

Ruin-roaming and wind-surfing

TIP

If you enjoy retsina, try to avoid bottles with corks and fancy labels: these are produced for tourists and overpriced. If you can't find local retsina from the barrel, stick to the commercial brands with metal crowns or screw tops.

Palékastro ⓯, 9 km (5½ miles) to the south of Vái, is a pleasant, large village situated in a barren, rocky landscape yet with a good selection of hotels and restaurants. More relaxing is smaller **Angathiá**, 2 km (1¼ miles) to the east. Bordering the sea is **Hióna Beach**, a good stretch of pebble and sand. Close to the beach lie the ruins of ancient **Palékastro** (sometimes called **Roussolákos**) which was a late Minoan settlement. Although this is the largest Minoan town uncovered to date, no palace has yet been found and it has been suggested that Roussolákos may have been under the jurisdiction of Káto Zákros. Pieces of a gold and ivory statuette known as the Koúros of Palékastro, now in the Sitía museum, were uncovered here but, other than stairways and streets and the foundations of dwelling houses, the site does not have much to offer the casual visitor.

At the northern end of the Minoan ruins, a sanctuary of the Hellenic era, identified as the famous Temple of Zeus Diktaios was found. Within it was stone on which was engraved a 4th-century BC hymn to Zeus, believed to be an invocation at the Dance of the Koúretes. It has been suggested that the temple and other Hellenic ruins found here may be the remains of ancient Dragmos. Just to the north a narrow signposted road leads down to **Kouroménos**, a nearly deserted pebble beach which is one of Crete's best windsurfing areas and where boards may be rented.

A rough track south of Hióna Beach leads after about 3 km (1¾ miles) to **Pétsofas** where a Minoan Peak Sanctuary dedicated to the goddess yielded a cache of votive offerings, mainly human and animal figurines in clay. There are magnificent views from the top of the hill.

BELOW: sunbeds for hire, Hióna Beach.

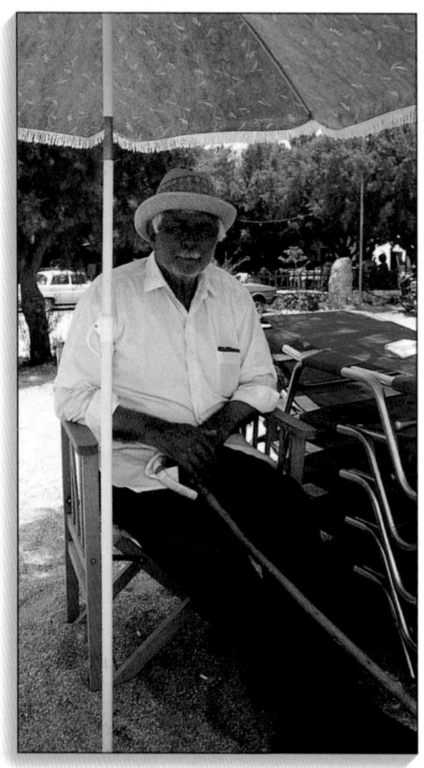

From Palékastro village the road abandons the sea and winds southwards for 18 km (11 miles) across windswept hills to the undistinguished town of **Zákros**, also called **Áno Zákros**, from where it is 8 km (5 miles) by a winding road down to **Káto Zákros** ⓰ with its extensive Minoan ruins. Rather than drive from Upper to Lower Zákros, you might enjoy the glorious 8-km (5-mile) walk through a deep ravine riddled with caves in which the Minoans buried their dead. Allow three hours for this stroll, a short part of which is a scramble through "The Valley of the Dead" during which blissful peace is interrupted only by the bleating of the occasional goat.

Modern Káto Zákros, with its long stretch of pebbly beach shaded by pine trees and bordered by a string of tavernas, is a beguiling hamlet as a result of the region being a protected archaeological area. Ancient Káto Zákros appears to have suffered a terrible catastrophe in 1450 BC, resulting in its buildings collapsing and then burning. Nikólaos Pláton, who excavated Káto Zákros, believes that this gives credence to the theory that it was an eruption of volcanic Santoríni (Thíra) that ended the Minoan civilisation. Lumps of pumice among the ruins, said to have been deposited by the tidal wave which followed the eruption, support Pláton's theory but not all agree. Unlike the other Minoan palaces, the existence of Zákros was completely forgotten. Thus it was never looted and when Pláton excavated in the 1960s he found more than 10,000 artefacts, including large quantities of ivory.

The ruins are approached at their northeast corner by a paved Minoan road coming from the harbour which was strategically situated for trade with the Levant and Egypt. You can get an overall view of the palace and its layout by climbing on to the narrow stepped and cobbled streets of the ruined Minoan town, similar to Gourniá *(see page 219)*, which occupies raised ground to the north of the palace. The streets are flanked by the remains of houses and commercial buildings used by the ordinary people, many of whom would have been employed at the harbour or worked in the palace.

The ruins are much more readily understood than at the other major sites as they consist of only one palace. It dates from the New Palace era (1700–1400 BC). An earlier settlement does exist at a lower level but is under water and attempts have not been made to excavate it. Even the New Palace ruins are not in great condition because they are often waterlogged.

The palace, like other Minoan palaces, had a long central court and a well for sacrificial offerings. Bordering this, on the south were workshops and on the north were the kitchen and storerooms. The west wing housed a Ceremonial Hall, a lustral basin which served as a washrooom for those entering the central shrine, the treasury and archives where hundreds of Linear-A clay tablets were discovered. The East wing contained the royal apartments.

Between Káto Zákros and the south coast, some roads are of poor quality and tourists are very thin upon the ground: this is Crete's "empty quarter". This rough road with many hairpin bends travels first through olive groves, then through a deep ravine before reaching **Xerókambos** ⓱ and its splendid, long, wide, deserted, shadeless, sandy beach. If this is not your idea of nirvana then, both to the north and south of this beach, are isolated sandy coves.

Maps: Area 228 Site 235

There are an estimated 25 million olive trees in Crete, many of them more than 1,000 years old.

BELOW: rock tombs in the "Valley of the Dead".

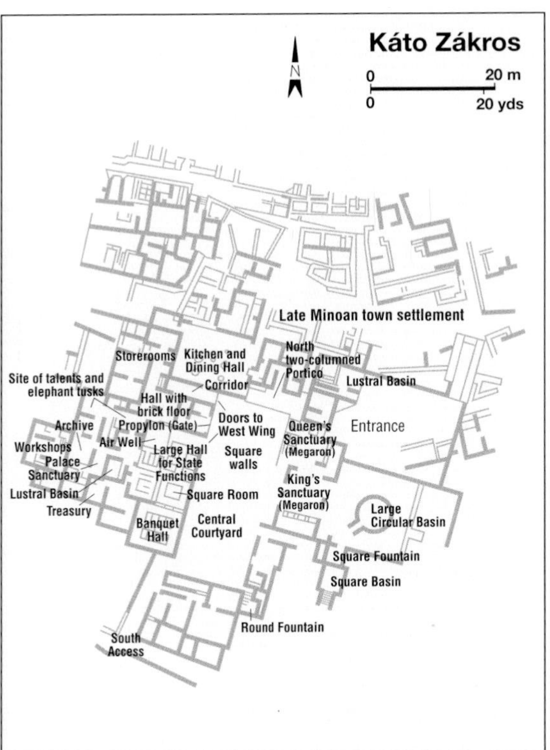

The beach sign means "Nudism is forbidden". Nude sunbathing is actually illegal, except on a few designated beaches, and is offensive to many Greeks.

A new sealed road climbs northwest from Xerókambos through dramatic scenery for 14 km (9 miles) to the farming village of **Zíros**. En route you pass the simple, seductive hamlet of **Hamétoulo** with a score of houses, a cobbled street and a church. Zíros, situated at an altitude of 440 metres (1,466 ft), on a fertile plateau surrounded by cliffs, dates back at least to Venetian times. Its church of Aghía Paraskeví is decorated with frescoes that are believed to be the last wall-paintings (1565) of the Cretan Renaissance.

From Zíros the choice is between descending on a poor road for 13 km (8 miles) to **Goúdhouras** which, although awash with plastic greenhouses, has a beach, or proceeding due west on a sealed road to join the main road to the south from Sitía. On the latter route, 4 km (2½ miles) after leaving Zíros you reach the farming village of **Handhrás** (Chandrás). Almost immediately before reaching Handhrás, you can make a short detour to the north, to reach the abandoned, medieval village of **Voilá** 18 where two ornamental Turkish stone fountains still function. The ruins in the village are dominated by the 15th-century double-aisled church of Ághios Yeórghios and a tower from the Turkish period.

Just beyond Handhrás is the village of **Etiá** which has a partly restored three-storey Venetian mansion that was built at the end of the 15th century. And so to **Lithínes** where a left turn puts you on the Sitía road. The Libyan Sea comes into view and after an 8-km (5-mile) journey you will arrive at the coast at **Análipsi**.

Here, rather than turning west for Ierápetra, double back east and after 6 km (4 miles) observe on the left the white-painted walls of the 14th-century **Kapsá Monastery (Moní Kapsá)** built snugly into the cliffs at the entrance to a gorge. Monks will show you, encased in a silver casket, the body of Yerondoghiánnis or Old John, a 19th-century eccentric, renowned for his piety and miraculous

BELOW: fishing-nets drying in Ierápetra.

cures. The monastery attracts large crowds of visitors to its annual *panighýri* (local celebration of a holy day) on 29 August, the feast day of St John, one of the most popular late summer festivals in eastern Crete.

Retrace your route along the main road to soon arrive at the sprawling resort of **Makrýghialos** 19 which has a long sandy tamarisk-shaded beach and some attractive relatively peaceful coves. Excursion boats leave from here for the island of **Koufonísi** (21 km/13 miles), the largest of a small remote archipelago known in ancient days as the White Islands. There are good beaches and ruins, including a small theatre, to be explored. In classical times the island was well known for its purple dye made from murex seashells and was much fought over by Ierapythna and Itanos.

Crete's spine of mountains acts as a barrier to rain, so bad weather in the north is often not experienced in the south, and vice versa.

The sunniest place in Europe

Continue along the south shore to **Aghía Fotiá** and its pleasant beach, somewhat hidden off the road. From here it is 12 km (8 miles) of what by now is familiar plastic landscape to **Ierápetra** 20.

The largest town on the south coast and the southernmost in all Europe, Ierápetra is enjoying a boom, not as a result of tourism or the uncovering of archaeological sites, but because of market gardening. In the 1960s, Paul Coopers, a Dutch farmer, introduced those plastic greenhouses which have marred the countryside through which you have travelled, to utilise the fact that Ierápetra probably has more sun-hours than anywhere in Europe, thus turning the region into a regular cornucopia. A visit, especially on Saturdays, to the morning fruit market across from the archaeological museum provides some idea of the prodigious fruitfulness of the region.

BELOW: cutting bamboo cane, Ierápetra.

The town, backed by superb mountain scenery, is scarcely atmospheric. Start an exploration at Platía Kanoupakí where the town hall and tourist office are situated. Here too is the **Archaeological Museum** (Tues–Sun 8.30am–3pm). It is apt that in this rich fertile land a major work in the museum is a splendid 2nd-century statue of Demeter, the goddess of fertility.

A few steps lead to the seafront where a right turn places you on a short promenade at the rear of a disappointing beach. At the south end of the promenade, paved with multi-coloured marble and travertine slabs, stands a 13th-century Venetian fortress overlooking a harbour, that is home to brightly painted fishing boats. Close by stands a three-storey bell tower across from which is the 14th-century church of Aféndis Christós with its twin red-tiled domes. Turn inland (northwards) through the old Turkish quarter, a jumble of narrow lanes, to a house where Napoleon supposedly spent 26 June 1798 before sailing off to campaign in Egypt, less than 400 km (250 miles) to the south. A few steps to the west is a small square with an octagonal domed Turkish fountain and a Turkish mosque with a capless minaret. To the northeast are the restored churches of Ághios Yeórghios and Ághios Ioánnis: the latter served as a mosque for a time.

Ierápetra was the last Cretan city to fall to the Romans, who used it as a base for their conquest of Egypt.

If you are looking for beaches, you should board an excursion boat at Ierápetra for the 12-km (8-mile) voyage to **Chrýsi** (also called Gaïdhouronísi or Donkey Island), which offers a great choice of beaches and tranquillity.

BELOW: preparing pork *souvlákia*.
RIGHT: the bells of Moní Toploú.
FOLLOWING PAGE: a village elder in traditional dress.

West of Ierápertra

Continuing west from Ierápetra, after 14 km (8¾ miles) you will reach **Néa Mýrtos**. On a hill just beyond the village is a Minoan site known locally as **Fournoú Korifí**, a Pre-Palace Minoan hilltop settlement with a labyrinth of small buildings in which the famous pot-bellied and slim-necked goddess of Mýrtos, now in the Ághios Nikólaos museum, was found. The site was destroyed by fire about 2200 BC.

Two kilometres (1¼ miles) further along the main road, immediately before a bridge over the Mýrtos river, turn right into a quarry, from where a 10-minute walk leads to **Pýrgos**, also destroyed by fire around 2200 BC. Unlike Fournoú Korifí, Pýrgos was rebuilt and the scanty remains, which compete with glorious views for your attention, are mainly of a Neo-Palatial villa from *circa*1600 BC.

A little further on, surrounded by orange and lemon groves, is the flower-bedecked village of **Mýrtos ㉑**. The village was razed to the ground by the German army in 1943, as a reprisal for Resistance activities, but has re-created itself as a charming and attractive contrast to the drab market-garden landscape you traverse to arrive here. There is a long shingle beach and a choice of bars and tavernas.

Backtrack and at **Grá Lyghiá**, just before you reach Ierápetra, a minor road on the left takes you north past a dam and a quarry and finally, after 17 km (11 miles) to **Kalamáfka ㉒**, a delightful little village clinging to a cleft in the island's spine. A couple of kilometres (just over a mile mile) north of here is a spot from where you may gaze enraptured on both the Sea of Crete and the Libyan Sea. ❑

INSIGHT GUIDES

TRAVEL TIPS

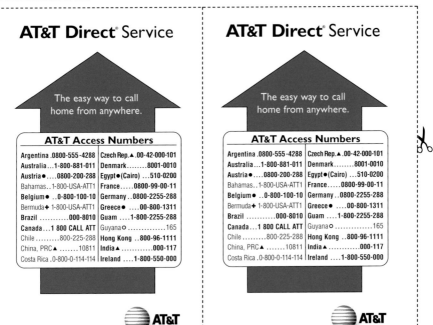

AT&T Direct® Service

The easy way to call home from anywhere.

AT&T Access Numbers

Argentina .0800-555-4288	Czech Rep.▲ .00-42-000-101
Australia ...1-800-881-011	Denmark........8001-0010
Austria● 0800-200-288	Egypt●(Cairo) ...510-0200
Bahamas..1-800-USA-ATT1	France.....0800-99-00-11
Belgium● ..0-800-100-10	Germany..0800-2255-288
Bermuda✚ 1-800-USA-ATT1	Greece● 00-800-1311
Brazil 000-8010	Guam 1-800-2255-288
Canada...1 800 CALL ATT	Guyana○ 165
Chile 800-225-288	Hong Kong ..800-96-1111
China, PRC▲ 10811	India▲ 000-117
Costa Rica .0-800-0-114-114	Ireland 1-800-550-000

Country	Access Number	Country	Access Number
Israel	**1-800-94-94-949**	**Portugal ▲**	**800-800-128**
Italy ●	**172-1011**	**Saudi Arabia ▲**	**1-800-10**
Jamaica ●	1-800-USA-ATT1	Singapore	800-0111-111
Japan ● ▲	**005-39-111**	**South Africa**	**0800-99-0123**
Korea, Republic ●	**0072-911**	**Spain**	**900-99-00-11**
Mexico ▽ ●	**01-800-288-2872**	**Sweden**	**020-799-111**
Netherlands ●	**0800-022-9111**	**Switzerland ●**	**0800-89-0011**
Neth. Ant. ▲❂	**001-800-USA-ATT1**	**Taiwan**	**0080-10288-0**
New Zealand ●	**000-911**	Thailand ❮	001-999-111-11
Norway	**800-190-11**	**Turkey ●**	**00-800-12277**
Panama	00-800-001-0109	U.A. Emirates ●	800-121
Philippines ●	**105-11**	**U.K.**	**0800-89-0011**
Poland ● ▲	**00-800-111-1111**	**Venezuela**	**800-11-120**

FOR EASY CALLING WORLDWIDE

1. Just dial the AT&T Access Number for the country you are calling from. *2.* Dial the phone number you're calling. *3.* Dial your card number.*

For access numbers not listed ask any operator for **AT&T Direct**® Service.
In the U.S. call 1-800-222-0300 for **AT&T Direct** Service information.
Visit our Web site at: **www.att.com/traveler**
Bold-faced countries permit country-to-country calling outside the U.S.

- ● Public phones require coin or card deposit to place call.
- ✚ Public phones and select hotels.
- ▲ May not be available from every phone/payphone.
- ○ Collect calling only.
- ▽ Includes "Ladatel" public phones; if call does not complete, use 001-800-462-4240.
- ❂ From St. Maarten or phones at Bobby's Marina, use 1-800-USA-ATT1.
- ❮ When calling from public phones, use phones marked Lenso.
- * AT&T Calling Card, AT&T Corporate, AT&T Universal, MasterCard®, Diners Club®, American Express®, or Discover® cards accepted.

When placing an international call ***from*** the U.S., dial 1-800-CALL ATT.

WW ©6/00 AT&T

CONTENTS

Getting Acquainted

Planning the Trip

Practical Tips

Getting Around

Where to Stay

Where to Eat

Sightseeing

Festivals

Outdoor Activities

Nightlife

Shopping

Language

Further Reading

Getting Acquainted

The Place

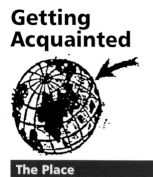

Area: Crete is 253 km (157 miles) long, and between 13 and 60 km (8 and 37 miles) wide.
Coastline: 1,046 km (650 miles).
Highest Point: Mount Ida (Ídhi) at 2,456 metres (8,058 ft).
Population: 540,000.
Capital: Iráklion.
Currency: Drachma
Language: Greek and Cretan dialect
Religion: Greek Orthodox.
Electricity: 220 volts/50 Hz AC.
Weights and Measures: Metric.
Time Zone: GMT +2 hours, Eastern Standard Time +7 hours.
Summertime: last Sunday in March to last Sunday in October.
National Carrier: Olympic Airways.
Dialling Code: +30 (Greece) +81 (Iráklion).

Climate

The southernmost of the Greek islands, Crete has an average of 320 sunny days per year; an average temperature of 30–35°C (86–95°F) in the summer (occasionally rising as high as 40°C/104°F) and 10–18°C (50–65°F) in the winter. In spring (April and May) the weather is clear but not yet debilitatingly hot: this is a lovely time to visit, when the island is relatively empty of tourists and the countryside is at its greenest.

The hottest summer months are July and August when, in addition to the hot sun, there is a fierce northwesterly wind called the *meltémi* which can blow across the Aegean for days at a time; the other (less common) wind is the *lívas*, which comes up from the Sahara laden with dust and sand.

During the autumn months (September and October) it is still hot enough to sunbathe and swim in the sea. Winters in Crete are mild, though it can suddenly become cold for short spells. About 70 percent of the annual rainfall comes between November and February. Rainfall varies widely from year to year, and can be as low as 30 cm (12 ins) overall.

In general, the south coast of Crete is both hotter and drier than the north. The mountains of the interior act as a block to the rain, so bad weather in the north is often not experienced in the south (and vice-versa). From autumn to late spring the mountains are covered in snow.

Economy

Until the advent of tourism, agriculture was the mainstay of the economy, even though only 30 percent of the land can be cultivated. The most important crops are olives, sultanas, grapes for table and wine, tomatoes, cucumbers, citrus fruits, bananas and carob. Sheep and goats are kept for wool, meat and cheese.

Government

Greece is a republic with a president, elected by parliament, who holds ceremonial executive power. The parliament is a single chamber of 300 deputies, led by the prime minister. There are three main parties: Néa Dhimokratía (New Democracy), PASOK (socialist) and KKE (communist).

There are 11 cities and 1,447 villages on Crete. Crete is divided into four governmental regions called *nomí*: Haniá, Réthymnon and Iráklion, with their respective capitals of the same names; and Lassíthi, with Ághios Nikólaos as its capital. More than half the 540,000 population lives in Nomós Iráklion. The *nomí* are subdivided into districts, known as *eparchíes*. In 1972, Iráklion replaced Haniá as the capital of the island.

Etiquette

Nude bathing is officially forbidden in Crete except on a few designated beaches. In practice it is more widespread, but be aware that Crete is still a very conservative society and it is extremely offensive to some Cretans, especially the older generation. Choose a beach that is either well secluded or well established as a nudist beach. Topless bathing may be tolerated on the beaches but it is generally frowned upon by the Greeks.

Public Holidays

On these days all banks, post offices, shops and offices are closed. If a holiday falls on a Sunday, Monday is also a holiday.
1 January New Year's Day *(Protochroniá)*/St Basil's Day.
6 January Epiphany *(Theofánia)*
Feb/Mar "Clean Monday" *(Kathará Dhefthéra)*: beginning of Lent, 48 days before Easter.
25 March Feast of the Annunciation *(Evangelismós)* and Independence Day.
Apr/May Greek Orthodox Easter *(Páscha)*: Good Friday to Easter Monday.
1 May Labour Day *(Protomayá)*.
Variable Pentecost *(Aghíou Pnévmatos)*, seven weeks after Easter Monday.
15 August Assumption of the Virgin *(Kímisis tís Panaghías)*.
28 October *Óchi* ("No") Day, aniversary of the defiance of Mussolini's ultimatum.
25 December Christmas Day *(Christoúghenna)*.
26 December Gathering of the Virgin *(Sínaxis tís Theotókou)*.

Planning the Trip

What to Bring

The following items might come in handy on Crete: a decent map of the island *(see Maps & Guidebooks below)*; an alarm clock for early-morning buses or ferries; two torches for exploring caves; an AC travel plug/adaptor for electrical appliances; mosquito repellent and plug-in vapour-release systems (both widely available on Crete); binoculars (for bird-watching); film (expensive on the island); suntan lotion (more expensive here, though widely available) and medical supplies (easily found on the island but generally more expensive).

What to Wear

In the summer, bring light clothing made of natural fabrics and a sweater or wind-cheater for the evening, when it can get quite cool. Sunglasses and a hat are also recommended, as well as comfortable walking shoes for visits to archaeological sites such as Knossós or trips up into the mountains.

Waterproof clothing should be taken for visits in the winter, spring and autumn. Also, during the winter months, warm clothing is needed, since it can get quite damp and buildings are often poorly heated. For visits to churches and monasteries, trousers should be worn by men (shorts are unacceptable) and skirts or dresses by women (no bare shoulders). Women especially should dress modestly when visiting rural villages away from the main tourist areas. As for formal attire, it is rarely needed in Crete.

Entry Regulations

Visitors from EU countries have unlimited visitation rights in Greece; your passport will not be stamped on entry or exit. Citizens of Canada, the USA, Australia and New Zealand need only a valid passport and can stay for a period of up to three months. No visa is necessary. For longer stays a resident's permit must be obtained from the local police in Crete.

There are no longer any duty-free allowances for travel within the EU. Visitors from non-EU countries may bring the following goods duty-free into Greece: 200 cigarettes or 100 cigarillos or 50 cigars or 250 g tobacco (18 years or over); 2 litres wine or 1 litre spirits or 2 litres liqueurs (18 years or over); 60 ml perfume; 250 ml eau de toilette.

Visitors using a prescription drug should bring a copy of the prescription to avoid any possible problems at customs. Note that the drug codeine (fairly common in headache pills) has been officially banned in Greece.

Visitors from non-EU countries can take home the same quantities of duty-free goods as are listed above. Note that the export of antiquities and archaeological artefacts from Greece is strictly prohibited.

Visitors to Greece do not need any inoculations, though tetanus and typhoid boosters are recommended. British and other EU nationals are entitled to free medical care in Greece (UK residents should take an E111 form, available at any British post office). It should be noted, however, that public health facilities are limited in Crete and private doctors are sometimes the only satisfactory option. Comprehensive travel insurance is a sensible precaution. Available from travel agents, banks and insurance brokers, this covers private medical treatment as well as loss of personal property.

Tour Operators

Many British companies offer accomodation, travel, excursions and activity holidays. Note that villas and apartments in Crete are nearly always rented out through foreign tour operators and must be arranged from home. It is much safer to book before travelling if you are going in high summer, when accomodation is in high demand. National newspapers and specialist magazines also often carry private advertisments for villas and apartments to rent. Reliable British companies include:

Freelance Holidays
40b Grove Road, Stratford-upon-Avon, Warwickshire CV37 6PB.
Tel: 01789 297705
Fax: 01789 292017
E-mail: info@freelance-holidays.co.uk
Website: www.freelance-holidays.co.uk.

Useful Websites

www.interkriti.gr – thousands of pages on places, history, customs, facilities, people etc. Good search engine.
www.crete.tournet.gr – described as an electronic tourist guide, with plenty of pictures and information.
www.dilos.com/region/crete/map_cr.html – a navigable map of the island.
www.explorecrete.com – an online magazine, with reviews, information, maps, photographs and much of interest.
www.cretamusic.gr – a website created by United Artists of Traditional Cretan Music.
www.dmoz.org/Regional/Europe/Greece/Regions/Crete – perhaps the most useful of all: contains links to all the above and to dozens of other specialist sites, covering everything from cycling in Crete to women in Minoan culture.

Pure Crete
79 George Street, Croydon,
Surrey CR0 1LD.
Tel: 020 8760 0879
Fax: 020 8688 9951
E-mail: info@purecrete.com
Website: www.purecrete.com.

Simply Crete
King's House, Wood Street,
Kingston-upon-Thames,
Surrey KT1 1VG.
Tel: 020 8541 2201
Fax: 020 8541 2280
E-mail: crete@simply-travel.com
Website: www.simply-travel.co.uk.

Smart Holidays
Red Hill House, Clifford Chambers,
Stratford-upon-Avon, Warwickshire
CV37 8JF.
Tel: 01789 267623
Fax: 01789 267887
Website: www.smart-holidays.co.uk.

Travel Club of Upminster
Station Road, Upminster,
Essex RM14 2TT.
Tel: 01708 225000
Fax: 01708 229678
E-mail: upminsterT@aol.com;
Website: www.travelclub.org.uk

Greek Tourist Offices

The National Tourist Organisation of Greece (Ellinikós Organismós Tourismoú or EOT) has offices in most European capitals, North America and Australia. They will provide free maps and brochures on Crete in English.

Australia: 51 Pitt Street, Sydney, NSW 2000; Tel: 02-9241 1663-5, Fax: 02-9235 2174.

Canada: 1300 Bay Street, Toronto, Ontario M5R 3K8; Tel: 416-968 2220; Fax: 416-968 6533;
1233 rue de la Montagne, Suite 101, Montreal, Quebec H3G 1Z2; Tel: 541-871 1535, Fax: 541-871 1498.

UK: 4 Conduit Street London W1R 0DJ; Tel: 020 7734 5997; Fax: 020 7287 1369.

USA: Olympic Tower, 645 Fifth Avenue, New York, NY 10022; Tel: 212-421 5777, Fax: 212-826 6940; 611 West Sixth Street, Suite 2198, Los Angeles, California 92668; Tel: 213-626 6696, Fax: 213-489 9744; 168 North Michigan Avenue, Chicago, Illinois 60601; Tel: 312-782 1084, Fax 312-782 1091.

Greek Embassies

Greece has diplomatic representation in all the major capitals of the world, including:

Australia: 9 Turrana Street, Yarralumla, Canberra, ACT 26000. Tel: 02-673 3158.

Canada: 76–80 MacLaren Street, Ottowa, Ontario K2POK6. Tel: 613-238 6271.

UK: 1a Holland Park, London W11 3TP. Tel: 020 7229 3850.

USA: 2221 Massachusetts Avenue NW, Washington DC 20008. Tel: 202-667 3169.

Maps & Guide Books

Island maps are notoriously inaccurate, particularly those distributed by car rental agencies. You are better off buying a decent map before you leave home. Nelles, Freytag & Berndt, Bartholomew, Hildebrand, HarperCollins and GeoCenter are all adequate. Insight Guides' laminated *Fleximap: Crete* is excellent and hard-wearing. The best maps for walking in Crete are produced by Harms Verlag: there are five in their 1:80,000 series, covering the island from west to east.

On Crete itself, there are a number of local guidebooks published in English with information on the island's flora and fauna, museums and archaeological sites. These can be found at the foreign-language bookshops or at some *períptera* (kiosks). *See also Further Reading.*

Money

The Greek unit of currency is the drachma *(drachmí* in Greek; plural *drachmés)*. The commonest denominations are notes worth 50, 100, 500, 1,000, 5,000 and 10,000 drachmas, and coins of 10, 20, 50 and 100 drachmas. You may take any amount of foreign currency and traveller's cheques into Greece, although anything over US$1,000 (or equivalent) should be declared on entry, in case this money needs to be exported again.

There are banks in all major towns and resorts, but be prepared for long queues *(see Banks on page 249)*. Exchange facilities are also available at post offices (which often offer a better rate than the banks), travel agents, hotels and tourist offices. Always take your passport with you when exchanging money or cashing traveller's cheques, and check the rates and commission charges beforehand, as they vary considerably.

In the main towns, you can also withdraw local currency on a credit or debit card at cashpoints.

Eurocheques are accepted by banks and post offices but not by shops, while major credit cards are accepted by many shops, hotels and restaurants, as well as all car rental agencies. However, there are no credit card facilities in many villages, even small resorts such as Loutró.

Getting There

BY AIR

There are no international scheduled flights direct to Crete from Britain, so most visitors arrive on charter flights either as part of a package holiday or on a flight-only deal. There are direct charters to Iráklion and Haniá from regional airports in the UK (flight time: approx. 4 hours), as well as from Ireland and other European cities (no direct flights from the US).

Greek airline regulations require that visitors arriving on charters must stay for a minimum of three days and a maximum of four weeks and must have accommodation on Crete. (In practice, on a flight-only package, this means being issued an accommodation voucher which you have no intention of using.)

All scheduled flights involve changing planes in Athens. For airlines apart from Olympic Airways, this means changing terminals. (To be on the safe side allow about 1 hour for this, as the two terminals are a bus or taxi ride apart).

Olympic Airways, the main carrier, operates direct flights from Britain (London Heathrow) and from the US (New York) to Athens.

Olympic has up to 7 flights per day to Iráklion (flight time 50 mins) and 5 flights per day to Haniá (flight time 45 mins). Two other Greek carriers also run scheduled flights: Cronus Airlines have 2–3 planes per day to Iráklion and 1–2 per day to Haniá; Aegean Airlines have 6 per day to Iráklion and 3 per day to Haniá.

Most airlines require passengers to confirm their return passage a few days before departure. This is advisable to avoid overbooking problems.

Olympic Airways

In the UK:
11 Conduit Street,
London W1R OLP.
Tel: 020 7399 1509
Fax: 020 7493 0563.

In the US:
645 Fifth Avenue,
New York 10022.
Tel: 212-735 0200
Fax: 212-735 0215.
624 South Grand Ave, Suite 1709,
Los Angeles, CA 90017
Tel: 213-624 6441
Fax: 213-624 0760.

BY BOAT

Bear in mind that ferry schedules change frequently, especially between the summer and winter seasons. The best place to gain up-to-date information is from the Greek Tourist Office, from any travel agent in Greece (the latter also sell ferry tickets) or on the internet.

From the Greek mainland: ANEK and Minoan shipping lines operate daily car and passenger ferry services from Piraeus (the port of Athens) to Iráklion and Haniá (Soúdha Bay). Iráklion is 164 nautical miles and Haniá is 147. Both trips take approximately 12 hours and run through the night, leaving Piraeus in the early evening (berths and cabins are available).

ANEK also offers a daily service from Piraeus to Réthymnon. In addition, Lane Sea Lines run regular ferries to Ághios Nikólaos and Sitía, and ANEN Lines run ferries between the Peloponnese and the island of Kíthira, from where they proceed to Kastélli in western Crete.

From other Greek islands

There are frequent ferries from many of the Cycladic islands (daily from Santoríni/Thíra). A regular ferry service also operates from Rhodes to Ághios Nikólaos and Sitía.

From Italy

Ferries run regularly from Brindisi, Ancona, Bari, Trieste and Venice in Italy via the Greek island of Kérkira (Corfu) to Pátra and Igoumenítsa on the Greek mainland (from here you have to travel 225 km/140 miles overland to Piraeus by car, bus or train). At time of publication Blue Star Ferries offer a direct service from Iráklion to Venice once a week.

From Cyprus and Israel

Ferries run weekly to Iráklion from Limassol, Cyprus and Haifa, Israel.

BY CAR

Taking a car to Crete can be an expensive business; hiring a car on the island is a much cheaper alternative.

To drive all the way, the main route from London to Athens is through France and Italy, a distance of approximately 2,400 km (1,500 miles), not including the ferry crossing from Italy to Greece. The route via the former Yugoslavia is possible but it is no longer recommended: ask your local motoring organisation before setting out. Otherwise, if you are determined to travel overland all the way to Greece, the best route is via France, Belgium, Germany, Austria, Hungary, Romania and Bulgaria, arriving over the border in northeastern Greece.

Before setting out, consult the Greek tourist office or a motoring organisation such as the AA for advice on insurance requirements and any special regulations for countries en route. Many countries, including Greece, insist that you carry a first-aid kit, warning triangle and fire extinguisher. For a small fee the AA will provide up-to-date itineraries, including details of major roadworks and other possible delays.

A national driving licence, vehicle registration documents and third-party insurance are all compulsory, and comprehensive cover is strongly recommended. If you are passing through any non-EU countries, an international driving permit and green insurance card will also be required (otherwise your cover will be third-party only).

Greece by Coach

The cheapest – and most strenuous – way of travelling to Greece from the UK is by coach, which takes three and a half days via France and Italy. Eurolines provides the most reliable service; buy tickets from any National Express office. For further information from the UK: **Eurolines**, 52 Grosvenor Gardens, London SW1W OAU. Tel: 020 7730 8235.

BY TRAIN

The main rail route from London to Athens takes around three and a half days, travelling through France and Italy, and crossing to Greece by ferry from the Adriatic port of Brindisi.

Regular train tickets are valid for two months and allow as many stops as you like on a pre-selected route; all ferry crossings are included.

Rail passes: An Inter-Rail pass represents good value for money, and entitles the holder to unlimited 2nd class travel on the national rail network of the countries of the zones purchased. There are 'under 26' and '26 and over' passes available. Contact your nearest train station or travel agent for more information.

BY YACHT

The harbour authorities at the points of entry are contactable on

the following phone numbers:
Iráklion (081) 244912
Réthymnon (0831) 22276
Haniá (0821) 98888
Ághios Nikólaos (0841) 22312
Sitía (0843) 22310
These ports have harbour, customs and health officials as well as a passport and foreign exchange control service. Fuel, water and provisions can be obtained, and transit logs must be stamped upon entry and departure.

Disabled Travellers

There are very few facilities for assisting the disabled on Crete. Wheelchair users are advised to plan their trip carefully before they leave – the mountainous terrain of the island's interior and the poor state of the roads and pavements are a major obstacle to getting around. Organisations such as **Holiday Care Service** (Tel: 01293 774535) in the UK are worth contacting for advice.

Travelling with Kids

The Greeks love children and they are welcome almost everywhere in Crete. For younger children, baby-sitting services are offered by many hotels as well as establishments offering just rooms (enquire before you check in).

Buses are free for anyone under eight years of age. The sea is generally safe for kids, but do keep a keen eye on them, as lifeguards are not commonplace in Crete; also be aware of the hazards of overexposure to the sun and dehydration.

Low-Price Museums

Students and people under 26 are entitled to reduced admission fees to museums and archaeological sites. Students will need to produce a valid international student card, and under-26s will need a FIYTO youth card (available from STA Travel in Britain or Council Travel in the US).

Practical Tips

Foreign Embassies in Greece

All the main embassies in Greece are based in Athens. Addresses include:
Australia: D. Soútsou 37, 11521 Athens; Tel: (01) 645 0404
Canada: Yenadhíou 4, Ypsilántou, 11521 Athens; Tel: (01) 727 3400
UK: Ploutárchou 1, 10675 Athens; Tel: (01) 723 6211-9
USA: Vasilíssis Sofías 91, 11521 Athens; Tel: (01) 721 2951-9

UK Consulate in Crete:
Papalexándrou 16, Iráklion; Tel: (081) 224012

Tourist Offices in Crete

The National Tourist Organisation of Greece (EOT) maintains offices throughout Greece. They will provide, free of charge, maps and brochures on Crete (in English), bus and ferry schedules, opening times of museums and archaeological sites, as well as hotel listings – but beware, their information is not always correct, or up-to-date.

EOT offices

Iráklion: Xanthoulídou 1 (opposite the Archaeological Museum); Tel: (081) 226081 or (081) 228203; fax: (081) 226020
Réthymnon: El. Venizélou Avenue (on the beach); Tel: (0831) 29148
Haniá: Kriári 40; Tel: (0821) 92943; Fax: (0821) 92624

Municipal Tourist Offices

Ághios Nikólaos: Aktí Koúndourou; Tel: (0841) 22357
Sitía: 5 Anthéon St; Tel: (0843) 25967

Commercial Tourist Offices

Haniá: Aptera Travel, Makrí Tíchos, Néa Kydonía; Tel: (0821) 33303; Fax: 33304.
Horeftákis Tours, Skalídhi St., Kastélli; Tel: (0822) 23250.
Kalamáki Travel, Ág. Fanoúrios, Kalamáki; Tel: (0821) 31995; Fax: 32245.
Polífimos Travel, Soúghia; Tel/Fax: (0823) 51022.
Réthymnon: Réthymno Travel, 64 Sof. Venizélou St; Tel: (0831) 22480; Fax: 54977.
Iráklion: Travels of Crete Ltd, 97 Ethnikís Antistáseos Ave; Mail: P.O.Box 1410, 7110 Iráklion; Tel: (081) 222763; Fax: 223357; Mobile: 0944 784055; Telex: 262464 LYTOGR.
Lassíthi: Minotours Hellas, 72100 Ístro; Tel: (0841) 61168; Fax: 61043.

Rural Tourism

Haniá: Vámos AE, Vámos, Haniá 73008; Tel: (0825) 23100.
Based in the Apokóronas district of Haniá, this organisation offers a wide range of activities and promotes ecological tourism.
Lassíthi: Rural Tourism Office, 5 Anthéon St, 72300 Sitía; Tel: (0843) 25967; Fax: 25341.
An extremely helpful, enthusiastic and well-organised tourist office, easily the best on the island, which can supply information, maps and routes, and also organises one-week tours for groups.

Business Hours

It is hard to generalise about shops' opening hours, but typically they will be open from around 8.30am–1.30, then close for lunch and a siesta, opening again from 6–9pm. Mondays and Saturdays they may not reopen in the afternoon, and Sunday they may be closed all day. The evening opening times are usually an hour earlier in winter months.

However, village shops are often a law unto themselves. Supermarkets are usually open 8.30am–9pm, without closing for lunch, but may close earlier on

Saturdays, while "mini-markets" and tourist shops are open much longer hours, although most shut up completely for the winter.

Banks

In general, opening hours are 8am–2pm Mon–Fri (or to 1.30pm on Friday). In the larger towns, one bank will re-open its change desk from 5 or 5.30–7pm and for a few hours on Saturday. Some now have exchange cashpoints providing an automated 24-hour service. Bureaux de change have much longer opening hours than banks.

Post Offices

Local post offices are open 8am–2.30pm Mon–Fri. Main post offices in large towns and post office "caravans" in tourist areas are open 8am–8pm Mon–Fri, 8am–2pm Saturdays and closed on Sundays (however the caravans may have more flexible hours).

Religious Services

Cretans are 98 percent Greek Orthodox. There are no Anglican or other Protestant churches on the island, nor are there any mosques where services are held. Catholic churches are to be found in Iráklion, Haniá and Réthymnon. There is also a synagogue in Haniá. Times for church services are as follows:

Catholic Church of Iráklion, 2 Patrós-Antoníou; Tel: (081) 346191 – Mass every Saturday 6pm and Sunday 10am.

Roman Catholic Cathedral (Church of the Assumption), 46 Hálidhon St, Haniá; Tel: (0821) 93443 – Mass every Saturday 7pm and Sunday 10am.

Pentecostal Church, 51 Sfakíon St, Haniá (behind Olympic Airways) – daily Mass and a service in English every Sunday 7pm.

Catholic Church of Réthymnon, Mesolonghíou-Salamínos; Tel: (0831) 26416 – Mass every Saturday 6pm and Sunday 10am.

Ághios Nikólaos (in the Orthodox church) – Mass every Sunday 6pm.

Tipping

Service is included on most bills, but tips are still appreciated. The percentage given is usually quite small compared to other European countries. In smaller restaurants or tavernas, a tip of 5–10 percent is appropriate; in bars and cafes about 5 percent, or whatever loose change you might have.

In hotel dining rooms and smarter restaurants, a 10–15 percent service charge is usually already included, so either leave nothing or whatever change is left over after the bill has been paid.

Taxi-drivers do not expect tips, but they are not averse to them either – 10 percent is about right, or round up the fare to the nearest 100 drachmas. Toilet attendants also expect a small contribution, as do hotel porters and chambermaids.

Etz Hayim Synagogue, off Kondiláki St, Old Haniá; contact Nichólas Stavroulákis-Hannan (0821) 86286 for Information.

Crime

The crime rate in Crete is extremely low. Nevertheless, it is wise to keep cars and hotel rooms locked, and to watch your handbag in public. If you do have anything stolen, contact the police or tourist police *(see Emergency Numbers, below)*.

Foreign visitors are strongly advised against importing or using drugs in Greece. Possession of even small amounts can result in jail sentences of up to a year. Anyone caught dealing can expect a much longer sentence.

Health

The main health hazard in Crete is overexposure to the sun: wear a hat and sunglasses during the summer months and use a high-factor suntan lotion, especially for the first week or so. Also, be sure to drink plenty of fluids to avoid any danger of dehydration.

INSECTS AND PESTS

There are a lot of mosquitoes in some areas, notably near fresh water, so take and use insect repellent. Slow-burning anti-mosquito coils can be bought cheaply in Crete, and are effective in a bedroom at night, as are the small electrical devices that plug into a standard socket (not so easily found in Crete).

There are no poisonous snakes to worry about *(see page 87)* but there are three underwater hazards you should be aware of – sea urchins, jellyfish and weevers. Sea urchins are the most common: if you step on one of these use a sterilised needle and olive oil to extract the spine. Jellyfish stings can be relieved by ammonia or urine. Weevers are an extremely rare fish that bury themselves under the sand with only their venomous spines protruding; if you do tread on one, immerse your foot in very hot water and call for medical help immediately.

DRINKING WATER

Tap water is safe to drink in most places on the island (but not in Soúghia or Loutró), although it's usually bottled water that's offered to you in restaurants and tavernas. In people's homes, there is often a hot and cold tap for general purposes and a separate tap for drinking water.

CHEMISTS

Pharmacies *(farmakía)* are recognised by a red or green cross on a white background. Greek pharmacists are highly trained and can usually advise on treatments for minor complaints. They are also able to dispense a number of medicines that in other countries are available only on prescription. In the larger towns, pharmacists operate a rota to provide 24-hour cover; details are posted in pharmacy windows.

Lost Property

Honesty is a matter of pride among Cretans so, if you leave something behind in a shop or restaurant, the chances are that the proprietor will have scrupulously kept it to one side for you. If you do have any problems, however, then contact the Tourist Police *(see box).*

Media

NEWSPAPERS

Foreign newspapers are available at *períptera* (kiosks) and bookshops in all the major towns and resorts. They are usually a day old and the mark-up is substantial.

Considerably cheaper and also widely available are the English-language daily *Athens News* and weekly *Hellenic Star*. The larger hotels are often the best place to find magazines and weekly papers.

RADIO AND TV

One of the channels of Greek National radio, ERA5, broadcasts news bulletins in English three times a day (9.10am, 2.10 pm and 9.30pm).

With a short-wave radio you'll also be able to pick up the BBC World Service and Voice of America in the early morning and evening.

Most hotels have TV lounges where CNN and Euronews are usually available. Otherwise, Greek TV (nine channels available on Crete) includes a lot of British and US films, sitcoms and soaps, usually subtitled in Greek rather than dubbed.

Films are always shown at cinemas in their original language with Greek subtitles.

Pornography

Many kiosks and newsagents now sell hard-core pornographic magazines and videos, which are often prominently displayed (and not necessarily on the top shelf), so bear this in mind when travelling with minors.

Communications

POST

Postboxes are bright yellow. If there are two slots, *esoterikó* means inland (within Greece) and *exoterikó* means overseas. Post offices *(tachydromeía)* are also recognisable by their bright yellow signs. Main branches will usually change money in addition to handling mail.

Stamps *(grammatósima)* can be purchased at any post office or *períptero* (kiosk); the latter usually charge a small commission. Air-mail letters take anywhere from four days to a week to get to most European countries and just over a week to reach North America; for postcards allow anywhere from two weeks to a month.

The Poste Restante system is widely used in Crete. Mail should be clearly marked Poste Restante, with the addressee's surname underlined and the name of the town to which it is being sent. Be sure to bring a passport or some other proof of identity when collecting mail and, as the mail is filed alphabetically, always ask them to check both surname and first name categories.

TELEPHONES

Local calls can be made from hotel lobbies, *períptera* (kiosks), *kafenía* (cafes) or telephone booths with a blue band: for these you need to purchase a *tilekárta* (phone card), available from any *períptero*. For international calls use either a telephone booth, a *períptero* with a metered phone or any OTE (Organismós Tilepikinonión Elládos) office.

The OTE is the cheapest option, and the only one if you plan to reverse the charges. But you need patience: be prepared for long queues and, when you finally succeed in getting a booth, be prepared to have to dial your number a few times before getting through. Operator-assisted calls can also take anything up to an hour to connect.

For international calls, dial 00, then the country code (44 for the UK, 1 for the US and Canada).

Some other useful numbers:
Operator: 151
International operator: 161
Local directory inquiries: 131
International directory inquiries: 169

Mobile phone users should note that, due to the mountainous terrain, there can be "pockets" where no network is available.

INTERNET

There are an increasing number of internet cafes and other internet

Emergency Numbers

If you need emergency assistance, dial the following:
Police: 100
Ambulance: 166
Fire: 199
ELPA (Greek automobile association): 104

There are Tourist Police in some centres concerned solely with visitors:
Iráklion: (081) 283190
Haniá: (0821) 53333
Réthymnon: (0831) 28156 or 53450
Ághios Nikólaos: (0841) 26900

In a medical emergency, try the Tourist Police first. If they cannot help, either call an ambulance on 166, or contact your nearest hospital:
Iráklion: (081) 237502
Haniá (Mourniés): (0821) 22000
Réthymnon: (0831) 27814 (6 lines)
Ághios Nikólaos: (0841) 25221 (9 lines)

access points on the island. Here are a few:

Iráklion

Istós Cyber Cafe, 2 Malikoúti St; Tel: (081) 222120.
Netc@fe, 4 1878 St; Tel: (081) 229569.
Políkendro, 2 Andrógeo St; Tel: (081) 399212.

Réthymnon

Galeró Internet Cafe, by the Rimondi Fountain; Tel: (0831) 22657.

Haniá

Vranás, corner of Sarpáki/Aghíon Dhéka, Mitropóleos Square; Tel/Fax: (0821) 58618.
e-K@fe.com, 59 Theotokopoúlou St; Tel: (0821) 73300. Open daily 8am–2am (open 24 hours 15 July–15 Aug).
Internet Cafe, 15 Hortátson Square (by western steps of market); Tel: (0821) 55440. Open 9am–1am every day except Sunday.
The T-Shirt Shop
Corner of Zambelíou/Kondiláki St, Haniá; Tel: (0821) 93839. Access charged by the hour, 15-minute minimum.
Internet Souvláki, Gíro Gíro Óloi, Néa Katastímata, 63 Kidonías St, Haniá; Tel: 72929.
Polífimos Travel, Soúghia; Tel: (0823) 51022. Internet access charged by the hour. A phone/fax service is also available.

Ághios Nikólaos

Perípou Polichóros (books, CDs and internet café), 25 28th Octovríou St; Tel: (0841) 24876. Open daily 9.30am–1am.

Sitía

Café Ianós, 159 El. Venizélou St; Tel: (0843) 22180.

Ierápetra

Orphéas Cyber-Cafe, 25 Koundouriótou; Tel: (0842) 80462.

Getting Around

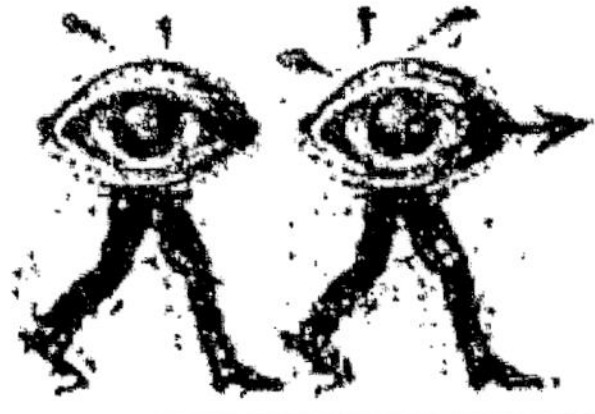

By Car

Driving is on the right and road signs follow standard European conventions, although on country byways you may come across some place-name signs in Greek only. There is a good network of roads on the island, and what your road map may still show as a gravel road may turn out to be paved, as many have been recently asphalted with EU money.

The Cretan style of driving takes some getting used to: on highways motorists pass on the right or left without warning and frequently use the hard shoulder as an extra lane (it is customary to pull into this lane to let other drivers overtake). Motorcyclists generally ignore the concept of the one-way system; in villages red lights are commonly viewed as a suggestion rather than a rule.

High speeds are neither recommended nor often possible. There are too many unexpected hazards: a paved road that suddenly becomes a dirt track without warning, a huge pothole or rock in the middle of the road, or an entire herd of sheep appearing out of nowhere.

The speed limit on national highways is 100 kph (62 mph) for cars and 70 kph (44 mph) for motorbikes; on country roads it is 70 kph (44 mph) and in towns 50 kph (31 mph).

Although usually ignored, the use of seatbelts in cars is required by law, as are helmets for motorcyclists. Every so often the police clamp down and on-the-spot fines are imposed. Parking and speeding tickets must be paid at the local police station or car rental agency – be sure to ask for a receipt. Driving under the influence of alcohol is illegal and breathalyser tests are becoming more frequent on the island.

Should you break down or require emergency road assistance while driving on the island, the number to ring is 104, which is the Automobile and Touring Club of Greece (ELPA) who will also help members of affiliated motoring organisations such as the AA or RAC.

Distances by Road

From Iráklion to:	
Knossós	5 km (3 miles)
Archánes	15 km (9 miles)
Phaestos	62 km (39 miles)
Kastélli	36 km (22 miles)
Hersónissos	26 km (16 miles)
Ág. Nikólaos	69 km (43 miles)
Mátala	70 km (44 miles)
Réthymnon	78 km (48 miles)
Aghía Galíni	70 km (44 miles)
Haniá	156 km (97 miles)
From Réthymnon to:	
Moní Préveli	37 km (23 miles)
Amári	39 km (24 miles)
Aghía Galíni	62 km (39 miles)
Hóra Sfakíon	70 km (44 miles)
Haniá	78 km (48 miles)
From Haniá to:	
Kastélli	42 km (26 miles)
Omalós	42 km (26 miles)
Soúghia	68 km (42 miles)
Hóra Sfakíon	72 km (45 miles)
Paleochóra	75 km (47 miles)
From Ághios Nikólaos to:	
Kritsá	11 km (7 miles)
Eloúnda	12 km (8 miles)
Ierápetra	36 km (22 miles)
Sitía	73 km (45 miles)
Moní Toplоú	94 km (58 miles)
Palékastro	97 km (60 miles)
Káto Zákros	115 km (72 miles)

CAR HIRE

There are scores of car rental agencies on the island offering the normal range of hire cars as well as four-wheel-drive vehicles. International companies such as Avis and Hertz are considerably more expensive than their local counterparts, who are generally just as reliable. Whoever you rent from, be sure to check carefully the insurance being offered – full coverage is strongly recommended – and whether it is included in the price quoted. Also remember that the "unlimited kilometres" deal is usually best if you are going any kind of distance. Payment by credit card is usually preferred; if not, a large cash deposit will be requested. You will need to produce an international driving permit or a valid national licence that has been held for at least one year (a passport is also sometimes requested). The minimum age for renting a car in Crete varies from 18 to 21, depending on the agency.

Motorcycle Hire

Motorbikes and mopeds are widely available in all the resort towns. Mopeds are ideal for short distances on reasonably flat terrain, but the interior of Crete is too mountainous for anything but a motorbike. Whatever you hire, make sure that the vehicle is in good condition and that the price includes proper insurance. And be sure to wear a helmet – all rental outfits have them, though often they won't actually give you one unless you ask.

FUEL

Service stations are plentiful in towns, but harder to find in rural areas. Always set out with a full tank if you're planning to travel any distance. The price of fuel is comparable to other European countries and unleaded petrol is available in all the main tourist resorts.

Filling stations are generally open 7am–7pm on weekdays and till 3pm Saturdays; a few also stay open all night and on Sundays.

By Bus

Buses are the only form of public transport on the island. Run by a group of companies known as KTEL, they are modern, reliable and inexpensive. There are frequent services connecting Iráklion, Ághios Nikólaos, Haniá and Réthymnon, as well as services to the main archaeological sites, the Samariá Gorge and many villages.

Each city has its own bus terminal (or terminals) – just ask for the "KTEL". Timetables (also in English) can be obtained there, as well as at travel agencies and tourist information offices.

Coach Tours

Coach tours are offered by most travel agents. They include trips to the major archaeological sites, the Samariá Gorge and various beaches, as well as excursions into the mountains. If you don't have your own transport, this is an option worth considering.

Hitch-hiking

Public transport is reasonably cheap in Crete, so hitching is really only necessary if you are trying to get somewhere out of the way (or if you've missed the last bus back). Although Crete is a relatively safe place to hitch, female travellers are advised not to travel alone and to dress modestly.

By Taxi

Taxis are plentiful in the main towns and cheap. They can be flagged down on the street, found at ranks or ordered by phone. There is a basic charge (higher if booked by phone) and then a metering system of tariff "1" for daytime and town centre and "2" for after midnight and out of town. There can also be surcharges for airports, luggage and at Christmas and Easter.

For trips further afield, a fare should be agreed in advance – if there are several of you a long trip by taxi can prove quite economical, and may not add up to much more than a number of bus fares.

Rural villages generally have at least one taxi. You can usually arrange for the driver to drop you off somewhere and pick you up later, or you can ask him to take you on a private tour (negotiate the fare before setting off).

Note that a tip of 10 percent is customary for taxi drivers.

By Boat

A good way to travel along the south coast of Western Crete is to use the boat service. There are regular connections between Elafonísi, Paleochóra, Soúghia, Aghía Rouméli, Loutró and Hóra Sfakíon, as well as boats to Gávdos from Paleochóra (three times a week), Soúghia (once a week) and Hóra Sfakíon (four times a week). Current timetables are available from the Greek Tourist Offices or from the local harbour authorities:
Paleochóra Tel: (0823) 41214.
Hóra Sfakíon Tel: (0825) 91292.

In the northeast there are connections between Ághios Nikólaos and Sitía with **Lane Sea Lines**, 5 K. Sfakianáki St, Ág. Nikólaos; Tel: (0841) 25249; or 60 Vincéntzos Kornáros St, Sitía; Tel: (0843) 25555.

ISLAND-HOPPING

From Kastélli-Kíssamos in the northwest, there are three boats a week to Kíthira operated by ANEN Lines; Tel: (0822) 22655.

There are many opportunities for cruises (destinations include Santoríni, Délos, Mýkonos, Hýdra and Turkey) and island-hopping. For further information try:
Paleológos Shipping Agency, 5 25th August St, Iráklion 71202; Tel: (081) 346185; Fax: 346208.

Or enquire at the Greek Tourist Offices and/or the harbour authorities listed below:
Kastélli: Tel: (0822) 22024
Iráklion: Tel: (081) 244912
Réthymnon: Tel: (0831) 22276
Soúdha Bay: Tel: (0821) 89240

EXCURSIONS BY BOAT

It is possible to sail from Kastélli/Kissámos to the former pirate island of Gramvoúsa on the northwest tip of Crete. Two companies run daily boat trips: **Gramvoúsa-Bálos Maritime Co:** Tel/Fax: (0822) 24344; Mobile: 0977 013323 **Kastélli-Gramvoússa-Kísamos Shipping Co:** Tel: (0822) 22655; Fax: (0822) 23464

On the harbour front of Haniá there are a number of boats making the trip around the island of Theodoroú, which today is a sanctuary for the Cretan ibex. One example is **Evángelos Cruise Lines** which offers daily cruises in a glass-bottomed boat and a catamaran, lasting from 3 to 6 hours, and including provision of snorkelling equipment when breaks for swimming are taken.

In Paleochóra there is the opportunity to go dolphin and whale spotting. One of several operators is **E-motion Travel** (Tel/Fax: 0823 41755). Captain Stélios Yialinákis, joint owner of the company, is an expert on knowing where and when to meet up with these animals.

In eastern Crete, the island of Spinalónga with its substantial Venetian fortress, was once a leper colony. Regular excursions can be made from the harbours of Ághios Nikólaos and Eloúnda. It is also possible to charter a small boat from the fishing village of Pláka.

From Ierápetra, on the south coast of Lassíthi, there are daily trips to the quiet island of Chrisí, also known as Gaidaronísi (literally donkey island).

The beaches of Ághios Yeórghios and Ághios Pávlos on the southern coast of Réthymnon are visited regularly by boats from Aghía Gallíni.

At the mouth of the Kourtaliótiko Gorge, with the Megálou river running through it, is Prévali beach. This can be reached by regular boat services from Plakiás (run by Leftéris: 0832 31941) and also from Aghía Galíni.

Where to Stay

Hotels

Most visitors come to Crete on a package tour that includes pre-booked accommodation. This means that during the high season many of the larger, more luxurious resort hotels are fully booked in advance by foreign tour operators. But there are decent hotels of all classes to be had in all the towns.

EOT tourist offices can often provide a comprehensive list of hotels and pensions in the area. Alternatively, when you arrive in a town, park your car and explore the old quarter on foot – you'll usually find a suitable hotel or pension fairly quickly. On a warm, starry night "roof-space" can be very pleasant – sleeping on a mattress on the roof of a budget hotel or taverna (but be sure to use plenty of mosquito repellent and light a spiral smoke coil).

Our accommodation listings cover hotels and pensions in and around the main tourist resorts of Iráklion, Réthymnon, Haniá, and Lassíthi "counties" *(nómi)*. Hotels and pensions are graded by the tourist police as Luxury, A, B, C or D: all except the top category (Luxury) have to keep within set price limits.

Price Categories

Our hotel price bands are based on the cost of a double room with ensuite bathroom for one night in high season:

$$$$	over 50,000 drachmas
$$$	25,000–50,000 drx
$$	12,000–24,000 drx
$	up to 12,000 drx

Iráklion

Iráklion Town

Astória Capsís Hotel
Elefthérias Square
Tel: (081) 229002
Fax: (081) 229078
Located in the main square, close to the Archaeological Museum, the hotel has 116 comfortable rooms and 15 suites. Open all year. **$$$**

Átrion
9 Chronáki St
Tel: (081) 229225
Fax: (081) 223292
A quiet, superior "B" class hotel with 70 rooms in the heart of Iráklion. Open all year round. **$$**

Galaxy
67 Dimokratías Ave
Tel: (081) 238812
Fax: (081) 211211
A superior 5-star hotel in the centre of the city, with 140 deluxe rooms, 4 suites and a pool. Open all year round. **$$$**

Iríni
4 Ideomenéos St
Tel: (081) 226561
"C" class hotel situated in a quiet central area between the museum and the Venetian port. With 46 double and 13 single rooms, it is open 12 months of the year. **$$**

Lató
15 Epimenídou St
Tel: (081) 228103
Fax: (081) 240350
Overlooking the Koúles fortress on the old harbour, this family-run "B" class hotel has 50 rooms with a capacity of 90 beds. **$$$**

Olympic
Kornárou Square
Tel: (081) 288861
Fax: (081) 222512
Conveniently located in the city centre for easy access to the museum and other sites, this hotel has 73 rooms with standard amenities. **$$**

Dafnés

Dafnés Guest House
Tel: (081) 792191
Fax: (081) 280630
Situated in the quiet village of Dafnés (14 km/9 miles from Iráklion on the Míres road), this

traditional village house was renovated in 1999 into an "A" class guest house with 4 rooms. Open all year round. **$$**

Goúves

Memories Apartments
Tel: (0897) 41844
Fax: (0897) 41791
Situated 16 km (10 miles) east of Iráklion, Goúves village is where this newly built luxury complex offers self-catering apartments 800 metres/yards from the sandy beach. **$$**

Hersónisos

Galaxy Villas
Koutouloúfari 70014
Tel/Fax: (0897) 22910
This is a pleasant complex of villas set in the village of Koutouloúfari, approximately 1 km (½ mile) from Hersónisos and 25 km (16 miles) from Iráklion. **$$$**

Nana Beach
PO Box 20, Hersónisos
Tel: (0897) 22950
Fax: (0897) 22954
This is an all-inclusive resort complex on a private beach situated between Liménas Hersonísou and Mália. **$$$**

Royal Mare Village
Tel: (0897) 25025
Fax: (0897) 21664
This deluxe hotel offers 415 spacious rooms, housed in bungalows, by its own private beach. **$$$$**

Kókkinos Pyrgos

Libyan Sea
Tel: (0892) 51621
Fax: (0892) 52134
Mobile: 0944 179993
This is a small hotel, just 10 metres/yards from the sea on the coast of Messará Bay. Open all year round. **$**

Léndas

Hotel Levin
Tel: (0892) 95237
Located in the small village of Léndas, the ancient port of Górtyn, on the Libyan Sea, the hotel has 8 studios and 2 apartments with sea views. **$**

Mátala

Die Zwei Brüder (The Two Brothers)
Two minutes' walk from Mátala beach, a small, clean hotel with 20 double rooms. **$$**

Sun Rise
Tel: (0892) 45490
Situated 300m/yds from the village centre and 500m from the beach, Sun Rise offers a number of 2-room apartments in a small, newly built complex with excellent views of the sea. **$$**

Golden Phoenix
Tel: (0892) 45238
Has new, well-maintained, fully equipped apartments 300m/yds from the beach. **$**

Stalídha

Cactus Beach
Tel: (0907) 32494
Fax: (0907) 31589
Located 30 km (18 miles) east of Iráklion, Cactus Beach is a large hotel-resort complex with 185 rooms, just 20m from the beach. **$$$**

Tsoútsouros

Venetía
Tel: (0891) 92258
Fax: (0891) 92320
Eight self-catering apartments situated beside the delightful Tsoútsouros Bay. **$$**

Zarós

Kéramos
Tel/Fax: (0894) 31352
These spacious rooms, in the mountain village of Zarós are run by the Papadovasilákis family, who offer amazing hospitality and an unbelievable Cretan breakfast. Excellent value. **$**

Réthymnon

Réthymnon Town

Bráscos
Corner of Moátsou and Daskaláki Streets
Tel: (0831) 23721
Fax: (0831) 23725
A 3-star hotel with 88 rooms, situated in the town centre opposite the public gardens, 450m/yds from the beach. **$$**

Price Categories

Our hotel price bands are based on the cost of a double room with ensuite toilet for one night in high season:

$$$$	over 50,000 drachmas
$$$	25,000–50,000 drx
$$	12,000–24,000 drx
$	up to 12,000 drx

Fortezza
16 Melisinoú St
Tel: (0831) 22828
Fax: (0831) 54073
Takes its name from the Venetian fortress close by, in the old town. A modern hotel with 54 rooms, 150m/yds from the beach. **$$**

Idéon
10 Nikoláou Plastíra St
Tel: (0831) 28667
Fax: (0831) 28670
A four-storey "B" class hotel on the seafront; all modern amenities. **$$**

Kýma
1 Agnóstou Stratiótou Square
Tel: (0831) 55503
Fax: (0831) 22353
A modern 40-room hotel situated at the edge of the old town opposite the beach. Open all year round. **$$$**

Palazzo Rimóndi
Agent's Tel: (0842) 89933
With 21 studios and apartments in a renovated 15th-century building located in a quiet side street in the heart of the old Venetian town. **$$$**

Pearl Beach
Beach Road, Perivólia
Tel: (0831) 51513
Fax: (0831) 54891
At the end of the beach promenade, a 2-km (1-mile) walk from the old town, this "B" class hotel was completely renovated in 2000. **$$**

Theártemis Palace
30 M. Portáliou St
Tel: (0831) 53991
Fax: (0831) 23785
A comfortable "A" class hotel with swimming pool, in the centre of town. Recently refurbished. **$$$**

Venéto Suites
4 Epimenídhou St
Tel: (0831) 56634
Fax: (0831) 56635

Ten suites and studios in a beautifully renovated 15th-century monastery and, later, Venetian townhouse in the old city. **$$$**

Adhelianós Kámpos

Grecotel Réthymna Beach
Tel: (0831) 71002
Fax: (0831) 71668
Seven km (4 miles) east of Réthymnon, this "A" class resort complex has 520 rooms and bungalows, on its own private beach. **$$$$**

Aghía Galíni

Févro Hotel
Tel: (0831) 91275
Fax: (0831) 91475
Only 250m up from the beach, there are 50 spacious rooms, with views to the Libyan Sea. **$$**

Pórto Galíni
Tel: (0831) 91284
Fax: (0831) 91084
Close to the beach, this small 22-room hotel has all the usual amenities as well as special rooms for disabled people. **$$**

Balí

Balí Beach Hotel
Tel: (0834) 94210
Fax: (0834) 94252
Located on the village beach, this hotel consists of 90 rooms, with views of the sea. **$$**

Missíria

Grecotel Creta Palace
Tel: (0831) 55181
Fax: (0831) 54085
Three km (1½ miles) east of Réthymnon a luxury resort complex with 366 rooms and bungalows, incorporating all the expected amenities. **$$$$**

Odyssia
18 Mandilará St
Tel: (0831) 27874
Fax: (0831) 54906
A beach hotel with 69 rooms, most with a view of the sea. Internet facilities. Children welcome. **$**

Plakiás

Afrodíte Pension
Tel/Fax: (0832) 31266
Off the main strip, with south-facing views of the Libyan Sea and wonderful gardens, this small, clean pension offers good value. **$**

Anemone
Tel: (0832) 31972
Family-run accomodation 2 minutes' walk from the village centre, with good-sized balconies and sea views. **$**

Horizon Beach Hotel
Tel: (0832) 31476
Fax: (0832) 31154
A small hotel (26 rooms) offering a quiet family vacation on the beach, 400m/yds west of Plakiás. **$$**

Santa María
Tel: (0832) 31342
Fax: (0832) 31403
These 3 apartments and 4 studios, surrounded by a large, well-kept garden, are in the centre of the village and close to the sea. **$**

Rodhákino

Sun Rise
Tel: (0832) 31787
A complex of 10 rooms, with hotel service, 50m/yds from the sandy beach in the Bay of Kóraka. **$**

Haniá

Haniá Town

Casa Delfíno
9 Theofánous St
Tel: (0821) 93098
Fax: (0821) 96500
A beautifully restored 17th-century Venetian family house with 20 luxury apartments surrounding a courtyard in the old harbour area. Open all year round. **$$$**

Casa Venéta
57 Theotokopoúlou St
Tel: (0821) 75930
Fax: (0821) 75931
A new four-storey building, with wooden stairs and mezzanines, constructed behind a renovated Venetian façade in the Topanás area. **$$**

Contéssa
15 Theofánous St
Tel: (0821) 98565
A fine Venetian building (extensively altered in the Turkish period), which offers large, spacious rooms. Near the old harbour. **$$**

Dóma
124 Venezélou St
Tel: (0821) 51772
Fax: (0821) 41578
A converted 19th-century mansion, formerly the British vice-consulate, just to the east of the town centre, overlooking the sea. **$$$**

Ifigénia
Old Harbour area.
Has rooms and studios to let in several buildings in the Venetian quarter. Contact Michális Boúlakas at the Hotel Captain Vassílis, Theotokopoúlou 12 A Párodos
Tel/Fax: (0821) 94357
Mobile: 0944 501319. **$$**

Kríti Hotel
Nikefórou Foká and Kíprou streets
Tel: (0821) 51881
Fax: (0821) 41000
A modern hotel with 98 rooms, between the beach of Koum Kapi and the town market. **$$$**

Nóstos
42–46 Zambelíou St
Tel: (0821) 94743
Fax: (0821) 94740
A superbly renovated building (probably the 17th-century church of the "Virgin of the Renieris") situated on the harbour front, with 12 studios and a roof garden. **$$**

Pension Eva
1 Theofánous and Zambelíou St
Tel: (0821) 76706
A small, 6-bedroom pension in a renovated Venetian house with wooden ceilings and brass beds. **$$**

Porto Del Colombo
corner of Theofánous and Muschón streets
Tel/Fax: (0821) 70945
An impressively restored Venetian townhouse in the narrow, picturesque backstreets of the old town. Open all year. **$$**

Traditional Retreat

For a truly away-from-it-all retreat-style vacation, renovated traditional stone houses in the old village of Miliá, near Élos (southwest of Haniá), are available to rent. The village does not have electricity. For details, Tel/Fax: (0822) 51569.

Price Categories

Our hotel price bands are based on the cost of a double room with ensuite toilet for one night in high season:

$$$$	over 50,000 drachmas
$$$	25,000–50,000 drx
$$	12,000–24,000 drx
$	up to 12,000 drx

Theréza
8 Angélou St, Old Harbour
Tel/Fax: (0821) 92798
A three-storey Venetian house, renovated and refurbished with great care. Superb views of the harbour from the roof terrace. Open all year. **$$**

Yeráni

Creta Paradise
Tel: (0821) 61315
Fax: (0821) 61134
An "A" class resort-hotel with 148 rooms and 38 bungalows by the beach, between Plataniás and Yeráni. **$$$**

Yeorghioúpolis

Pilot Beach Hotel
Tel: (0825) 61002
Fax: (0825) 61397
Bungalow-style "A" class hotel, with 165 rooms and its own beach, situated 1 km from the village (38 km/24 miles east of Haniá). **$$$**

Kal´yves

Kalíves Beach
Apokorónou
Tel: (0825) 31881
Fax: (0825) 31134
A modern, well-appointed hotel situated by the beach on Soúdha Bay, with a view of the White Mountains to the south. **$$$**

Kastélli

Hotel Hermes
Kastélli Kissámou
Tel: (0822) 24109
Fax: (0822) 22166
A modern hotel close to the beach on the outskirts of town. Makes an ideal base for exploring northwest Crete. **$$**

Kondomarí

Aegean Palace
Kondomarí, POE 73104
Tel: (0821) 62668
Situated just 15 km (9 miles) west of Haniá, in an unspoilt location, the hotel consists of 45 suites, 10 of which have their own pools. **$$$**

Loutró

Hotel Porto Loutró (I & II)
Tel: (0825) 91433
On the beach, these two small but comfortable Cretan-style hotels were built by the owners some 10 years ago. Most rooms have balconies and overlook the bay. **$$**

Paleochóra

Alexía
Tel: (0823) 42004
On the eastern side of the Paleochóra peninsula, by the pebble beach. Quiet, clean and excellent value, with self-catering facilities. **$**

Áris
Tel: (0823) 41502
Fax: (0823) 41546
A small, 25-room family hotel, situated 300m/yds from the beach. All rooms have balconies with either a sea view or a garden view. **$$**

Kóstas
Tel/Fax: (0823) 41248
Has 6 unpretentious and inexpensive self-catering rooms overlooking the sea, just to the south of the quay. **$**

Pyrgos Psilonérou

Summer Lodge (**Stamátis Pension**)
Pírgos Psilonérou, Haniá 73014
Tel: (0821) 62470
Fax: (0821) 62564
An attractive, 17-room, family-run pension with its own swimming pool and gardens, set in the olive groves 14 km (9 miles) west of Haniá. **$**

Soúghia

Santa Iríni
Tel: (0823) 51342
On the seafront, with good-sized, clean rooms and air-conditioning. **$**

Villa Rinío
Tel: (0823) 51537
In a quiet area of the village, 200m/yds from the sea, offers rooms with self-catering facilities. **$**

Lassíthi

Ághios Nikólaos

Akrotíri Hotel
Tel: (0841) 24891
Offers accommodation for 60 visitors in self-catering studios, in a quiet area by the beach, 2 km (1 mile) from the centre of town. **$$$**

Crystal Hotel
Tel: (0841) 24407
Fax: (0841) 25394
Set back from the main road, this 38-room hotel near the town centre is 10 mins from the beach. **$$**

Lató Hotel
Tel: (0841) 24581
Fax: (0841) 23996
On the beach, 1.5 km (1 mile) from Ághios Nikólaos and 6 km (4 miles) from Eloúnda village, Ladó has 37 rooms in its hotel complex which is set in lush gardens. They also manage the Karavostási (stone house) 8 km (5 miles) from the town, with 3 self-catering studios on the coast. **$$**

Mínos Beach Art 'Otel
Tel: (0841) 22345
Fax: (0841) 22548
This is an elegant, deluxe coastal resort consisting of bungalows surrounded by well-tended gardens, renowned for the collection of contemporary art on display. **$$$$**

Sgourós
Kitroplatía Beach
Tel: (0841) 28931
Fax: (0841) 25568
A family-run hotel, 10m/yds) from the sea and 300m/yds from the town centre, with accomodation for 60 visitors. **$$**

Eloúnda

Eloúnda Beach
Tel: (0841) 41412
Fax (0841) 41373
Overlooking the Mirabéllo Bay and the island of Spinalónga, with its Venetian fortress, the Eloúnda Beach is an internationally acclaimed deluxe hotel. **$$$$**

Eloúnda Mare
Tel: (0841) 41102
Fax: (0841) 41307
The only Relais and Chateaux hotel in Greece, this deluxe complex offers bungalows with pools. **$$$$**

Aktí Olous
Tel: (0841) 41270
Fax: (0841) 41425
This "B" class hotel is located in the sheltered bay of Eloúnda, 300m/yds from the village. Its 79 twin rooms have recently been renovated. **$$**

Ierápetra

Aríon Palace
Tel: (0842) 25930
Fax: (0842) 25931
An "A" class hotel 1.5 km (1 mile) from the town centre, with 82 rooms and panoramic views. **$$$**
Pétra Mare
Tel: (0842) 23341
Fax: (0842) 23350
Situated right on the beach near the centre of town, this large "A" class resort-complex has 227 spacious rooms. **$$$**
Ástron
56 M. Kothrí St
Tel: (0842) 25114
Fax: (0842) 25917
This newly-built "B" class hotel, with 70 rooms on 4 floors, is by the sandy beach in Ierápetra town. **$$**

Palékastro

Marína Village
Tel: (0843) 61284
Fax: (0843) 61285
Set in tranquil, rural surroundings, this complex has 32 rooms and a most amiable host in Antónis Relákis, who also owns the Hióna Studio, on the beach nearby. **$$**
Thália
Tel: (0843) 61448
Fax: (0843) 61588
Situated in a quiet side-street in the centre of the village, this small, family-run hotel has 10 pleasant rooms. **$**

Síssi

Castello Village
Tel: (0841) 71124
Fax: (0841) 71462
This "B" class hotel on the coast, 40 km (25 miles) east of Iráklion airport, has 93 apartments and caters for families with children. **$$$**
Síssi Bay
Tel: (0841) 71384
Fax: (0841) 71284
A 50-room "A" class hotel 150m/yds from a sandy beach and 200m/yds from the village harbour with its picturesque fishermen's boats. **$$$**

Sitía

El Greco
13 G. Arkadíou St
Tel/Fax: (0843) 23133
A small "C" class hotel with 19 rooms, set in a quiet, central location. **$$**
Ploímon
Tel: (0843) 25445
Fax: (0843) 61285
Five "A" class self-catering apartments, which can each accommodate up to 4 people, located on the outskirts of town. **$$**
Crystal
17 Kapitán Sífi
Tel: (0843) 22284
Fax: (0843) 28644
With sea views and only 50 metres/yards from the beach, this "C" class hotel has 41 rooms. **$**

Zákros

Alex
Tel: (0843) 93338
Seven "C" class self-catering apartments in rural surroundings. **$**
Athená
Tel: (0843) 26893
Fax: (0843) 26894
Located on the beach at Káto Zákros, four "A" class apartments offering self-catering facilities (details available from the Taverna Agroyáli). **$**

Youth Hostels

There are a few official youth hostels in Crete located in or near some of the major tourist resorts. They offer simple but clean accommodation and cheap meals or cooking facilities. Youth Hostel Association (YHA) membership cards are rarely (if ever) asked for in Crete – though to be on the safe side it is probably still worth obtaining one before leaving home.

At the time of writing, the list of Youth Hostels published by the EOT and available from tourist offices is woefully inaccurate (eg. the hostel in Ághios Nikólaos has been closed for 9 years!). Four hostels certainly do exist. These are:
Iráklion: 5, Víronos St
Tel: (081) 222947
Réthymnon: 41–45 Tobázi St
Tel: (0831) 22848
Plakiás: (on the south coast)
Tel: (0832) 32118
Sitía: 4 Therísssou St.
Tel: (0843) 22693

There are no youth hostels in Haniá or Ághios Nikólaos.

Rooms to Rent

Dhomátia in Greek – which is normally signposted in English as "Rent Rooms" or "Rooms to Let" – are generally cheaper and often more congenial than hotel rooms. The local tourist office does not provide listings of such rooms, so it is usually a matter of finding them for yourself.

In smaller villages away from the coast, rooms can sometimes be in private family houses: the local *kafeníon* is the best source of information. For example, there are no obvious rooms to rent in Archánes – an important archaeological site – but if you ask in the first *kafeníon* on the left as you enter the town from Iráklion, you will find that the owner knows of rooms available.

In the larger resorts, outside of the Old Town areas, rooms are often in characterless concrete blocks, and their owners will usually seek you out at the ferry or bus terminal.

Note that it is standard practice for "rooms" proprietors to ask you to hand over your passport, but it is better to persuade them to write down or photocopy the information, so that you can keep your passport as identification.

Campsites

Camping in Greece, a booklet produced by the Panhellenic Camping Association and the Hellenic Chamber of Hotels, is available from EOT tourist offices, and lists all the amenities available on each site. However it contains many errors concerning addresses and telephone/fax numbers. Below, we hope, are the current correct details. (Note: camping on unrecognised sites is forbidden.)

IRÁKLION

Caravan
Liménas Hersonísou 70014
Tel: (0897) 22025
On the coast 26 km (16 miles) east of Iráklion.
Creta Camping
Goúves 71500
Tel: (0897) 41400
Fax: (0897) 41792
17 km (11 miles) east of Iráklion.
Hersónisos Camping
Anissarás 70014
Tel: (0897) 22902
On the eastern edge of Hersónisos, 5 km (3 miles) before Mália.
Komós
Pitsídia 70200
Tel: (0892) 45596
Located 65 km (40 miles) southwest of Iráklion, between Pitsídia and Mátala and 10 minutes from the beach.
Mátala Camping
Mátala 70200
Tel: (0892) 45720
Fax: (0892) 45331
Close to Mátala beach and the famous caves.

RÉTHYMNON

Aghía Galíni
Tel: (0832) 91386
Fax: (0832) 91239
East of the village, near the beach. Open all year.
Apollonía
Plakiás 74060
Tel: (0832) 31507/31318
Fax: (0832) 31607
On the south coast 40 km (25 miles) from Réthymnon.
Elizabeth
Missíria, Réthymnon 74100
Tel: (0831) 28694
Set 5 km (3 miles) east of Réthymnon, beside the beach.

HANIÁ

Camping Haniá
Ághii Apóstoli 73100
Tel: (0821) 31138
Fax: (0821) 33371
4 km (2½ miles) west of Haniá.
Kíssamos Camping
Kastélli 73400 (near town centre)
Tel: (0822) 23444
Mýthimna
Drapaniás, Kísamos 73400
Tel: (0822) 31444/5
Fax: (0822) 31000
4 km (2½ miles) east of Kastélli in the district of Kissámou.
Nopíghia
Kísamos 73400
Tel: (0822) 31111
Fax: (0822) 31700
6 km (4 miles) east of Kastélli.
Paleochóra Camping
Paleochóra 73001
Tel: (0823) 41120
Fax: (0823) 41744
Northeast from the village, close to the beach and open-air disco.

LASSÍTHI

Gournía Moon
Gournía 72200
Tel/Fax: (0842) 93243
15 km (9 miles) east of Ághios Nikólaos on the national road, close to Ístro.
Koutsounári Camping
Koutsounári, Ierápetra 72200
Tel: (0842) 61213
Fax: (0842) 61186
7 km (4 miles) to the east of Ierápetra on the south coast. Also open in the winter for caravans.
Síssi
Mirabéllou 72400
Tel: (0841) 71247
Fax: (0897) 23566
26 km (16 miles) northwest of Ághios Nikólaos.

Where to Eat

Eating Out

There are literally thousands of places to eat on the island, offering a wide variety of culinary delights. As well as *estiatória* (restaurants) and tavernas there are *psistariá* (rôtisseries), *maghérika* (eating-houses), *mezedhádhika* (places for *mezédhes*), *ouzerí* (for *oúzo* and *mezédhes*), *psarotavérnas* (fish restaurants), *souvlazídhika* (*souvláki* houses) and last, but not least, *fastfoudádhika* (self-explanatory!).

However, these days there is a general trend, particularly in the more urban and/or touristic restaurants and tavernas, to move away from the *étima* (ready-cooked) foods such as those done in casseroles *(katsaróles)* or in baking trays *(tapsiá)* towards *tís óras* (food that is fried or grilled to order). This is because it is easier and quicker to prepare, keeps longer in refrigerators and generally has a higher profit-margin.

So the experience of eating out does not honestly reflect the wide range and diversity of traditional Cretan cuisine. This also means that there are very few main course dishes *(kíria piáta)* available to vegetarians, although they have a wide choice of starters (*orektiká*) – fried vegetables, beans, salads, chips and *tzatzíki*.

Iráklion

Iráklion Town

Giovanni
12 Koraí St (parallel to Dedálou St)
Tel: (081) 346338
In a fine, neo-classical building, Giovanni specialises in Greek and Italian cuisine.

Ionía
corner of Evans and Yiánari streets
A *fagádhiko* offering a variety of Greek, meat, fish and vegetable dishes since 1923. Avoid their house wine.

Ippókampos
Overlooking the harbour, close to the junction of 25th August St. and Sofoklís Venizélou Ave.
Tel: (081) 280240
Ippókampos is famed for its *mezédhes* and is usually packed with locals.

Kiriákos
51 Dhimokratías St
Serves typically Cretan cuisine, with meat, fish and vegetable dishes all cooked in the traditional way.

Loúkoulos
Korai St
Tel: (081) 224435
An Italian restaurant in a neo-classical building. Upmarket and expensive but good. Vegetarians catered for.

New China
Koraí St
Tel: (081) 245162
A Chinese restaurant with a courtyard and trees. Like all Chinese restaurants on the island, it is more expensive than local cuisine.

Terzákis
Next to the church of Ághios Dhimítrios, close to the junction of Marinélis St and Víronos St.
Similar in cuisine to Ippókampos but more expensive.

Vyzándio
3 Vizándio St
Tel: (081) 244775
A typical modern taverna, offering Greek and international dishes at reasonable prices.

Áno Archánes

Dhíktamos
3 Pérkolo St
Pleasant, intimate surroundings with friendly service and quality Cretan food. Sensible prices.

Goúves

Chickadees Restaurant
In the main street, offering international and American-style cuisine.

Kamáres

Zacharías Kafeníon
opposite the trail to the Kamáres Cave
Very pleasantly situated overlooking the valley, and quirkily decorated, there is no set menu (just ask for what he has available).

Mália

Der Engel
On the beach road, offers above-average international cuisine presented by the Dutch owners.

Seasons
On the fishing harbour, serves excellent European cooking in a well-established Dutch restaurant.

Mátala

Die Zwei Brüder (The Two Brothers)
A well-established eating and meeting place with reasonable prices.

Rogdhiá

O Exóstis Taverna
Tel: (081) 841206
Set high above the Gulf of Iráklion, with great views, excellent Cretan food, fair prices and friendly service from Andhréas, the owner.

Zarós

Óasis
in the high street
A small, congenial place, where Manólis has *souvláki, tís óras* and some *étima* as well as excellent home-made wine.

Vótamos
next to the Ídhi Hotel
Tel: (0892) 31302
A well-established *psarotavérna* with its own trout *(péstrofa)* farm. Very popular with locals and, of course, the fish is fresh.

Réthymnon

Réthymnon Town

Fanári
16 Kefaloyiánnidhon St
Tel: (0831) 54879
A good taverna specialising in traditional Greek *mezédhes.*

Globe (Ydrógeios)
33 El. Venizélou
Tel: (0831) 25465
Situated opposite the beachfront promenade, the owner and chef, Ághis, prepares Cretan specialities, pasta dishes, pizzas, crepes and much more. Menu includes a reasonable choice for vegetarian diners.

Kafeníon Stá Brisákia
Moschovíti St (behind the Rimondi Fountain)
Small, quiet *kafeníon* that offers a wide selection of home-cooked *mezédhes* with barrelled wine or *tsikoudhiá.*

Koumbés
3 Akrotiríou, Koumbés
Tel: (0831) 52209
Overlooking the sea in a suburb to the west is this excellent *psarotavérna* with fresh fish caught by the owner himself, Ilias Kapetanákis.

Kyría María
20 Moschovíti St (behind the Rimondi Fountain)
Tel: (0831) 29078
Open all day long and providing good basic Cretan cooking. Some vegetarian options are always available.

La Creperie
10 Arambatzóglou St, Old town
Tel: (0831) 50230
The first and best place for crêpes in town, Tótis has been cooking them up for over 6 years. Good espresso.

Óthon
Plátanos Square
Tel: (0831) 55500
Open every day, this *estiatório* offers a wide variety of Greek and European dishes in the old town.

Venéto
4 Epimenídhou St
Tel: (0831) 56634
Attached to the suites in a beautifully renovated 15th-century building *(see Where to Stay, page 254)*, this restaurant has a menu based on Greek and Mediterranean cuisine.

Zambía
20 Stamathioudháki St, Koumbés (by the municipal swimming pool)
Tel: (0831) 24561
A justly popular restaurant serving good fish and traditional Greek dishes.

Arghyroúpoli

Paleós Mílos (The Old Mill)
Tel: (0831) 81209
Yiórgos and Sylvia run this restaurant, stunningly set among the springs of what was once ancient Lappa. Grilled meats are the speciality.

Chromonastíri

Vardís
Tel: (0831) 75227
A typical Cretan taverna located in the village 13 km (8 miles) southeast of Réthymnon town. Open all day.

Margharítes

Vrísi Taverna
The taverna lies on the outskirts of this village in the Milopótamos region, 32 km (20 miles) east of Réthymnon. Very pleasant, with typical Cretan food.

Missíria

Stelína
Tel: (0831) 53192
Has a great variety of Greek and vegetarian dishes. Closed Mondays.
Zísis
Tel: (0831) 28814
Offers a wide range of traditional Greek cuisine. Closed Tuesdays.

Mírthios

Taverna Platéa
Overlooking Plakiás on the south coast, the taverna has excellent Cretan food and fantastic views.

Pánormos

Sofoklís Taverna
Tel: (0834) 51297
Situated on the fishing harbour, 22 km (13 miles) to the east of Réthymnon, it specialises in Greek and Cretan cooking.

Plakiás

Kástro Taverna
Tel: (0832) 32246
Half-way up the hill between Plakiás and Mírthios, it has a good and extensive menu. Quiet surroundings with great views.
Krí-krí Taverna
Tel: (0832) 31101
Opposite the beach, Krí-krí has excellent oven-baked dishes and an international menu, including pizza.
Lyssós
Down some steps to the riverside location, Lyssós is hospitable and very comfortable. Many meat dishes from Greece and Cyprus. Fine village wine.

Stavroménos

Taverna Alékos
Tel: (0831) 72234
Situated 11 km (7 miles) east of Réthymnon, a family-run establishment offering typical Cretan food.

Haniá

Haniá Town

Anáplous (Upstream)
corner of Sífaka and Melchisedhék
Tel: (0821) 41320
In the district of Macherádhika and set in a ruined Turkish house, Níkos and Ángelos offer Cretan specialities including pork baked in clay, and vegetarian dishes.
Apostólis
3 Aktí Enóseos
Tel: (0821) 41767
A good-quality *psarotavérna* overlooking the inner harbour.
Árti
15 Skoufón St
Tel: (0821) 75867
Restaurant with international cuisine prepared by a Swiss chef. Small, pleasant courtyard at the back.
Kariátis
12 Katecháki Square
Tel: (0821) 55600
Located behind the former customs house, this unique Italian restaurant enjoys a good reputation for its pastas and pizzas.
O Kormoránοs (The Cormorant)
46 Theotokopoúlou St
Tel: (0821) 86910
A *mezedhádhiko* with barrelled wine and *tsikoudhiá*. Also open during the day for snacks and sandwiches. Excellent value.
Rudi's Bierhaus
26 Sífaka St
Tel: (0821) 50824
In the Macherádhika area, Rudi has created a unique beerhouse with over 100 different beers from all over the world. These are complemented by excellent *mezédhes* of imported cheeses and Austrian cooked meats, served on wooden platters. He also has a great collection of jazz music.
Tamám
49 Zambelíou St
Tel: (0821) 96080
In the old Hamam (steam-baths), Márkos has an interesting and varied menu including range of Cretan specialities and vegetarian dishes.
Tó Karnágio
8 Katecháki Square
Tel: (0821) 53366
Set back from the harbour, by the former customs house, a well-established restaurant with "European-style" service. Quality Cretan cuisine and vegetarian dishes.
To Katófli
13 Aktí Papanikolí, Néa Hóra
Tel: (0821) 98621
Opposite the beach, to the west of the harbour, this small taverna specialises in Cretan food.
Tó Pighádhi Toú Toúrkou (The Well of the Turk)
1–3 Kalínikou Sarpáki, Splántzia
Tel: (0821) 54547
Run by an English woman, Jenny, who specialises in Middle Eastern dishes. A long-established restaurant.

Áno Stalós

O Levéntis
Tel: (0821) 68155
A family-run village taverna 6 km (4 miles) west of Haniá, excelling in home-cooked Cretan food.

Afráta

Roxáni
Tel: (0824) 23169
Situated on the Rodhopoú Peninsula, this village taverna is renowned for Roxíni's *kalitsoúnia.*

Epanochóri

Odysséas Kafeníon
On the road to Soúghia, this traveller's rest (they also have rooms) supplies dishes of the day. Stunning views.

Gávdhos Island

Óasis
Sarakíniko village
A popular eatery with baked pies and pizzas as well as vegetarian and vegan dishes.

Horafákia

Iríni
Tel: (0821) 39470
This taverna is on the Akrotíri Peninsula, and has traditional Greek home-cooking and a wide variety of *étima.*

Hóra Sfakíon

Lefká Óri
Tel: (0825) 91209
In this restaurant, at the western end of the harbour front, Andréas cooks some of the best traditional dishes in the area.

Kalyves

Aléxis Zorbás
Tel: (0825) 31363
In the district of Apokóronas, and pleasantly situated by the Venetian mill, this family taverna is open all year round. Large portions.

Kastélli

To Kelári (The Cellar)
Tel: (0822) 23883
On the beachfront promenade, Stelios takes great pride in his local cuisine.

Paleochóra

Caravélla
Tel: (0823) 41131
Close to the quay and offering wonderful sea views, Yeórghios and his brother are specialists in good quality fresh fish.

Chrístos
Tel: (0823) 41359
This restaurant is situated on the promenade running next to the pebble beach. The cooking is done by Chrístos' wife and daughter, who produce a vast array of meat and fish dishes.

Third Eye
Located in a back street between the village centre and the sandy beach, this excellent vegetarian restaurant has been established for 12 years.

Polyrhínia

Odysséas
Tel: (0822) 23331
A real taste of the Cretan countryside and traditional cooking, using home-grown ingredients. 7 km (4 miles) south of Kastélli.

Soúghia

Polífimos
In a pleasant garden setting, this taverna specialises in local lamb cooked in wine, and rabbit stew.

Lassíthi

Ághios Nikólaos

Du Lac
by the Voulisméni Lake
A long-established restaurant with pretty setting and Greek and international cuisine. Tourist prices but popular with the locals. Street entrance on 28th Octovríou St.

Pórtes
3 Anapávseos
Tel: (0841) 28489
Recommended for its large selection of *mezédhes.*

Stámna
200m from the Hotel Mirabéllo, Havánia
Tel: (0841) 25817
An Italian and Greek restaurant serving superb quality food.

Aghathiás

Nikólas O Psarás (Nicholas The Fisherman)
Tel: (0843) 61598
20 km (12 miles) east of Sitía, this taverna offers fresh fish caught by Nikólas and Cretan specialities prepared by his wife, Vangelía.

Aghía Fotiá

Nerómilos
Tel: (0843) 25576
Offers simple grilled food and a wonderful view in this little village, 5km (3 miles) east of Sitía.

Eloúnda

Akrochoriá
Tel: (0841) 42091
On the road leading to Eloúnda. An excellent place for fresh fish, lobster and seafood grilled over charcoal.

Hióna

Kakaviá
Tel: (0843) 61227
On the beautiful Hiona beach, just down from Palékastro on the east coast, Michális and Ólga have 35 years' experience cooking fish and their speciality is *kakaviá* (fish soup). Aided by their two sons, the atmosphere is very friendly.

Ístro

El Greco
Tel: (0841) 61637
In the beach resort of Ístro, 10 km (6 miles) south of Ághios Nikólaos. Has a range of Greek specialities, fresh fish and lobster.

Káto Zákros

Akroghiáli
Tel: (0843) 93316
Has a friendly atmosphere and a beachside setting on the east coast. Níkos Perákis enjoys a reputation for his local fresh fish and meat.

Koútsouras

Votsalákia
Tel: (0843) 51247
Good option located in this small village (44 km/27 miles east of Makrí Yialós, on the south coast), Votsalákia has a beachside setting and stays open as long as the locals sit there and drink *tsikoudhiá.* It specialises in fresh fish. Reasonable prices.

Lassíthi Plateau

Taverna Antónis
Tel: (0844) 31581
Off the tourist trail, it can be found between the two small villages of Psychró and Pláti. In a quiet and beautiful environment, Antónis has a good selection of charcoal-grilled meats.

Makrí Yialós

Cave of the Dragon
Tel: (0843) 51494
Located 3 km (1½ miles) east of the village, on the south coast, this taverna has great views across the bay from its hillside location.Traditional Cretan food and home-baked bread.

To Limáni
Tel: (0843) 52457
Down by the harbour, specialising in meat and fish dishes. A favourite with locals and tourists alike.

Maridhátis

Taverna Maridátis
Close to the beach and 5 km (3 miles) from Palékastro, in the direction of Vái, is where Manólis and his partner Níki prepare fresh fish, meat and traditional *mezédhes*.

Méssa Moulianá

Kefalóvrisi
Tel: (0843) 95462
Located 50 km (31 miles) east of Ághios Nikólaos this taverna has superb Cretan cuisine, served in the shade of plane trees.

Neápoli

Yéfseis Restaurant
Tel: (0841) 32397
A well-known favourite with the locals, sited in the main square of this small town, 15 km (9 miles) northwest of Ághios Nikólaos.

Palékastro

Helena Restaurant
Tel: (0843) 61234
Located 50m (164ft) from the central square, in the direction of Sitía. Here, Yeórghios Relákis and his wife, Helena, have had a wealth of experience in producing delicious Cretan food.

Sitía

Creta House
Konstantínou Karamanlís St
Tel: (0843) 25133
Offers traditional fare and some of the best *mezédhes* in town.
Koliós Remezo
El. Venizélou St
Tel: (0843) 28609
Presents Greek and Cretan dishes, with grilled *kalamári* being the house speciality.
The Balcony
V.Kornárou St
Tel: (0843) 25598
Prepares a large selection of international recipes, but is a more expensive option.

Sightseeing

Monasteries and convents

IRÁKLION

Monasteries

Ághios Geórghios Epanosífi south of Archánes; Tel: (0894) 51231. Open daily 8am–8pm.
Apezánou south of Míres; Tel: (0892) 97390. Open daily 8am–7pm.
Koudoumá west of Trís Ekklisíes (south of Iráklion); Tel: (0892) 41324.
Panaghía Odhigítria north of Kalí Liménes; Tel: (0892) 42364. Open only on Sunday mornings after church.
Valsamónero Vorízia, southwest of Iráklion. Open daily 9am–3pm except Mondays.
Vrondíssi west of Zarós; Tel: (0894) 31247. Open daily 8am–8pm.

Convents

Kerá Kardhiótissas southeast of Mochós (east of Iráklion); Tel: (0897) 51203. Open daily 8.30am–1pm and 4.30–7.30pm.
Panaghía Kaliviani west of Míres; Tel: (0892) 22151. Open daily 6.30am–8pm.

Monastic silence

When visiting monasteries it is important to dress appropriately (shorts are unacceptable on both men and women) and not to make unnecessary noise. It is also bear in mind that, although some monasteries are open all day, it is important to be especially quiet during the mid-afternoon "siesta".

Panaghía Pallianí near Veneráto (southwest of Iráklion); Tel: (081) 791331. Open daily 8am–12.30pm and 4–8pm.
Savathianón Rogdhiá, northwest of Iráklion; Tel: (081) 841296. Open daily 4–7pm.

RÉTHYMNON

Monasteries

Arkádhi south of Amnátos; Tel: (0831) 83116. Open daily 8am–1.30pm and 2.30–8pm.
Arsáni Stavroménos, east of Réthymnon; Tel: (0831) 71228. Open daily 8am–noon and 4–7pm.
Préveli south of Réthymnon; Tel: (0832) 31246. Open daily 8.30am–1.30pm and 3.30–8.30pm.
Profitis Ilías Roústika, southwest of Réthymnon; Tel: (0831) 91205. Open daily 9–11.30am and 3–6pm, but the church is no longer open to the public after the theft of some icons by Italian tourists.

Convents

Metamorphóseos Sotíros Koumbés suburb of Réthymnon; Tel: (0831) 29103. Open daily 8am–1pm.

HANIÁ

Monasteries

Aghía Triádha Akrotíri; Tel: (0821) 63310. Open daily 6am–2pm and 5–7pm.
Gouvernéto Akrotíri; Tel: (0821) 63319. Open daily 8am–12.30pm and 4.30–7.30pm.
Goniá Kolimbári; Tel: (0824) 22281. Open daily 8am–noon and 4–8pm. Saturdays 4–8pm only.

Convents

Chrysoskalítissa on the southwest coast; Tel: (0822) 61261. Open daily 7am–sunset.
Korakiés Akrotíri; Tel: (0821) 64571. Open daily 10.30–11.30am and 5.30–6.30pm.
Zoodhóchou Pighís Chrisopighí, on the southern outskirts of Haniá; Tel: (0821) 91125. Open daily 8am–12.30pm and 4–6pm.

LASSÍTHI

Monasteries

Ághios Yeórghios Selinári, east of Mália; Tel: (0841) 71438. Open daily 8am–8pm
Ághios Ioánnis Kapsá south of Sitía; Tel/Fax: (0843) 51458. Open by appointment only or as part of an organised tour.
Panaghía Faneroméni south of Ághios Nikólaos; Tel: (0842) 93220. Open daily 8am–2pm and 4–8pm.
Toploú east of Sitía; Tel: (0843) 61226. Open daily 9am–6pm.

Archaeological sites

Archaeological sites are usually well signposted. Opening hours vary considerably from site to siten. Summer hours are longer than winter hours. Most close on public holidays .

IRÁKLION

Aghía Triádha near Phaestós; Tel: (0892) 91360. Open daily 8.30am–3pm.
Górtyn Tel: (0892) 31144. Open daily 8am–6pm.
Knossós Tel: (081) 231940. Open daily 8am–7pm
Koúles Fortress Old Harbour, Iráklion; Tel: (081) 224630. Open daily 8am–7pm except Mondays, noon–7pm
Mália Tel: (0897) 31597. Open Tue–Sun 8.30am–3pm.
Niroú Háni east of Iráklion; key from custodian in *kafeníon* during "normal hours".
Phaestós Tel: (0892) 42315. Open daily 8am–7pm.
Týlissos west of Iráklion; Tel: (081) 831498. Open daily 8.30am–3pm.
Vathípetro near Archánes. Open daily 8.30am–3pm.

RÉTHYMNON

Arméni Minoan Cemetery north of Arméni village. Open Tue–Sun 8.30am–3pm.
Fortezza (fortress) Réthymnon town; Tel: (0831) 28101. Open Tue–Sun 8am–8pm (last admission 7.15pm).

HANIÁ

Aptera Fort and other sites open continuously. However the monastic settlement and Roman cisterns are fenced off and are only open Mon–Fri 8am–7pm, Sat–Sun 8am–3pm.
Lissós Soúghia; Tel: (0823) 51336. Open continuously

LASSÍTHI

Gourniá Tel: (0842) 93028. Open Tue–Sun 8.30am–3pm.
Zákros Tel: (0843) 26897. Open Tue–Sun 8am–7pm.
Spinalónga Island former leper colony; Tel: (0841) 42366. Open daily 10am–6pm. Only accessable by caiques which leave hourly from Pláka (5-minute trip) and Eloúnda (20 minutes).

Museums

Most of these are closed one day a week, and on public holidays and religious festivals.

IRÁKLION

Archaeological Museum of Iráklion
8 Xanthoulídou St; Tel: (081) 226092. Open daily 8am–7pm, except Mondays, 12.30–7pm.
Historical Museum
7 Lisimáchou Kalokairinoú St, off Sof. Venizélou St, Iráklion; Tel: (081) 283219. Open Mon–Fri 9am–5pm, Sat 9am– 2pm.
Battle of Crete Museum
Hatzidáki/ Doukós Bofor, Iráklion; Tel: (081) 346554. Open daily 9am–1pm.
Ikon Museum
Church of Aghía Ekateríni, Aghía Ekateríni Square, Iráklion; Tel: (081) 288825. Open Tue–Sat 8.30am–1.30pm, also 5–7pm on Tue, Thu and Fri.
Natural History Museum
157 L. Knosoú, Iráklion; Tel: (081) 324711. Open Mon–Sat 9am–7pm, Sun 10am–8pm.
Archaeological Museum of Archánes
Archánes Town; Tel: (081) 751898. Open Wed–Mon 8.30am– 3pm.
Cretan Historical and Folklore Museum (Mikális Níkos Psaltákis) 6 km (4 miles) from Knossós and 3 km (1½ miles) from Archánes; Tel: (081) 751853. Open Wed–Mon 9.30am–2pm.
Lychnostátis Open-air Museum
between Hersónisos and Mália; Tel: (0897) 23660. Open Tue–Sun 9.30am–2pm.
Museum of Cretan Ethnology
Vóri Village, near Míres and Timbáki; Tel: (0892) 91110. Open daily 10am– 6pm.
Níkos Kazantzákis Museum
Village Square, Mirtiá; Tel: (081) 742451. Open Fri–Tue 9am–1pm, also Sat–Mon and Wed 4–8pm.

RÉTHYMNON

Archaeological Museum
opposite the Fortezza; Tel: (0831) 29975. Open Tue–Sun 8.30am–3pm.
Marine Museum
Arambatsóglou St; Tel: (0831) 74484. Open Tue–Sun 8.30am–3pm.
Historical and Folk Art Museum
30 Vernárdhou St; Tel: (0831) 23398. Open daily 9am–1pm, also Mon–Tue 6–8pm, Wed–Sun 7–9pm.
Leftéris Kanakákis Gallery of Contemporary Art
5 Himáras St; Tel: (0831) 55847. Open Tue–Fri 9am–1pm and 7–8pm, Sat–Sun 11am–3pm.
Folklore Museum
Situated next to the Zografákis Taverna, Arghyroúpoli; Tel: (0831) 81269.
Open daily 8am–midnight.

HANIÁ

Archaeological Museum
21 Hálidhon St; Tel: (0821) 90334. Open Tue–Sun 8.30am–2.30pm.

Byzantine Museum
in the former church of San Salvatore, Theotokopoúlou St; Tel: (0821) 96046. Open Tue–Sun 8.30am–2pm.
Historical Museum and Archives
20 Sfakianáki St; Tel: (0821) 52606. Open Mon–Fri 9am–1pm.
Naval Museum
Aktí Koundourióti (Firkás), Harbour front; Tel: (0821) 91875. Open daily 9.30am–4pm.
War Museum
in the barracks on Tzanakáki St/ Neárchou St; Tel: (0821) 44156. Open Tue–Sat 9am–1pm.
Folklore Museum
46b Hálidhon St; Tel: (0821) 90816. Open Mon–Sat 9am–3pm, 6–9pm.
Puppet Exhibiton
46 Hálidhon St; Tel: (0821) 73444. Open Wed–Mon 9am–3pm, 5–8pm.
Folklore and Historical Museum
Azoghyrés, Paleochóra. Keys from curator in village *kafeníon.*
Historical Folklore Museum
Gavalochóri, Apokóronas Province; Tel: (0825) 23222. 8am–8pm.

LASSÍTHI

Archaeological Museum
74 Paleológou St, Ághios Nikólaos; Tue–Sun 8.30am–3pm.
Folklore Museum
1 Paleológou, Ághios Nikólaos. Open Sun–Fri 10am–4pm.
Archaeological Museum of Neápoli
9.30am- 2.30pm.
Folklore Museum of Neápoli
Platía El. Venizélou; Tel: (0841) 31369. Tue–Sun 10am–1pm, 6–9pm.
Cretan Folklore Museum
Ághios Yeórghios, Lassíthi Plateau. Open daily 9am–4pm.
Museum of Elefthérios Venizélos
Ághios Yeórghios, Lassíthi Plateau. Open daily 9am–4pm.
Archaeological Museum of Sitía
El. Venizélou St. Tue–Sun 8.30am–3pm.
Folklore Museum of Sitía
Kapitán Sífi 26. Mon–Fri 9.30am–2.30pm and (except Wed) 5–8pm.
Archaeological Collection of Ierápetra
Tue–Sun 8.30am–3pm.

Festivals

Cultural Festivals

IRÁKLION

The **Summer Arts Festival** of theatre, music, dance and folklore runs from July to September, with most performances held in either the Níkos Kazantzákis or Mános Hatzidhákis open-air theatres. Additional performances are organised around the suburbs of Iráklion.

Programmes and tickets are available from the Municipal Building, 2 Andrógeo St from 9am to 2.30pm daily, and from the Níkos Kazantzákis Theatre 9am–2.30pm and 6.30–9.30pm daily. Festival Hotlines: (081) 242977/399211/ 241950; Fax: (081) 227180.

RÉTHYMNON

The **Renaissance Festival**, with music, dance, theatre and "happenings" from July to September, is organised by the municipality. Most performances occur in the Erofíli theatre at the Fortezza, with exhibitions at the "Dímito" Art Gallery. For further information call (0831) 50740 or Fax (0831) 29879. Erofíli Theatre: (0831) 28101. Dímito Gallery: (0831) 55416.

HANIÁ

The **Municipal Cultural Centre** – Tel: (0821) 87098; Fax: (0821) 74332 – organises a series of events including theatre, music, dance, visual arts exhibitions and "evening celebrations in the neighbourhood" every summer from June to September. Most performances take place in the Eastern Moat Theatre.

The **Festival of Nations**, a week-long celebration with music, food and displays from a mix of European, Baltic, Near Eastern and North African peoples is held in the Kípos (park) on Tzanakákis St and the Park of Peace and Friendship on Papandréou St (Dhimokratías) during July.

Kastélli-Kísamos

In July and August the **Gramvoúsa Festival** is held in Kastélli, with a number of events including concerts of Cretan music and *Rizítika* singing. Information from the town hall. Tel: (0822) 23519.

Gavalochóri

In early September, the village of Gavalochóri, in the Apokóronas region of Haniá, is host to a Folklore Festival, with music, dance and traditional crafts on display.

LASSÍTHI

Ághios Nikólaos

Every summer the Municipal Cultural Centre presents the **Lató Festival**, with performances of music, theatre and dance ranging from the traditional to the contemporary, by artists from Crete, Greece and abroad. Information: Tel: (0841) 22357; Fax: (0841) 26398.

Sitía

The **Kornária Festival**, held in honour of Vincénzos Kornáros, takes place during July and August. It includes performances by numerous Greek and foreign folk dance groups, as well as theatre, art exhibitions, lectures and talks. Information from the tourism office, 5 Anthéon St; Tel: (0843) 25967.

Ierápetra

In July and August there are music concerts, drama productions and art exhibitions at the **Kýrvia Festival**. Information can be found at tourist agencies or the Town Hall. Tel: (0842) 22562.

Workshops

The KER **dance workshop** runs summer courses in a wide variety of techniques (from butoh to improvisation), taught by an eclectic range of professional dance performers. Held during July and August, they attract an international mix of students. Information: Éfi Kaloútsi, KER Workshop, 22a Dhaglí St, Halépa, Haniá 73100; Tel/Fax: (0821) 52295.

World Spirit runs courses in creative writing, painting, acting and drumming in the village of Loutró, on the south coast of the Haniá region. For further information contact: World Spirit, 12 Vale Road, Altringham, Cheshire, England WA14 3AQ; Tel/Fax: +44 161 928 5768.

Smart Holidays can supply **Activity Holidays** including icon painting and ceramics. For further information contact:
Minotours Hellas, 72100 Ístro, Crete; Tel: (0841) 61168; Fax: (0841) 61043
or
Kalamáki Travel, 73100 Haniá, Crete; Tel: (0821) 31459; Fax: (0821) 32245.

Annual Events

Apókreas are three weeks of pre-Lenten celebrations ending on the last Sunday of Apókreas with major carnivals in Kastélli, Soúdha, Réthymnon and Sitía.

Kathará Dhefthéra (Clean Monday), seven weeks before Easter Monday, marks the beginning of Orthodox Lent. Traditionally, it is the day to fly kites and feast on boiled seafood (as oil is given up for Lent) and *lagána* (Lenten bread).

As well as being the Feast of the Annunciation, 25 March is **Independence Day** in Greece, marked with parades in all the major towns to celebrate the revolt against Turkish rule in 1821, and church services to honour the announcement of the Incarnation to the Virgin Mary.

Protomayá (Labour Day) on 1 May is a popular day for picnics in the countryside, where people pick flowers and make wreaths to decorate their cars and homes.

Religious Festivals

Easter is the most important event of the religious calendar in Crete, but many saints' days are cause for celebrations.

6 January Ághia Theofánia (Epiphany): water is blessed in commemoration of the Baptism of Christ.

25 March The Annunciation of the Virgin, celebrated in Paleochóra.

1st Sunday after Easter Ághios Thomás, celebrated at Vrondíssi Monastery near Zarós.

23 April Ághios Yeórghios (St George), patron saint of shepherds, celebrated in many rural villages. A sheep-shearing festival is held in Así Goniá.

8 May Ioánnis o Theológos (John the Evangelist) celebrated at Préveli Monastery.

24 June Ioánnis o Pródromos (John the Baptist), celebrated in many parts of the island.

29 June Pétrou ké Pávlou (Peter and Paul), celebrated at Gavalóchori near Haniá.

20 July Profítis Ilías, celebrated on mountaintop shrines and villages named after the Prophet Elijah.

26 July Aghía Paraskeví, celebrated at the Skotíno Cave.

27 July Ághios Pandeleímonas: festivities at Fournés, near Haniá.

6 August Metamórfosis toú Christoú (Transfiguration of Christ), celebrated on Mount Yioúchtas with a major two-day festival (5th/6th) in nearby Archánes.

15 August Apokímisis tís Panaghías (the Assumption of the Virgin) is celebrated throughout Crete, particularly at the monasteries of Faneroméni, Chryssoskalítissa and Kolimbári.

25 August Ághios Títos (patron saint of the island): a large procession in Iráklion.

27 August Ághios Fanoúrios, celebrated at Valsamónero Monastery, southwest of Iráklion.

29 August Ághios Ioánnis (John the Baptist), includes a pilgrimage to Ághios Ioánnis on the Rodhopoú Peninsula, and mass baptisms of boys named Ioánnis.

8 September Yénesi tís Panaghías (Birth of the Virgin Mary).

14 September Ípsosi Timíou Stavroú (Exaltation of the Cross), celebrated in Axós, Anóghia and Réthymnon, with a procession to the convent of Metamorfóseos Sotíros.

7 October Ághios Ioánnis Erimítis (St John the Hermit), with celebrations at Gouvernéto Monastery, Akrotirí, Haniá and at Azoghyrés, near Paleochóra.

26 October Ághios Dimítrios, observed at many chapels.

3 November Ághios Yeórghios o Methistís (Saint George who "gets you drunk"), a day for tasting the new wine and the fresh *tsikoudhiá (rakí)* in the Sfakiá region.

8 November Big celebrations to mark the anniversary of the massacre at Arkádhi Monastery on 8 November 1866. It is also the festival of Michaíl and Gavriíl (Archangels Michael and Gabriel).

11 November Ághios Minás, patron saint of Iráklion.

21 November Panaghías Isódia (the Virgin Mary's introduction to the Temple), celebrated in Haniá and Réthymnon, of which she is the patron saint.

25 November Aghías Ekaterínis (St Catherine): a running race is held in Sitía in honour of their patron saint.

30 November Ághios Andhréas (Saint Andrew), with a festival in Maláxa, near Haniá.**6 December** Ághios Nikólaos: festivities in "Ag Nik", where St Nicholas is the patron saint.

On 20–27 May, there are celebrations in Haniá town and different villages each year to commemorate **Máchi tís Krítis** (the Battle of Crete) – the German invasion in 1941. And in late June, Naval Week is celebrated with fireworks in Soúdha and other harbour towns.

Óchi Day, 28 October, celebrates with parades and folk dancing the Greeks' answer (*Óchi* meaning "No") to Mussolini's 1940 ultimatum.

Christoúghenna (Christmas Day) is not as important as Easter or the Feast of the Assumption in the Orthodox year, though there are religious services and feasting.

Presents are not given until **Paramoní Protochroniá** (New Year's Eve), which is also a favourite time for heavy gambling with cards or dice.

Harvest Festivals

The fertile island gives thanks for its fruitfulness with a series of harvest festivals throughout the year:

April Snail Festival in Vámos, east of Haniá.
Orange Festival in Skinés, southwest of Haniá.
June Cherry Festival in Karános, south of Haniá.
July Watermelon Festival in Hersónisos, east of Iráklion.
Late July Réthymnon Wine Festival – a week of music, dancing and wine sampling held in the public gardens.
16–22 August Soultanína Festival, organised by the municipality of Sitía in celebration of the *soultanína* grape grown there.
Early September Sardine Festival at Néa Hóra harbour, Haniá, and in nearby Soúdha.
Early October Cabbage Festival in Aghía Varvára, south of Iráklion.
Mid-October Chestnut Festival in Élos and other villages southwest of Haniá celebrates the chestnut harvest with folk dancing.

Activities

Cretans are great sports enthusiasts, though for the most part as spectators only. Whenever a major football match is televised, the *kafenía* in the big cities are crammed with enthusiastic supporters. But this enthusiasm rarely manifests itself when it comes to engaging in sport themselves. Don't let this discourage you: Crete offers all kinds of sporting possibilities from cycling to diving and horse-riding to mountaineering.

Cycling & Walking

In Haniá, **Trekking Plan** (Aghía Marína, Kidonías; Tel/Fax: 0821 60861; Mobile: 093 241 7040) offer organised guided cycling programmes, including mountain bike and extreme biking, as well as excursions for children.

In Réthymnon, **The Happy Walker** (56 Tombázi St; Tel: 0831 52920) organise a choice of different walks, in small groups and escorted by an experienced guide, on the inland trails.

Similar guided tours, either on foot or by bike, through the rural areas of Eastern Crete are arranged by **Diéxodos Adventure Unlimited**, Ághios Nikólaos, Havánia 72100; Tel/Fax: (0841) 28098.

The Tourist Information Office in **Ághios Nikólaos** has an excellent booklet, produced by the Council of Káto Mirabéllou, containing 17 walking/cycling routes. And the Tourist Office of **Sitía** (5 Anthéon St; Tel: 0843 25887) has information about walking tours and cycle trails in the region.

When walking, wear sturdy, comfortable shoes and a hat, and take a jacket or sweater (even in the summer). It is also important to use suntan lotion, and to take food and plenty of water.

An early start is advisable, especially in the summer when it can get oppressively hot in the middle of the day. Bear in mind that everything grinds to a halt for the afternoon siesta (from around 2 to 6pm), including some monasteries you may wish to visit. In mountain villages the *kafeníon* is the local "information office" for overnight accommodation; it is also the place to go for such things as the key to the local church.

Diving

On account of the many underwater archaeological sites around the island, scuba diving is restricted to government-designated areas. But snorkelling is permitted everywhere, and it can be quite a rewarding pursuit, especially around Mirabéllou Bay, where from Eloúnda Beach you can swim out to see the sunken Graeco-Roman city of Oloús.

There are several diving schools on the island:

Blue Adventures Diving, 69 Daskaloghiánni St, Haniá; Tel/Fax: (0821) 40608; Mobile: 094 546 736. Offer courses for beginners as well as the more experienced diver from the cruise boat *Atlantis* or from inflatable dinghies. Bookings are made at the diving shop (address above) which is one of the best equipped in Crete.

Creta's Diving Centre, 6 Aktí Papanikolí, Haniá 73100; Tel/Fax: (0821) 93616. They have a wide variety of scuba diving courses and excursions, along with daily sunset cruises and an accessories shop.

Divers Club, Aghía Pelaghía 71202 (northwest of Iráklion town); Tel: (081) 243604; Fax: (081) 322085; Mobile: 0944 565462. Offer courses from basic training to advanced, where it is possible to become qualified as a diving instructor.

Scuba Kreta Diving Club, Nana Beach Hotel, Hersónisos; Tel: (0897) 24915; Fax: (0897) 24916; Central Reservations: (0897)

24076. Operating since 1991, they provide both diving education and recreational diving. A member of the Greek Underwater Federation.

Creta's Happy Divers in Ághios Nikólaos have two diving centres: on the beach of Hotels Hermes and Coral, close to Ag Nik centre; Tel: (0841) 82546; and at Eloúnda Beach Hotel, Eloúnda north of Ag Nik; Tel: (0841) 41850.

Horse-Riding

There are a number of riding centres on the island.

Komós Horse Riding Centre, located close to the village of Pitsídia (near Mátala), offers rides in the olive groves of the Messará Plains or on the beach of Kommós, as well as pony-riding for the young. Contact Níkos Fassoulákis on (0892) 45040.

Karteros Horse and Wagon Safari, near Goúves on the north coast, offers lessons, mountain/ seaside rides and the "safari". They pick up from most major hotels in the Mália/Hersónisos area and the day out also includes lunch on their farm. Tel: (081) 380244; Fax: (081) 380059.

The **Horse Riding Club** at Tersanás, Akrotíri; Tel: (0821) 39366; Mobile: 093 209 1118, has three sand-based arenas and offers a selection of rides in the surrounding area, including rides up to the monasteries of Aghía Triádha and Gouvernéto. The centre also offers a restaurant, cafeteria and swimming pool, as well as accommodation.

Derés Horse Riding Centre, in Derés village west of Haniá; Tel: 0824 31339; Fax: 0824 31900; Manager: Yiánnis Pissadákis.

Pegasus Horse Riding Club, Makrís Tíchos/Vamvakópoulo; Tel: (0821) 76046, is open from 8am to late, summer and winter. They have organised rides on farm tracks in the foothills and a paddock for children and beginners of all ages.

Mountaineering

There are numerous possibilities for hiking and climbing in Crete. Excursions into the mountains are organised by the Greek Alpine Club (EOS), which has branches in Iráklion, Réthymnon and Haniá. Guides and equipment are also available for climbers wishing to scale the heights of Mount Psiloritis (Ida) or peaks in the Lefká Óri (White Mountains).

The **Mountaineering Club of Haniá** was established in 1930 and is a member of the Association of Greek Mountaineering Clubs. Its activities include mountain climbing, skiing, canoeing down the rivers in Western Crete and speleology. The club maintains four shelters in the Haniá region:

Tavrís, at 1,200m (4,000 ft) on the Askýfou Plateau, sleeps 42.

Chrístos Houliópoulos, at 1,970m (6,567 ft) on Svourítis peak in the central Lefká Óri, sleeps 25.

Kallérgis, at 1,680m (5,600 ft) above Samariá Gorge, sleeps 50.

Vólikas, at 1,400m (4,667 ft) on Vólikas Keramión, sleeps 40.

Visitors interested in joining any of their excursions can contact the club either by visiting the offices in Haniá (90 Tzanakáki St) or phoning (0821) 74560.

The **Mountaineering and Skiing Club of Iráklion** was established in 1940 and is also a member of the Greek Mountaineering Clubs association. Today the club has about 200 active members. Its activities include mountain climbing, cross-country walking and skiing.

Most weekends the club organises excursions to various locations in Crete, which are open to non-members. The difficulty of these excursions varies from extremely easy (3–4 hours' walking on footpaths) to very hard (eg. climbing to the top of Psiloritis at 2,456m/8,187 ft).

The club also has its own shelter in the area of Asítes, close to Iráklion. If you want to visit the shelter, make arrangements with the club in advance, since it has limited sleeping facilities. Contact the Mountaineering and Skiing Club of Iráklion on (081) 227609 between 8.30pm and 10.30pm any day.

For more information on mountaineering, contact the **Mountaineering Club of Réthymnon** is at 12 Dhimokratías St; Tel: (081) 227609.

Watersports

Watersports are one of the main attractions for many visitors. The seas around the island are warm enough for swimming from April through until early November. They are generally safe as well, though the waves can get rough when the

Photography

Film and film processing, though widely available, are not cheap on the island, so it is sensible to bring a supply of film with you. Don't leave film or cameras in the heat for long periods, and protect them from water and sand.

There are some restrictions on taking photography. It is illegal, for example, to photograph any military installations, including the entire Soúdha Bay region near Haniá and the area around Iráklion airport.

Photography is sometimes permitted in museums and on some archaeological sites, but if it is a fee is usually charged. This is generally fairly small for hand-held equipment but a higher charge is made for cameras on tripods. (But beware: as the use of a tripod makes you "professional", and a permit may be required from the archaeological authorities.) Taking pictures inside churches is usually forbidden because flash-guns may damage the frescoes.

When photographing local people it is best, and more polite, to ask their permission first.

meltémi wind blows – so take care, as lifeguards are not common.

Most of the big coastal resort hotels hire out watersports equipment (usually to both guests and non-guests). Waterskiing is popular at all the major resorts and some of them also have facilities for paragliding and jet-skiing.

A number of waterparks have appeared in recent years, offering rides and pools for all the family.

Limnoúpolis, Varípetro (off the Haniá/Omalós road); Tel: (0821) 33246.
Aquasplash, Hersónisos; Tel: (0897) 24582.
Water City, On the Anápolis/ Iráklion road; Tel: (081) 781316.

Sailing

Apart from the possibilities of chartering boats/yachts from local harbours and marinas, there are the following clubs:

Nautical Club of Haniá
Tel: (0821) 24384
Nautical Club of Réthymnon
Tel: (0831) 29881
Iráklion Sailing Club
Tel: (081) 242120
Aelos Sailing Club, Ághios Nikólaos
Tel: (0841) 24037
Nautical Club of Sitía
Tel: (0843) 24323

Tennis

Most tennis courts on the island are to be found in the larger hotel complexes. If you are not a resident, it is sometimes possible to gain access by enquiring at reception and offering to pay a fee.

The few municipal courts that exist are usually busy with teaching programmes and tournaments but you can always try your luck. The courts in Haniá are on Papandhréou St (Dimokratías) opposite the Rolí (clock tower); Tel: (0821) 44010. Or contact the Tennis Club of Iráklion (Ómilos Antisférisis), 17 Dhoúkas Bofor St; Tel: (081) 344545.

Nightlife

Entertainment

Bars, discos and clubs abound in the holiday resorts, but there is nothing distinctively Greek about them. In fact, in most cases, you feel you could be just about anywhere. Resort hotels often lay on evenings of "authentic traditional entertainment", which includes music, dancing and even costumes – the only thing missing are the Cretans themselves.

The **Kritiká Kéndra**, traditional nightclubs located on the outskirts of town or even further out in the country, are the venues for wedding and baptism celebrations as well as evenings of live Cretan music. People also come here to eat and drink, but mainly to participate in Cretan dances. These are the places to go to experience a real Cretan evening. As tourists are rarely seen, you will be made most welcome, for demonstrating your interest in local culture. However there is not much point in turning up before midnight.

Skyláthika (from the Greek word *skýlos*, "dog", so probably best translated as "dog-houses") are similar but sleazier clubs imported from the mainland, their dance music furnished by inferior *bouzoúki* ensembles playing "electric dog music".

A *skyláthiko* is the final stop of many a late-evening tour of the nightspots, and is one of the few places where you might see Greeks drinking heavily (whisky is sold by the bottle at grossly inflated prices).

You may see International Show Clubs advertised in the busier resorts – but do not expect some kind of Las Vegas-style entertainment. The cabaret is generally supplied by Balkan strippers and Eastern Bloc lap-dancers. You have been warned.

And last, but certainly not least, there is the *vólta*, or evening stroll, in which virtually the entire populace partakes. This is the time to catch up with local gossip, to see and be seen.

Cretan Music

Watch out for posters advertising *lýra* and *laoúto* concerts. Even if you don't read Greek, they usually include a photograph of the musician(s) performing, and you should be able to work out the date and venue – or ask a passer-by.

The *lýra* is Crete's own native instrument, a three-stringed fiddle made of mulberry or maple, which is played upright with a bow. The *laoúto* is the Cretan equivalent of the *bouzoúki*, but smaller, more like a mandolin. Both are used to accompany songs, as well as playing instrumental music.

Two top performers to look out for are Vasílis Skoulás, an accomplished singer and *lýra* player from Anóghia, and Psaradónis, the most controversial of Cretan performers because of his unique style and often bizarre interpretation of the Cretan repertoire.

Cinema

Most towns of any size have a cinema. In addition, most of the major towns and some of the larger tourist areas have open-air cinemas during the summer months. All films are shown in their original language with Greek subtitles, although many cartoons are dubbed into Greek for the local children.

The municipality of Haniá presents an excellent programme, including new releases, popular re-runs and classic world cinema from May to September in the open-air cinema in the park on Papandhréou Ave. They also publish a comprehensive programme containing film reviews and related articles, but only in Greek.

Shopping

What to Buy

The island's tourist resorts are full of souvenir shops selling overpriced junk. But if you can manage to steer clear of these places, there are some genuine treasures to be had. These include hand-woven blankets, embroidery work, metal and wood crafts, ceramics and earthenware, as well as spices and herbal teas – all of which have been important export commodities as far back as Minoan times.

Leather and ceramics

Crete, and above all Haniá, is famous for its leather goods: bags in all sizes, rucksacks, sandals and especially boots of cowhide, some of which is imported from Nigeria. There are unglazed ceramic storage jars *(pithári)* of the kind produced on Crete 4,000 years ago as well as a large selection of everyday earthenware to choose from, some of it very attractive.

Fabrics

Hand-woven, hand-embroidered or crocheted blankets and fabrics, once important products of the native crafts industry, have been ousted by cheaper industrial copies. Inexpensive items include sheep's wool knits and countless cotton products from T-shirts to teatowels, as well as linens with colourful stripes on a white background. These get much softer once they've been washed a few times.

Knives

Cretan knives, originally part of the traditional costume, are long and curved with thick white handles and silver scabbards. Old ones are rare and expensive, but new ones come in various shapes and sizes as souvenirs. Other varieties are available, from chopping knives to the curved blades used for pruning.

Jewellery

Gold and silver jewellery is relatively inexpensive in Crete and Greece generally. There is an abundance of jewellery shops, often selling machine-made merchandise, but you'll also find a number of skilled gold and silversmiths on the island.

Food and drink

For the gourmets, there are a number of culinary delights worth bringing home, including the sharp, firm cheese called *graviéra*; honey *(méli)*, especially the kind derived from thyme blossoms; black and green olives in brine; wine and *tsikoudhiá*, Crete's version of *rakí*.

The place to go for most of these is the local market, where you'll also find a whole array of herbs and spices, from *dhíktamos* (local mountain tea) and *rígani* (oregano) to Cretan saffron and spicy cinnamon bark. You can also stock up on *passatémpo* from any street cart – paper bags full of peanuts, pistachios, roasted chickpeas, pumpkin seeds, etc.

Music

Music lovers might like to seek out cassettes or CDs by the best-known and loved Cretan musicians. Recommended recordings:

Kóstas Mountákis: *Afiéroma Stón Megálo Kritikó* (Minos)
Sadly recently deceased, Mountákis was one of the grand old men of Cretan music. This is a collection of his greatest hits.

Níkos Xiloúris: *Ta Xilouréika* (Fabelsound)
Xiloúris, who died young, had the most famous voice in Crete. This early recording is a fine example of traditional Cretan song, accompanied by *lýra* and *laoúto*.

Protomástores: 1920–1955 (Aerákis; including Rodinós, Skordalós, Foustaliéris, Mountákis and others)
A boxed 10-CD set with an excellent booklet giving a lot of historical information (in English) about the music and the musicians. The individual CDs are also available, each with its own booklet.

Vasílis Skoulás: *Seryiávisma Stín Kríti* (Aerákis)
Arguably the best of many great recordings by this accomplished singer and *lýra* player.

Where to Shop

Many of the souvenirs listed above can be found all over the island. Listed below are some specialist retailers (often also the producers) who can supply top-quality goods at reasonable prices.

Artworks and picture framing

Mánthos Papadákis, a skilled artisan, can be found in his workshop, Archipélagos, at 26 Souliou St, Réthymnon; Tel: (0831) 26565).

Avocado products

In Arghyroúpoli, west of Réthymnon, Stélios (the ex-mayor) and his wife Joanne run the "Lappa Avocado" shop. Open daily from 9.30am to 8pm, it sells a range of avocado products (soaps, oils and

Coffee-making Paraphernalia

Market vendors and small household goods shops sell the traditional *bríkia* – the small copper pots with long handles that areused to make Greek coffee. With a bit of luck, you should also be able to find the matching long-handled copper spoon and whisk.

A chinaware store is the best place to get the tiny cups to go with the set: the classic *kafeníon* variety are white and virtually unbreakable.

Finally, to complete your Greek coffee-making ensemble, you'll need a brass coffee grinder. The smaller versions of these mills make excellent pepper grinders.

cosmetics) incorporating the oil extracted from the fruit cultivated on Stelios' plantation.

Belts and bags

Michális Kanakákis produces excellent hand-made leather belts, bags and other accessories which are available from The Leather Factory, 23 Soulíou St, Réthymnon; Tel: (0831) 55666.

Byzantine icons

At "Byzántio", 14 28th Octovríou St, Ághios Nikólaos; Tel: (0841) 26530, Níkos Tzirís hand-paints copies of traditional icons from the Byzantine era as well as producing works in the Byzantine style.

Carpets

Michális at Roka Carpets is the only man in Crete who still weaves on a traditional loom. Using sheep's wool from his village his brightly coloured traditional designs are achieved with natural vegetable and plant dyes. You'll find him weaving in his shop Mon–Sat: 61 Zambelíou St, Haniá; Tel/Fax: (0821) 74736.

Ceramics

Manólis Kallérgis has his workshop in the village of Margarítes, 24 km (15 miles) east of Réthymnon, where he produces an appealing range of both glazed and unglazed decorative and table ware. Open every day but if the workshop is closed, ring the doorbell, as he lives above; Tel: (0834) 92262.

Crochet and embroidery

The Rural Women's Co-operative of Volgáro, a village 40 km (25 miles) from Haniá on the road to Elafonísi, was founded in 1995. Here they produce Cretan embroideries *(ifantá)* and crochet work *(plektá)*. They also prepare jams, noodles, *paximádhia*, olives etc. Tel: (0822) 51002/51319.

Food

"To Mirovólon", in Vámos village, Apokóronas, Haniá, has a wide selection of traditional produce, including *xinóchontros*, *hilopíttes*, *ladhotíri* and *petimézi*, as well as marmalades, olives and *tsikoudhiá* – all produced by the local villagers.

Iráklion Market, on 1866 Street in the centre of the city, is packed with fruits, vegetables, meat, fish, spices, herbs, honey and nuts as well as kitchen utensils, clothing, sponges, cassettes, knick-knacks and bric-a-brac. Open Mon–Sat.

Glasswork

Robert Zambetákis, 33 3rd September St, Sitía; Tel: (0843) 26646, works in stained-glass, fusing (where colour is added to the glass while it is in the fire) and sandblasting. He produces attractive decorative items from bowls to lampshades.

Handicrafts

The Verékinthos Craft Village is on the national road just south of Haniá. But don't be fooled by its name, as it is not a true village, but rather the western section of a light industrial estate.

Here a large number of units are occupied by local artisans and craftspeople producing ceramics, silver and gold jewellery, leather goods, glass-works, embroideries and textiles in both traditional and contemporary designs.

The opening times are fairly flexible as each workshop is a law unto itself but, as many of the artists actually live on their premises, they may be "open" long hours (but do avoid going during the siesta). Tel: (0821) 81261/80118.

Jewellery

Aristídes Tsapákis produces his own hand-made rings, bracelets, broaches and necklaces at "21", 21 Soulíou St, Réthymnon; Tel: (0831) 55209.

Knives

The area in Haniá known as *macherádhika*, around Sífaka St, has been famous for its knife-makers for hundreds of years. Here you will find "O Arménis" (the Armenian) Michális Pachtikós and his workshop. Tel: (0821) 54434.

Leather goods

The best known area on the island is Haniá's "Leather Lane" in Skridlof St, with its plethora of boots, bags, sandals and belts, many of them still made on the premises.

Street Markets

These colourful, bustling and lively markets *(Laikí Agorá)* are well worth a visit. They take place in all the major cities on the island and in many inland market towns.

Operating from very early in the morning until around 1–2pm, they are basically farmers' markets, purveying fresh seasonal produce from the local area, including fruits, vegetables, nuts, olives, cheeses, eggs, chickens, rabbits, wines and *tsikoudhiá*.

Alongside all this are stalls with household goods and tools as well as cheap clothing and footwear, the speciality of the Roma (gipsy) traders.

Here are some of the larger markets:

Iráklion every Saturday, by the Old Harbour (as well as the daily market on 1866 Street).

Réthymnon every Monday, by the Skolí Horofilakís; and every Thursday, opposite the public gardens.

Haniá every Thursday, near the church of Ághios Konstantínos, Néa Hóra; and every Saturday, in Mínoös Street, to the east of the harbour.

Kastélli every Sunday (winter only), near Elefthérios Venizélou Square.

Ághios Nikólaos every Wednesday, in Ethnikís Antistáseos St, near the fire station.

Sitía every Tuesday, on Plastíra Street.

Ierápetra every Saturday, by the Próto Yymnásio (First High School).

To find out if there are markets in other areas, and when, just ask one of the locals.

Musical instruments

Adónis Stefanákis in the village of Zarós *(see page 136)*. Tel: (0894) 31166/31249.

Manólis Frankiadhákis in Vorízia (ask for directions from the *kafeníon*) still makes *askoubandoúra* (Cretan bagpipes) and *floghéra* (Cretan shepherds' flutes).

Pithári

The ideal place to find these large earthenware storage jars, produced since Minoan times, is in the historic potters' village of Thrápsano, 33 km (20 miles) southeast of Iráklion. Here there are many workshops manufacturing them and other ceramic items. As the jars are very large, shipment can be arranged from the workshop to the purchaser's door.

Silk products

The Women's Co-operative in Kalamítsi Amigdháli (7 km/4 miles southeast of Vámos, Haniá) not only produce a large variety of articles made from silk but also breed their own silkworms. Open daily 10am–5pm.

Wood-turning products

Níkos Sirágas has his workshop at 2 Petalióti St in Réthymnon, just off the beach road. He has been working with wood for 20 years and is one of the few remaining Cretans to practise this craft. He produces bowls and vases from olive and carob (both very hard woods) and each piece is unique. He is also renowned for sculpures made by carving the roots of olive trees. Tel: (0831) 23010/52248.

Language

The Greek Language

Modern Greek, as spoken in Crete today, is still very close to Ancient Greek, as used in the Classical period (5th–4th centuries BC). It uses the same alphabet and much of the same vocabulary, and it retains much of the same complex grammar, though the pronunciation of some sounds has changed radically.

This guide to Greek phrases cannot deal with the complexities of the grammar – there are three genders, all with different case endings in singular and plural – but it aims to provide the simplest (if not the most elegant) way of saying some basic things. It's worth investing in a good phrase-book, and possibly a pocket dictionary.

All Greeks learn English at school, and many speak it very well. The many tourists who have visited Crete since the 1960s have given the locals plenty of opportunity to practise their English. There are also many Cretans who have lived abroad (in America, Australia or elsewhere) and have picked up an excellent command of English there. More importantly, Greeks aren't used to foreigners knowing any Greek at all, and even a couple of words from you in their native language are likely to provoke admiration and encouragement.

Pronunciation Tips

The words and phrases in this language section are transcribed into the Roman alphabet; the only items given in Greek characters are a few words and phrases commonly used in notices. Most of the sounds of Greek aren't difficult for English speakers to pronounce. The vowel sounds are fairly straightforward: *a* is pronounced as in northern English "bath"; *e* as in "red"; *i* as in "ski"; *o* is like the vowel sound in English "long"; *ou* is as in "through"; and *y* (as a vowel) is always an "ee" sound as in "silly".

The letter *s* in this guide is always pronounced "s", never "z". The sound represented here as *th* is always pronounced as in "thin", not "that". The Greek letter delta (often transcribed as simply *d*) is represented here by *dh*, to indicate a softer sound, rather like the beginning of "then".

A more difficult sound is the Greek chi, which is like a rough *h* at the beginning of a word, and more like the "ch" in Scottish "loch" elsewhere. Similarly, we have transcribed the Greek letter gamma in several ways, according to where it falls: before *a* or *o*, it is a hard *g* as in "gas" or "got"; before other vowels, it comes out as a sound that has no equivalent in English – somewhere between a rough *y* and a soft *gh*.

Even some of the most common Greek words tend to be quite long: four or five syllables are quite usual. The position of the stress in words is of the utmost importance, and Greeks will often fail to understand you if you don't stress the right syllable; in this guide, stress is marked by an accent (á): compare *póli* "town" (pronounced something like "Polly") and *polí* "much", "many" or "very" (pronounced "poll-ee")

Greek word order is flexible, so you may often hear phrases in a different order from the one in which they are given here.

Like the French, the Greeks use the plural of the second person when they are addressing someone politely. We have used the polite (formal) form throughout this language section that follows. the only exceptions to this are where an expression is specified as "informal".

Greetings

Good morning *kaliméra*
Good evening *kalispéra*
Good night *kaliníhta*
Hello/Goodbye *yásas* (informal) *(yásou)*
Mr/Mrs/Miss *kírios/kiría/dhespinís*
Pleased to meet you (formal) *héro polí*
What is your name? *pos léyeste?/pos íne t'onomá sas?* (informal) *(pos se léne?)*
I am English/American *íme ánglos/amerikanós* (feminine) *(anglídha/amerikanídha)*
Irish/Scottish *irlandhós/skotsézos* (feminine) *(irlandhéza/skotséza)*
Canadian/Australian *kanadhós/ afstralós* (feminine) *(kanadhéza/ afstraléza)*
I'm here on holiday *káno dhiakopés edhó*
Is this your first trip to Greece/Crete? *próti forá ércheste stin Eládha/Kríti?*
Do you like it here? *sas arési edhó?*
How are you? *ti kánete?* (informal) *(ti kánis?)*
Fine, thanks, and you? *kalá, esís?* (informal) *(esí)*
Cheers/Your health! (when drinking) *yámas!*
Do you like...? *sas arési...?*
Very much *pára polí*
It's lovely/beautiful *íne polí oréa*
Never mind/It doesn't matter *dhembirázi*

Communication

Yes *ne*
No *óchi*
Thank you *efcharistó*
You're welcome *parakaló*
Please *parakaló*
Excuse me (to get attention) *parakaló*
Excuse me (to get past) *signómi*
Excuse me (pardon?) *signómi*
Okay/All right *endáxi*
Can I ask you something? (normal way of beginning a request for information) *na sas rotíso káti?*
Could you help me? *boríte na me voithísete?*
Certainly *vevéos* (or *efcharístos*)
Can I help you? *boró na sas voithíso?*
Can you show me...? *boríte na mou dhíxete...?*
I want... *thélo...*
Wait a minute! *periménete!*
I'm lost *échasa to dhrómo*
I don't know *dhen xéro*
I don't understand *dhen katálava*
Do you speak English/Greek? *xérete angliká/eliniká?*
Please speak more slowly *parakaló miláte pió argá*
Say that again, please *parakaló, hanapéste to*
Here *edhó*
There *ekí*
Up/above *páno*
Down/below *káto*
Now *tóra*
Early *norís*
Late *argá*
What? *ti?*
When? *póte?*
Why? *yatí?*
Where? *pou?*
Where is the toilet? *pou íne i toualéta?*

Our Transliteration System

In Crete, most town and village names on road signs, as well as most street names, are written in both the Greek and the Roman alphabets. There's no single, universally accepted system of transliteration into Roman, so you will have to get used to seeing different spellings of the same place on maps and signs and in this book. For instance, the word Αγιος ("saint", masculine) in place names may be spelled "Agios", "Aghios", "Ayos" or "Ayios".

Below is the transliteration scheme we have used in this book: beside each Greek letter or pair of letters is the Roman letter(s) we have used. (Note that sometimes this will vary according to which letter follows it, or whether the letter occurs at the beginning or in the middle of a word.) Next to that is a rough approximation of the sound in an English word.

Greek		Roman	Sound
Α α		**a**	cat
Β β		**v**	vote
Γ γ		**g**	**g**ot
	or	**gh**	softer version of **g**et
	or	**y**	throaty **y**et
Δ δ		**dh**	**th**en
Ε ε		**e**	**e**gg
Ζ ζ		**z**	**z**oo
Η η		**i**	sk**i**
Θ θ		**th**	**th**in
Ι ι		**i**	sk**i**
Κ κ		**k**	**k**iss
Λ λ		**l**	**l**ong
Μ μ		**m**	**m**an
Ν ν		**n**	**n**o
Ξ ξ		**x**	ta**x**i
Ο ο		**o**	l**o**ng
Π π		**p**	**p**en
Ρ ρ		**r**	**r**oom
Σ σ/ς		**s**	**s**et
Τ τ		**t**	**t**ea
Υ υ		**y**	sk**i**
Φ φ		**f**	**f**ish
Χ χ		**h**	lo**ch**
	or	**ch**	lo**ch**
Ψ ψ		**ps**	ma**ps**
Ω ω		**o**	l**o**ng
ΑΙ αι (ai)		**e**	h**ay**
ΑΥ αυ (au)		**af**	d**af**t
	or	**av**	l**av**a
ΕΙ ει (ei)		**i**	sk**i**
ΕΥ ευ (eu)		**ef**	h**eff**er
	or	**ev**	**ev**er
ΟΙ οι (oi)		**i**	sk**i**
ΟΥ ου (ou)		**ou**	t**ou**rist
ΓΓ γγ (gg)		**ng**	a**ng**le
ΓΚ γκ (gk)		**ng**	a**ng**le
ΓΞ γξ (gx)		**nx**	a**nx**ious
ΜΠ μπ (mp)		**b**	**b**eg
	or	**mb**	li**mb**er
ΝΤ ντ (nt)		**d**	**d**og
	or	**nd**	u**nd**er
ΤΣ τσ (ts)		**ts**	hi**ts**
ΤΖ τζ (tz)		**dz**	be**ds**

Telephone Calls

The telephone *to tiléfono*
Phonecard *tilekárta*
May I use the phone, please? *boró na tilefoníso parakaló?*
Hello (on the phone) *embrós*
My name is... *légome...*
Could I speak to... *boró na milíso me...*
Wait a moment *periménete mia stigmí*
He/she isn't here *dhen íne edhó*
When will he/she be back? *póte tha íne ekí?*
Should he/she call you back? *na sas pári?*
I'll try again later *tha xanapáro argótera*
I didn't hear what you said *dhen ákusa*

Times and Dates

(in the) morning/afternoon/evening *to proí/to apóyevma/to vrádhi*
the middle of the day *to mesiméri*
(at) night *(ti) nýchta*
yesterday *chtes*
today *símera*
tomorrow *ávrio*
the day before yesterday *proxtés*
the day after tomorrow *methávrio*
now *tóra*
early *norís*
late *argá*
a minute *éna leptó*
five/ten minutes *pénde/dhéka leptá*
an hour *mia óra*
half an hour *misí óra*
a quarter-hour *éna tétarto*
at one/two (o'clock) *sti mia/stis dhío (i óra)*
a day *mia méra*
a week *mia vdhomádha*
on the first *tin próti*
(of the month) *(tou minós)*
on the second/third *stis dhío/tris*

In the Hotel

The hotel *to xenodhochío*
Do you have any rooms? *échete dhomátia?*
I've booked a room *écho kratísi éna dhomátio*
I'd like... *tha íthela...*
a single/double room (with double bed) *éna monó/dhipló dhomátio*
a twin-bed/three-bed room *éna dhíklino/tríklino*
a room with a bath/shower *éna dhomátio me bánio/dous*
How long will you stay? *póso tha mínete?*
One night *éna vrádhi*
Two nights *dhío vrádhia*
How much is it? *póso káni?*
Is breakfast included? *mazí me to proinó?*
It's expensive *íne akrivó*
Is it quiet? *íne ísiho?*
Is there a balcony? *échi balkóni?*
Do you have a room with a sea-view? *échete dhomátio me théa pros ti thálasa?*
Is the room heated/air-conditioned? *to dhomátio échi thérmansi/air condition?*
Can I see the room, please? *boró na dho to dhomátio, parakaló?*
What floor is it on? *se pio órofo íne?*
On the first floor *stom bróto órofo*
Is there a lift? *échi asansér?*
The room is too hot/cold/small *to dhomátio íne polí zestó/krío/mikró*
It's noisy *échi polí fasaría*
Could you show me another room please? *boríte na mu dhíxete álo dhomátio, parakaló?*
I'll take it *tha to páro*
Sign here, please *mya ipografí, parakaló*
What time is breakfast? *ti óra servírete to proinó?*
Please give me a call at... *parakaló, xipníste me stis...*
Come in! *embrós!*
Can I have the bill please? *mu kánete to logariasmó, parakaló?*
Can you call me a taxi, please? *tha kalésete éna taxí, parakaló?*
dining room *trapezaría*
key *klidhí*
towel petséta
sheet *sendóni*
pillow *maxilári*
soap *sapúni*
hot water *zestó neró*
toilet paper *hartí toualétas*

Days of the Week

(on) Monday *(ti) dheftéra*
(on) Tuesday *(tin) tríti*
(on) Wednesday *(tin) tetárti*
(on) Thursday *(tin) pémpti*
(on) Friday *(tin) paraskeví*
(on) Saturday *(to) sávato*
(on) Sunday *(tin) kiryakí*

At a Bar or Café

bar/café *bar/kafenío* (or *kafetéria*)
patisserie *zacharoplastío*
I'd like... *tha íthela...*
a coffee *éna kafé*
Greek coffee *elinikó kafé*
filter coffee *galikó kafé/kafé fíltro*
instant coffee *neskafé* (or *nes*)
cappuccino *kaputsíno*
white (with milk) *me gála*
black *horís gála*
with sugar *me záchari*
without sugar *horís záhari* (or *skéto*)
a cup of tea *éna tsái*
a lemon tea *éna tsái me lemóni*
orange/lemon juice *portokaládha/lemonádha*
fresh orange juice *éna himó portokáli*
a glass/bottle of water *éna potíri/boukáli neró*
with ice *me págo*
a whisky/brandy *éna whisky/cognac*
a beer *mia bíra*
(draught) *(apó varéli)*
an ice-cream *éna pagotó*
a pastry *mia pásta*
Anything else? *típot'álo?*
sweet pastries *baklavá/kataífi*

In a Restaurant

Have you got a table for... *échete trapézi ya...*
How many are you? *pósa átoma íste?*
There are (four) of us *ímaste (téseris)*
Could we change tables? *borúme n' aláxume trapézi?*
I'm a vegetarian *íme hortofágos*
Can we see the menu? *boroúme na dhoúme ton katálogo?*
What have you got to eat? *ti éhete na fáme?*
Come and see what we've got *eláte na dhíte ti éhume*
We would like to order *thélume na parangílume*
What will you have? *ti tha párete?*

What would you like to drink? *ti tha pyíte?*
Have you got wine by the carafe? *échete krasí híma?*
a litre/half-litre *éna kiló/misókilo*
of white/red wine *áspro/kókino krasí*
Would you like anything else? *thélete típot' álo?*
No, thank you *óchi efharistó*
glass *potíri*
knife/fork/spoon *machéri/pirúni/koutáli*
plate/napkin *piáto/petséta*
The bill, please *to logariasmó, parakaló*

Reading the Menu

MEZÉDHES

andzoúghies **anchovies**
tsatsíki **yoghurt with garlic**
dolmádhes **vine-leaves stuffed with rice**
eliés **olives**
fáva **pease pudding**
kolokithákia tiganitá **courgettes fried in batter**
loukánika **sausages**
melidzánosalata **pureéd aubergine**
saganáki **fried cheese**
taramosaláta **smoked fish-roe dip**
tyropittákia **cheese pies**

MEAT DISHES

arní **mutton, lamb**
biftéki **hamburger (without bap)**
brizóla **(pork or veal) chop**
domátes yemístés **stuffed tomatoes**
hirinó **pork**
kapnistó **smoked**
keftédhes **meat-balls (fried or grilled)**
kimás **minced meat**
kokkinistó **stewed in tomato sauce**
kotópoulo **chicken**
krasáto **stewed in wine sauce**
kréas **meat**
kounéli **rabbit**
makarónia me kimá **spaghetti with minced meat**
makarónia me sáltsa **spaghetti with tomato sauce**
moschári **veal, beef**
mousakás **moussaka**
paidákia **lamb chops**
pastítsio **minced meat and pasta topped with béchamel sauce**
piláfi me kimá **rice with minced meat**
piláfi me sáltsa **rice with tomato sauce**
piperiés **stuffed peppers**
sta kárvouna **grilled**
sti soúvla **on the spit**
sto foúrno **roast**
soutzoukákia **meatballs**
souvláki **spit-roast**
tiganitó **fried**
youvarlákia **stewed**
yíros me píta **doner kebab (slices of grilled meat served in pitta bread)**
yemistés **stuffed**
(me rízi/kimá) **(with rice/minced meat)**

SEAFOOD

astakós **lobster**
bakaliáros **dried salted cod**
barboúnia **red mullet**
frésko **fresh**
garídhes **prawns**
glósa **sole**
chtapódhi **octopus**
kalamarákia **squid**
katepsigméno **frozen**
kávouras **crab**
koliós **mackerel**
kidhónia **clams**
marídhes **whitebait**
mídhia **mussels**
psári **fish**
sardhéles **sardines**
strídhia **oysters**
soupiés **cuttlefish**
xifías **swordfish**

VEGETABLES AND VEGETARIAN FOOD

angináres **artichokes**
angourodomáta **tomato and cucumber salad**
arakás **peas**
domátes **tomatoes**
domatosaláta **tomato salad**
fakés **brown lentils**
fasólia **stewed white beans**
fasolákia **green beans**
(fréska) **(stewed in tomato sauce)**
hórta **various kinds of boiled greens**
horiátiki **"Greek salad" (tomato, cucumber, onions, olives, feta cheese)**
láchano **cabbage**
karóta **carrots**
koukiá **broad beans**
kolokithákia **courgettes**
kounoupídhi **cauliflower**
maroúli **lettuce**
melidzánes **aubergine/eggplant**
pandzária **beetroot**
patátes **potatoes**
(tiganités/sto foúrno) **(chips/roast)**
piperiés **peppers**
radhíkia **dandelion leaves**
rapanákia **radishes**
revíthia **chickpeas**
saláta **salad**
spanáki **spinach**
spanakópita **spinach pie**
tyrópita **cheese pie**
vlíta **boiled greens**
yíghandes **stewed butter beans**

BASIC FOODS

aláti **salt**
avgá (tiganitá) **(fried) eggs**
féta **sheeps-milk cheese**
kremídhia **onions**
ládhi **(olive) oil**
marmeládha **jam, marmalade**
méli **honey**
moustárdha **mustard**
omeléta **omelette**
pipéri **pepper**
psomí **bread**
rízi **rice**
skórdho **garlic**
tyrí **cheese**
voútiro **butter**
xídhi **vinegar**
yaoúrti **yoghurt**
záchari **sugar**

FRUIT (TA FROÚTA)

mílo **apple**
veríkoka **apricots**
banánes **bananas**
kerásia **cherries**
síka **figs**
stafília **grapes**
lemóni **lemon**
pepóni **melon**

portokáli **orange**
rodhákino **peach**
achládhi **pear**
fráoules **strawberries**
karpoúzi **watermelon**

Visiting a Site

Is it possible to see the archaeological site/church? *boroúme na dhúme ta archéa/tin eklisía?*
Where can I find the key/custodian? *pou boró na vro to klidhí/fílaka?*
We've come a long way to see it. It's a pity it's closed *írthame apo polí makriá na to dhúme. Kríma pou ína klistó*

Sightseeing

art gallery *pinakothíki*
beach *plaz*
bridge *yéfira*
castle *kástro/froúrio*
cathedral *mitrópoli*
church *eklisía*
excavations *anaskafés*
forest *dhásos*
fresco *aghiografía*
garden *kípos*
icon *ikóna*
lake *límni*
library *vivliothíki*
market *agorá*
minaret *minaré*
monastery/convent *monastíri*
monument *mnimío*
mosque *dzamí*
mountain *vounó*
museum *musío*
old town *paliá póli*
park *párko*
river *potamós*
ruins eripia/*archéa*
sea *thálasa*
temple *naós*
information *pliroforíes*
open/closed *anichtó/klistó*

At the Shops

shop *magazí/katástima*
What time do you open/close? *ti óra aníyete/klínete?*
Are you being served? *exiperitíste?*
Whose turn is it? *pios échisirá?*
What would you like? *oríste/ti thélete?*
I'm just looking *aplós kitázo*
How much does it cost? *póso échi?*
Do you take credit cards? *pérnete pistotikés kártes?*
I'd like... *tha íthela...*
this one *aftó*
that one *ekíno*
one of these *éna tétio*
Have you got...? *échete...?*
Yes, of course *málista/ne vévea/vevéos*
(Unfortunately) *(dhistihós)*
we haven't got (any) *dhen éhume*
size (for clothes & shoes) *número*
Can I try it on? *boró na to dhokimáso?*
What size do you take? *ti número pérnete?*
It's too expensive *íne polí akrivó*
cheap *ftinó*
Don't you have anything cheaper? *dhen éhete típota pio ftinó?*
Please write it down for me *to gráfete parakaló?*
It's too small/big *íne polí mikró/megálo*
colour *chróma*
black *mávro*
blue *ble*
brown *kafé*
gold *chrisó*
green *prásino*
grey *grízo*
pink *roz*
red *kókino*
silver *arghiró*
white *áspro*
yellow *kítrino*
It's lovely *íne polí oréo*
No thank you, I don't like it *óchi efharistó, dhe m'arési*
I'll take it *tha to páro*
I don't want it *dhen to thélo*
This is faulty: *aftó échiéna*
Can I have a replacement? *elátoma. Boró na to aláxo?*
Can I have a refund? *boró na páro píso ta leftá?*
Anything else? *típot' álo?*
Pay at the cash desk *plirónete sto tamío*
a kilo *éna kiló*
half a kilo *misókilo*
a quarter (of a kilo) *éna tétarto*
two kilos *dhío kilá*
100 grams *ekató gramária*
200 grams *dhiakósa gramária*
more *perisótero*
less *ligótero*
a little *lígo*
very little *polí lígo*
with/without *me/horís*
That's enough *ftáni*
That's all *tipot'álo*

TYPES OF SHOP

bakery *foúrnos*
bank *trápeza*
barber's *kourío*
bookshop *vivliopolío*
butcher's *hasápiko/kreopolío*
chemist's *farmakío*
department store *megálo katástima*
dry cleaner's *stegnotírio*

Numbers

1	*éna/mia*
2	*dhío*
3	*tris/tría*
4	*tésera*
5	*pénde*
6	*éxi*
7	*eptá*
8	*ochtó*
9	*enéa*
10	*dhéka*
11	*éndheka*
12	*dhódheka*
13	*dhekatrís*
14	*dhekatéseris*
15	*dhekapénde*
16	*dhekaéxi*
17	*dhekaeptá*
18	*dhekaochtó*
19	*dhekaenéa*
20	*íkosi*
30	*triánda*
40	*saránda*
50	*penínda*
60	*exínda*
70	*evdhomínda*
80	*ochdhónda*
90	*enenínda*
100	*ekató*
200	*dhiakósa*
300	*trakósa*
400	*tetrakósa*
500	*pendakósa*
1,000	*hílies/hília*
2,000	*dhio hiliádhes*
a million	*éna ekatomírio*

fishmonger's *ichthiopolío/psarádhiko*
florist *anthopolío*
greengrocer's *manáviko*
grocer's *bakáliko*
hairdresser's (women's) *komotírio*
kiosk (for newspapers and a variety of other goods) *períptero*
laundry *plindírio*
liquor store *káva*
market *agorá*
photographer's *fotografío*
post office *tachidhromío*
stationer's *hartopolío*
supermarket *supermárket*
tobacconist *kapnopolío*
travel agency *taxidhiotikó grafío/praktorío*

Transport

airport *aerodhrómio*
aeroplane *aeropláno*
boarding card *kárta epivívasis*
boat *plío/karávi*
bus *leoforío*
bus station *stathmós leoforíon*
bus stop *stási*
coach *poúlman*
ferry *feribót*
first/second class *próti/dhéfteri thési*
flight *ptísi*
hydrofoil *iptámeno*
motorway *ethnikí odhós*
No smoking *apagorévete to kápnisma*
port *limáni*
return ticket *isitírio me epistrofí*
single ticket *aplo isitírio*
station *stathmós*
taxi *taxí*
train *tréno*
WC *toualéta*

ON PUBLIC TRANSPORT

Can you help me, please? *boríte na me vithísete, parakaló*
Where can I buy tickets? *pou na kópso isitírio?*
At the counter *sto tamío*
Does it stop at... *káni stási sto...*
You need to change at... *tha prépi n'aláxete sto...*
When is the next train/bus/ferry to... *póte févyi to tréno/leoforío/feribót ya...*
How long does the journey take? *pósi óra káni to taxídhi?*
What time will we arrive? *ti óra tha ftásoume?*
How much is the fare? *póso íne to isitírio*
Next stop, please *stási parakaló*
Can you tell me where to get off? *tha mu píte pou na katévo?*
Should I get off here? *edhó na katévo?*
Excuse me, I want to get off *signómi na katévo*
delay *kathistérisi*

AT THE AIRPORT

Where are the offices of BA/Olympic? *pou íne ta grafía tis British/Olymbiakís?*
I'd like to book a seat to... *tha íthela na kratíso mia thési ya...*
When is the next flight to... *póte tha íne i epómeni ptísi ya*
Are there any seats available? *párchoun i thésis?*
How many suitcases have you got? *póses valítses échete?*
Can I take this with me? *boró na to páro aftó mazí mou?*
My suitcase has got lost *háthike i valítsa mou*
My suitcase has been damaged *i valítsa mu épathe zimiá*
The flight has been delayed *i ptísi échi kathistérisi*
The flight has been cancelled *i ptísi mateóthike*
I can put you on the waiting list *boró na sa válo sti lísta anamonís*

DIRECTIONS

right/left *dhexiá/aristerá*
Take the first/second right *párte ton próto/dhéftero dhrómo dhexiá*
Turn right/left *strípste dhexiá/aristerá*
Go straight on *tha páte ísia/efthía*
after the traffic lights *metá ta fanária*
Is it near/far away? *ína kondá/makriá?*
How far is it? *póso makriá íne?*
It's five minutes' walk *íne pénde leptá me ta pódhia*
It's ten minutes by car *íne dhéka leptá me to aftokínito*
100 metres *ekató métra*
opposite/next to *apénandi/dhípla*
up/down *páno/káto*
junction *dhiastávrosi*
house/building/apartment block *spíti/ktírio/polikatikía*
Where is/are... *pou íne...*
Where can I find a bank/bus stop/hotel/petrol station? *pou boró na vro mia trápeza/mia stási/éna xenodohío/éna venzinádhiko?*
How do I get there? *pos na páo ekí?*
Can you show me where I am on the map? *boríte na mou díxete sto hárti pou íme?*
Am I on the right road for... *ya... kalá páo?*
No, you're on the wrong road *óchi, pírate láthos dhrómo*

ON THE ROAD

Where can I rent a car? *pou boró na nikiáso aftokínito?*
What is it insured for? *ti asfália échi?*
Can another driver drive it? *borí na to odhighísi álos odhigós?*
By what time must I return it? *méchri ti óra prépi na to epistrépso?*
driving licence *dhíploma*
licence plate *pinakídha*
petrol *venzíni*
petrol station *venzinádhiko*
oil *ládhi*
How much should I put in? *pósi na válo?*
Fill it up please *óso pérni*
lead-free *amólivdhi*
My car won't start *to aftokínito dhen pérni bros*
My car has broken down *hálase to aftokinitó mou*
I've had an accident *ícha éna atíchima*
How long will it take to repair? *pósi óra thélete na to ftiáxete?*
Can you check... *boríde na elénxete...*
There's something wrong with... *káti échi... (plural káti échun...)*
the accelerator *to gázi*
the brakes *ta fréna*
the clutch *to ambraghiáz*
the engine *i michaní*
the exhaust *i exátmisi*

the fanbelt *i zóni*
the gearbox *i tachítites*
the headlights *ta fanária*
the radiator *to psighío*
the spark plugs *ta bouzí*
the tyre(s) *to lásticho (ta lásticha)*
the windscreen *to parbríz*

Emergencies

Help! *voíthia!*
Stop! *stamatíste!*
I've had an accident *ícha éna atíchima*
Watch out! *proséche!*
Call a doctor *tilefónise éna yiatró*
Call an ambulance *tilefónise éna asthenofóro*
Call the police *tilefónise tin astinomía*
Call the fire brigade *tilefónise tous pyrosvéstes*
Where's the telephone? *pou íne to tiléfono?*
Where's the nearest hospital? *pou íne to pio kondinó nosokomío?*
I would like to report a theft *éghine mia klopí*
Thank you very much for your help *efcharistó polí pou me voithísate*

Health

Is there a chemist's nearby? *ipárchi éna farmakío edhó kondá?*
Which chemist is open all night? *pio farmakío dianykterévi?*
I don't feel well *dhen estهánome kalá*
I'm ill *íme árostos* (feminine) *(árosti)*
He/she's ill *íne árostos/árosti*
Where does it hurt? *pu ponái?*
It hurts here *ponái edhó*
I suffer from... *páscho apo...*
I have a *éxo*
headache/sore throat/stomach ache *ponokéfalo/ponólemo/ kilіópono*
Have you got something for travel sickness? *échete típota yia ti naftía?*
It's nothing serious *dhen íne sovaró*
Do I need a prescription? *hriázete sindaghí?*
It bit me (of an animal) *me dhángose*
It bit me (of an insect) *me tsímbise*
It stung me *me kéntrise*
bee *mélisa*
wasp *sfíka*
mosquito *kuonoúpi*
sticking plaster *lefkoplástis*
tissues *hartomándila*
toothpaste *odhondókrema*
diarrhoea pills *hápia yia ti dhiária*

Notices

ΤΟΥΑΛΕΤΕΣ **toilets**
ΑΝΔΡΩΝ **gentlemen**
ΓΥΝΑΙΚΩΝ **ladies**
ΑΝΟΙΚΤΟ **open**
ΚΛΕΙΣΤΟ **closed**
ΕΙΣΟΔΟΣ **entrance**
ΕΞΟΔΟΣ **exit**
ΑΠΑΓΟΡΕΥΤΑΙ **forbidden/no entry**
ΕΙΣΙΤΗΡΙΑ **tickets**
ΑΠΑΓΟΡΕΥΤΑΙ ΤΟ ΚΑΠΝΙΣΜΑ **no smoking**
ΠΛΗΡΟΦΟΡΙΕΣ **information**
ΠΡΟΣΟΧΗ **caution**
ΚΙΝΔΥΝΟΣ **danger**
ΑΡΓΑ **slow**
ΔΗΜΟΣΙΑ ΕΡΓΑ **road works**
ΠΑΡΚΙΝ/ΧΩΡΟΣ ΣΤΑΘΜΕΥΣΕΩΣ **car park**
ΑΠΑΓΟΡΕΥΤΑΙ Η ΣΤΑΘΜΕΥΣΗ **no parking**
ΤΑΞΙ **taxi**
ΤΡΑΠΕΖΑ **bank**
ΤΗΛΕΦΩΝΟ **telephone**
ΤΗΛΕΚΑΡΤΕΣ **phone cards**
ΕΚΤΟΣ ΛΕΙΤΟΥΡΓΙΑΣ **out of order**

Further Reading

General

Crete, John Freely (Wiederfeld & Nicholson)
The Cretan Journal, Edward Lear (Denise Harvey & Co). A record of the artist's journey in 1864. ***The Great Island***, Michael Llewellyn-Smith (Allen Lane).
The Greek Islands, Lawrence Durrell (Faber & Faber).
Under Mount Ida, Oliver Burch (Ashford).

Réthymnon

Rethymno – A Guide to the Town, A. Malagari & H. Stratidakis (Malagari & Stratidakis).
Fortezza – The Fortress of Rethymno, Stella Kalogeraki (Mediterraneo Editions).
Byzantine Wall-paintings in Rethymnon, Ioannis Spatharakis (Spatharakis & Mitos).

Haniá

The Old City of Hania, Michalis Adrianakis (Adam Editions).
Fenny's Hania, Tony Fennymore (Fenny's Crete Publications).
The County of Khania Through its Monuments, Maria Andreadaki-Blasaki (Ministry of Culture).

Archaeology, History & Mythology

Archanes, J & E Sakellarakis (Ekdotike Athenon SA).
Guide to Cretan Antiquities, Costis Davaras (Eptalofos SA).
History of Crete, Theocharis E. Detorakis.
The Iliad and ***The Odyssey***, Homer, translated by E.V. Rieu (Penguin Classics).
The Greek Myths, Robert Graves (Pelican Books). The definitive book on the subject.
Monasteries & Byzantine Memories of Crete, Nikos Psilakis (Editions Karmanor).

Jewish Sites & Synagogues of Greece, Timothy J. DeVinney & Nicholas D. Stavroulakis (Talos Press).

Knossós and Minoan Crete

The Bull of Minos, Leonard Cotterell (Bell & Wyman Ltd).
A Handbook to the Palace of Minos, J.D.S. Pendlebury (MacDonald).
Palaces of Minoan Crete, Gerald Cadogan (Routledge).
Knossos – Unearthing a Legend, Alexandre Farnou (Thames & Hudson).
Villa Ariadne, Dilys Powell (Efstathiadis Group).
The Knossos Labyrinth, Rodney Castleden (Routledge).
The Secret of Crete, H.G. Wunderlich (Efstathiadis Group).

The Battle of Crete

Crete – The Battle and the Resistance, Antony Beevor (Penguin).
The Cretan Runner, George Psychoundakis, translated by Patrick Leigh Fermor (Penguin).
The Fall of Crete, Alan Clarke (Efstathiadis Group).
The Lost Battle – Crete 1941, Callum MacDonald (Macmillan).

Literature

Zorba The Greek, Níkos Kazantzákis, translated by Carl Wildman (Faber & Faber).
Best known work of Crete's best known author. (Also look for Kazantzákis' *Freedom or Death*, *The Last Temptation of Christ* and *Christ Recrucified*.)

Flora, Fauna, Geology etc

A Birdwatching Guide to Crete, Stephanie Coghlan (Arlequin Press)
Flowers of Greece and the Balkans, Oleg Polunin (Oxford Paperbacks).
Mediterranean Wild Flowers, Chris Grey Wilson & Marjorie Blamey (HarperCollins).
Flora of the Cretan Area, N. Turland, L. Chilton & J.R. Press (HMSO)
Wild Flowers of Crete, George Sfikas (Efstathiades Group)
The Making of the Cretan Landscape, Oliver Rackham and Jennifer Moody (Manchester University Press)

Cookery

Cretan Cooking, Maria & Nikos Psilakis (Psilakis).
The Foods of Greece, Algaia Kremezi (Stewart, Talori & Chang).
Origins and Uses of Aromatic Plants, Herbs and Spices in Our Life – ***The basis of the Mediterranean diet***, Savvakis S.A. – ©Savvakis D. Michael Editions ISBN: 960-86129-1-8

Other Insight Guides

Included in the 400 or so titles created by Apa Publications, the world's largest collection of visual guidebooks, are **Insight Guides** to various areas of Greece, as well as to nearby countries and islands in the Mediterranean, such as Turkey and Cyprus.

Three *Insight Guides* to Greece, the Greek Islands and Athens are companion volumes to this book, providing the big picture and perfect photographs.

For the short-stay traveller there are *Insight Pocket Guides* to Crete, the Aegean Islands, Rhodes and Athens. Written by locally based authors or experts on the destinations concerned, they contain tailor-made itineraries linking the essential sights and sections on shopping, eating out and nightlife. They include personal recommendations on where to stay and eat, as well as a large fold-out map that fits into a wallet in the back of the guide.

There are also *Insight Compact Guides* to Greece, Athens, Crete and Rhodes. These small, fact-packed, highly portable books are perfect for on-the-spot reference.

In addition to guidebooks, Insight publishes an excellent range of hard-wearing laminated maps. Among the range of titles on Greece are *Insight Fleximap: Athens*, *Insight Fleximap: Crete* and *Insight Fleximap Corfu & the Ionian Islands*.

Feedback

We do our best to ensure the information in our books is as accurate and up-to-date as possible. The books are updated on a regular basis, using local contacts, who painstakingly add, amend and correct as required. However, some mistakes and omissions are inevitable and we are ultimately reliant on our readers to put us in the picture.

We would welcome your feedback on your experiences using the book "on the road". The more information you can give us, the better.

We will acknowledge all contributions, and we'll offer an Insight Guide to the best letters received.

Please write to us at:
Insight Guides
APA Publications
PO Box 7910
London SE1 1WE
Or send e-mail to:
insight@apaguide.demon.co.uk

ART & PHOTO CREDITS

AKG London back cover centre left, 18, 34
Heather Angel back cover centre right, 80/81, 202T
Archiv Gerner 22, 23, 24, 25, 44, 71, 72, 73, 112, 124R
Nomi Baumgarti 138, 140, 240
Benaki Museum 46
Jenny Bennathan 86R
Marcus Brooke back flap top, front flap bottom, 5B, 57, 60, 64, 114, 115, 117, 125T, 129, 130L, 142T, 143, 177, 183, 184, 197, 206, 212, 212T, 213, 227, 232, 234
Lance Chilton/Marengo Publications 84L/84R, 85, 87L/R, 139, 165, 168, 171, 201
Bruce Coleman 86L
Friedericke Fritz 195
Glyn Genin back cover top right, spine centre, 1, 4/5, 4BL, 10/11, 19, 21, 30, 45, 61, 65, 70, 98, 100T, 102, 102T, 103, 104, 109, 120T, 124L, 124T, 125, 128T, 132/133, 141T, 145, 146/147, 148, 150T, 152, 154T, 158T, 160T, 162/163, 170, 170T, 174/175, 178T, 179, 180, 180T, 181, 182, 185, 186, 187T, 190, 194T, 196T, 200T, 202, 203, 206T, 211, 214T, 215, 216, 217, 220, 230R, 231, 232T, 233, 235, 236, 236T, 237, 239
Udo Gerner 39, 41, 69, 96/97, 105, 118, 126L, 137, 188/189
Regina Hagen 47, 88/89, 135, 157L/R, 158, 159, 164, 169, 187, 218, 230L
Terry Harris 12/13, 63, 68, 77, 128, 130T, 136T, 138T, 154, 166T, 221
Blaine Harrington front flap top, 2/3, 62, 67, 210, 214, 218T, 224/225
Fotoarchiv Hirmer spine top, 2B, 31
Thomas Kanzler 90/91
Michele Macrakis 43, 49, 52/53, 54, 56, 59, 92/93, 116, 121, 123, 160, 199, 219
Museum of Heraklion 16/17, 27R, 28, 29, 33, 108
NHPA 82, 83, 205L/R
Steve Outram 55, 58, 74/75, 78, 79, 111, 153, 161, 208/209
Gerd Pfeiffer 42, 194, 196
Jeffery Pike 149, 156, 229,
Aris Saris/STF 48
Hans Gerd Schulte 113, 144
Jens Schumann back flap bottom, 50/51, 66, 119, 127, 131, 141, 176, 198, 200, 226, 238
Stefan Seidel 191, 207
Rick Strange 126R
Topham Picturepoint back cover bottom, 4BR, 20, 26, 27L, 32, 38, 40, 112T, 116T, 144T, 184T
Bill Wassman 99, 101
Hans Wiesenhofer 6/7, 8/9, 76, 122, 134, 151, 204

Picture Spreads

Pages 106/107: *Top row, left to right:* Steve Outram, C. Vergas/Ideal Photo, Steve Outram, AKG Berlin. Dolphin fresco: Glyn Genin. *Centre row:* Steve Outram, D. Ball/Ideal Photo. *Bottom row:* all by Steve Outram.
Pages 172/173: *Top row, left to right:* Robert Thompson/NHPA, E.A. Janes/NHPA, Lance Chilton/Marengo Publications, Lance Chilton. *Centre row:* Lance Chilton. *Bottom row:* Robert Thompson/NHPA, Lance Chilton, Robert Thompson/NHPA, Robert Thompson/NHPA
Pages 222/223: *Top row, left to right:* David Tipling/BBC, Brian Rogers/Biofotos, Hans Christoph Kappel/BBC, Nigel J Dennis/NHPA. *Centre row:* Peter Pickford/NHPA, Vicente Garcia Canseco/NHPA. *Bottom row:* Jose B Ruiz/BBC, Alan Williams/NHPA, Jean-Louis Le Moigne/NHPA, John Buckingham/NHPA.

Map Production by Colin Earl

Cartographic Editor **Zoë Goodwin**
Production **Linton Donaldson**
Design Consultants
Carlotta Junger, Graham Mitchener
Picture Research **Hilary Genin**

Index

Numbers in italics refer to photographs

a

b

l

m

r

s

t

v

“I was first drawn to the Insight Guides by the excellent “Nepal” volume. I can think of no book which so effectively captures the essence of a country. Out of these pages leaped the Nepal I know – the captivating charm of a people and their culture. I’ve since discovered and enjoyed the entire Insight Guide series. Each volume deals with a country in the same sensitive depth, which is nowhere more evident than in the superb photography.”

Sir Edmund Hillary

Insight Guide
New York City

Insight Guide
Denmark

Insight Guide
Singapore

Budapest

Costa del Sol

Corsica

London

Hong Kong

Ireland

Chile

New Orleans